About This Book

This book starts where you are likely to start—at the point when you first start Microsoft Access, and a whole new world opens up before your eyes. You might be in a state of panic, shock, or total excitement.

This book provides hands-on tutorials, useful tips, and technical information to get you started and keep you going with Access. It takes you from the most basic and elementary database tasks, such as setting up tables and printing quick reports, to advanced techniques, such as sophisticated queries and linked-table databases. And it tries throughout to be friendly, fun, and easy to understand.

You'll see the following specific features throughout the book:

- ☐ **Do/Don't boxes:** These give you specific guidance on what to do and what to avoid doing in specific Access database tasks.

- ☐ **Notes:** These provide essential background information so that you cannot only do things with Access, but have a good understanding of what you're doing and why.

- ☐ **Access Jargon:** These explain database jargon in plain English, so you can impress your friends at parties when the conversation turns to database management.

- ☐ **The Access Way sidebars:** These give tips, tricks, or warnings specific to Access 2.

Who Should Read This Book

Whether you just need help with a specific database task or want a step-by-step tutorial on every aspect of the program, you will find what you need in this book. For beginners, there's coverage of the basic concepts of database management and the basic techniques of using Access. For readers who are more technically advanced, there's reference information about various aspects of using the program. And for people who just need to "dip into" the book and learn about a specific topic, the clear organization of the sections and lessons makes it fast and easy for them to find what they need.

Conventions

The most notable conventions in the book are as follows:

☐ Access commands, which are in code listings or embedded in regular text, appear in monospace type. For example, "Enter the expression `=DatePart("d",[Date of Record])` on the first row of the Sorting and Grouping box" contains a command in monospace.

☐ Access menu choices are indicated by the name of the menu, followed by a vertical slash character (|), then the name of the menu choice.

Throughout the book, the emphasis has been on providing useful information in a way that is fast, easy, and fun.

Teach Yourself
Access 2
in 14 Days, Second Edition

Teach Yourself
Access 2
in 14 Days,
Second Edition

Paul Cassel

SAMS
PUBLISHING

A Division of Macmillan Publishing
201 West 103rd Street, Indianapolis, Indiana 46290

*This book is dedicated to my daughter, Tirilee Lynne Cassel,
who got it all together on Saint Patrick's Day. May she
always proudly wear the green.*

International Standard Book Number: 0-672-30488-0

Library of Congress Catalog Card Number: 93-87657

97 96 95 94   4 3 2

Composed in AGaramond and MCPdigital by Macmillan Publishing

Printed in the United States of America

Trademarks

About the Author

Paul Cassel has been designing and programming database systems on a wide range of computers for more than 15 years. His clients have included Intel Corp., Los Alamos National Laboratory, Pacific Gas & Electric, federal and state governments, the Navajo Nation, and many small to medium-sized companies. He currently travels nationally giving lectures, teaching seminars, and consulting about numerous small computer topics, including Microsoft Access. He's also co-host of the weekly Egghead Software Hour radio show.

Since 1981, he has done PC database development in dBase, FoxPro, R:Base, Paradox, and most recently, Access, which is his favorite Windows database package. He lives in the high desert of New Mexico with his wife, whom he exasperates, and his two children, whom he confuses.

Overview

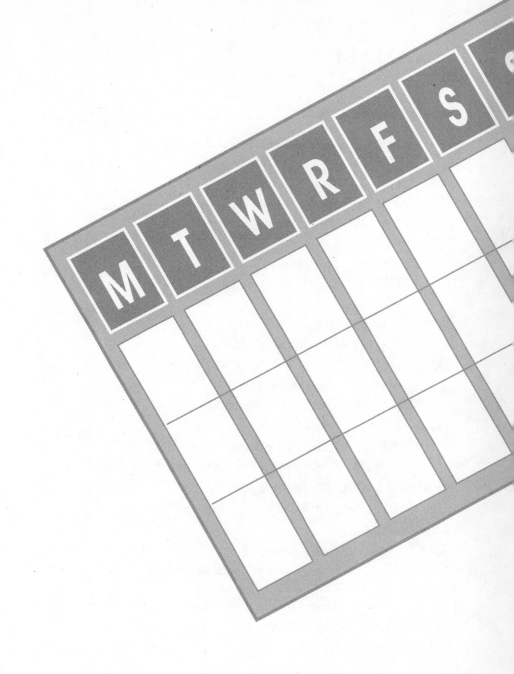

Contents

Extra Credit

Appendixes

Acknowledgments

While this book bears my name as author, it couldn't have come about without a collaborative effort from many people. Whatever mention I can make of them here cannot match their true contribution.

First of all, I'd like to thank Greg Croy, whom others have called, and I have come to believe is, the best acquisitions editor in the business. Dean Miller, the development editor, held this project together and on course. Joe Williams' efforts at copyediting turned my rough manuscript into something resembling English. Leslie K. Koorhan, as technical editor, caught and corrected the numerous technical errors and inconsistencies that inevitably find their way into anything I write.

Once again it was Carolyn Linn, the production editor, never hesitating to do what needed to be done, who ended up pulling the all-nighters when the deadlines loomed close.

Nothing is perfect. No doubt this book contains some omissions or inaccuracies. Any of these are wholly my fault. However much this book is complete and accurate is due to the efforts of the above-named people.

Introduction

Why I Wrote This Book

I wrote *Teach Yourself Access 2 in 14 Days* because I'm crazy about Access. Simply put, I think it's a terrific program.

When Microsoft first introduced Access in the fall of 1992, many people in the Paradox and dBASE developer communities reacted in fear of this potential new threat on the block. I did, too. But then, I took a serious look at the latest wonder from the wizards of Redmond and realized that Access was truly the first of a new generation of data-base products.

My opinion was confirmed a few days later when a client called me in to enhance an old dBase application that was a complete mess. I wondered, "Should I try to clean up what they have, or just start from scratch with totally new dBase IV code?"

After analyzing the client's needs, I returned to my office to see what I could do about them. Within three hours and without writing a single line of code, I duplicated the client's dBase IV application and made all the improvements requested.

As you've guessed by now, I did it with Access. It was a very leisurely three hours, too. If I'd worked at it, I could have done the job in an hour and a half.

What This Book Will Do for You

Any database package that gives great results without a lot of work is my kind of program. And that's what Access and this book can do for you. After you've completed this 14-day course, you'll not only be able to create your own database applications, but you could even hang out your shingle as an Access developer.

What This Book Won't Do for You

This book teaches you much of what you need to know to create solid, powerful database applications. But no book can be a substitute for your own creativity, imagination, and practical experience. As you work with Access, you'll constantly find

new ways to do old things. As you do, you can refer back to this book for the essential foundations that show you how to turn your new ideas into productive database systems.

Teach Yourself Access in 14 Days doesn't attempt to cover every detail in Access. Instead it uses specific examples to demonstrate general principles. This book shows you "how to." It doesn't attempt to be a reference work. You can find full reference documentation in the online help system and the printed documentation, both of which come with Access.

How This Book Works

None of the exercises in this book require you to do much data entry. You'll be working as a database manager for a fictional college. The focus is always on learning database concepts and techniques—you didn't buy this book to get some practice typing in data. If you want a fast jump and want to avoid almost all data entry typing, see Appendix E, which will give you several options for acquiring *Teach Yourself Access in 14 Days'* sample data.

How This Book Is Structured

This book's lessons are presented in 28 chapters, each designed for a half-day session. Each chapter consists of several examples or lessons.

An extra credit chapter, "OLE 2, Menu Building, and More," follows the 14-day series of lessons.

To get the most out of the book, you should complete each lesson before going on to the next. Once you've finished the lessons, of course, you can then go back and dip into the book any time you need a quick refresher course on specific points.

But Most of All—HAVE FUN!

I've spent many hours working with Access and enjoyed each hour. After going through this book, you'll have the level of expertise needed to create database applications easily with Access—and have fun doing it!

So, enough talk. Let's get started. I hope that you enjoy Access as much as I do and find many productive uses for your newfound database skills. But remember: If you're not having fun, you're missing half the point of doing it!

Database Fundamentals

A database is an orderly collection of information. Sales-order, personnel, and bookkeeping systems are all examples of databases. A relational database system such as Access categorizes its information into logical groups. These logical groups are physically represented in the database by linked tables. Each table holds a particular category of data.

OK, What's a Table?

A table is a grid. The grid's rows correspond to data records, and the columns correspond to data fields. As an example, a particular table in a personnel database might have fields of SSN, Last Name, First Name, Street Address, etc. A record is all the fields for a row in a database table. Figure IN.1 is a table in Access.

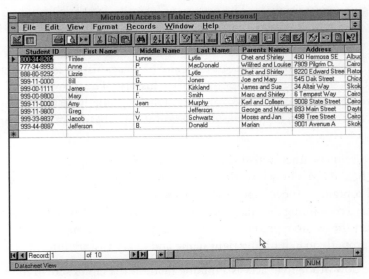

Figure IN.1. *One table from a registration system created using Access.*

Putting It in Action

Consider a personnel system of about 1,000 employees. Think of all the information such a system must contain and organize. There's personal information along with data about each employee's benefits, department, supervisor, salary history, credentials, reviews, and so forth.

When you organize all that information into a relational model, you break down the entire mass into logical categories. One table might contain an employee's name, address, and personal information, another one the employee's salary history, another one the department and supervisor information, another the employee's benefit package, and so on until all the information has been categorized.

You might be wondering why you should bother to fragment your information like this. The reason is efficiency. Any database system can manipulate and locate information faster if it's in small chunks. For example, Access, like any database management system, can sort, or order, a table much faster if it operates on a table with three fields rather than thirty.

A relational database can use data from any number of tables; therefore, any data existing in one table should never appear in another. The relational model makes any data duplication unnecessary. This is an important element to keep in mind when designing your database. The process of logically categorizing a mass of data into a relational model is called normalization.

The potential problem with breaking data into smaller chunks is loss of synchronization. If a person's name is in one table and his salary history is in another, how do you associate the name with the right salary history? The answer is linking fields that coordinate information in two or more tables. A properly designed relational database contains all the necessary links that permit the database to match records in different tables.

A typical personnel system uses the employee's social security number, or SSN, as a link field. Here's how it works. The record containing personal information has one field containing the SSN for the person represented in that record. In a separate table, a record containing the salary history also contains the SSN of the person whose salary history the record represents. Given this embedded information, a relational database can properly match up the right name and salary-history information.

Note how StudentID acts as a linking field for the tables shown in the relationships diagram in Figure IN.2. When asked to, Access can associate the proper Complete Courses or Student's Current Courses information with the information in the Student Personal table, even though the information is in separate tables. The trick is to have the same data for all StudentID fields in each table.

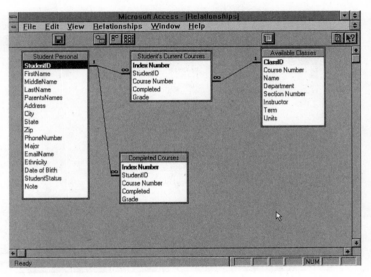

Figure IN.2. *The related tables.*

Referential Integrity

An important concept to understand is called *referential integrity.* A student registration system might have one table for student names and another for classes the students signed up to take. One student might sign up for many classes, but any seat in a class can have only one student assigned to it. A link between these tables is called a "one-to-many" because one student is linked to many classes. Figure IN.3 shows an Access query where one student has many classes.

Obviously, class registration information is useful only when linked to a particular student. In other words, a person must exist in the system before you can enter any class information. Using Access, you'd first enter a person in the system, and only afterward enter the classes that person is signed up for. The table with the Student Personal information is the "one" table. The Student's Current Courses table structurally shown in Figure IN.2 is the "many" table. Using Access, you can protect against adding unlinked class information into the system. This can happen if a data-entry person makes an error typing the StudentID that's supposed to be associated with a class. You can instruct Access to enforce a rule saying you can only enter class information for a StudentID that already exists in the Student Personal table.

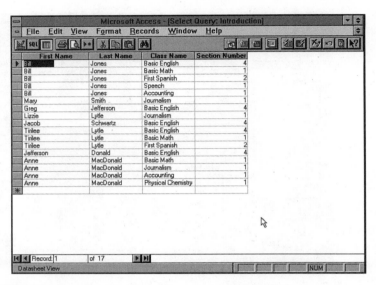

Figure IN.3. *An Access query illustrating a one-to-many link.*

In traditional PC-based relational database programs, you also need to protect against accidentally erasing linked information in the one table because doing so would result in meaningless data being left in the many table. What good is degree information if the person who earned the degree isn't in the system anymore? Access can prevent the creation of this unlinked data or orphan. Referential integrity is a complex way of stating that the system itself guards against unlinked pieces of information.

ACCESS JARGON

> **referential integrity:** The existence of a related value or attribute in a database depends upon another identical value or attribute.

Designing a Database

A database in Access can have any or all of these parts:

☐ **Tables** are the basic building blocks of a database. They are where the actual data resides.

☐ **Forms** create a framework for presenting or entering data in one or more tables. In Access, forms also have special abilities for manipulating and verifying data not available at the table level.

☐ **Queries** search and retrieve data from one or more tables based on entered criteria.

☐ **Reports** are a way to output data from tables or queries. Reports can summarize data.

☐ **Macros** are a simple way to coordinate operations in Access.

☐ **Modules** are functions and procedures programmed through the Access Basic language.

Design Well

A poorly designed database can bring you years of grief. Professional database designers spend a great deal of time analyzing the entire mass of data they'll be dealing with before actually creating the database. The very nature of Access gives you a great deal of flexibility when organizing your data, but nothing's a guarantee against thoughtless design.

When designing a database, you should categorize your data into the smallest parts consistent with a logically organized structure. Keep in mind one-to-many, one-to-one, and many-to-many relations. For example, if you're creating a database for a hospital, you should consider that one patient has only one bed but can have many doctors; doctors can have many patients; one patient can have many procedures; a particular prescription should go to only one patient, but many patients might have identical prescriptions; and so forth.

Four Steps in Database Design

Here are the four general steps you take to design a database:

1. Determine user requirements in terms of output. What is it you want to get out of the system? For example, you might move to a computerized personnel system because doing required government reporting overwhelms your paper-based system. In this case, you would make sure that your database system could create the needed reports.

2. Do a conceptual model. This should usually be a flow chart but can be a simple word diagram. Do this in a formal way, committing the flow chart or word diagram to paper for later reference.

3. Determine a strategy to implement the design. What resources does the project need and how can you commit them? How do you map the conceptual model from Step 2 into the particular database you've chosen for the

task? In other words, how do you translate your conceptual flow chart to actual Access tables, forms, and reports?

4. Working from the map in Step 3, physically create the database system.

Initially this process will take some time, and you'll make some false starts. As with so many things, after you've made a few passes over the territory, the process will become almost second nature.

Physically Designing the Computer Database

Once you've run through the four steps in database design, you will have a good idea of what tables you need, what should be in each table, and how the tables should be linked. You also need to determine the internal structure of each table.

A Table's Internal Structure

Each field in a database has two characteristics identifying it. The first is the field ID, or name. A field for last names can and logically should have the ID of Last Name. The second characteristic is the data type of the field. The Last Name field uses the data type called Text. Here is a list of Access's data types, with a brief description of each:

- ☐ Text—Alphanumeric characters

- ☐ Memo—Up to 32,000 alphanumeric characters; generally contain comments

- ☐ Number—Numeric values with or without decimal places

- ☐ Date/Time—Dates and Times

- ☐ Currency—Money

- ☐ Counter—A numeric value that automatically increments with each record added

- ☐ Yes/No—Logical or Boolean values

- ☐ OLE Object—Graphics, sounds, or other binary objects created outside of the Access program

You can attach many properties, such as size and formatting, to each data type. The Text type of data can have a size of up to 255 characters. When specifying how large a text field will be, you don't want to use more space than needed for the actual entries

you anticipate. Access reserves the amount of space you specify for the Field Size property. It's a waste of your resources to tell Access to reserve 40 spaces for a field that will never hold more than 10 characters. Usually, a field size of 20 characters suffices for Last Name, 15 for First Name, and 30 for Street Address.

Indexes and Keys Fields

There are two more small topics to cover before digging into the program. You can tell Access to index certain fields in a table. When you do, Access orders the data according to the index and also tracks the indexed records. If you often search on a particular field, you should instruct Access to make it an index field.

A key field is a field or set of fields in a table that uniquely identifies each record. Access orders or sorts the database based on the contents of key fields, and it works much more efficiently if every table in a database has a key field. For example, the SSN field is often a good choice for a key field because each person has a unique social security number.

ACCESS JARGON

> **key field:** a field or set of fields in a table that uniquely identifies each record, such as a social security number.

Multiple Field Keys

Sometimes there's no unique field in your database to use for a key field. In these cases, you can use multiple fields as a key. For example, you wouldn't want to use Last Name as a key field because that would only allow one instance of the last name Smith. However, combining the Last Name field with a First Name or Telephone field might work.

Summary

This introducton was short and dry, but very important. Just knowing how to use Access or any database program is only part of what you need to manage your data. Before firing up your computer, you must have a good idea of what your data consists of, have planned a logical structure for it, and have developed at least a rough map of how to link the various parts of it together.

Much in the first three stages of database design has been done for you in this book. This is a book about using Access, not a theoretical book on database concepts; therefore, it concentrates on the final stage, Step 4. As you work through the next few lessons, the theory behind Steps 1 through 3 will become apparent. By the time you are done with this book and ready to design your own applications, you should be able to apply correct design elements to your projects.

Day

1

1

A Short Access Tour

This morning you'll learn the following:

- ☐ How to install Access 2
- ☐ The meaning of the various installation dialog boxes and screens
- ☐ The parts of the Access user interface
- ☐ How to change the shape and location of toolbars

Installing Access

Before using Access, you must install it on your computer. The following example uses drive B: as the installation drive and installs Access on drive C:, in the subdirectory called "Access." Your particular installation or setup might differ from this example. Many computers install Access from drive A:, or because of space limitations you might want to install to a different logical drive (such as drive D:) or a different subdirectory. If you install from or to a different drive or subdirectory, just substitute your choices for the example's. If your Access setup is on a network, you should consult your network administrator for instructions.

One further caution. This example runs from the standard Windows 3.1 interface. Many people choose to run different user interfaces (or shells) with Windows. If you have an alternate shell, your installation will run the same as the example, but some of your screens will look different.

Ready to go? First, put your Access 2 disk number one, the one called "Setup," in drive B:. Click on the menu item called File on the Program Manager's menu bar. Click on Run. Fill the resulting dialog box's parameter line with

`b:\setup`

Your screen should look like Figure 1.1.

Setup will grumble around for a while and eventually advise you to shut down any running programs during the Access installation routine. If you're running any processes such as a disk defragmenter that will write to setup's target drive, now's the time to exit and shut that process down.

Now that the Access setup has your computer's complete attention, remove this warning screen by clicking on OK. If this is your first time installing Access, you'll be prompted to enter some specific user information. Access will then ask you to confirm your ownership of the product or to enter some personal information about you and your company. Click on OK after you've either confirmed your ownership of Access or entered the requested information.

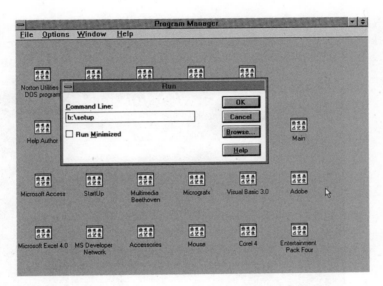

Figure 1.1. *Telling Windows to run the Access setup from drive B:.*

Access will then flash a screen showing your serial number information. Click on OK and you're finally at the screen where you tell the setup program where to install Access. Your screen at this point should resemble Figure 1.2. Note that in the case of Figure 1.2, the Access setup has detected an older version of Access already installed and is advising that this install overwrite the older one.

At this point you can either accept Setup's suggested drive and directory or click on the Change Directory button to specify a different path. This example accepts the suggested path. Click on OK to move to the next screen.

This screen gives you three optional configurations of Access, including one that enables you to customize which components to install.

Unless you're desperate for disk space, don't choose the Laptop configuration, since you'll lose many easy-to-use Access features. If you possibly can, choose the Complete/Custom option and then choose to install Access fully in the following screen. This book doesn't use the sample applications that ship with Access, but having them to experiment with as you work through the book will speed your learning process.

Click on Continue to bring up the screen where you pick a Program Manager group for Access. This example chooses Access 2 as a group name. Accept either Microsoft's choice for program group or choose one more to your liking. Click on OK and the real install program begins. After asking you to feed it disks, the setup routine will end

with either an error message (in case of a problem) or a success screen (if everything worked properly). This example's resulting program group, edited from the default Micosoft Office to Access 2, with its installed icons, is shown in Figure 1.3.

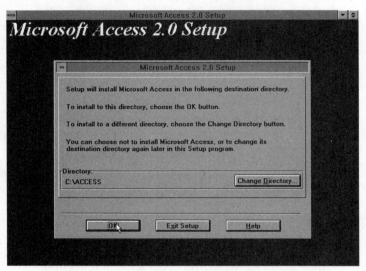

Figure 1.2. *Specifying where to install Access.*

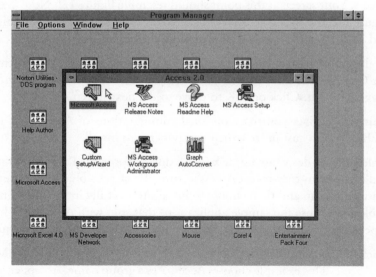

Figure 1.3. *Access fully installed into a group called Access 2.*

Depending on your options, your program group might look slightly different from Figure 1.3. For example, the setup shown has the extra-cost ADT installed in addition to Access itself.

Launching Access From Windows

You launch Access by double-clicking on the icon bearing its name. (See Figure 1.3.) The icon is the top-left one in the group called Access 2.0. Try it yourself. Access will show you a splash, or billboard screen, before starting. Your screen should then look like Figure 1.4.

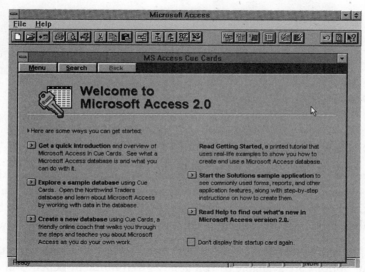

Figure 1.4. *Access launched, or started, showing the introductory cue card menu.*

Close the opening menu cue card, or if you prefer, explore around to see what these cue cards offer. If you're upgrading from Access 1.0 or 1.1, the What's New cue card should be of special interest to you. If you don't want to see this screen again when you start Access, check the box in the lower-right corner telling Access to hide this screen for future startups. After you're done with this visual menu system, click on its control menu icon. That's the short horizontal bar-in-a-box at the upper-left corner of the menu screen. Click on Close to enter the Access program. Your screen should resemble Figure 1.5.

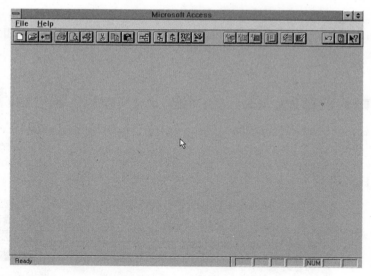

Figure 1.5. *Access launched without any database loaded.*

The Access Interface

Refer to Figure 1.5 (or your actual screen) if you have Access launched. The topmost part of the screen has "Microsoft Access" written on it. That part of the screen is called the title bar. Every window, or frame, within Windows has a title bar bearing a name or label. These names usually describe the function of the frame or window.

Dropping down one level you'll see the menu bar, where menu options appear. What menu options are available to you at any given moment depends upon what mode Access is in and whether your Access application has a custom menu system. At this point, Access has nothing loaded, so the only two menu choices are File, for file services, and Help, which is one way to get to the online help system.

Directly below the menu bar is the toolbar. There are many different toolbars in Access. You can also make your own custom ones. The purpose of toolbars is to enable you to quickly and easily perform common tasks while using the Access program. You can think of toolbars as shortcuts to many menu commands. You can also assign custom buttons on a toolbar to special routines that you've programmed into your applications; but for now, just think of toolbars as shortcuts to commonly performed tasks.

The toolbars in Access 2 are more plentiful and easier to use than in previous Access versions. Perhaps the two largest improvements incorporated in 2's toolbars are mobility and ToolTips. Look at ToolTips first.

Look at the toolbar. If you've never seen the Access toolbar, you probably can't decipher what each button on it does. Even Access veterans occasionally forget the buttons they seldom use. Microsoft, responding to customer demands for easier-to-use toolbars, added ToolTips to Access 2. Here's how ToolTips work: Move your cursor over the toolbar button on the extreme left of your screen. (That's the button with what looks like an asterisk behind a bunch of open window frames.) Don't click any mouse buttons. In a second or two a little balloon will pop up with the caption "New Database." Your screen should resemble Figure 1.6.

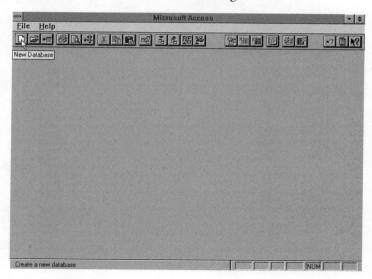

Figure 1.6. *A ToolTip in Access.*

This tells you that the button on the extreme left will, when clicked on, start the process of creating a new database. Also note that the status bar—that's the bar along the extreme bottom of your screen—pops up a slightly expanded explanation for this button's function.

Without ever clicking your mouse buttons, move your cursor over some other buttons along the toolbar. Be sure to leave the cursor on each button long enough to evoke the ToolTip. Compare the short ToolTip with the longer explanation on the status bar.

Don't worry if you don't understand what some of these buttons do at this time. In a short while, each button's function will become second nature to you. After you're familiar with how to get the ToolTip for any button, move on to the next section.

Arranging Toolbars

When Access starts, the toolbar is in a single row right below the menu bar. This works all right for many tasks, but you might prefer a different arrangement. Access is happy to comply with your wishes. Move your cursor to a place on the toolbar unoccupied by buttons. Refer to Figure 1.7 for a likely location to place your cursor.

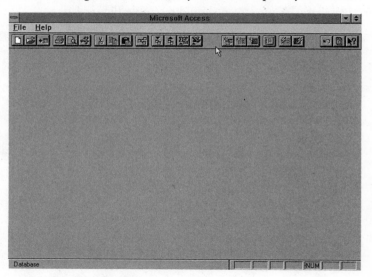

Figure 1.7. *Moving the toolbar.*

Now click your left mouse button and hold it down. While holding the button down, move the mouse down the screen. In Windows lingo, this is called "dragging." As you drag the toolbar down, it'll detach from the menu bar and change shape to one more square than when it was located right below the menu bar. Release the mouse button to drop the toolbar in a new location. Move your mouse over any border of the new toolbar. It'll change shape to a double-ended arrow. With the cursor over a border, click your mouse button and drag the toolbar's border. The toolbar changes shape depending on how much and in what direction you drag its border.

Also note that the toolbar, when detached from the menu bar, gains a title bar. In this case, the title bar for this toolbar is "Database." This tells you the toolbar you're seeing is the Database toolbar. You can move the newly shaped and sized toolbar by dragging when your cursor's on this title bar. Figure 1.8 is a moved and shaped database toolbar.

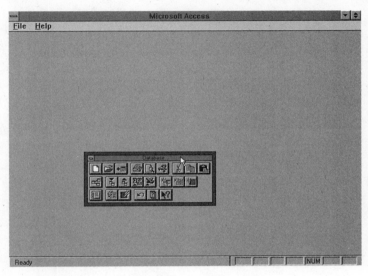

Figure 1.8. *A moved and resized database toolbar.*

If you want to restore your toolbar to its original place, drag it to just below the menu bar. Shuffle it around until you hit the hot spot that tells Access you wish to replace the toolbar. When you hit this hot spot, the toolbar will get a "ghost" outline showing its original shape. Release the mouse button and the toolbar will snap back to its initial shape and location.

Morning Summary

This morning you learned how to install Access 2, what the install screens mean, how to launch Access, the parts of the Access user interface, and how to change the shape and location of toolbars.

2

Wizards, Cue Cards, and Help

This afternoon you'll learn the following:

- ☐ What cue cards are
- ☐ What wizards are
- ☐ How to use cue cards
- ☐ How to use wizards
- ☐ How to use online help

Cue Cards

Cue cards are like coaches. They step you through various processes in Access. After you use Access for a while, many procedures will become almost second nature to you. However, even the most experienced Access users will occasionally find themselves facing a task they feel less than secure performing. Cue cards work well both as a training tool and a coaching tool for those times you feel unsure of yourself.

Like so many things in a visual apparatus like Access, you can best learn how to use cue cards by trying them out. Exercise 2.1 serves as an introduction to Cue Cards.

Exercise 2.1. Introduction to cue cards.

1. Launch Access if you have not already done so.

2. Note the button that is second from the right. This is the toolbar button that starts Cue Cards. It has what looks like two frames with a question mark in the middle of the front one. Click on that button. Your screen should look like Figure 2.1.

    You've just launched the Cue Card main menu. Each topic has a button with a "greater than" (>) sign next to it. When you're in Cue Cards, clicking on these signs moves you around in the Cue Cards system.

3. Click on the first button, the one labeled See a Quick Overview. Your screen should resemble Figure 2.2.

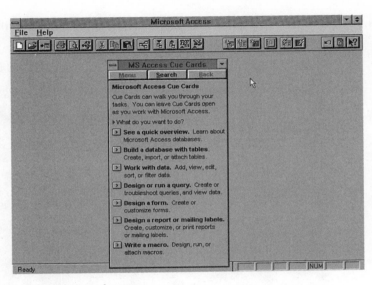

Figure 2.1. *The Cue Card main menu.*

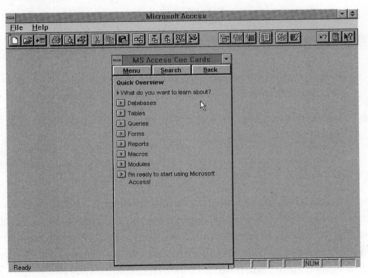

Figure 2.2. *The Quick Overview cue card.*

4. Access offers you a quick overview of several topics. Click on the button next to Databases. Your screen should resemble Figure 2.3.

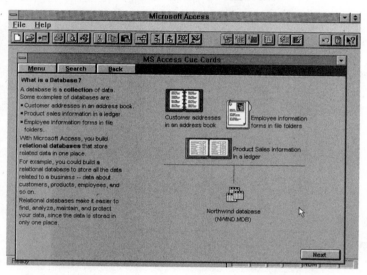

Figure 2.3. *The Databases cue card.*

5. Access brings up the cue card explaining what databases are. Click on the Next button in the lower-right corner of the screen.

6. Access moves on to the next page of the cue-card lesson. Click on the Next button again.

   Access now returns you to the submenu that launched the Databases cue-card series.

Cue Cards float on top of any other Windows object. This enables you to refer to them as you work. While the cue-card set you walked through only offered an overview of database concepts, most cue cards will step you through actual Access operations. Having the cue card float on top of Access while you work means you can easily refer to it as you go along. Most other help systems sink when you're in the main program, forcing you to call them back up at each step.

Use the cool switch (Alt+Tab) in Windows to switch from Access to another application. Access will shrink to an icon, but the cue card will remain on top, even when you are in the middle of another program. You can click on the minimize button

to shrink the cue cards to an icon if they get in your way. Restore Access to full screen again by cool-switching back to it. Floating cue cards are, overall, a great help—but they can get in the way sometimes.

If, when using it, a cue card gets in your way, you can minimize it to an icon by clicking on its minimize button. This gets the cue card out of your way but keeps it available if you need to refer to it.

Cue Cards have a little toolbar of their own right below their menu bar. Locate the button on the toolbar labeled Menu and click on it. That returns you to the opening menu. Exit Cue Cards by double-clicking on the control menu icon. (That's the box in the extreme upper-left corner of the window. It is a small square with a horizontal line in the middle of it.)

DO   DON'T

DO use cue cards as memory joggers or to lead you through operations you don't feel completely familiar doing.

DON'T forget you can minimize the cue cards to get them out of the way.

Wizards

Cue cards give you coachlike instructions, but you need to perform the steps themselves to get results. Wizards take the next logical step in an active help system. They ask you a few questions, and after you and the wizard agree what needs to be done, the wizard goes out and does it.

Most people use wizards when using Access. Even the most highly paid senior-level developers rely on wizards to do much of the grunt work in form and report design. In some areas, such as programming buttons on forms or reports, wizards make the chore so easy that even a fairly naive Access user can make applications that work just like the ones that are done by experts. True, there's nothing you can do with a wizard that you can't do manually, but ignoring wizards only makes for more work.

This wizard demo creates a table. Before you create a table, you need a database to put it in. Exercise 2.2 shows how to create a new database.

Exercise 2.2. Creating a new database.

1. Launch Access if you have not already done so.

2. Click on the New Database button on the toolbar. The New Database button is the one on the far left. It has an asterisk and several frames on it.

3. Access will return with a dialog box inviting you to name your new database. Enter myfirst.mdb. Your screen should resemble Figure 2.4.

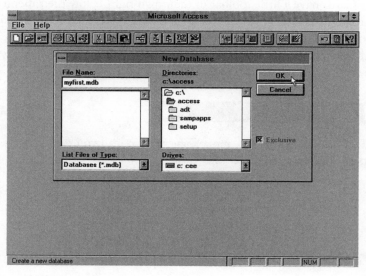

Figure 2.4. *Creating a new database.*

4. Click on OK. You've just created a new database called MYFIRST.

Enter the Wizard

Now you're ready to use a wizard to make a new table. Your screen should look like Figure 2.5.

The frame or window with MYFIRST written in the title bar is a container for all the objects you create to use in the MYFIRST database. Right now it's empty, since you've not yet made any objects for MYFIRST.

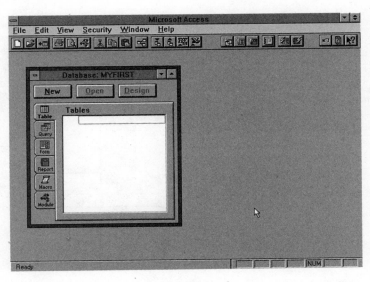

Figure 2.5. *The Database View of an empty database.*

ACCESS JARGON

> **Database View:** Access's term for a screen like the one in Figure 2.5, where you can see a database's object collection.

The Database View frame has a toolbar but no menu bar. Right now, the only button active on the toolbar is the one called New, since you can't open or design (modify) something you haven't created yet. Exercise 2.3 shows how to make a table using a wizard.

Exercise 2.3. Using a wizard to make a new table.

1. Click on the New button right below the title bar that says MYFIRST.

2. Click on the Table Wizards button to tell Access you want to use a wizard to make this table instead of defining it manually.

   Access will grind away for a while, loading the tools that the wizard needs to design a table. After it's done, it will bring up a design display. Your screen should resemble Figure 2.6.

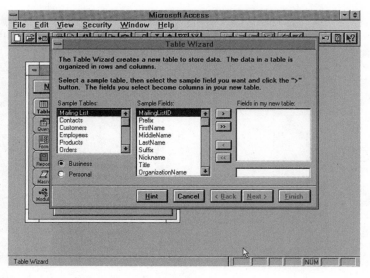

Figure 2.6. *Starting the Table Design wizard.*

3. Look at the bottom-left portion of the wizard screen. You'll see two option buttons, labeled Business and Personal. These specify which group of table types you can choose when using this wizard. The list box called Sample Tables lists the tables you can use as templates for your new table. The list box called Sample Fields shows the fields you can use in each sample table.

   Click on different sample tables and note how the Sample Fields list box changes. This is because each sample table has a different set of fields in it. When using the New Table wizard, you choose a sample table that contains fields close to what you want in your finished table. Don't worry if the furnished sample tables don't match your needs exactly. Later on you can add or edit what the wizard does.

4. Click on the option button labeled Personal to bring up the personal set of sample tables. Access will respond by bringing up a new set of sample tables.

5. Click on the Category sample table. Your screen should resemble Figure 2.7.

6. You next have to decide which fields from the sample table, Category, to include in your new table. You can add fields one at a time or all at once. Click on the button with the right-facing single greater-than sign (>). Access copies the field Category ID to the "Fields in my new table" list. Now click

on the button with the two right-facing greater-than signs (>>). Access copies all the fields from the sample table to the "Fields in my new table" list.

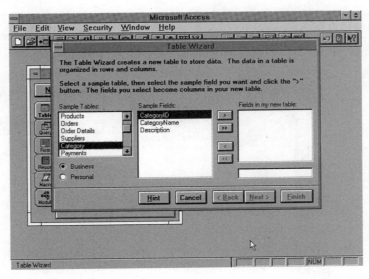

Figure 2.7. *Choosing a sample table.*

7. Oops! When that happened, you also got a double entry for Category ID, which Access considerately renamed Category ID1 since you can't have two identically named fields in one table. Remove the Category ID1 field by clicking on it to highlight it, then clicking on the left-facing greater-than sign (<).

8. Now that you have all the fields you want in your new table included in the "Fields in my new table" list box and no extras, click on the Next > button to move on to the next phase of table design.

9. Access rather uncreatively suggests the name Category for your new table. Enter My First as an equally uncreative but illustrative name for this table. Leave all other options, such as who sets the primary key, alone. Click on Next >.

10. Access brings up a screen with a checkered flag signaling that you're about to finish the wizard process. At this point you have the options of modifying the table's design, opening the table for data entry, or invoking another

wizard to create a form. You can also call up a cue card that will step you through the process of modifying the table's design if you opted for the first choice.

11. Click on "Enter data directly into the table" and click on the Finish button. At this point Access grinds away, creating and opening your new table, My First. After it's done, your screen should look like Figure 2.8.

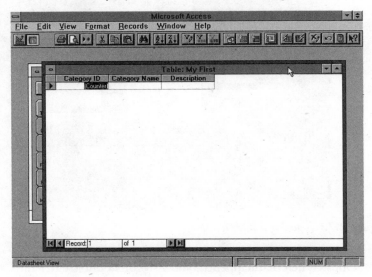

Figure 2.8. *The finished table.*

If you want to, press the tab key to move to the category name field and enter some data in it and the other fields. You move between fields in Access either by pressing the tab key or by pressing Enter. Figure 2.9 is the My First table with some sample data entered.

When you're satisfied, close the table by either double-clicking on its control menu icon or by clicking File on the menu bar and then clicking Close from the drop-down menu choices. You've just created a table in Access.

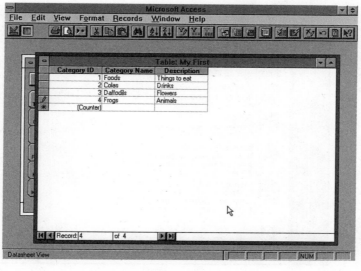

Figure 2.9. *Some sample data for the new table.*

Using Help

Sometimes the help you need can't be found through cue cards or with wizards. In those cases (such as clarifying the use of a particular function), you'll likely use Access's online help system. Exercise 2.4 steps you through some parts of Access's online help.

Exercise 2.4. Help with Help.

1. Launch Access if you have not already done so.

2. Click on the Help entry from the main menu bar.

3. Click on Contents from the drop-down menu list. Your screen should resemble Figure 2.10.

4. Move your cursor over the underlined topic called General Reference. Note that the cursor changes to a pointing hand. This signifies that you're over a jump or hypertext link. Click while keeping your cursor over General Reference. You'll then jump to the General Reference detailed help system.

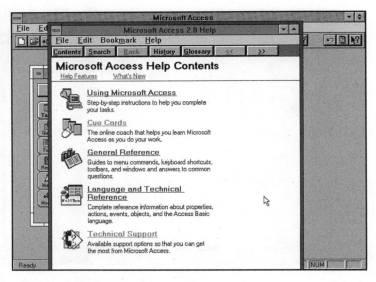

Figure 2.10. *The Help Contents section.*

5. Click on Glossary. This brings up a list of terms, all with dotted underlines. A dotted underline cues you that Help will pop up an informative window when you click on the word so designated. For example, click on the entry American National Standards Institute to pop up a definition for it. Your screen should resemble Figure 2.11.

6. You can also search for help by using keywords.

7. Click on the button called Search that is located on Help's toolbar. Access prompts you for a term to search on. Enter add.

8. Note that as you enter the letters that form add, Access scrolls to find the closest match to your entry. Click on the Show Topics button. Your screen should resemble Figure 2.12.

9. At this point you could click on any of the shown topics and Access would jump to that subject. Since we're really not interested in these topics yet, click on the Close button. Double-click on the Help system's control icon or pull down the File menu and choose Exit.

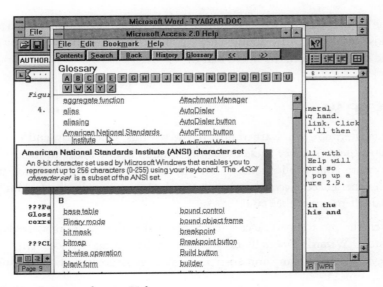

2

Figure 2.11. *A pop-up box in Help.*

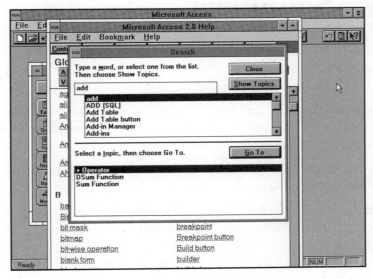

Figure 2.12. *Displaying topics in a successful Help search.*

You've just taken the five-cent tour of Access's help system and finished today's lesson. Close Access by either double-clicking on its control menu icon or by choosing File and then Exit from the menu bar.

Review

This afternoon you learned how to use wizards, Cue Cards, and the Access online help system. Each of these tools will come in handy many times as you use Access to create your applications. While cue cards are primarily targeted for new users, ven experienced Access hands will use them occasionally for seldom performed or difficult-to-remember tasks.

Even the most expert Access developer makes liberal use of wizards and the help system. Wizards especially do wonders in decreasing development time, and since they can't make many human-type errors, they assure you of clean implementations.

Day's Summary

Installing Access is as simple as inserting the setup disk in drive A: or B: and instructing Windows to run Setup from that disk. You'll have to tell Setup where to install Access, what components of Access to install, and what to name the group that will contain Access's icon; nonetheless, most of the installation is automatic.

You launch Access by double-clicking on its Program Manager icon. The top three layers of the Access interface are the title bar, the menu bar and the toolbar. The bottommost strip of the Access interface is the status bar.

You can adjust the shape and location of any Access toolbar by dragging it to where you want it and adjusting its outline using the mouse.

Access has three systems in addition to the printed documentation to help you use the program: cue cards, wizards, and online help. Cue cards have step-by-step instructions for certain operations, wizards interact with you to perform certain functions, and online help is (for the most part) a reference system similar to the printed manuals that come with Access.

Q&A

Q Can I adjust the size and location of the menu or status bars the same way I can the toolbars?

A No. Access only allows custom location of toolbars. You can create custom menu bars for your applications, but these will always remain in the menubar area.

Q When should I use cue cards instead of wizards?

A If the output from your wizard isn't close to what you want, you'll have to manually design your database object. If you're unclear about how to do this, you should use a cue card to help you.

Q Is there any reason to accept Setup's default location for Access? In other words, are there dangers if I install Access to a different place than Setup suggests?

A You can install Access wherever you please without any adverse consequences.

Workshop

Here's where you can test and apply what you have learned today.

Quiz

Possible answers to these questions are provided in Appendix A.

1. Why should you avoid the Laptop installation routine if at all possible?

2. What shape does the cursor assume when it's capable of reshaping a toolbar?

3. How do you launch Access from Program Manager?

4. Can you move or resize the menu bar?

Put Access into Action

1. Launch Access.

2. Open the Cue Card help system by clicking on its button located on the toolbar.

3. Locate and launch the cue cards telling you how to create a database.

4. Follow the cue cards to make a new database. Name the new database number2.

5. Exit Access. Use Windows' File Manager to erase or delete the file number2.mdb that you just made.

3

Entering Data Into Tables

This morning you'll learn the following:

- ☐ What database project we'll be covering
- ☐ How to plan the initial tables for the database
- ☐ How to use a wizard to create a table

The Database Project

The right way to learn Access, as with almost any small computer program, is to use it. Rather than go through a series of boring exercises that are unrelated to each other, as you work your way through this book you will devise a solution to a hypothetical problem. While this particular situation—a student registration and tracking application at a make-believe college—is fictional, you can directly apply the principles you will learn when making this application to your own particular situations.

For example, some of the things the fictional database must track include the students' vital statistics, the courses they take, and the status of their tuition payments. By changing the labels and making a few modifications, this system can also be used for the following:

- ☐ Tracking customer orders and account balances
- ☐ Maintaining a medical or dental practice
- ☐ Tracking retail sales and inventory
- ☐ Maintaining a personnel-management system

The principles you will learn through the process of building this system can be applied to almost any possible Access application. Actually, the college-management system you'll create as you work through this book is more complex than most user-created Access applications. The real problems that you'll use Access to solve will probably be much simpler than this sample application.

Planning the Database

Refer back to the introduction of this book if you need a refresher on planning databases and what the relational model is. Remember that in a relational database such as Access, you distribute or divide your data into logical groupings of tables. For

those needing near perfection, there's a complex mathematical model for performing this process; but most people don't need to worry that they've completely optimized their data. As in many other fields, close is good enough for most database work.

The goal of the relational model is efficiency. Take a look at Figure 3.1, which is the flat file (or non-relational) method to store data for a particular student. Note that for each course that this student has taken, the student's name, address, and phone information is duplicated. If you're only dealing with a few records, this duplication is not a problem. However, today's databases deal with thousands or even millions of records. Any database carrying around all that extra baggage would inevitably be bogged down under that extra load.

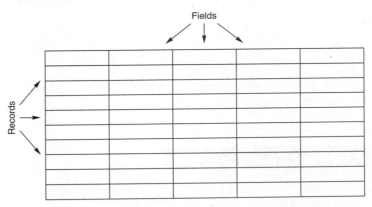

Figure 3.1. *The flat file database model showing duplicated information.*

Now take a look at Figure 3.2. This is the same data but in the relational model. Note that with this model, the data that was shown in Figure 3.1 is now broken into two tables. One table has the student's personal information, such as student ID or social security number, student name, student address, and phone. The second table doesn't duplicate all this information for each course the student has taken, as in the flat file model shown in Figure 3.1. Instead, the second table contains only the course information for this student plus the student ID for each course. The student ID is the link field that will allow Access to match up the student with the courses taken.

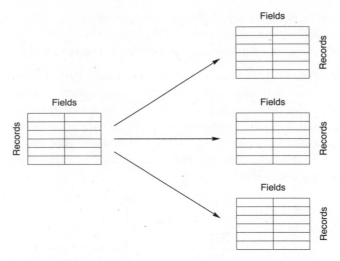

Figure 3.2. *The same information as in Figure 3.1, but shown using the relational model. Note the lack of data duplication.*

DO   DON'T

DO organize your data into tables to minimize or eliminate duplication.

DON'T get overly carried away breaking up your data. After you've organized it to the point of no or minimal duplication, stop. Further atomizing of your data will lead to inefficiencies.

Before the First Table

Any college database needs a table to store personal information about students, so that will be the first table you add to your database. Before you go further, you need a new database to store your database objects. Exercise 3.1 shows you how to create the new database.

Exercise 3.1. Creating the new database.

1. Launch Access if you have not already done so.

2. Move your mouse cursor over the farthest left button on the toolbar. (Refer to Figure 3.3.) Access will drop down a balloon-type help box reminding you that this button creates a new database.

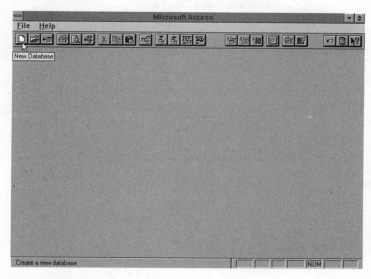

Figure 3.3. *Creating a new database.*

3. Click on the New Database button.

4. Access responds with a dialog box asking you to name your new database. The program suggests the rather drab db1.mdb as a name. Override Access's suggestion and enter College in the dialog box for the new database's name. You can either include the extension .mdb or leave it out and let Access attach the file extension automatically. Access uses the file extension .mdb to identify its native format databases.

5. Access will grind away for a while, and after verifying that all's OK with its world, it will create a new database and leave your screen looking like Figure 3.4.

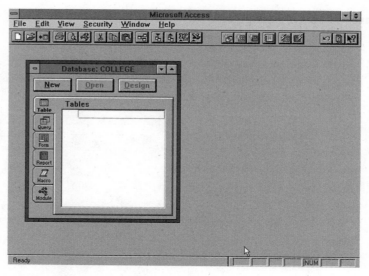

Figure 3.4. *The newly created College database.*

The First Table

Right now the College database is empty of any objects. Remember, the first order of business is to make a table to store all the student's personal information. Consider what information is "personal" and therefore belongs in this table. Here's where your particular needs must be considered. This application will initially store the following information in the Student Personal table:

> Student ID or social security number
>
> Name (last name, first name, and middle initial)
>
> Address
>
> Phone
>
> Emergency contact and/or parents
>
> E-mail address
>
> Major
>
> Notes

If you were making this database on your own, you might consider more, different, or fewer fields for this table. For example, if you were modifying this model for a

customer database, you'd include a company name and a contact person and probably leave out the emergency contact. Additionally, you'd need an alternative to the social security number to act as a Customer ID.

Now that we've settled on some of the fields we'll need for the first table, it's time to go ahead and create it.

Exercise 3.2. Creating the Student Personal table.

1. Make sure the Table tab in the Database box is selected. (Figure 3.4 shows the tab correctly selected.)

2. Click on the New button within the Database box.

3. Access responds by asking you if you want to use the Table Wizard or New Table. New Table is what you'd choose if you wanted to bypass the wizard. In this case, click on the Table Wizard button. Access responds with a screen like Figure 3.5.

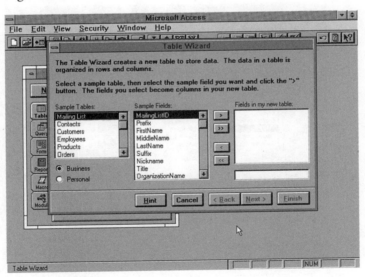

Figure 3.5. *The Table Wizard again in action.*

4. Make sure the option button, Business, in the lower-left corner is selected. Use your mouse to scroll through the Sample Tables list. Locate the sample table called Students and click on it.

5. Access is making it easy for us. Look at the Sample Fields list box and note that almost all the fields we want are included in this sample table.

DO   **DON'T**

DO check to see if Access comes up with a sample or solution that closely fits your needs. It's not necessary to reinvent the wheel.

DON'T force a fit. If you can't find a sample or solution that's close to your needs, don't be afraid of rolling your own from scratch.

---

6. Click on the >> button just to the right of the Sample Fields list to include all the sample fields into our new table. Then click on Region in the "Fields in my new table" list and click on the < button to eliminate the Region field from the new table. Your screen should resemble Figure 3.6.

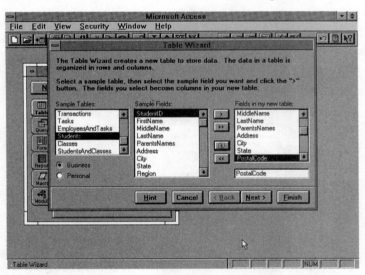

Figure 3.6. *The Table Wizard with the needed sample fields included.*

7. Click on the Next> button at the bottom right of the Table Wizard. This is the button right next to the Finish button. Access prompts you for a name for this table and suggests Students. Override Access's suggestion and name your table Student Personal.

8. Move to the middle of the wizard dialog box and change the choice from having Access set the primary key for you to Set the Primary Key Myself. In this case, Access's choice for a primary key would suffice nicely, but it's a good exercise to learn how to set keys manually, so we'll do that later on. Click on Next> to move to the next dialog box.

9. The Student ID will be unique to each record since you'll be using the students' social security numbers as Student IDs. Therefore, leave Access's choice of Student ID as the field that will be unique to each record, but select the bottom option button from the selections in the middle of the dialog box to tell Access that Student ID will be numbers or letters added when you add new records. Your screen should now look like Figure 3.7.

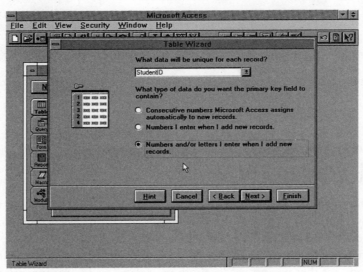

Figure 3.7. *Identifying the unique field for the Table Wizard.*

10. Click on the Next> button. Access gives you three final choices and signals you're at the end of this wizard by showing you the checkered-flag symbol. Click on the top option if it's not selected to tell Access that at the end of the wizard you want to modify the table's design. Click on Finish. Access will trundle around a bit, create the new table, and leave you in table Design View. Your screen should look like Figure 3.8.

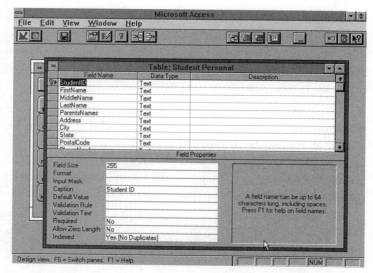

Figure 3.8. *The finished Student Personal table shown in Design View.*

A Look at Field Type and Properties

Refer to Figure 3.8 or your screen. The top part of the table design window shows a list of the field names and their data types. The bottom part of the window has a section labeled Field Properties. Each field in an Access table has three elements: the field name, such as StudentID; a field type, such as Text; and a set of properties. It's important that you set each field in your database to an appropriate field type. It's generally less important, but still a matter of concern, that your table fields have their properties set correctly.

Data Types

The data type for a field tells Access what type of data, or information, you plan on entering in that field. Access allows the following data types:

Text: Also known as Alphanumeric. This data type accepts any normal characters and is limited to a field length of 255 characters.

Number: This data type accepts numbers. You can specify the level of precision for a Number data type. Use the Number data type when you plan on applying arithmetical operations on a field or fields.

Date/Time: A specialized form of Number data type, for entering date or time information. Like the standard Number data type, the Date/Time data type enables you to perform arithmetical operations. For example, you can find the number of days between two dates if they are entered as Date/Time data types. (If you entered date or time information in a Text data type field, Access would accept the entry, but you couldn't perform arithmetical operations on the entries.)

Currency: This is another specialized Number data type, which fixes a certain number of decimal places. It is useful for entering monetary information.

Counter: When you make a field a Counter data type, Access will automatically apply sequential numbers to records as you enter them. The numbering begins at 1. Counter fields are great for primary keys since Access will never reuse a number once it has been assigned to a record in a table.

Yes/No: Accepts only two values—Yes or No.

OLE Object: Enables you either to link or embed an object created in another program that can act as an OLE server program. Access 2 is an OLE client-only program and cannot generate objects for embedding in other OLE-aware programs. This is a fairly complex subject that this book addresses on Day 11 and the extra credit day.

Memo: A field for adding notes or memoranda to a record.

Keep in mind that you can't index on either the Memo or OLE fields. Generally speaking, use the Text data type unless you're sure either that all your data will conform to one of the less flexible data types or that you'll need to perform math on a field's data. You cannot do math on a Text field, even if that field only contains numerical data.

DO	DON'T

DO try to get your data types correct the first time.

DON'T despair if you defined a data type incorrectly. In most cases, Access will allow you to change data types even after you've entered data into the table. In some cases you might lose some entered data, but Access will warn you if this could occur.

Morning Summary

This morning you learned how to create a new database and add a table to it using a wizard. You also were introduced to the various data types Access uses.

4

Table Field Properties

This afternoon you'll learn how to do the following:

☐ Modify a wizard-created table

☐ Manually create a table

☐ Create a simple two-table relationship

Modifying a Table

Access enables you to modify almost any aspect of an existing table, whether it is made manually or through the use of a wizard. In almost every case, a wizard-based table needs some sort of customizing. You saw this in Exercise 3.2 when you deleted the unneeded field called Region, which was supplied in the sample table, from your finished Student Personal table.

Many times you'll design a table and then realize that a particular field's data type is wrong, or you included a field you shouldn't have, or you left one out that you need. In all these cases, you would need to modify an existing table design.

The Student Personal table was fairly close to what you needed when it came out of the wizard. It needs only two modifications: changing the field name PostalCode to Zip, and adding a field for ethnicity. (The latter field is necessary for many government reports a college needs to make.)

The basic way to change a table's design is to click in the appropriate area of the table design grid and make whatever changes you want.

Exercise 4.1. Modifying a table.

1. If you've closed Access, the College database, or the Student Personal table, you'll need to reopen them. If necessary, launch Access, click on the menu item called File, click on Open Database, and choose College from the list box. With the Student Personal table highlighted, click on the Design button in the database box. Your screen should resemble Figure 3.8.

2. Locate the field called PostalCode. Double-click on the word PostalCode. This will highlight the word. Your screen should resemble Figure 4.1.

3. Type the word Zip. Access replaces the word PostalCode with Zip. You've just modified a field's name. Your screen should now resemble Figure 4.2.

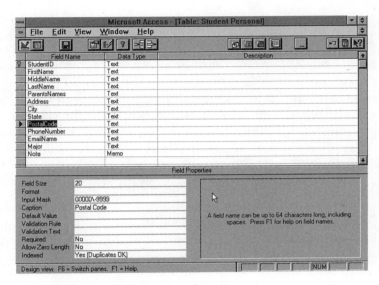

Figure 4.1. *Highlighting a field name to alter it.*

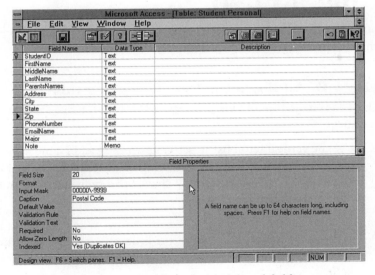

Figure 4.2. *The Student Personal table with the changed field name.*

> **The Access Way**
>
> Because of a long-standing database convention, Access wizards use field names lacking white space. This harkens back to a time when database programs limited their field names to eight characters and couldn't handle white space within these names. Those days are, for the most part, long gone; but many database veterans still get nervous seeing a field name such as First Name, so the designers of Access concede the point and concatenate First Name to FirstName.
>
> There's a practical side to this as well. Field names without white space export to these older-style database programs much better. However, feel free to add white space to your field names if you're fairly sure you won't have to contend with these older technologies.

Adding a Field

You can easily add a field to an existing Access database. Here's how to add a field called Ethnicity to the Student Personal table.

Exercise 4.2. Adding a field to an existing table.

1. Your screen should look like Figure 4.2. If not, make the necessary adjustments.

2. Use the vertical scroll bar to scroll down the Field Name list until you can see the field name Major. Move your cursor to the left border of the Field Name column. Your cursor will change to a right-facing arrow. Your screen should now resemble Figure 4.3.

3. Click once. Access highlights the entire row. When you click, be sure not to move the mouse cursor from the little gray square just to the left of the Major field. This can be a little tricky and might take you a few tries to get right.

4. With the entire row containing the field name Major highlighted, press the Insert key on your keyboard. Access will insert a new empty row and push the field Major down one row. Your screen should now resemble Figure 4.4.

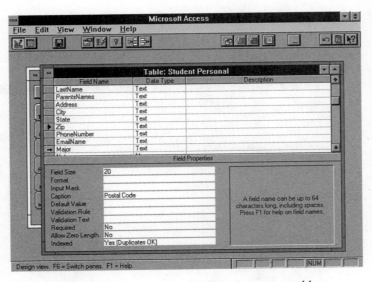

Figure 4.3. *Getting ready to insert a new field in an existing table.*

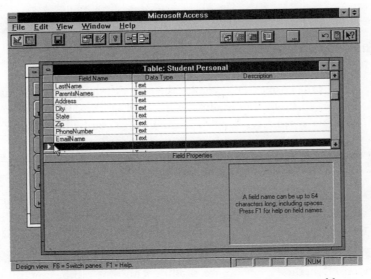

Figure 4.4. *Getting ready to add a new field name to an existing table.*

5. Click once in the Field Name column of the highlighted row. The row will lose the highlight and your cursor will be at the extreme left of the Field Name column. Type the word Ethnicity.

6. Tab to move your cursor to the Data Type column. Access will respond by suggesting the data type Text and will also reveal a pull-down tab to the right of the Data Type field. Your screen should now resemble Figure 4.5.

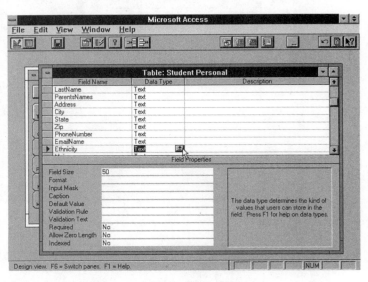

Figure 4.5. *Specifying the data type for Table field.*

7. Text is the correct data type for the new Ethnicity field, but just to take a look at what else you might choose, click on the down arrow to the right of the data-type entry. Access will show you a combo box of all its data types.

DO   DON'T

DO use whatever keyboard navigation methods you like. For example, pressing the Enter key after adding the field name Ethnicity would have moved the cursor to the Data Type column just as well as pressing Tab.

DON'T worry about following the keystrokes in this book precisely. If your preferred method for using Access differs in some minor way from the instructions in this book, use whatever makes you comfortable.

8. You've just added a new field to the Student Personal table. Close the Student Personal table either by double-clicking on its control menu icon or by pulling down the menu item File and choosing Close. When Access asks if you want to save the changes you made to the table, click on OK.

Rolling a New Table Manually

Sometimes a table you need doesn't resemble anything in the wizard's samples. In these cases you'll need to roll your own from scratch. Many database veterans are reluctant to let wizards take over their work and they opt for manual design even if a good prototype exists in the wizard. No matter how experienced you are, you should get a feel for manual table design since it's only a matter of time until you need to use table design skills. Actually, if you've done the two exercises in this chapter, you already have a good idea of what it takes to manually design a table in Access.

You need a table to store information about student course registrations. This table will contain a field for StudentID so it can be linked to the Student Personal table. It'll also need fields for course number, an indication whether the student finished the course, and the student's grade. Each semester this table will feed information into another table, which will, in effect, be the student's transcript.

Note: Our example is a somewhat simplified college registration system. In it we'll assume that all course numbers will point to unique courses and there are no sections to these courses. Although in real life many college courses contain sections, adding this complexity to our example would obscure the point of these exercises. If you're working on a real-world college registration system, adding items such as sections will be easy for you after you learn the basics in these exercises.

Creating the Table

After you close the Student Personal table in Exercise 4.2, your screen should look like Figure 4.6. If it doesn't, navigate around Access until it does. Exercise 4.3 shows you how to create a table manually.

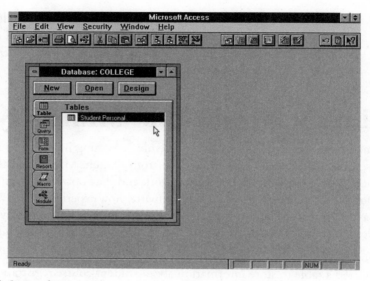

Figure 4.6. *Ready to create a new table without a wizard's help.*

Exercise 4.3. Creating a table without a wizard.

1. Click on the New button to start the table creation process. When Access asks you if you want to use Table Wizards or a New Table, choose New Table. Access will immediately open a blank table design grid as in Figure 4.7.

2. Your cursor will be on the first row in the leftmost column of the design grid. This is the column where, as you saw in the wizard process, Access stores field names. Take a moment to examine the square in the lower right corner of the table design grid. Right now it says, "A field name can be up to 64 characters long including spaces. Press F1 for help on field names." As you use Access, the program helps you along with valuable tidbits such as this. As you work through this exercise, watch not only the prompts in this box but also those along the status bar at the very bottom of your screen.

3. Enter the words Index Number for the first field name. Press tab to move to the Data Type field. Access will suggest the Text data type. Click on the pull-down tab to choose another data type. Locate the Counter data type and click on it. The Index Number field will be the key field for this table. While key fields are not absolutely necessary, Access operates more efficiently using tables with key fields, so we're including one here. The Counter data

type means that Access will automatically add unique numbers to this field for each record you create as you use this table.

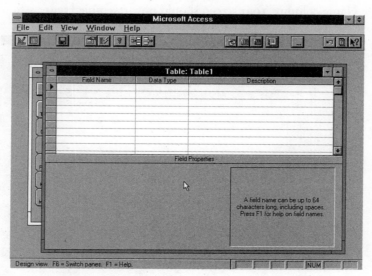

Figure 4.7. *The blank table design grid.*

4. The next field you need is StudentID so you can link this table to the Student Personal table. Press tab twice to move through the Description field to the second row of the Field Name column.

DO   DON'T

DO comment your tables and other database objects with full descriptions if users will be asked to maintain them. Access shows the contents of the field description column in the status bar during data entry for a table.

DON'T be cryptic or overly cute when commenting. The comments or descriptions you think are clever today might come back to haunt you tomorrow.

5. Enter StudentID. Tab to the Data Type field. Accept Access's defaults and tab twice to move to the next row.

6. Enter Course Number. Again tab to the Data Type column and again accept Access's default by tabbing twice to move to the fourth row in the Field Name column. Your screen should now resemble Figure 4.8.

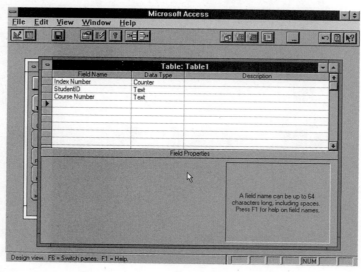

Figure 4.8. *In the middle of a manual table design session.*

Note: The field Course Number was left at the default Text data type even though the field will only contain numbers. This is because no math will ever be performed on this field.

7. Enter Completed as the next field name and choose Yes/No as its data type. Tab to the next Field Name row.

8. Finish this table's name and data types by entering Grade and leaving the data type as text. Don't tab away from the data type column just yet.

9. Since a grade won't ever take up the 50 spaces Access allows for a field size, click on the Field Size row in the Field Properties section of the table design grid. Change the default value of 50 to 2. Your screen will now resemble Figure 4.9.

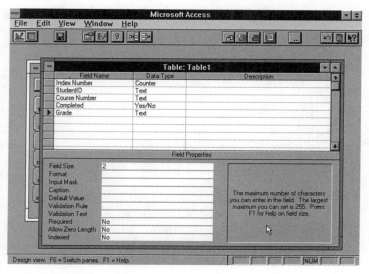

Figure 4.9. *Changing a field size.*

10. The only thing left to do is to tell Access you want the Index Number field to be the key field. A key field in Access contains unique data for each record, and Access indexes or orders the table primarily on that key.

11. Click on the first row in the first column of the table design grid; that is, click on the field name Index Number. Look at the toolbar until you find a button with a little down-pointing key on it. Move your cursor over this button and you should see the balloon help Set Primary Key drop-down. Click on this button. A little key will appear just to the left of the Index Number field name, indicating that you've just set Index Number to be the key field for this table. Your screen will now resemble Figure 4.10.

12. Now save and name this table. Click on the menu item File and choose Close. Access will respond with a message box asking you if you want to save the changes to Table 1. Click on Yes. When prompted for a table name, enter Students' Current Courses. Click on OK. Access will save the table and return you to the Database View that now shows two tables: Student Personal and Students' Current Courses.

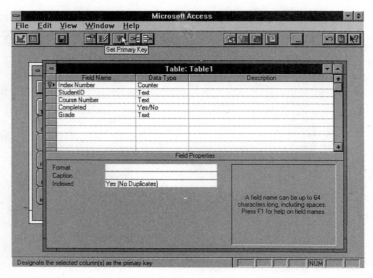

Figure 4.10. *Setting a key field for a table.*

The "Why" of a Relationship

Consider the functions of the Students' Current Courses table. You wouldn't want any entries in this table for nonstudents, and you also want to be able to match the courses taken with the appropriate students. In a relational database such as Access, links serve both these functions.

You'll want to establish a link between the Student Personal table and the Students' Current Courses table in order to do two things. You want to make sure you don't get any erroneous data in Students' Current Courses—that is, you don't want data for a course being taken without a student attached to it. So you'll want to make sure a record exists for a student in Student Personal before you try to make an entry for that student in Students' Current Courses.

You also want to be sure you can enter many records for any one student in Students' Current Courses, since one student can take many courses during a semester. A relationship wherein one record can be linked to many is called, not surprisingly, a one-to-many relationship. Making sure a record exists in the table on the "one" side before any records can be entered in the "many" side is called referential integrity.

If this seems complicated, don't worry about it for now. After you establish the link this afternoon, enter some data tomorrow, and continue to work with this database later on, the ways in which these elements fit together will become clear.

Making the Link or Relationship

Your screen should now be at the Database View, as it was when you finished Exercise 4.3. If it's not, navigate there before you start Exercise 4.4.

Exercise 4.4. Creating a one-to-many link.

1. Click on the menu item called Edit and then click on Relationships at the bottom of the drop-down list.

2. Click on the Add button in the Add Table dialog box. This will add the Student Personal table to the Relationships window. Click on the Students' Current Courses entry in the Add Table dialog box and again click on the Add button to add this table to the window. Your screen should now resemble Figure 4.11.

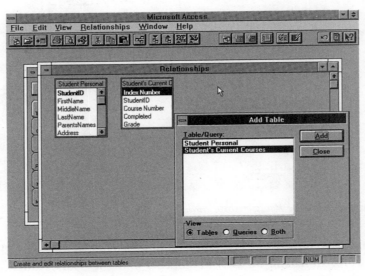

Figure 4.11. *Adding tables to the Relationships window.*

3. Click on the Close button in the Add Table dialog box.

4. Click on the entry StudentID in the Students' Current Courses list box. Note that the two fields, Index Number in the Students' Current Courses and StudentID in Student Personal, are represented in boldface. This indicates that these fields are the key fields for their respective tables.

5. Now for some tricky mouse work. You establish a link between tables by dragging your mouse from table to table within the relationships window. Here's how it works:

   Move your mouse cursor to the entry called StudentID in the Student Personal list box. Click the left button and hold it while you drag the cursor into the Students' Current Courses list box. Still holding the mouse button down, move the cursor over the StudentID field in the second list box and then let go. Access will respond with a dialog box. Your screen should now resemble Figure 4.12.

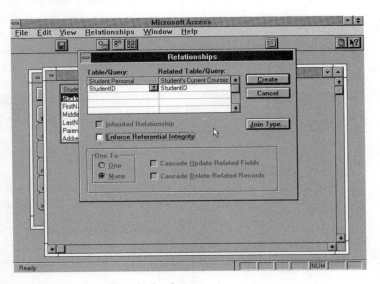

Figure 4.12. *The Relationships dialog box.*

6. Click on the check box called Enforce Referential Integrity. This will prevent making an entry in Students' Current Courses unless a previous entry exists in Student Personal. Click on the Create button and Access will respond by giving you a screen like the one in Figure 4.13.

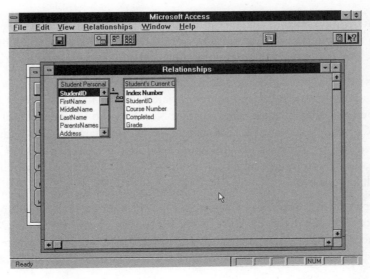

Figure 4.13. *The finished table link.*

Note that Access indicates a one-to-many link pictorially. Near the point where the link line enters the Student Personal list box, you see a numeral 1. This signifies the one side of the one-to-many relationship. Near where the link line enters the Students' Current Courses list box is a "lazy eight" sign representing infinity. This shows that the Students' Current Courses table holds down the many side of this one-to-many relationship.

Again, don't be concerned at this point if linking and relationships are difficult concepts for you. The next and subsequent chapters help to clarify these issues.

7. Click on the menu items File and then Close. Access will ask if you want to save the relationships changes. Click on Yes and that will land you back at the Database View.

Summary

The ongoing project we are using in this book is a student tracking and registration system for a mythical college. On this day you created two tables for this database. You created the first table, Student Personal, using a new table wizard. Since a good prototype apparently didn't exist, you made the second table, Students' Current Courses, manually.

Often you'll need to change some elements of a wizard-created table. You can easily do this from the table design grid. For example, to change a field name, just double-click on it to give it the highlight. Then type in the new field name.

It's important to set the right data type for fields. Access defaults to the Text data type, which, generally speaking, is appropriate for most fields. However, Access also has several less-flexible data types, such as Number, and specialized number types, such as Currency. Use one of the Number or Date/Time data types for fields in which you'll need to perform math. If you won't be doing any calculations on a field, the safe approach is to leave it as a Text data type—even if you anticipate that all its entries will be numbers.

Each field also has a set of properties. These properties, such as field size, vary with the data type. Key fields have the Indexed property always set to Yes (No Duplicates), since the nature of key fields is that the data for any record can appear only once in a table and Access will index (or order) a table primarily on the key field's entries.

Creating a table manually is operationally identical to altering the entries in a wizard-created table.

You create a link, or relationship, between two tables by first choosing the menu selections Edit|Relationships from the Database View. Then add the tables you want to add to the link structure by highlighting them in the Add Table dialog box and clicking on the Add button. You create the links themselves by dragging the mouse cursor from one table's list box to another. Finally, you finish the linking process by choosing options for the link in the Relationships dialog box.

Q&A

Q **I noticed several sample tables with names like Classes and StudentsAndClasses in the new Table Wizard. Why didn't we use those tables instead of rolling one from scratch?**

A You've got sharp eyes. Actually we could have used the Access-supplied sample tables for the second table we made today, but we did it manually for practice.

Q **I noticed many other field properties in the table design grid. When do you set these?**

A The most efficient time to set these properties is during the initial design, but you lose nothing but a little time if you skip this originally and come back to it later. We skipped most of the properties during today's

exercises in order to focus on basic table-design methods. When you're familiar with Access and making your own applications, try to set as many field properties as you can anticipate during the initial design phase.

Q **I created a field with the Text data type. It accepted date entries such as September 2, 1994, just fine. Why should I bother with the Date/Time data type?**

A Date/Time is a specialized number format. You can perform math on fields with this data type. Let's say you have a database with tables tracking loans, and you have fields for the starting and ending dates of those loans. If the data type is Text, you won't be able to use Access to calculate the time between these dates. If the data type is set to Date/Time, performing these calculations is simple. Later in this book you'll see how handy the Date/Time data type is for this purpose.

Q **Help! My Access came without wizards.**

A If you chose to install Access in the minimum or laptop configuration, Setup didn't install your wizards, so you need to rerun Setup and choose a full installation. (See Question 1 after Day 1 for a related answer.)

Also examine your MSACC20.INI file, located in your Windows directory, with a text editor such as Notepad. You should see the following entries:

```
[Libraries]
wzlib.mda=rw, Wizard Utility Functions
wzTable.mda=rw, Table Wizard
wzQuery.mda=rw, Query Wizards
wzfrmrpt.mda=rw, Form and Report Wizards
wzbldr.mda=rw, Property and Control Wizards
```

If you don't, you need to add these lines to your MSACC20.INI file. See your Access documentation for more information on the MSACC20.INI file.

Q **Why use the Text data type for the numbers-only Zip field?**

A A Number data type field cannot start with a zero, since in a Number data type, zeros on the left are meaningless and Access will drop them. If you enter the number 010 into a Number data type field, Access will strip the left zero and enter just 10. Some Zip codes begin with a zero, so we needed to specify the Text data type. Even if no Zip codes started with a zero, Text is the appropriate data type to use here, since you don't do math on Zip fields.

Workshop

Here's where you can test and apply the lessons you learned today.

Quiz

Possible answers to these questions are provided in Appendix A.

1. What's the first step in creating a new Access table?

2. You have an order-entry sales system that has two linked tables: Customers and Sales to Customers. Which table do you suppose is the "many" in this one-to-many link?

3. Why use a wizard when making a table?

4. What's the maximum size of a field with the data type set to Text?

5. What is the maximum number of characters (including spaces) for a field name in an Access table?

6. Let's say you're going to export a table called A List of My Friends to an old database system that can't handle white space in table names. What do you suppose will happen when you try to use this table in the older database system?

Put Access into Action

1. During the exercise, you altered the field name PostalCode in the Student Personal table to Zip. However, the field property Caption was left at PostalCode. The Caption property overrides the field name when a field is used on a form. While this is correctable, it's inconvenient. Open the Student Personal table in Design View and change the caption property for the Zip field to Zip.

2. Add a field called Date of Birth to the Student Personal table. Have the new field appear just below the Ethnicity field. Set the data-type format to Date/Time.

3. To get your Student Personal table back into sync with the book, delete the Date of Birth field from Student Personal. Hint: To do this, highlight the entire row containing the field and press the Delete key. If you accidentally delete the wrong field, press Ctrl+Z or select the menu choices Edit|Undo.

4. Close the Student Personal table, discarding all changes.

Day

3

5

Modifying Table Properties

Yesterday was devoted to basic table-making, with an introduction to table field properties. Today's lesson builds directly on that foundation. This morning you'll learn about the following:

- ☐ Adding data directly into a table
- ☐ Using an input mask
- ☐ The Field Size property
- ☐ Learning basic data-validation and default methods
- ☐ Rearranging field order in a table
- ☐ Resizing the appearance of a field

This might seem like a lot of territory to cover, but each new technique follows logically from the one that precedes it. The material about data validation, defaults, and input masks directly addresses the integrity of your data, so pay particular attention to those sections—especially if you're planning on creating a database application for others to use. Keep in mind that although much of this is rather dry, it is important.

Getting Started

The tables you made yesterday are empty storage units for the information that you want to keep in an orderly fashion. Tables in and of themselves do nothing—it's the data they can store that is the heart of your database project. Entering data into a table is as simple as typing it in. Exercise 5.1 guides you through the creation of your first record using Access.

Exercise 5.1. Entering data directly into a table.

1. Launch Access if you have not already done so.

2. Open the College database either by clicking on the menu items File|Open or by locating and clicking on the Open Database button on the toolbar. (The Open Database button has an open folder as its icon.)

   When Access opens College, the Database View should be on the Table objects and the highlight on the Student Personal table. Access shows database objects in alphabetical order at the Database View. If you want a particular table to appear at the bottom of the Database View window, start its name with a "zz." (You can also hide a table from a casual user's view.

These techniques are covered in later chapters.)

3. Click on the Open button to open the Student Personal table in Datasheet View. Datasheet View means that the table's ready for data entry, editing, or viewing (as opposed to Design View, in which a table's open to modify its design). Your screen should resemble Figure 5.1.

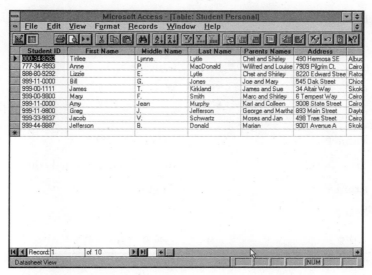

Figure 5.1. *A table in Datasheet View.*

The next steps are easier if you click on the maximize button in the Student Personal table's window. That's the button in the upper-right corner with the up-facing arrow.

4. Your cursor will be in the first field, StudentID. Enter 999-11-0000 as the StudentID for this record. The college has a policy of using a student's social security number as a student ID number. (The case of a student without a social security number is considered later in this chapter.)

5. After entering the student ID, press Tab or Enter to move on to the FirstName field. Enter Bill.

In a similar manner, continue entering the following information for this record:

Table 5.1. Data for Student Personal table.

Field	Data
MiddleName	G.
LastName	Jones
ParentsNames	Joe and Mary
Address	545 Oak Street
City	Chicago
State	IL
Zip (PostalCode)	39844
PhoneNumber	(317) 555-9873
EmailName	billg@speedy.fictional.edu
Ethnicity	Anglo
Major	English
Note	Hobbies include woodworking and skiing

Entering data directly into a table is as easy as typing it in. However, doing it this way is, to say the least, inconvenient, and there's no way to make sure you're entering valid data.

Quality Assurance, Data-Entry Style

If the only thing you want Access to do is store raw data, you need go no further; but it is capable of much more. One of the ways in which an electronic storage system such as Access is superior to a paper-based system is that the electronic system can examine input and then, based on rules you supply, accept or reject it.

You can edit data in an Access table in a similar manner to editing field names during the table design phase. Edit Bill Jones' StudentID by clicking in the StudentID field just to the right of the last zero. Drag the cursor all the way to the left of the StudentID number to highlight the entire field. Enter `Hello World!` and tab to the FirstName field. The text Hello World! now replaces Bill's StudentID. Hello World! isn't anywhere close to a valid social security number or a student ID, but Access permitted it.

The reason Access accepted Hello World! as a StudentID is because you didn't tell it not to. Also, although each StudentID will follow the form of ###-##-#### (with data substituted for the # characters), you had to manually insert the dashes. You can solve the problems of having to insert dashes manually and of inappropriate entries at the same time. Before moving on, edit Bill's StudentID back to 999-11-0000.

ACCESS JARGON

view: Access heavily utilizes the word "view," which replaces the more descriptive term "mode" for many Access activities. So while you might think you are in Table-Design *Mode*, Access's term for this is Table-Design *View*. This seems to fit in with Microsoft's corporate leadership in visual tools such as Visual Basic and Visual C++. The term "view" is surely overworked in Access, but once you get used to it, well, you'll be used to it.

Exercise 5.2 shows how to add an input mask.

Exercise 5.2. Adding an input mask.

1. Locate the Design View button on the toolbar. (Refer to Figure 5.2.)

2. Click on the Design View button. This switches you from table Datasheet View to Design View. Your screen should resemble Figure 5.3.

3. Click on the field name StudentID because you'll initially be setting a field property for this field. Clicking in the row with a field name tells Access to bring up the properties for this field.

4. Examine the Field properties list box at the lower part of the table design grid. One of the properties is called Input Mask. Click in the now empty field just to the right of the Input Mask property label.

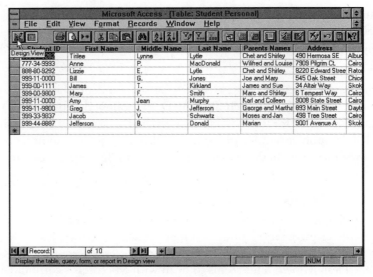

Figure 5.2. *Switching from Datasheet to Design View.*

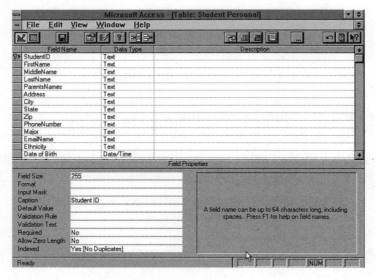

Figure 5.3. *The table returned to Design View.*

Note that when you clicked on the field for input mask, a button with three dots appeared on the right of the field. This is a build button. If you clicked on it, it'd bring up an appropriate builder or wizard. At this point, clicking on this button or on the build button of the toolbar brings up an Input Mask Builder Wizard. This exercise creates an input mask manually—even though the exact mask you'll build is available for the price of a few simple clicks in a wizard.

5. Enter AAA-AA-AAAA;1;" " for an input mask. The A's in the input mask are placeholders saying you must enter a total of nine alphanumeric characters for this field. Press Tab to move to the next field. Access adds two backslashes before each dash, but otherwise accepts the entry.

Access Input Masks

Access input masks have three parts. The first part is the look of the mask. Entering ??-?? enables the acceptance of any four characters but separates them with a dash. Access added the backslash before each dash in Exercise 5.2 because the backslash indicates to Access that the next character is to be literally interpreted. If you had an input mask such as ?\??, Access would accept any two characters separated by a question mark.

The second part of the input mask comes after the semi-colon. This can either be blank, a numeral 1, or a 0. A blank or a 1 in this space tells Access to only store the field's data. A 0 in this place tells Access not only to store input data but the formatting characters.

The third and final part of an input mask tells Access what character to use as a placeholder. This example uses " " or white space to tell Access that you want blanks as placeholders.

After entering your input mask, your screen should resemble Figure 5.4.

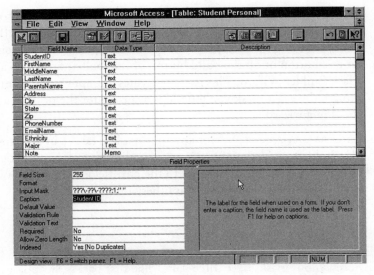

Figure 5.4. *An input mask after Access inserts the literal characters.*

Trying Out the Input Mask

Return to Datasheet View by either clicking on the Datasheet View button in the toolbar—it's the one second from the left—or clicking on the menu selections View|Datasheet. Access will tell you that you must save your changes before entering Datasheet View. Since that's what you want, click on OK.

Click on the StudentID field on row two of the table to get ready to enter a new record. Try to enter Hello World! Two things then occur. First, Access adds dashes after Hel and lo, and second, it refuses to accept the entire text. The input mask told Access to insert a dash after the third and fifth character and not to accept more than nine characters for this field.

You could have told Access only to accept numbers for this field, but that would have caused a problem with students (such as visiting exchange students) who lack a social security number. In the case of these students, the college generates a Student ID based on the student's birthday and last name.

Here's how the college system works for students without a social security number. For students such as this, the college creates a StudentID using the student's birth date in the form DDMMYY and the first three letters of the student's last name.

A student born on July 12, 1972, with the last name Johnson would have the StudentID of 071272JOH. A student born on May 5, 1967, having a last name of Smith would have a StudentID of 050567SMI, and so forth. The possible inclusion of alpha characters such as JOH and SMI in the StudentID field is why the input mask accepts letters as well as numbers.

Press Esc to cancel this record's data entry. Click back on the StudentID field for row two. Now enter the incomplete StudentID 99998098. Press tab or Enter. Access will give you one of its standard message boxes telling you that your entry doesn't meet the requirement of the input mask you've defined. Click on OK to acknowledge this message.

Press Esc to cancel data entry. Return to Design View. Add an input mask to the PhoneNumber field by clicking on that field and then adding (AAA) AAA-AAAA;1;"#" for the Input-mask Field property. The big difference between this and the previous input mask is that here Access prompts the user for the right number of digits by using the placeholder # instead of a white space. As with StudentID, this field accepts alpha characters in the phone number. Thus, it accepts phone numbers in the form (317) 555-1234 as well as (317) KL5-1234. Return to Datasheet View.

Add a second record to this table using the following data:

Table 5.2. Data for Student Personal table.

Field	Data
StudentID	999-00-9800
FirstName	Mary
MiddleName	F.
LastName	Smith
ParentsNames	Marc and Shirley
Address	6 Tempest Way
City	Cairo
State	IL
Zip (PostalCode)	35854
PhoneNumber	(317) 555-9038

continues

Table 5.2. continued

Field	Data
EmailName	99955.495@compuserve.com
Ethnicity	Indian
Major	Mathematics
Note	On full scholarship

Note how much easier it is to enter data when an input mask exists.

DO   **DON'T**

DO use input masks, especially in applications where you expect a lot of data entry, since input masks greatly ease data-entry chores.

DON'T ignore the second part of the input-mask field. Generally speaking, you don't want to embed input-mask literals in your data, but if you do, you must tell Access specifically that you do.

Changing Field Order

Changing the order of fields in a table is something you might want to do from time to time. Keep in mind that the order in which fields appear in the design grid doesn't force you to have fields in the same order in Datasheet View, forms, or reports.

Moving a Field

Click on the Design View button to bring up the table design grid. Exercise 5.3 moves the Major field to just under the PhoneNumber.

Exercise 5.3. Changing the field order of a table.

1. Click on the gray border just to the left of the Major field. Access highlights the entire row. Your screen should look like Figure 5.5.

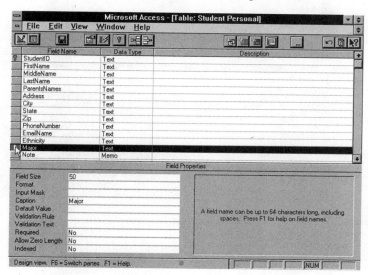

Figure 5.5. *Getting ready to move a field.*

2. Release your mouse button, then move the cursor back to the gray area you clicked on to give the row a highlight. Make sure you've maneuvered the mouse so its cursor looks like a slightly left-leaning arrow.

3. Click your mouse again and hold. You should see a small "ghost" rectangle below the mouse cursor. This rectangle visually represents that you can now move the field. Keep the mouse button pressed and drag the cursor up until the moving dark line appears just below the PhoneNumber field.

4. Release the mouse button. Access will drop the Major field to the space below PhoneNumber. Your screen should resemble Figure 5.6.

5. Return to Datasheet View, telling Access it's OK when it reminds you that you must save changes before changing view.

6. Scroll over so you can see the PhoneNumber and the field just to its right. The field to the right of PhoneNumber now is Major rather than EmailName.

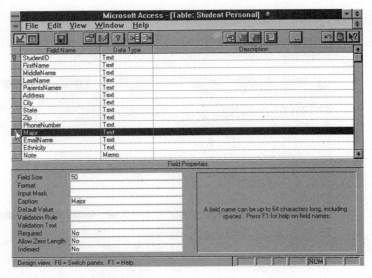

Figure 5.6. *A field moved and dropped to a new location.*

Changing the Apparent Field Order

When you change the field order in the field design grid, you also change the order in which the fields will appear in the Datasheet View. However, you can make changes in the Datasheet View that won't change the field order in the Database Design View. Exercise 5.4 illustrates this.

Exercise 5.4. Changing the apparent field order.

1. If you're not in Datasheet View, click on the toolbar or choose the necessary menu selections to bring that view up.

2. Click on the gray area just above the LastName field. This gray area has the label "LastName" in it. The entire LastName column will get the highlight. Your screen should resemble Figure 5.7.

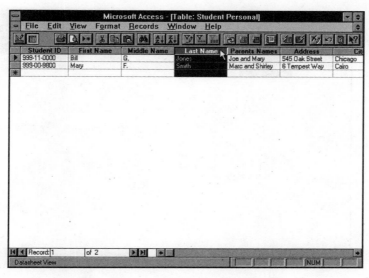

Figure 5.7. *Getting ready to move a column in Datasheet View.*

3. Move your cursor over the now-highlighted gray area again. You've hit the appropriate place when the cursor changes to look like a left-leaning arrow. Click again without moving the mouse, but this time hold the mouse button down. You'll get a "ghost" rectangle at the base of the cursor. Drag the cursor to the left until a black line appears between the fields StudentID and FirstName. Release the mouse.

   The LastName field now appears just to the right of the StudentID field. Your screen should resemble Figure 5.8.

4. Switch to Design View. Note the LastName field remains below the MiddleName field just as it did before you moved it in the Datasheet View.

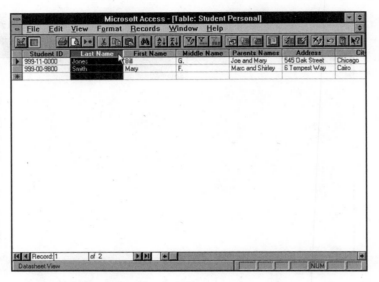

Figure 5.8. *A field moved in the datasheet.*

Changing field locations or widths in the Datasheet View *does not* change their location in Design View. Changing field locations in Design View *does* change field locations in the Datasheet View.

Changing Field Widths and Row Heights

The Field Size property for Text fields determines the capacity of the fields but doesn't affect how wide they're shown in the Datasheet View. Naturally that leaves some fields appearing too small while others are too wide in the default Datasheet View. Changing apparent field sizes from Access's default in the Datasheet View is quite simple, as Exercise 5.5 demonstrates.

Exercise 5.5. Changing apparent field widths and height.

1. Return to Datasheet View if you have not already done so.

2. Most street addresses are longer than the default size that Access has allowed for fields in our table, so the next step shows you how to make this field appear a bit wider.

Move your cursor into the gray area where field names appear. Now move the cursor to a point between the Address and City fields. The cursor changes to a wide vertical beam with left- and right-facing arrows. Your screen should resemble Figure 5.9.

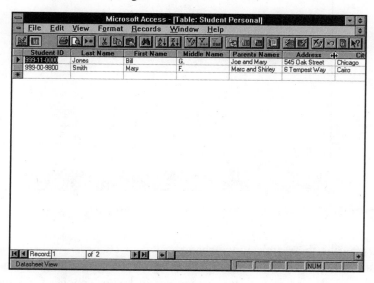

Figure 5.9. *Getting ready to alter a field's width.*

3. Click and hold the mouse button. Keeping the mouse button down, drag the cursor to the right. The Address field widens. When it's roughly one-and-a-half times larger than it was initially, release the mouse button. The field is now wide enough for most street addresses. Your screen should resemble Figure 5.10.

That's all there is to making a field wider.

To make a field *deeper,* or in other words to increase row height, proceed as you did in the preceding steps, only move your cursor to the gray area at the left of the leftmost field. Then move the cursor between two rows until the cursor becomes a horizontal bar with up- and down-facing arrows. Click and drag the row to its new height.

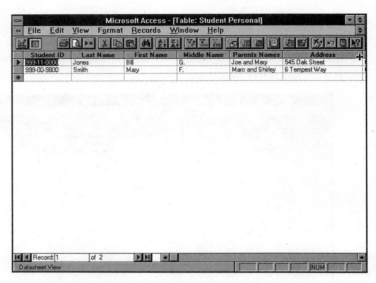

Figure 5.10. *A field made wider in the Datasheet View.*

Access calls these appearance changes "layout changes." When you close a table, Access asks you if you want to save these layout changes to field width and height. This gives you the freedom to make apparent or layout changes for a session and then discard them when closing the table. Or you can accept Access's offer and make the changes persist until the next datasheet session.

You might wonder why you'd ever want to change a row height in a datasheet. There are two common uses for greater row height. If you store pictures in a database, the standard row height won't show them very well, so increasing the row height is just the ticket. Also, if you have long Text or Memo field entries, trying to view those entries in one long text row is impractical. If you change the row height to accommodate more than one line, Access will wrap the long text entry to fit in as many lines as you want.

Well, that's it for this morning. Close the Student Personal table. When Access asks you if you want it to save the layout changes, click on NO.

Morning Summary

This morning you reviewed how to enter data directly into tables, how to create an input mask to format the appearance of data, and how to change the appearance of tables by altering the order and width of its columns and the width of its rows.

6

Data Types and Validation

This afternoon's lesson delves deeper into the dry yet important subject of table field properties. Specifically, it covers the following:

☐ The field properties for various data types

☐ Setting a default value for a field

☐ The differences in the Field Size property for Number and Text data type fields

☐ The Format property

☐ The Validation Data property

☐ The Validation Text property

More Field Properties

There are several other field property settings that can make your data entry easier and/or assure your data's integrity. Take a look at these properties by doing this: open the Student Personal table in Design View, click on the FirstName field, and look at the Field Properties list box. If you maximize the design grid window, your screen should resemble Figure 6.1.

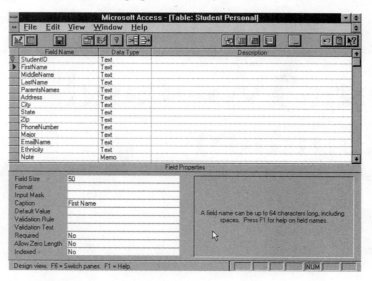

Figure 6.1. *The field properties for a Text field.*

Now click on the field called Note. The Properties list box changes to list only those field properties that a Memo field can have. Click on the field called State and the list box switches back to Text data type properties.

Each data type has a particular set of properties associated with it. The Note field lacks an Index property since you can't index a field with the data type of Memo. Figures 6.2 through 6.9 show the field properties associated with the various field types in Access.

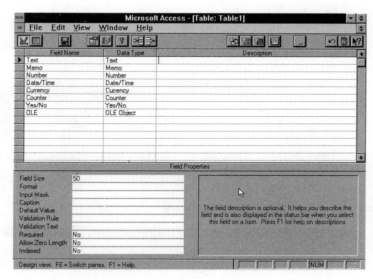

Figure 6.2. *The field properties of a Text data type.*

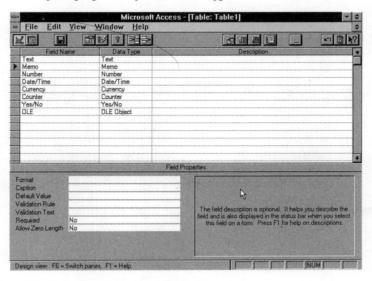

Figure 6.3. *The field properties of a Memo data type.*

81

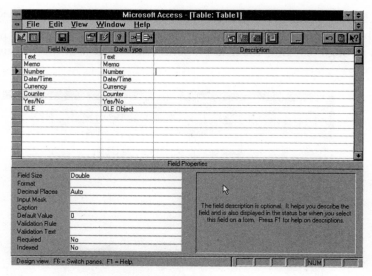

Figure 6.4. *The field properties of a Number data type.*

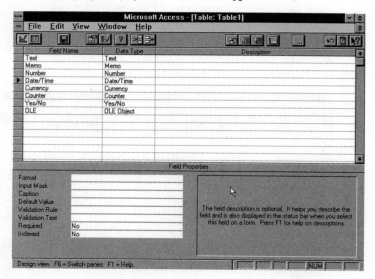

Figure 6.5. *The field properties of a Date/Time data type.*

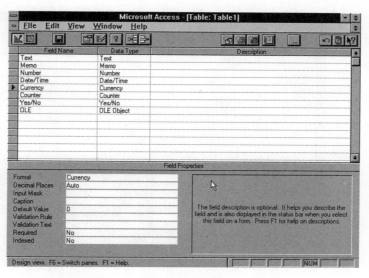

Figure 6.6. *The field properties of a Currency data type.*

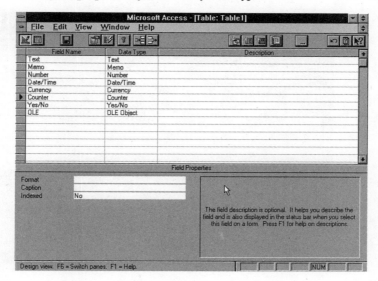

Figure 6.7. *The field properties of a Counter data type.*

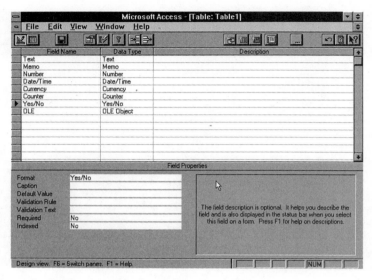

Figure 6.8. *The field properties of a Yes/No data type.*

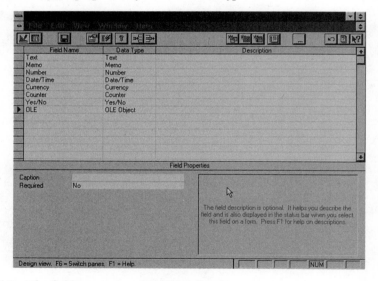

Figure 6.9. *The field properties of an OLE data type.*

Most of these field properties are at least somewhat self-explanatory from their labels, but one isn't. In a Text data type, the field size means the amount of space that Access allows for an entry. So a text field with a field size of five cannot hold the 11-space text entry "Hello World!" (The blank and the exclamation point each take one space.)

Take a look at Figure 6.4, which notes the field properties for a Number data type. There's an entry for field size there too, but in the case of a Number data type, field size has a completely different meaning than with a Text data type. Field size in a Number data type means number precision. The various sizes for a Number data type are as follows:

Byte: whole numbers from 0 to 255

Integer: whole numbers from -32,768 to 32,767

Long Integer: whole numbers from -2,147,483,648 to 2,147,483,647

Double: decimal numbers with 10 places of precision

Single: decimal numbers with 8 places of precision

Each of these data types requires a different amount of storage inside your computer. For example, Access reserves eight bytes of space for a number with a field size of "double," while it only reserves a single byte for a number with the field size of "byte."

The reason for having large field-size type numbers is to assure precision in calculations. The more precisely a number is stored inside Access, the more precise the calculations using that number will be. This is particularly important in repeating calculations, where the results of one calculation are fed back in for more iterations. The most common class of iterative calculations are interest calculations, where a period's interest is added to the principal to form the basis of the principal for the next period's calculation.

It's Default of Access

A very handy field property is the default value for a field. When you specify a default value for a field, Access automatically supplies that value during data entry. One nice thing about default values is that you can override them, so setting defaults exacts no penalty in your application.

> | **DO** | **DON'T** |
> | --- | --- |
>
> **DO** assign default values liberally in your applications. Even if you end up overriding them most of the time, you'll end up saving time overall.
>
> **DON'T** be concerned about potential penalties or gotchas that a default field value might create. There are none.

Our fictional college is in Northern Illinois and most of the students are from Illinois. Therefore, it makes sense for us to set a default value to IL for the state field in our Student Personal table. Exercise 6.1 shows how it's done.

Exercise 6.1. Setting a Default field property.

1. Make sure the Student Personal table is open in Design View.

2. Click on the State field in the Field Name column.

3. Click in the Default Value area of the Field Properties list box.

4. Enter IL for a value. Your screen should resemble Figure 6.10.

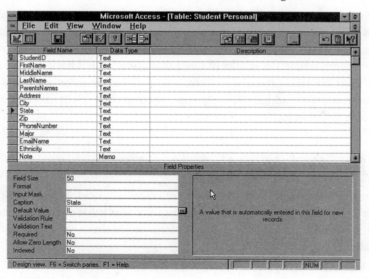

Figure 6.10. *Creating a default value for a field.*

It's that easy.

5. Now switch back to Datasheet View, saving the changes when Access reminds you that you must. Enter a record with the following data:

Table 6.1. Data for Student Personal table.

Field	Data
StudentID	999-11-9800
FirstName	Greg
MiddleName	J.
LastName	Jefferson
ParentsNames	George and Martha
Address	893 Main Street
City	Daytona
State	IL
Zip (PostalCode)	35888
PhoneNumber	(317) 555-2983
Major	Speech
EmailName	gregj@speedy.fictional.edu
Ethnicity	Black
Note	Honor society candidate

Did you notice that before you got to the State field, Access not only filled in this field for Jefferson's record but subsequent records as well? Look at Figure 6.11, which shows how Access is now supplying a default value for the State field.

6. Here's how to use a field with a default value. If the record you're entering uses the default value, just tab or hit Enter when you get into this field. If you need to change the default value to another, just tab into the field with the default value and enter the right data.

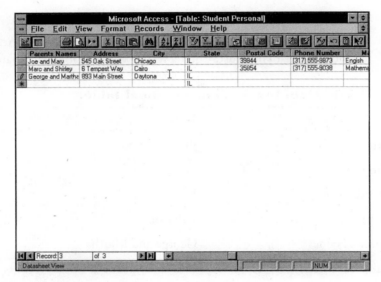

Figure 6.11. *The Default field property in action.*

ACCESS JARGON

default: If you're bothered by the term "default" for a value that's automatically assigned by Access to a field, you're not alone. Default, which means "failing in an obligation" to most English speakers, is standard computerese for any automatically assigned value. This is one term that Access didn't make up. It's borrowed from a long-standing computer tradition.

Data Validation

In many cases, you'll want to limit field entries to one or a certain array of selections. One way to do this in Access is to set the Data Validation field property. The exercise that follows isn't an optimal use of the Data Validation property, but working through this and reviewing the table of data-validation examples will give you a good idea of this field property's use.

Exercise 6.2. Setting the Data Validation field property.

This exercise limits the possible entries for the Ethnicity field to ensure data consistency. A data-entry person might enter any of the following values for an Anglo:

White

white

Caucasian

Anglo

European extraction

When the college makes certain government reports, it'll want to group students by ethnicity. If data-entry people are free to enter their own terms for identifying ethnicity, extracting and grouping this data will be an enormous chore, since you'll have to tell Access to extract any possible values for all the possible ethnic labels various data-entry people might use. So for this table, confine the permissible entries to the following: Anglo for all non-Hispanics of European heritage, Hispanic for those of Spanish heritage, Black for those of African heritage, Asian for those of Asian heritage, and Indian for those of native-American heritage. This system doesn't pretend to meet actual government reporting criteria; it is only illustrative of the how to set a Data-Validation field property.

1. Put the Student Personal table in Design View if it is not there already.

2. Click on the Ethnicity field. This tells Access that you want to set a field property for this field.

3. Click on the Validation Rule property.

4. Enter Anglo or Hispanic or Black or Indian or Asian.

5. Press tab to move away from this field.

   Access will alter the Validation Rule to proper syntax, which in this case is: "Anglo" or "Hispanic" or "Black" or "Indian" or "Asian". When Access checks for these validations, the check is case insensitive.

6. Return to Datasheet View, saving the changes when Access reminds you that you haven't. Access will give you an additional message box reminding you that data-validation rules have changed and some previously entered data

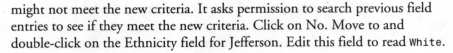

might not meet the new criteria. It asks permission to search previous field entries to see if they meet the new criteria. Click on No. Move to and double-click on the Ethnicity field for Jefferson. Edit this field to read White.

7. Try to tab away from this field. Access gives a rather rude but informative message box saying that the new entry violates the data-validation rule for this field. Click on OK and then press Esc to return this value to its original entry.

In the following exercise, you'll change the error message to a more courteous one.

Exercise 6.3. Making a data validation error message.

1. Return to Design View, click on Ethnicity, and then click on the field property Validation Text.

2. Enter Please enter either Anglo, Black, Hispanic, Asian or Indian for this field.

3. If it bothers you that you can't see all the text you're entering, press Shift+F2 to enter the Zoom view. This will give you a nice large editing area for entering this message. When you're done editing and entering your new message, just click on OK to exit Zoom view.

4. When you're done entering the validation text, return to Datasheet View. Click on OK when Access gives you the save reminder.

5. Repeat the procedure you employed when trying to change Jefferson's Ethnicity value from Black to White. Access still won't accept the entry because it violates the validation rule you set, but this time gives it you your custom message-box message. Press OK to close the message box, then press Esc to return Jefferson's ethnicity field to its original value.

The following table lists some additional examples of validation rules for table fields:

Table 6.2. Validation rule examples.

Example	Meaning
=5	Must be 5.
Between 1 and 5	Between 1 and 5 inclusive.
Between #2/3/90# AND #1/31/92#	Any date from February 3, 1990 to January 31, 1992 inclusive.

Example	Meaning
Like "A[a-z]B"	Must begin with the letter A, contain any letter from a to z as the second letter and end with B.
Like "V####"	Must start with V followed by four digits. Valid entries are V5888; V9023; V0000.
="USA"	Must be USA.
In ("Arizona", "New Mexico")	Can be either New Mexico or Arizona.
Not "New York"	Anything other than New York.
Not Between 1 and 10	Any number not between 1 and 10 inclusive.

6

The Required Property

The Required property is another field property you'll use extensively. This field property extends for all field types. It's somewhat self-explanatory. Access won't accept a record without an entry in the field or fields where this property is set to Yes.

A Date-Specific Property

The Date/Time data type has several predefined Format properties. Figure 6.12 is an example table in Design View with the Format property combo box pulled down to show the different predefined formats along with their examples.

All data types have a Format property. The Date/Time data type has several predefined formats. These are as many as most people need, but you can create your own formats. For information on this search online help using "Format" as a search criteria.

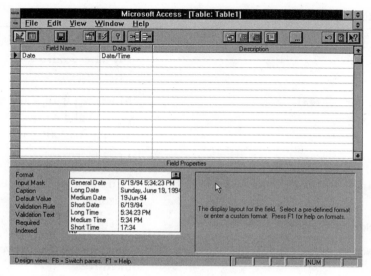

Figure 6.12. *The formats for the Date/Time data type.*

Two Number-Specific Properties

As discussed previously, the Number data type has the property called Field Size, which is different from the field size for text fields. If left to default, Access will choose "double" for the field size of a number. This is safe but wasteful of space if the particular field doesn't require double-type precision. If you're sure all your numerical data for a particular number field will be whole (that is, nondecimal numbers), specify "byte," "integer," or "long integer" for this property, depending upon what you project the range of the numbers will be.

The only caution here is when you're going to relate two fields where the key field on the one side of a one-to-many relationship is a Counter type. The matching field for a Counter field is long integer. So if your primary field in a relationship is Counter, make the data type and format of its link field as a long integer number.

The other special property for number fields, one that they share with the Currency data type, is the Decimal Places property. Access defaults to auto for a Decimal Places field property. Auto means that the format for the field (that is, how it appears) determines the number of decimal places shown. Note: The number of decimal places shown doesn't change the precision of the number. A number with the field size double will be the most precise type, no matter what the Decimal Place property is set to.

That's it for our discussion of field properties. As promised, it was a rather dry subject, but a necessary one because field properties are so important in designing your Access applications.

Summary

Changing the location of a field in the table design grid changes its location in the Datasheet View. You can also change a field's location and size in the Datasheet, but doing so won't affect either the field's position in the design grid or the Field Size property.

Access has many settings for various field properties. You can specify a default value for a field that you can override or a validation rule that you cannot. Access will give you an informative (but abrupt) error message if you try to enter a value in a table that violates data validation rules. You can change this message to one of your own choosing by changing the Validation Text property.

One of the most commonly used field properties is the Required property. If you set this property to Yes, Access will require an entry in this field before accepting a record. Key fields have their Required property set to Yes by inference.

Fields with the Number data type use the property called Field Size to specify how much precision they have. This directly affects the amount of data storage space Access reserves for entries in this field. While double is the most precise field size for the Number data type, letting all your number fields remain at the default double size will waste space in your computer. Use the most economical field size for your numbers consistent with your need for precision.

The Number and Currency data types share the property called Decimal Places. This controls how the data's shown, not the underlying precision of the field.

Finally, the Date/Time data type has some unique format properties predefined. You can show data in Access using predefined format types, or you can define your own.

Q&A

Q **If I change the size and location of a field in Datasheet View, will Access preserve those changes?**

A When you close the datasheet, Access will ask you if you want to save your layout changes. If you click on Yes, those changes will be preserved. Otherwise they'll be discarded.

Q **Can I enter decimal numbers in a field with the data type integer?**

A You can enter them, but Access will round them off to the next highest whole number.

Q **Can I enter fractions, such as 1/2, in a number field?**

A Access has no native way to accept fractions in a number field. You can enter 1/2 in a text field as a text entry, but you can't use it in calculations since it's a text value. You can enter the value 1/2 in a number field by entering its decimal equivalent, .5.

Q **Can I change data type for a field after I've already entered some values?**

A Yes, but you might lose data. For example, consider a Text data type field containing numbers for all records except one where the field reads "Sam." Converting the data type from Text to Number will cause you to lose the Sam entry. Access will give liberal warnings before it discards any of your data, but if you insist, it will go ahead with the conversion.

Q **How can I delete a record from a table?**

A Click to the left of the leftmost column in the gray area. This is called the record selector section. The record next to which you clicked will get the highlight. Press the Del or Delete key to delete this record. If you want to delete a series of records, you can click and drag on the record selector to choose many records. If you want to delete records according to a criterion (such as all records with a date older than 2/3/94), you'll need to do a delete action query. This topic is covered in Chapter 17, "Append and Delete Action Queries."

Workshop

Here's where you can test and apply the lessons you learned today.

Quiz

Possible answers to these questions are provided in Appendix A.

1. You're in Datasheet View. How can you tell when your cursor is located in the correct position to change a field's apparent width? Apparent height?

2. Will moving a field in Datasheet View change that field's position in the field-design grid?

3. Will the validation rule "A#" accept the value A1?

4. If you set a Default property for a field, can you override it during normal data entry? If not, what must you do to override the default value?

5. Will the validation rule "Between #1/2/90# and #2/1/90#" accept the value 1/5/91?

6. Why bother making input masks?

Put Access into Action

1. Open the Student Personal table in Design View.

2. Change the default value for City from blank to Chicago.

3. Try entering a record using data of your own. Did the default value work? Delete this record by clicking on the gray area just to the left of the record (the record selector) and pressing the Delete key. Confirm with Access that you want to delete this record.

4. (This one is a toughie.) Return to Design mode. Using the following bits of information, design an input mask that allows up to 12 letters for any entry in the FirstName field, capitalizes the first letter of the name automatically, and enters the balance of the name in lowercase. The following are some characters used in input masks and their meanings:

   > means what follows in the mask is uppercase

   L means you must enter a letter

   < means what follows is lowercase

   ? means any character or space including blanks

If you need to, search the online help system using the key words "input mask." This is one place the wizard won't help you.

5. If you give up on Number 4, you can find the solution after the quiz answers for this chapter.

6. Delete the input mask for the FirstName field. (Optional.)

7. Close the Student Personal table, saving or discarding changes (depending upon what you chose to do in Step 6). Exit Access.

7

An Introduction to Forms

M T W R F S S

Today's subject—an introduction to forms—is a lot more interesting and just plain more fun than what came yesterday. Forms are, primarily, attractive ways to show, edit, or enter data. Beyond that, forms have intrinsic properties that help in database administration.

This morning you'll learn

☐ What a form is

☐ How to make a quick form

☐ How to navigate in Form and Datasheet views

☐ How to use a Form Wizard

☐ How to add data to the new form

☐ About form control properties

What's a Form?

A form is an arrangement of controls you use to view, add, or edit data in Access. You've seen that you can view, add, or edit data in Datasheet View, so you might wonder why you should bother with forms if they only shadow what can be done without them. There are two basic reasons to use forms:

1. They make the job of editing, adding, and viewing data easier.

2. They add many features and capacities over a datasheet when it comes to adding, editing, or viewing data.

When you see all the features you can add to your database by using forms, you'll want to use them in even your simplest database applications.

Making a Form

In the bad old days of B.A.—that is, Before Access—creating database forms was something of a chore. It has been said that compared to other database systems, Access requires a lot of computer horsepower to run. That's true, but the reason Access requires so much computer is that, compared to lesser products, there are many more things that you can do with it. Form design is one of those areas where Access shines, partially because of its excellent design and partially because it's a native Windows application.

You paid a lot of money for a computer that could run Access well; now you're about to reap some benefits from that investment. Watch how easily Access handles the job of making a simple data-entry form in Exercise 7.1.

Exercise 7.1. An instant form.

1. Launch Access and open the College database.

2. Open the Student Personal table in Datasheet View.

3. Locate the Auto Form button on the toolbar. See Figure 7.1 for help if you have trouble finding this button.

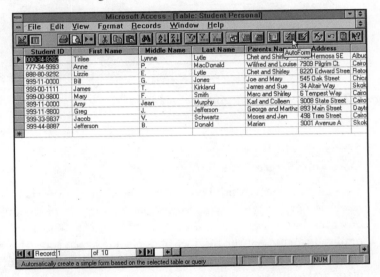

Figure 7.1. *Starting an instant form from the Datasheet View.*

4. Click on the Auto Form button. Access will grind away. When it's done, your screen should resemble Figure 7.2. If your screen varies somewhat from Figure 7.2, try maximizing your screen using the button in the upper right corner of the form's window.

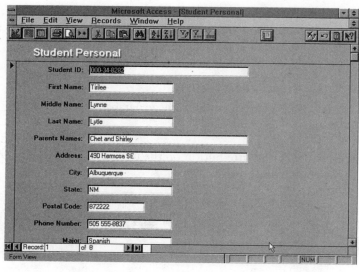

Figure 7.2. *The results of the Auto Form button.*

Does Your Screen Look Different?

The screens shown in this book have all been shot at the standard VGA resolution of 640 x 480. Your video adapter might be set to any of several other resolutions, such as 800 x 600 or 1024 x 768. The numbers in these resolutions represent the number of dots your screen shows horizontally and vertically. So a 640 x 480 screen has 640 dots along the horizontal plane and 480 dots along the vertical.

If your screen shows more or less than the standard screens in this book, your displays will differ, perhaps significantly, from those shown. Most displays today use the standard VGA or higher. If your screen has a higher resolution than standard, it'll hold more information and in effect, you'll have a wider view of Access than shown in the figures.

That's it. You've just created your first form in Access.

Looking Over the Form

Using the Auto Form button in the toolbar is the same as using the auto option in Form Wizard. (We'll learn about interacting with the wizard a little later.) Refer back to Figure 7.2 or your screen. You might recognize the data shown in the new form as the first record in the Student Personal table. Not all of the fields are shown, since the Auto Form button simply stacks fields and doesn't attempt to fit them all on one screen.

In this case, the EmailName, Ethnicity, and Note fields are below the form's horizon. Click near the bottom on the vertical scroll bar to the extreme right of the display. Access moves the thumb button on the scroll bar down and reveals the last three fields—but at the cost of hiding the first four, this time above the horizon. Your scrolled screen should resemble Figure 7.3.

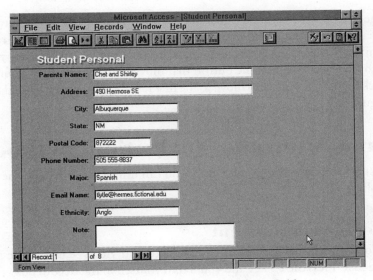

Figure 7.3. *The Auto Form scrolled to show the last three fields.*

You use the scroll bars in Access to navigate around a form within a particular record. Click toward the top of the vertical scroll bar and Access will reveal the first four fields and hide the last three, as in Figure 7.2.

Moving to New Records

There are several ways to navigate through your records in Access forms. The simplest is to use the VCR buttons at the bottom of the screen right above the status line. These VCR buttons, or record navigation buttons, are to the right and left of the specific record count box. In Figures 7.2 and 7.3 the specific record box tells you that you're at Record 1 of 3. This means the datasheet supplying the data for this form has three records and you're looking at the first one of them.

Clicking on the inner-right VCR button, the one just to the right of the numeral 3, will move you one record down in the datasheet. Try it yourself. After you click on this button, your screen will bring up the record for Mary Smith and the specific record count box will read "Record 2 of 3." This is the "move one record forward" button. Its equivalent for moving one record backward is to the left of the numeral 1 and looks the same (except it faces in the opposite direction).

The VCR button to the far right looks like the "move one forward" button, except that it has a vertical bar added to its graphic. This is the "jump to the last record" button. Similarly, there's an opposite-facing button to the left that moves you to the first record. Try clicking on the button that moves you to the end of your records. Now click on the left button to move to the first record. Your screen should again resemble Figure 7.2.

Some Alternate Navigation Methods

To navigate quickly around a form, you can utilize the keyboard, the menus, or the toolbar.

Keyboard Shortcut

If you know the record number you wish to find, Access has an express train you can ride to it. Press the F5 key and you'll find yourself in the Record box with the current record highlighted, as in Figure 7.4.

Notice two things. First, the number 1 in the notation "Record 1 of 3" has the highlight. Second, the status bar directly under this section of the screen reads "Enter New Value." Enter a number from 1 to 3 and press Enter, and Access immediately jumps to that record.

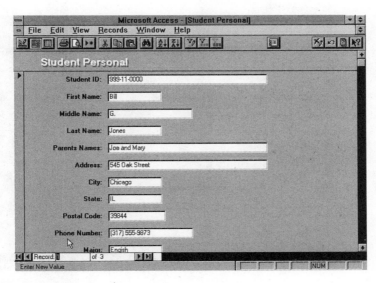

Figure 7.4. *Speeding to a record number.*

Menu Shortcut

Click on the menu choice Records. Click on the fly-out menu choice Go To. Your screen should resemble Figure 7.5.

Clicking on the various choices from this fly-out menu enables you to move through your records almost instantly.

Toolbar Shortcut

The standard toolbar for forms has two buttons that are useful for record navigation. The "move to new record" button is the one with a right-facing triangle and an asterisk. Click on that button and Access will move you to a new blank record.

The third-from-the-left button on the toolbar is the Datasheet View button. When in Form View, you can quickly switch to Datasheet View by clicking on this button. Figure 7.6 shows the results of clicking on the Datasheet View button while viewing Record 2 of 3 in the Student Personal table's form.

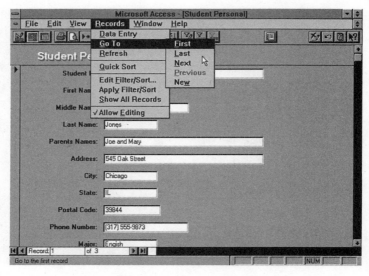

Figure 7.5. *Using the menu to navigate through records.*

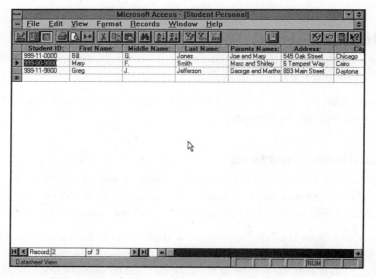

Figure 7.6. *The jump to Datasheet View from the Form View.*

Note that Access kept track that you were on Record 2 of this table and left you there after the jump to Datasheet View. Click on the StudentID field in the last record, the one for Greg Jefferson.

DO   DON'T

DO use whatever navigating method you prefer to move around your records.

DON'T think there's an absolute right or wrong way. The right way for you is the way you like. The wrong way is the way you dislike.

Now click on the Form View button, the second one from the left. Access will return you to Form View, but with Jefferson's record (Record 3) now the current one. Your screen should resemble Figure 7.7.

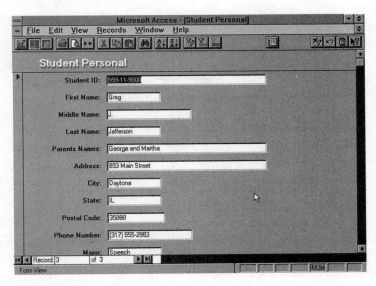

Figure 7.7. *Jumping back from Datasheet to Form View.*

Making a Form by Using a Wizard

Close the Auto Form either by choosing the menu selections File|Close or double-clicking on the form's control menu icon. When Access asks you if you want to save the form, click on No. Close this table.

Back at the Database View, click on the Form tab, the one that is third down at the Database View. Click on the New button to start a new form. This launches the form-making process.

Exercise 7.2 shows how to make a form by using a wizard.

Exercise 7.2. Using a wizard to make a form.

1. Pull down the Select A Table/Query combo box and click on Student Personal. Your screen should resemble Figure 7.8.

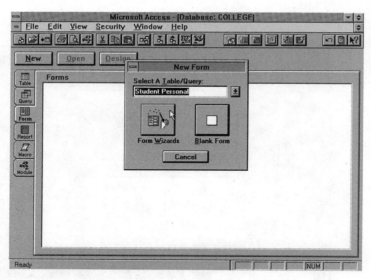

Figure 7.8. *Making a new form.*

2. Click on the large Form Wizards button to start the wizard process for a form based on the Student Personal table. Your first choice is the type of form you want the wizard to conjure up for you. Accept the default choice of Single Column and click OK. (Note that if you had chosen the Auto Form option, your form would have ended up looking identical to the form you made using the Auto Form button on the toolbar.)

The Access Way

There's no difference between the forms made by using the Auto Form toolbar button and those made by choosing Auto Form from the Form Wizard.

3. The next decision you must make is what fields to include in your new form. Forms don't have to include all the fields from the datasheet on which they're based. In some cases you'll want to restrict the fields on a form because you don't want unauthorized viewing of certain fields in a table. You'll be using this form for entering and editing records in all fields, so click on the >> button to add all the Student Personal's fields to this new form.

4. Click on the Next> button to move on.

5. This next dialog box gives you choices about the form's look. Experiment by clicking on the various option buttons in this dialog box to see what they mean. When you're satisfied, click on the Standard option button, then click on the Next> button to move on.

6. Edit the suggested name for this form to read "Student Personal Data." Your screen should resemble Figure 7.9.

7. Click on the Finish button. Access will grind away and finally deliver up a form. Your screen should resemble Figure 7.10.

Making a basic form by using a wizard is just that simple. Consider yourself a master of the simple Form Wizard.

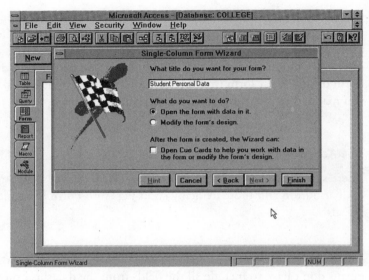

Figure 7.9. *The final dialog box for a Form Wizard.*

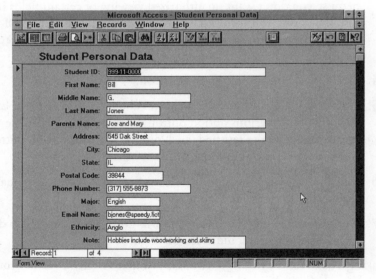

Figure 7.10. *The finished form.*

Adding Data Through a Form

Click on the toolbar button New to move to an empty record, or choose the navigation method you prefer. Enter the record shown in Figure 7.11. After you've entered the data for a field, you can move to the next empty field either by hitting the Tab key or Enter.

Notice that Access preserved the input mask for both the Phone Number and StudentID fields. Try editing Lytle's ethnicity to Chinese. Access will give you the same error message as if you tried doing this in the Datasheet View. Press Esc to return Lytle's Ethnicity field to Anglo.

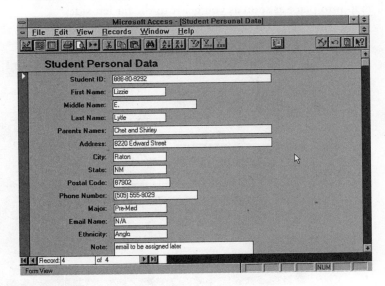

Figure 7.11. *A new record entered through a form.*

The Access Way

Access will preserve your table's field properties when you use the table through a Form View. You also can add many other properties exclusive to a particular form. These form properties will be in addition to the underlying properties you already set when designing your table.

Form Controls

Just as you can manually design a table, you can manually design a form. Look at the button on the far left of the toolbar. That's the button to switch into Form Design View. Click on that button now. Your screen should resemble Figure 7.12.

Your screen might differ in two basic ways from that of Figure 7.12. Your toolbox—that's the toolbar on the far left shown in a vertical orientation in Figure 7.12—might be below the menu bar and across the top of your screen. Additionally, you might have one or more floating property list boxes open. If your toolbox isn't oriented as in Figure 7.12, click on an empty place within it and drag it to the left side of the screen. It'll snap into place as soon as you get it to the far left side.

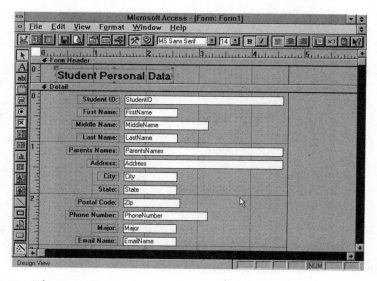

Figure 7.12. *The Form Design View.*

Feel free to close any floating property list boxes at this time. Figure 7.13 represents the screen in Figure 7.12 with the addition of two floating list boxes.

Close these boxes by either double-clicking on their control menu icons or by locating their toggle buttons on the horizontal toolbar and clicking on these buttons.

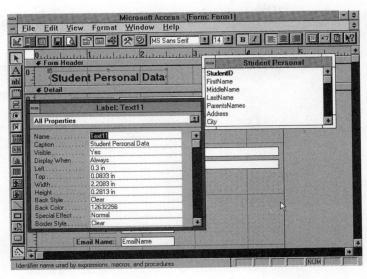

Figure 7.13. *Floating property list boxes.*

7

DO   DON'T

DO check the figures from time to time to make sure you're following along with the exercises.

DON'T worry if your screen grows slightly out of synch with the book. Some variances can't be helped.

Each element of a form is a control (or, as some prefer to say it, a form object). Just like fields in a table, each form control has a set of properties. These properties vary from one control to another.

The form in Figure 7.12 is quite simple. It has only one type of control, the text box. To get a feel for other types of form controls, run your mouse cursor down the buttons in the toolbox. (Again, that's the toolbar to the extreme left of the screen in Figure 7.12 and 7.13.) Pause over each button long enough for the balloon help to pop up. You'll come across controls such as label, text box, option group, toggle button, and so forth. Each of these controls has a different set of properties and each of them shares a few properties with other controls.

Take a look at Figure 7.14. It contains a partial list of all the properties for a text box control.

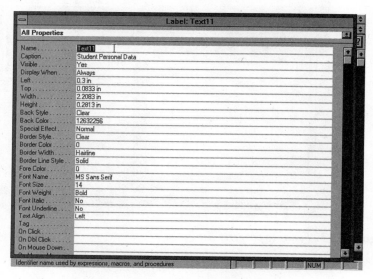

Figure 7.14. *Some of the properties of a text box control.*

That's a pretty imposing list, isn't it? Memorizing all those properties for all the controls and all their options would be a daunting task. Luckily, Access makes it fairly easy for us by doing two basic things.

First, you can categorize your properties according to function, so you're not overwhelmed with choices. You do this by pulling down the combo box at the top of the Properties list box and choosing one of the categories. Figure 7.15 shows the text box control's properties limited to those properties that affect layout. Look at the top of the list box; you'll see that you've told Access not to show All Properties, as in Figure 7.14, but only Layout Properties. It's still a long list, but at least it's manageable.

The second thing Access does to help us manage form control properties is to offer us "point and shoot" choices. Look at Figure 7.16. This shows the choices you have for setting the Special Effect property in a text box control.

You get these choices just as you did in table design—by clicking next to the property you want to examine or alter and by pulling down the list when Access gives you the indication it has a list from which to choose. Later on you'll learn some other ways that Access helps you when you are setting properties.

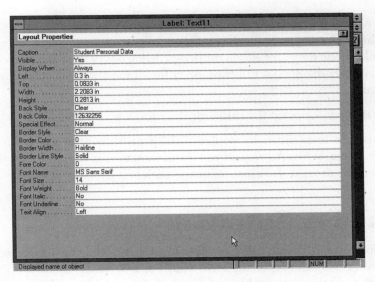

Figure 7.15. *Text box control properties that affect layout.*

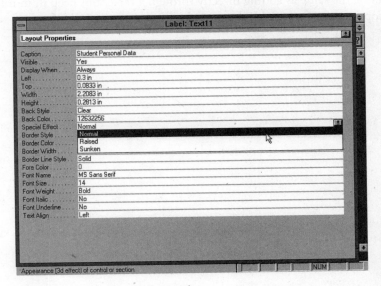

Figure 7.16. *Choosing a property from a list.*

In many cases, Access will automatically set properties for you as a consequence of another choice you made during form design. For example, if you chose to have a sunken look for your fields in the design dialog box of the wizard, Access would have already set the Special Effect property for all the text box controls on this form to Sunken.

That about wraps up the lesson for this morning.

Close the form either by double-clicking on its control menu icon or choosing File¦Close. When Access asks you if you want to save your form, click on Yes. Enter the name Student Personal Data and click on OK.

Morning Summary

This morning's lesson covered what a form is, including how to create one using the Auto Form button. Making forms using Form Wizards is quite simple, but in many cases you'll choose to modify what a wizard creates. Adding data to a table using a form can be the same as adding directly through a table, but keep in mind that there are properties for form fields that can alter data entry with the form.

8

Introduction to Form Controls

The elements of form design this lesson introduces will act as a foundation for many operations you'll perform in Access. This afternoon's lesson explains the following:

- ☐ The meaning of bound and unbound controls
- ☐ How to manipulate form controls
- ☐ How to select more than one control at a time
- ☐ How to add a control to a form
- ☐ How to delete form controls
- ☐ How to change the appearance of form controls

Bound and Unbound Controls

There are two general categories of controls in Access forms: bound and unbound. A bound control is one that's tied to some underlying element, usually in Access (although in the case of the specialized OLE type controls, a form control can be bound to something external to Access). An example of a bound control is the StudentID field in the Student Personal Data form you created using the wizard in this morning's lesson. That field is tied to the StudentID field in the Student Personal table. The control will show whatever information is in the StudentID field for the current record.

Unbound controls aren't tied to anything. These are generally used for information display, manipulating or decorating forms, and (as you'll see later in the book) reports. The label StudentID: to the left of the StudentID bound field shown in Figure 7.2 acts as a label informing you that the text field is showing the StudentID information.

Moving and Sizing

When Access inserts text box controls into a form through a wizard, it uses the Field Size property of the Text field to determine how wide to make that field. Take a look at Figure 7.2 again. The StudentID field is much bigger than it needs to be to hold any student ID information. Also, both of the forms made with the Auto Form button and the wizard don't quite fit on one standard VGA screen. The following exercises address both these issues.

Sizing

To make all the fields or form controls fit on one screen, you need to both alter the size of some overly wide ones and move some of them up from the bottom of the form. Keep in mind that the terms "field" and "form control," or just "control," refer to the same thing. A form control is the way to show a field on a form.

Exercise 8.1 illustrates how to resize a form control.

Exercise 8.1. Resizing a form control.

1. Launch Access and open the College database if you have not already done so.

2. Click on the Form tab in the Database View.

3. Click on the Design button to open the Student Personal Data form in Design View. Your screen should resemble Figure 8.1.

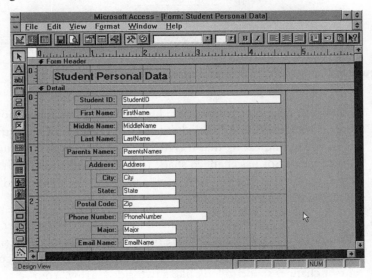

Figure 8.1. *A form opened in Design View.*

4. If your screen has some floating list boxes in it, close them by either double-clicking on their control menu icons or by locating their toggle buttons on the horizontal toolbar and clicking on those buttons.

5. Click on the StudentID field in the large white place where the StudentID information shows when this form is in Form View. Your screen should look like Figure 8.2.

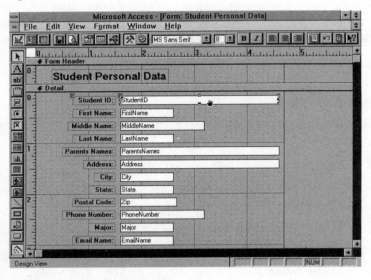

Figure 8.2. *Highlighting a form control.*

When you click on a control, you highlight it. Take a close look at your screen or Figure 8.2. A highlighted control gains a series of squares around its periphery indicating that it is highlighted. Also look at Figure 8.2 and notice the cursor has changed shape to look like a hand. The hand cursor visually indicates that you're now able to move the highlighted control by dragging it with your mouse.

6. You don't want to move this control, just resize it. The smaller squares around the control's periphery are hot spots for resizing chores. Move your cursor to the center square at the right side of the StudentID control. Your cursor changes shape to look like a two-sided arrow. Your screen should resemble Figure 8.3.

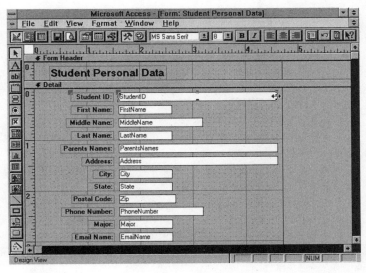

Figure 8.3. *The cursor visually indicating that it can now resize a control.*

8

DO	DON'T

DO proceed very slowly and carefully through this and the following sections, especially if you're not comfortable or familiar with mouse actions. Highlighting fields without inadvertently moving them, hitting the right hot spots, and dragging are all difficult for those who are less than expert in mouse operations.

DON'T become discouraged if you feel clumsy exercising your form design skills with a mouse. Skill will come in time. Meanwhile, keep in mind the Access "undo" facility. If you accidentally move, size, or delete a form control, you can undo it either by pressing Ctrl+Z or choosing the menu items Edit|Undo. Almost everybody uses this facility when learning about Access form design.

7. Keeping your cursor over this hot spot, click and hold your mouse. Drag the cursor to the left until the StudentID field is a little over an inch long. Refer to Figure 8.4, which shows the field during the sizing operation. Note the ruler on the top of the form design grid, which indicates the length of the field and the position of the cursor.

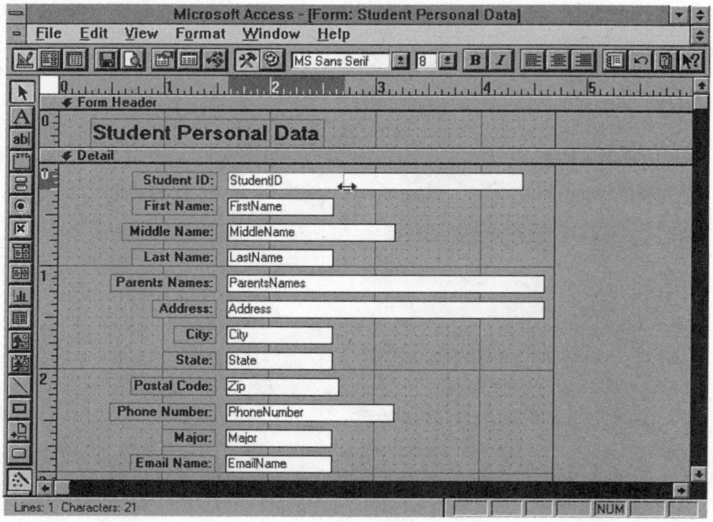

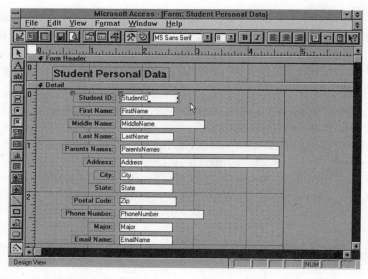

Figure 8.4. *Resizing a field.*

8. Release your mouse button and the field snaps into its new size, looking like Figure 8.5.

Figure 8.5. *The resized field.*

9. Using this same technique, resize the Phone Number field so that it is roughly the same size as the Zip or Postal Code fields.

The Access Way

You might find that you can't finely adjust the size of your fields because Access snaps them to certain points. Access has the options Grid and Snap To Grid. The grid is a series of virtual points in the Form Design View. You can control how fine this grid is by setting the relevant form properties. When Access is set to Snap To Grid, each control on the form must locate and size to one of these points. When doing this exercise, it makes no difference if your Snap To Grid is on or off. It is equally unimportant to size and locate the controls exactly.

That's all there is to sizing controls. The only other thing to bear in mind is that the other hot spots for resizing work differently. For example, the two hot spots in the middle of the controls act to size them vertically, not horizontally like the one you just used.

The Access Way

The two large squares in the upper-left corner of both the control and the field label are not hot spots for sizing but rather a way to move a control independently of its label or to move a label independently of its control. We'll learn about these different hot spots later.

Controls on the Move

You can move controls either with or independently of their field labels. You saw in the preceding section that when you click on a control, your cursor changes to a hand shape. This indicates you can now move a field with its label. The following exercise moves two controls with their labels so the entire form fits on one screen.

Exercise 8.2. Moving form controls.

1. Click toward the bottom of the vertical scroll bar to reveal the bottom of the form. If necessary, click on the up arrow at the top of the vertical scroll bar to adjust your screen so that you can not only see the last two fields but several above them as well. Your screen should resemble Figure 8.6.

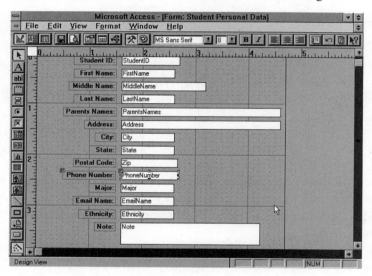

Figure 8.6. *Setting up to move form controls.*

2. Click in the Ethnicity control, in the area where the form displays ethnicity information when it's in Form View. Your cursor should change to look like a hand. Continue to hold your mouse button down, or if you let go, click again when the cursor looks like a hand. Your screen should resemble Figure 8.7.

3. If you missed—that is, if you find yourself clicking around in the field, unable to get the hand cursor back again—click away from the control. (Anywhere else on the form will do.) Then try clicking back on the Ethnicity control, but this time click and hold. You should find getting your hand cursor easy using this technique.

4. Continue to hold the mouse button down. Drag the Ethnicity field to a place directly to the right of the Zip/Postal Code field. Release the mouse button. Just before releasing the mouse button, your screen should resemble Figure 8.8.

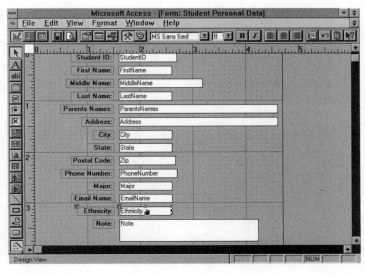

Figure 8.7. *A form control ready to move.*

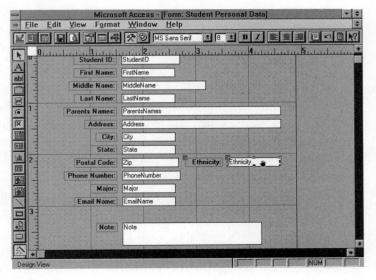

Figure 8.8. *The form control after a move.*

5. Move the Note field the same way. Click in the white area where the Note data appears, hold the mouse button after clicking, and drag the field so its label is directly to the right of the PhoneNumber field. Your screen should resemble Figure 8.9.

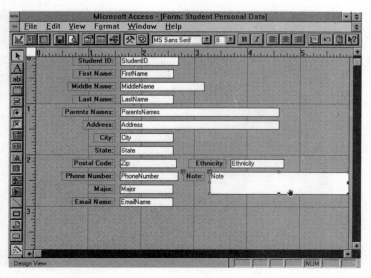

Figure 8.9. *Moving another form control.*

Note that the form itself was too narrow to accommodate this field in its new position, so Access courteously widened the form for you when you dropped the field into its new location.

6. Locate your cursor over the large square in the label part of this control. The label for the Note field is the box that says "Note:" in it, not the place where the Note data appears. When you move your cursor over the large black square, it changes to a hand. Click and drag. You'll be able to move the label independently of its control. Similarly, you can move a control independently of its label. Return the Note label to its former spot.

7. Resize the field using the techniques you learned in Exercise 8.1 to make it about one-half inch less wide and as deep at the bottom margin of the EmailName control. After you're done, your screen should resemble Figure 8.10. If you have trouble locating the hot spot that controls the vertical control size, examine Figure 8.10. The cursor in that figure is right on the hot spot you need.

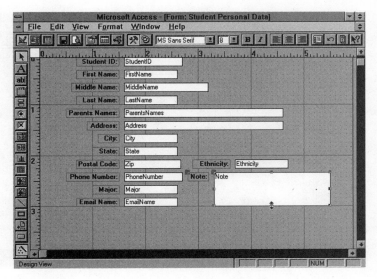

Figure 8.10. *Finished with the resizing and moving operations.*

8

The Access Way

There are many global options you can set in Access. Some of these affect how Access works. Some of these, if set differently from their defaults, will put your copy of Access at odds with the configuration used for these exercises.

The next exercise requires you to have the Selection Behavior option set to Partially Enclosed. To make sure this is the case, click on the View menu selection, then click on Options. Access gives you a dialog box with several choices. Click on Form and Report Design. Look at the list that follows. Locate the property Selection Behavior and, if necessary, change its option to Partially Enclosed. Your screen should resemble Figure 8.11.

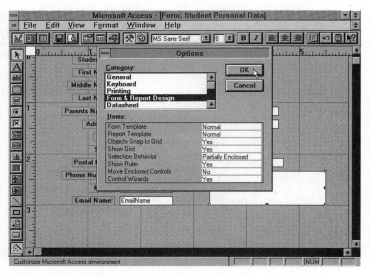

Figure 8.11. *Setting global options.*

Click on OK to exit this dialog box.

DO   **DON'T**

DO check your global options if your version of Access seems to be behaving differently from the book's.

DON'T be overly concerned about experimenting with global options. Most are self-explanatory. It's difficult to get into trouble by altering these options. Feel free to configure Access so it works the way you prefer.

Choosing Multiple Controls

Often you'll want to act on several controls at once. You can choose several controls quickly and easily by using a marquee selection. Exercise 8.3 shows you how.

Exercise 8.3. Marquee selections.

1. With your screen as you left it after Exercise 8.2, move your mouse cursor to the left of and slightly above the Postal Code label for the Zip field.

2. Click and hold your mouse button. Drag the mouse down and to the right. You'll see a contrasting "rubber band" type rectangle that grows as you move your mouse. Your screen should resemble Figure 8.12.

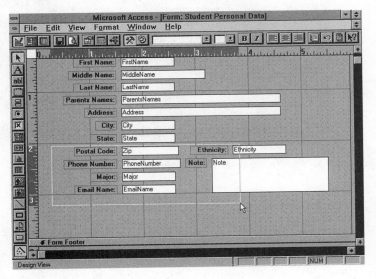

Figure 8.12. *Creating a marquee selection.*

3. Continue dragging the rubber-band box until it covers at least part or all the form controls to the right of or below Postal Code. Release the mouse button. All the fields you had covered with the rubber-band box now are highlighted. Your screen should resemble Figure 8.13.

4. Move your cursor into any of the highlighted areas. It'll turn into a hand, as shown in Figure 8.13. If you click and drag now, you'll move all these fields at once. This will preserve their relative positions to each other, but not to the form in general or to any other nonhighlighted controls.

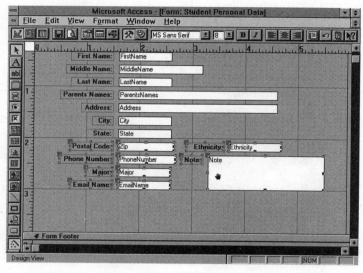

Figure 8.13. *The finished marquee highlight.*

The Access Way

You set control properties by first selecting a control or controls and then altering the relevant properties. You can set the properties for all of a form's controls at the same time by making the menu selection Edit|Select All or by pressing Ctrl+A. You can affect several adjacent controls through marquee selections. Finally, you can select any number of nonadjacent controls by holding down the shift key as you click on the controls.

5. Click anywhere outside of the areas having the highlight in order to remove the highlight from these controls.

Adding and Deleting Controls

You can delete a control from a form by selecting it and then either pressing the Delete key or choosing the menu selections Edit|Cut. Click on the FirstName field to give it the highlight. Press the Delete key and Access removes the field from your form.

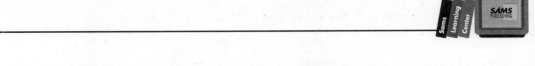

Click on the Form View button in the toolbar. Your form moves into Form View and your screen resembles Figure 8.14. Click on the Datasheet View button in the toolbar. Note that Access has eliminated the FirstName field from this view also. Return to Design View.

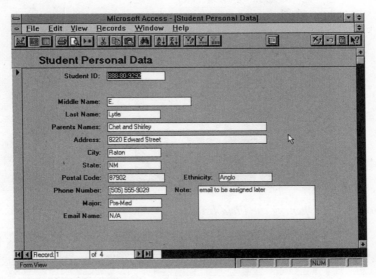

Figure 8.14. *The Form View.*

Locate and click on the Field List button in the toolbar. Refer to Figure 8.15 for help in finding this button.

Locate and click on the text box control in the Toolbox. (The Toolbox is the vertically oriented toolbar on the extreme left of your screen.) Click and hold on the FirstName field in the Student Personal list box—the box you opened when you clicked on the Field list box button.

Without releasing the mouse button, drag the FirstName field onto the form, juggling it around until it's in its former position. Release the mouse button. Your screen should resemble Figure 8.16.

If you have Snap To Grid on, you might not be able to align this field in its former position. If this is the case, click on the menu choices Format|Snap To Grid in order to turn off grid-snapping. Place the FirstName control precisely where you want it, then choose Format|Snap To Grid again to reactivate grid-snapping.

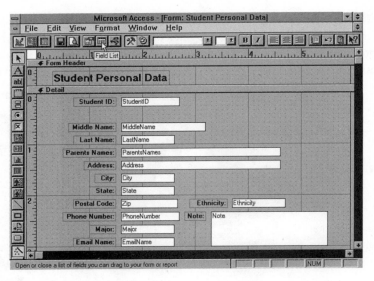

Figure 8.15. *Opening the Field list box.*

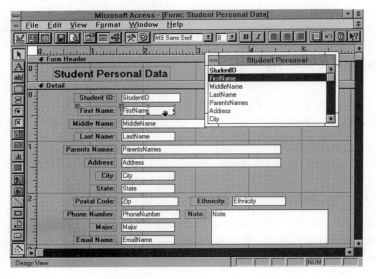

Figure 8.16. *Manually placing a field in a form.*

Changing Appearances

This afternoon's final topic is how to alter the appearance of form elements. This is generally done through the palette, but you can alter these elements, depending upon what's happening in an Access application, by using macros or through Access Basic.

Remember how the Auto Form's controls had a sunken look? Exercise 8.4 shows how Access did that.

Exercise 8.4. Using the palette.

1. Start with your form just as you left it after Exercise 8.3.

2. Press Ctrl+A to select all the controls on this form.

3. Close the Field list box by clicking on its button in the toolbar.

4. Open the palette by clicking on its button on the toolbar. (Refer to Figure 8.17.)

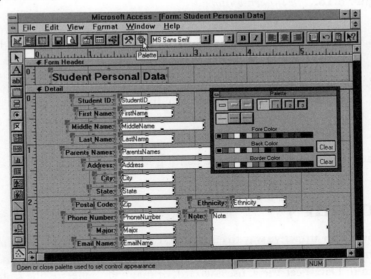

Figure 8.17. *The palette in Form Design View.*

5. The sunken button is the third from the left on the top row of the palette box. Click on this. (Refer to Figure 8.18.)

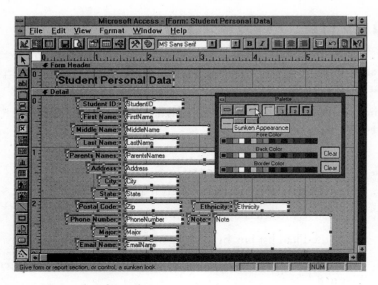

Figure 8.18. *The sunken button.*

6. Click on the Form View button and note that now all the fields or controls on your form have a sunken look.

7. Return to Design View and experiment with changing the color and the look of various controls until you develop a good feel for how the palette works. When you're done, return the form to resemble Figure 8.18 and close it, saving your changes.

That's it for this afternoon. More exciting adventures await you tomorrow morning.

Summary

A form is an attractive way to enter, edit, or view data stored in datasheets. There are several ways to create a form. You can click on the Auto Form button in the toolbar when in Datasheet View, use a wizard, or manually generate one from scratch.

Once you have a form, you can navigate through records by using menu choices, the VCR navigation keys, or direct jumps to record numbers. The Page Up and Page Down keys work as well, but they aren't as convenient, especially if your form takes up more than one vertical screen.

Forms maintain the properties of the underlying datasheets and can add properties of their own. Forms can contain bound and/or unbound controls. Bound controls are tied to some underlying item, usually inside of Access (although in the case of some type of controls, you can link to applications external to Access).

Forms have three views: Design, Form, and Datasheet. You can design your form in Design View, whereas the other two views give you access to your data. You change a control in a form by first selecting it by clicking on it, then applying whatever modifications you want. You can select several controls at once by holding down the shift key as you select, using a marquee selection, or by pressing Ctrl+A to choose all form elements.

You delete form controls by selecting those you wish to delete and then pressing the Delete key. Alternatively, you can choose the menu selections Edit|Cut to cut controls from a form. You add bound controls to the form by dragging the fields from the Field list box to the form design grid. The palette lets you set the static display attributes for your form controls.

Q&A

Q The text implies you can change a control's display when the form's open in Form View. Why would you want to do this?

A When you review a form's layout properties, you'll see many items that you might want to alter, depending on the state of the form or its data. For example, one property that a control has is called Visible. You might want to make some controls visible or not, depending upon the current data or the state of another control.

Q Why will Access not show a field in Form Datasheet View if that field's not on the form?

A The reason is security. Say you have a form with restricted information. You might clear people to see that form because it lacks the fields containing sensitive data from the underlying table. The way Access works, users of this limited form could not violate security by choosing the Datasheet View. You can also limit the Datasheet View by setting the appropriate form property.

Q **Is there any difference between adding, editing, or deleting data through a form rather than doing it directly into a table?**

A There can be—not in the data, but in how a person can address it. Remember, each control on a form has a slew of properties that act in addition to the properties of the fields in a table and the table's properties. You might not, for example, have any data validation set at the table level, but rather at the form level. This would have the effect of no data validation when entering data directly into a table. Instead, that validation would be effective only when using the form.

One reason to do this is so you can vary the data validation depending on which form is used to enter data into the table. Many forms can be bound to one table. As you'll see later on, one form can contain several tables as well.

Q **Forms look to me like rearranged table fields. Can they do more than that?**

A Forms can be very powerful tools in organizing and displaying your data. This chapter only covered the basics. Later on you'll learn about other form controls, such as check boxes, option groups, and command buttons, which, when used correctly, will greatly enhance your applications.

Q **Is there a rule of thumb saying when to use a form for data entry and when to do it through the Datasheet View directly?**

A There's no real rule of thumb, but since most people find data entry to be much easier in Form View than with the datasheet, why not use forms all the time? Even if you ask Access to generate an Auto Form for each data entry session and then you discard the form, you'll likely save time using a form for data entry. As you learn more about forms, you'll see that they can do many things that are impossible (or at least very awkward) to do from a datasheet.

Workshop

Here's where you can test and apply the lessons you learned today.

Quiz

Possible answers to these questions are provided in Appendix A.

1. How do you know when a form control has the highlight?

2. What visual indication does Access give you when you can move a form control?

3. What does the mouse cursor look like when it's over a hot spot and able to size a field or control on a form?

4. If you delete a field from a form in Form Design View, will you be able to see that field when you switch to Form Datasheet View?

5. How can you select (or give the highlight to) two noncontiguous controls on a form?

6. How can you select (or give the highlight to) four contiguous controls on a form?

Put Access into Action

1. Launch Access and open the College database if you have not already done so.

2. Open the Student's Current Courses table in Datasheet View.

3. Create a form using the Auto Form button on the toolbar. Your screen should resemble Figure 8.19.

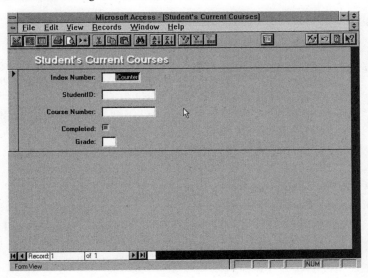

Figure 8.19. *An Auto Form.*

4. Change to Form Design View. Rearrange and resize the controls on this form to resemble Figure 8.20, which shows the rearranged controls in Form View. Hint: The size of the form itself was shortened vertically. Move your cursor to the bottom of the form and it'll take on a shape like you saw when resizing table fields. Click and drag to resize the form itself.

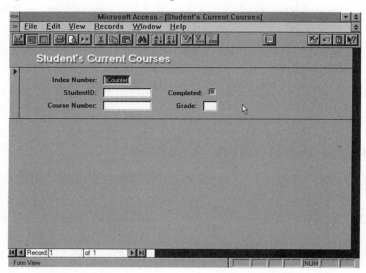

Figure 8.20. *The reworked Auto Form.*

5. Return to Form Design View. Select the Completed check box control. Open up the Properties list box. Locate the Default Value property either by scrolling through the All Properties list or choosing Data Properties. Enter Yes for a default property. Return to Form View. What change do you see in the Completed check box? Move on to the next section if you choose. If not, close this form, discarding changes.

For the Adventurous in Spirit

6. From Form View, try adding a record to this table through the form. Tab away from the (Counter) field, enter a StudentID that's *not* in the Student Personal table, and enter any data you want for the rest of the fields. When you try leaving the Grade field, will Access accept your data?

Remember that this table is linked to the Student Personal table. If the error message box is obvious to you, click on OK to close it, then press Esc to void this entry. If the message box didn't make sense to you, click on the help button and read Access's explanation for why it entered an error condition.

In either case, after you're done, press Esc to void this entry, then close the form and discard the changes.

8

Day

5

9

A Look into Queries

This morning you'll learn

- [ ] What an Access query is
- [ ] How to construct simple queries
- [ ] How to use criteria in queries
- [ ] How to use queries to reorder your data

Queries perform many functions in Access. Relational databases such as Access work best when the data they contain is broken into small logical chunks. Queries perform the function of rejoining those small chunks when you need to. Primarily, queries in Access perform the following functions:

- [ ] Extracting data according to criteria you set
- [ ] Performing actions on extracted data
- [ ] Linking several tables or queries to present data as you wish to view it
- [ ] Grouping, sorting, and calculating data from tables and queries

Queries in Access is a large topic, but one that's not particularly difficult to master if taken one step at a time. In short, you use queries to ask Access about your data or tell Access to manipulate it.

 **Note:** Starting with this chapter, *Teach Yourself Access 2 in 14 Days* relies on the book's sample data for the examples shown. The book starts with the sample data and then builds on it for more complex examples. Details on how you can get this sample data can be found in Appendix E.

A Simple Query

You construct a simple query in Access by telling Access you want to create a new query, then telling it what fields to include. Exercise 9.1 shows you how to construct a simple query.

Exercise 9.1. The simple query.

1. Launch Access and open the College database if you need to. Click on the second tab from the top in the Database View. It's the tab labeled Query. Click on the New button to start a new query. Click on New Query to bypass the wizard for this exercise. Your screen should look like Figure 9.1.

Different Screens

For the sake of simplicity, this chapter shows only those tables and queries relevant to the exercises. Your screens might differ from the book's examples if you have more of the sample data added to your College database. It's important that you have at least the sample data shown in this chapter so you can follow along with these exercises. You can safely ignore any extra data you have loaded either from the sample data or from your own working with Access.

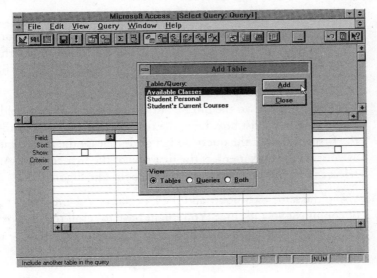

Figure 9.1. *Ready to construct a new query.*

2. Click on the Student Personal table shown in the Add Table list box. Click on the Add button. This tells Access that you wish to query the Student Personal table. Because this is the only table you wish to query at this time, click on the Close button. Your screen should resemble Figure 9.2.

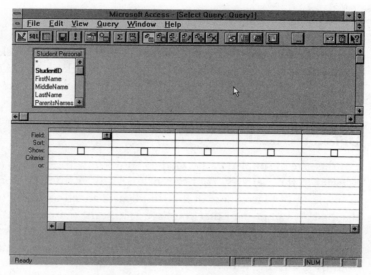

Figure 9.2. *The query design grid with one table added.*

Right now Access knows you want to query the Student Personal table, but doesn't know which fields you want to query. To tell Access that, you must place fields in the query design grid. You do this by dragging fields from the Field list box to the query design grid.

3. Click and hold down the mouse button on the FirstName field in the Student Personal list box. Drag the field from the list box to the first row of the first column of the query design grid. Release the mouse button as soon as your mouse cursor enters the first row of the first column. After you release the mouse button, your screen looks like Figure 9.3.

4. Using the same technique, add the LastName and City fields to the first row of columns two and three. You might have to scroll the list box to find the City field. When you're finished, your screen should resemble Figure 9.4.

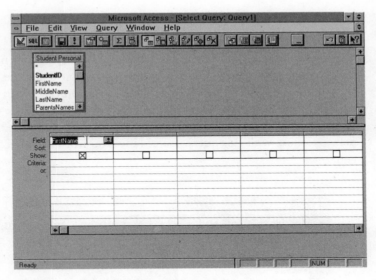

Figure 9.3. *A field inserted in the query design grid.*

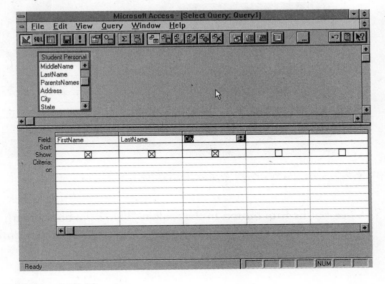

Figure 9.4. *A multifield query.*

The Access Way

You can resize and arrange the query design grid to suit your needs and tastes. Move your cursor around the query design grid and see how at certain hot spots the cursor changes its shape to indicate it can now manipulate the size or shape of the windows that make up the grid. Figure 9.5 is an example of how Figure 9.4 might have been changed to make working with this query easier. How you work with Access is up to you.

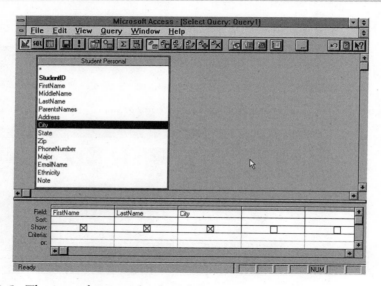

Figure 9.5. *The query design grid reshaped for easier use.*

5. Click on the Run button in the toolbar. That's the button with the exclamation point on it. Access runs the query, resulting in a screen similar to Figure 9.6.

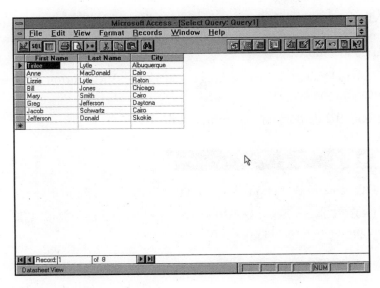

Figure 9.6. *Running the simple query.*

Pat yourself on the back. You've just constructed and successfully run an Access query.

The Access Way

Access queries are "live." Changes made to them are reflected in underlying tables or queries. Look at Figure 9.6. If you were to edit the name Tirilee to Tyralee in the query, you'd also change the entry Tirilee in the Student Personal table to Tyralee.

This is in contrast to most other PC database programs, where queries are dumped into dead tables. Edits into dead tables don't affect the underlying data. If you're used to this type of data base, keep the concept of Access's live data queries in mind when editing queries in the Datasheet View.

Also, if you're used to dead table queries you might, at first glance, feel Access's live queries are a dangerous feature. It's actually as safe as you make it. Additionally, it can greatly increase Access's power and flexibility over those programs that dump queries into dead tables. You'll see examples of Access queries' power and flexibility as we pursue the query subject.

Well, that was easy. It also wasn't particularly useful. This particular query just takes some of the fields in an Access table and shows all the records for those fields. Access can do lots more.

Return to Design View by clicking on the Design View button in the toolbar. It's the button on the far left.

Exercise 9.2 demonstrates sorting in a query.

DO	**DON'T**

DO remember that queries retain live links to their underlying tables.

DON'T forget how handy that can be when you need to edit data in more than one table at the same time.

Exercise 9.2. Sorting in a query.

1. Locate the Sort row in the query design grid. It's the second from the top.

2. Click in the first column of the grid in the Sort row. Access returns a down arrow indicating this field is a combo box with a pull-down list. Click on the down arrow. Your screen should resemble Figure 9.7. (Your screen will look slightly different if you didn't make the changes shown in Figure 9.5.)

3. Click on Ascending. You've just told Access to present your data sorted ascending based on the data in the FirstName field. Choose the menu selections File|Save As and save this query as Temp. Run the query by clicking on the Run button. Your screen should resemble Figure 9.8.

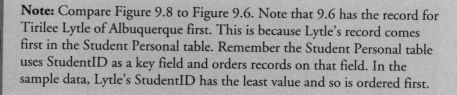

Note: Compare Figure 9.8 to Figure 9.6. Note that 9.6 has the record for Tirilee Lytle of Albuquerque first. This is because Lytle's record comes first in the Student Personal table. Remember the Student Personal table uses StudentID as a key field and orders records on that field. In the sample data, Lytle's StudentID has the least value and so is ordered first.

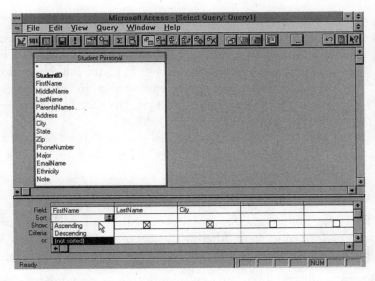

Figure 9.7. *Adding a sort to the query.*

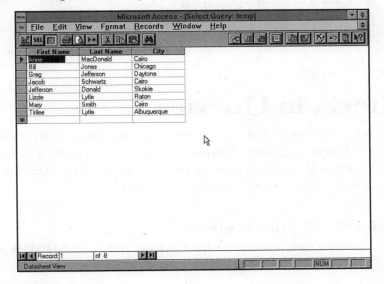

Figure 9.8. *A sorted query.*

When you told Access to order the query according to first name, the name Tirilee was last alphabetically, or to put it another way, it had the greatest value, so it came last as shown in Figure 9.8. Note also that Access has the smarts to keep records together. In both Figures 9.6 and 9.8 Access has the LastName field Lytle and City field Albuquerque attached to the Tirilee FirstName field.

The Access Way

There's an important difference between edits made to Access queries and sorts performed in them. Altering the sort order for a table in an Access query does not alter the order of the data in the underlying table.

Occasionally you'll want to view your data in varying orders. The easiest way to do this is to construct one query for each sort view you want. Access allows multiple queries on the same table and each query can have its own criteria and sort order.

Criteria in Queries

Access queries also perform the very important function of extracting subsets of your data. If, for example, you want to view all the records in a table for which the City field is Cairo, you can easily do so. Exercise 9.3 shows how to convert the general query made in Exercises 9.1 and 9.2 into one with a criterion.

Exercise 9.3. A criteria query.

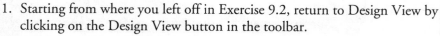

1. Starting from where you left off in Exercise 9.2, return to Design View by clicking on the Design View button in the toolbar.

2. Click on File and choose Save.

3. Locate the Criteria row in the query design grid. It's the fourth row down from the top. Enter Cairo in the Criteria row under the City field column. Press Enter. Access adds quote marks to your specified criterion. Your screen should resemble Figure 9.9.

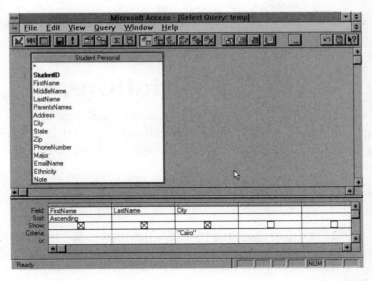

Figure 9.9. *Constructing a criteria query.*

4. Run the query by clicking on the Run button in the toolbar. Access runs the query. Your screen should resemble Figure 9.10.

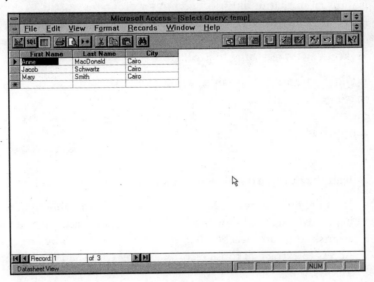

Figure 9.10. *The criteria query in Datasheet View.*

Access ran the query as before, but this time extracted only those records where the City field matched the criteria of Cairo.

Some Criteria Variations

Access has a wide variety of criteria you can enter into a query. Using a little imagination and some knowledge, you can extract your data in almost any manner you can think of. Exercise 9.4 goes into some variations on the criteria theme.

Exercise 9.4. Variations of criteria.

1. Click on the Design View button to return to Design View for this query.

2. Edit the Criteria Cairo to read C*. Press return. Access modifies your criteria to the proper Access syntax of Like "C*".

DO   DON'T

DO experiment with different criteria entries determining which ones work the way you expect them to and which ones yield unexpected results. Access is unusual in that unlike most computer programs, it tries to do what you mean, not only what you say. So when you enter the criterion C*, Access correctly interprets this to mean you want to extract all records that look "Like a C with anything following."

DON'T assume Access can figure out what you want all the time. Like any machine intelligence, Access has its limits. Until you're sure you understand query criteria, carefully check Access's output to make sure you got what you expected to get.

3. Run the query. Your screen should resemble Figure 9.11.

If you're familiar with DOS commands, you probably figured out what happened. Access, following DOS conventions, accepted the wildcard asterisk to mean "accept whatever" in this space. So by entering C* you told Access to extract all those records starting with the letter C and anything that follows.

4. Return to Design mode. Edit the criterion C* to read Ch*. Run the query again. Your screen should resemble Figure 9.12.

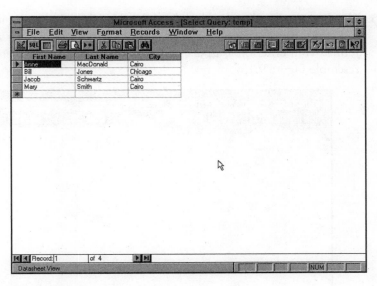

Figure 9.11. *A wildcard query criterion.*

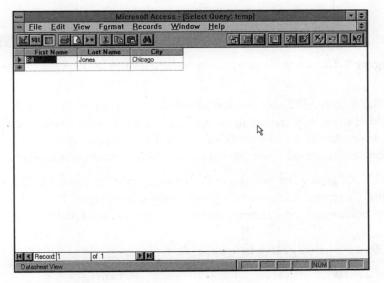

Figure 9.12. *A modified wildcard criterion.*

5. Here's a way people get wrong data when making criteria queries. Return to Design View and modify the criteria Ch* to Ch. Press return and Access returns your criterion as Like "Ch". Run the query. Your screen should resemble Figure 9.13.

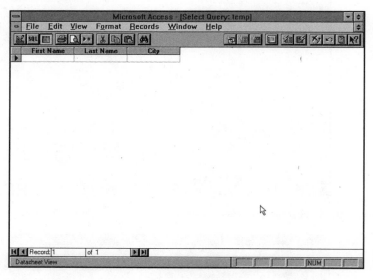

Figure 9.13. *A criteria query giving unexpected results.*

What happened? Your criteria now tells Access to return any records where the City field is Like "Ch" rather than any city beginning with Ch as the criterion "Ch*" instructs Access. You've modified your wildcard criteria query to a literal request to locate cities named Ch in your database. Naturally, there is no such city.

Table 9.1 gives a few examples of other query criteria. Note that criteria expressions closely resemble table validation expressions. In Chapter 19 you'll encounter filter expressions and the following expression examples work there also.

Table 9.1. Some criteria examples.

Criteria	Return
"Cairo"	Field must match Cairo.
"Cairo" or "Chicago"	Field can match either Cairo or Chicago.

Criteria	Return
=#2/20/95#	Matching the data February 20, 1995. Note when entering data criteria in Access you must surround the date with two number signs (#'s). This is how Access recognizes you're entering a date rather than the literal.
Between #1/3/94# And #6/7/95#	Anything between January 3, 1994 and June 7, 1995 inclusive.
In ("Cairo", "Chicago")	Another way to match either Cairo or Chicago. A syntactical alternative to or.
Not "Cairo"	Any record not Cairo. The opposite of "Cairo".
< Date( )- 30	Orders more than 30 days old.
Year([Order Date])=1998	Dates in 1998.
Like "C*"	Starts with C and anything else.
Like "*a"	Starts with anything, ends with a.
Like "[J-M]*"	Starts with J through M inclusive and ends with anything.
Left([City], 1)="O"	Anything with O in the far left position.

Using *OR* and *AND* Criteria

If a human wants to see all his company's files for customers who live in either Chicago or Cairo, he'll ask his assistant to "Get me those files where the customer lives in Cairo and Chicago." This makes sense in human speech, but the relentless logic of computers interprets this request to "Get me those files where the customer lives in BOTH Cairo and Chicago." This clearly isn't what the human desired.

Logically speaking, the human should have asked for those files where the customer lives in Cairo or Chicago. This is one important area in which Access does what you tell it to do rather than what you might mean it to do. Exercise 9.5 illustrates the distinction.

Exercise 9.5. OR's and AND's in criteria.

1. Return to Design View from the failed query in Exercise 9.4. Edit the City criterion back to Like "C*" to return all records in which the city begins with the letter C. Run the query to make sure you return four records.

2. Return to Design View and edit the first Criteria row under the First Name column to read Like "J*". Your screen should resemble Figure 9.14.

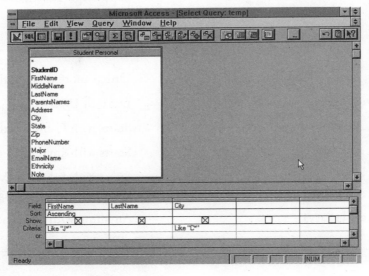

Figure 9.14. *The AND criterion.*

3. Run the query. Your screen should resemble Figure 9.15.

   You told Access to extract all those records in which the City field starts with C and the First Name starts with J. Only one record in our database now meets these criteria. Look what happens when we make a slight change to make this an OR criterion.

4. Return to Design View. Click and drag to highlight the criterion Like "J*" under the FirstName field.

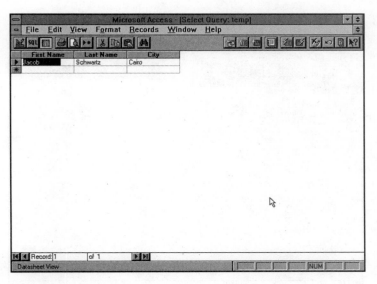

Figure 9.15. *Running the AND query.*

5. Press Ctrl+X to cut this criteria expression to Windows' clipboard. Click on the second line of the Criteria grid under the FirstName column next to the word "or." Press Ctrl+V to paste your criteria to the new row. Your screen should resemble Figure 9.16.

9

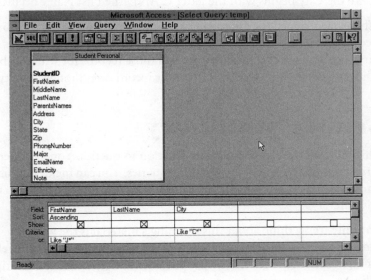

Figure 9.16. *Constructing the OR criteria.*

6. Now run the query. Your screen should resemble Figure 9.17.

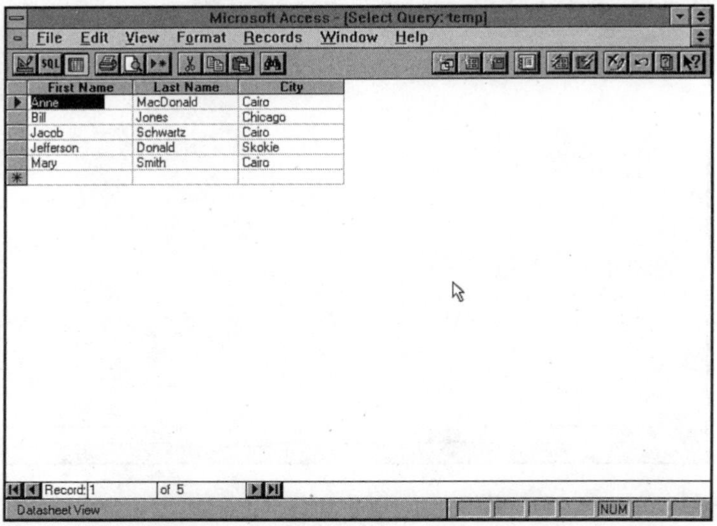

Figure 9.17. *The* OR *query's return.*

Note the difference between the query results shown in Figure 9.15 and Figure 9.17. In the criteria entered for Figure 9.15, you told Access to show you all the records where the City begins with the letter C AND the First Name begins with the letter J.

When you changed the criteria to be on two rows, you told Access to extract all those records where the FirstName field begins with J OR those records where the City name begins with C. This query gave all those records for which either criterion was valid, so you also got Jefferson Donald's record even though his city is Skokie.

Morning Summary

This morning you got a good introduction to queries. You use queries in Access to extract sets of data from tables or other queries. You can include as many fields as you want in a query. Additionally, you can use criteria in queries to extract records meeting this criteria.

The only tricky thing about this morning's material is the way Access interprets AND and OR query criteria. By placing multiple criteria on one line you're telling Access you want to use an AND set of criteria. By putting multiple criteria on multiple rows, you're telling Access you intend an OR extraction.

10

Multitable Queries

This afternoon you'll learn

- ☐ Why we skipped Query Wizards in the morning
- ☐ How to construct queries using multiple tables
- ☐ How links work in queries
- ☐ How to use criteria in multitable queries

Breaking your data into logical chunks makes it much easier for Access to manipulate, but on many occasions you'll want to reconstruct your data into various large pieces. For example, the College database stores students' names in the Student Personal table, course information in Available Courses table, and courses the students are currently signed up for in the Student's Current Courses table.

What if you want to see a class list? The information is all in the College database but scattered throughout these three tables. The way to join all this data into a coherent whole is through a query. Before moving on to this topic, however, this chapter introduces Query Wizards. *Teach Yourself Access 2 in 14 Days* skipped this step in the morning's lesson to give you some hands-on experience with queries. Unlike some other wizards, Access supplies Query Wizards only for the most complex type queries.

Looking at a Wizard

If your query's still open from the morning's lesson, close it, discarding changes. You can optionally save the Temp query for later experimentation, but *Teach Yourself Access 2 in 14 Days* won't use it for subsequent exercises.

Navigate to the Database View. Click on the Query tab if you're not at the query window. Click on New. Click on the Query Wizards button. Your screen should resemble Figure 10.1.

Access only has wizards for these very complex queries. There's no wizard for doing a simple query like you did this morning. At this level, the wizards won't do you any good. The scope of what they do is beyond this chapter's level, too, but Figure 10.1 shows you what Query Wizards are available in Access 2.

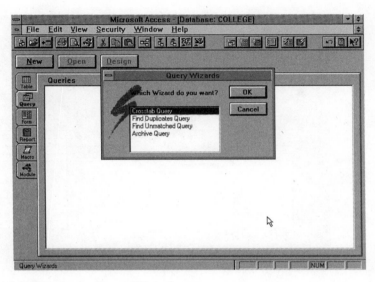

Figure 10.1. *Starting a Query Wizard.*

If you feel adventurous, continue on with any of these wizards, but to follow with the afternoon's lesson, click on Cancel to end this wizard so you can move on to this afternoon's agenda.

A Simple Multitable Query

The first exercise this afternoon shows you how to construct a simple two-table query. Later on you'll add another table and enter some criteria to construct a rather sophisticated query.

Exercise 10.1. A two-table query.

1. At the Database View, click on the query tab if necessary. Click on the New button. Click on the New Query button to skip the wizards. Your screen should resemble Figure 10.2.

2. Click on the Student Personal table in the Add Table list box. Click on the Add button.

3. Click on the Student's Current Courses table in the Add Table list box. Click on the Add button.

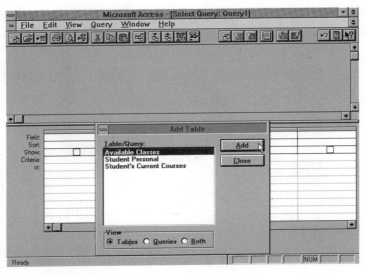

Figure 10.2. *Selecting a table for the two-table query.*

4. Click on the Close button to close the Add Table list box. Your screen should resemble Figure 10.3.

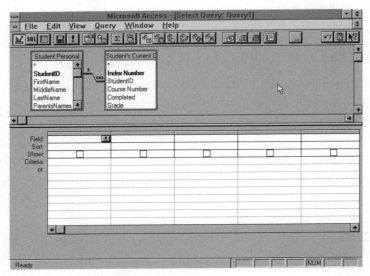

Figure 10.3. *Starting the two-table query.*

Access remembers that there's a link between these tables and shows it remembers by drawing a line between the tables, illustrating what fields are the link fields as well as which side of the link is the one side and which is the many side.

Optional: Adjust your query design grid and the list boxes to look like Figure 10.4. This simplifies creating the following queries, but isn't required to complete the exercises.

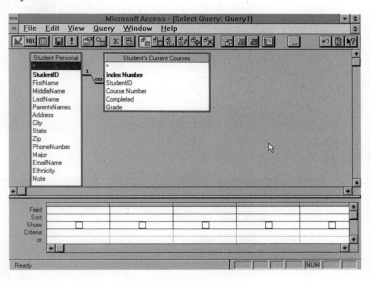

Figure 10.4. *A query design grid adjusted for clarity.*

5. You want to tell Access to show you the classes students are currently taking. Drag the following fields from Student Personal into the query design grid, starting with column one: StudentID, FirstName, MiddleName, LastName. Your screen should resemble Figure 10.5.

6. Now to add the courses these students are signed up for. Click in the Student's Current Courses list box on the Course Number field and drag that into the first empty column. Your screen should resemble Figure 10.6.

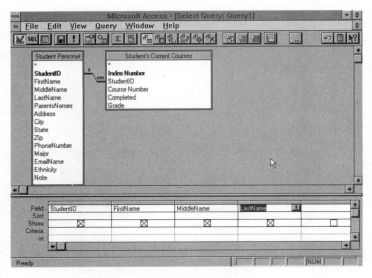

Figure 10.5. *Starting the multitable query construction.*

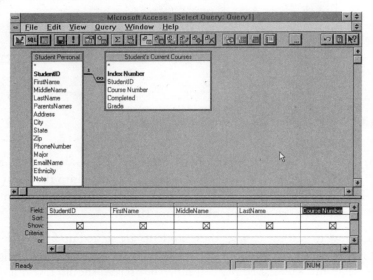

Figure 10.6. *Fields from two tables in the query design grid.*

7. Click on the Run button in the toolbar. Access evaluates the query design grid and returns the results shown in Figure 10.7.

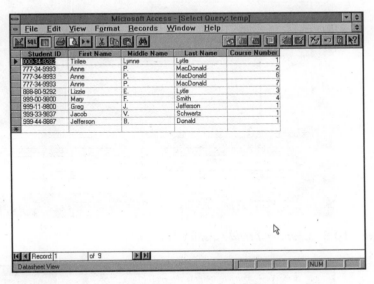

Figure 10.7. *The multitable query running.*

Well, that's all right, but not terribly useful as it sits. First, you wanted only the students' names but you also have the StudentIDs. The class number information is the index number of the class assigned by Access in the counter field. This doesn't really tell us much about the name of the class, the section, or the credit hours.

Note that although the StudentID field is in the Student's Current Courses table, it's not included in the query. Access still has the smarts to link up the right student with his or her courses.

The first modification is to eliminate the StudentID field from the query's display. Return to Design mode and click on the Show check box under the StudentID field. Your screen should resemble Figure 10.8.

Run the query again. Your screen should resemble Figure 10.9.

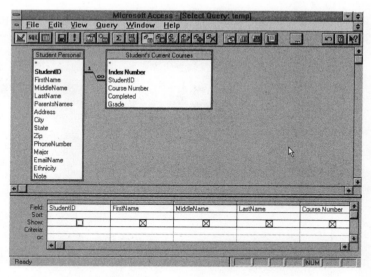

Figure 10.8. *Stopping a field's display in a query.*

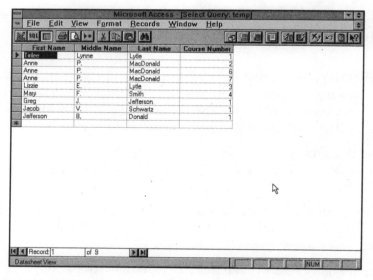

Figure 10.9. *The results of suppressing a field's display in a query.*

Removing a Field from a Query

The only reason to include a field in a query while suppressing its display is if you want to include some criteria for that field for a query's return, but you don't want to display the field. Since you don't want to enter a criterion for StudentID in this query, you can safely delete it from the query design grid. Save this query by clicking on File|Save As, giving it the name Temp if it doesn't conflict with the previous optional query that you may have saved. If it does conflict, make up a name for this query.

DO	DON'T

DO include only those fields in queries you want to either display or enter criteria for.

DON'T bother to litter up your query design grid with extraneous fields just for the sake of links. Access links all right with these fields left out.

Return to Design View. Move to the StudentID column in the query design grid. Move your cursor to right above the name StudentID in the design grid. The cursor switches to a down-facing arrow. Click to give the entire column the highlight. Your screen should resemble Figure 10.10.

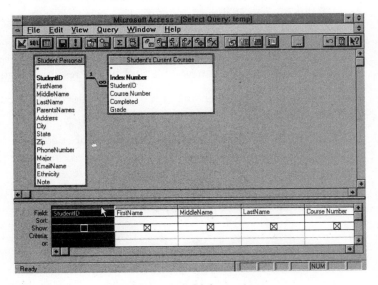

Figure 10.10. *Getting ready to delete a field from a query.*

Press the Del or Delete key to clip this field from the query design grid. Run the query to see that Access still returns the same results even with no StudentID field anywhere in the query.

> **The Access Way**
>
> Access doesn't need inclusion of link fields in a query to know how to link tables in queries. It's smart enough to understand the underlying relationships even with the link fields excluded.

Adding Another Table

This query is shaping up, but it still doesn't include the information about course title and credit hours you want. This information is in the Available Courses table, which isn't yet part of this query.

Exercise 10.2. The three-table query.

1. Return to Design View. Locate the Add Table button in the toolbar. It's the button with a table and a yellow cross. Refer to Figure 10.11. When you've located this button, click on it.

   Access brings up the Add Table list box. Locate the Available Classes table. Click on it and click on the Add button. Click on Close to close the Add Table list box. Arrange the new table's list box to resemble Figure 10.12.

   Note that Access remembers the link between Student's Current Courses and Available Classes.

2. Click on the Show check box in the Course Number column. Now drag the following fields from the Available Courses table to the query design grid, placing them in the first available empty column: Course Number (from Available Courses table), Name, Instructor, Units. Note that you might have to scroll horizontally to find empty columns.

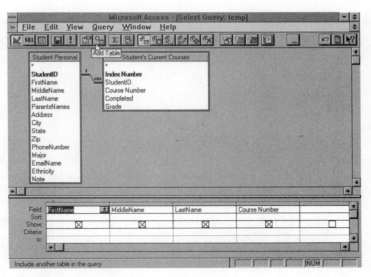

Figure 10.11. *Adding a table to a query.*

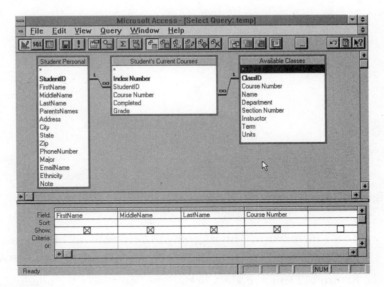

Figure 10.12. *The new table in the query design grid.*

The Access Way

Access enables you to dump one field on top of an occupied column and automatically shifts the new field to a new column. This works all right, but it's confusing when you see it for the first time.

3. After you've dragged the fields into the query design grid, click on the Run button. Adjust the widths of the fields in the Datasheet View like you adjusted the column widths in a table. Your screen should resemble Figure 10.13.

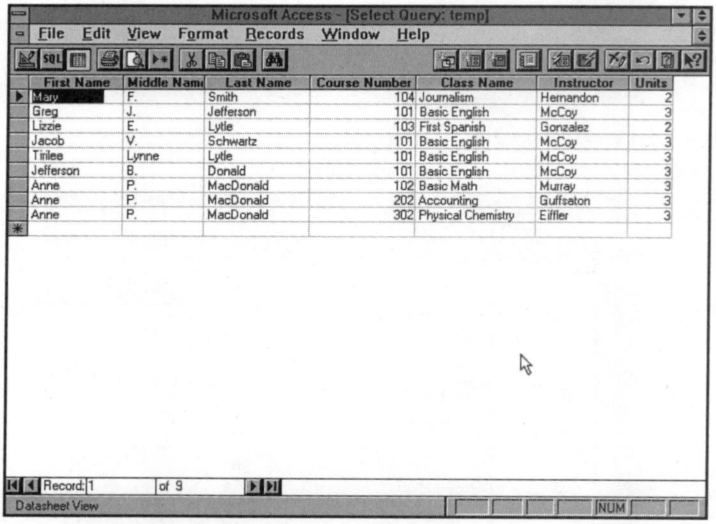

Figure 10.13. *The completed query.*

That's more like it. This is getting to be a useful set of information. The only thing that's confusing is that the query is in no particular order.

4. Return to Design mode. Click on the Sort row in the nondisplayed Course Number field—the one from the Student's Current Courses table. Pull down the combo box and click on Ascending. Your screen should resemble Figure 10.14.

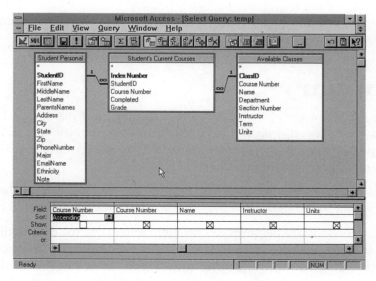

Figure 10.14. *Adding a sort to a nondisplayed field.*

5. Click on the Run button. Your screen should resemble Figure 10.15, which is the desired query.

10

Figure 10.15. *The finished three-table query.*

This query shows all the students and their courses, along with course information grouped by course. Save this query for later work.

Summary

You start new queries just like you start creating other Access objects. Move to the Database View, click on the Query tab, then click on the New button. You'll manually construct most of your queries since the Query Wizards only have sophisticated methods programmed into them.

You add tables or other queries to your new query by highlighting the table or query you want to add in the Add Table list box and clicking on the Add button.

After you've added the tables you want into your query, you click on the Close button in the Add Table list box and start dragging fields from the list boxes to the query design grid. Once in the query design grid, you can treat fields several ways. You can extract data according to criteria expressions such as `Like "Ch*"`, you can sort on a field's data, and you can choose to display or suppress a field from the final query.

Keep in mind the difference between human and computer syntax when creating criteria using the operatives `OR` and `AND`. `OR` tells a computer to widen the criteria. `AND` tells the computer to narrow the criteria. Humans generally use `AND` like the computer's `OR`.

Finally, until you're comfortable with Access query methods, carefully check what Access returns to you. The expression `Like "C*"` returns Cairo and Chicago. The expression `Like "C"` won't return either.

Q&A

Q Since you can edit queries, why bother having tables?

A You need to base a query on either a table or another query, which in turn is based eventually on an underlying table. You can't query nothing. You don't need data entered in a table to base a query on it, but you need some final structure for your data to reside in.

Q *Teach Yourself Access in 14 Days* has said I can base queries on other queries. How do I put a query into a new query's design grid?

A The Add Table list box has a three-button option group at its bottom. The three choices are Tables, Queries, and Both. Click on either the Queries or

Both button and Access includes queries in the list. Click on the query you wish to include and then click on the Add button. You include queries essentially the same way you do tables.

Q **I have a table with three entries: Smith, Jones, and Jenkins. I want to return only Smith's and Jones' records. Is it better to make a query with criteria `Smith OR Jones` or should I use `NOT Jenkins` as the criteria?**

A Access doesn't care. Use whichever you prefer. The advantage of using `Smith OR Jones` is that your return will assuredly give only Smith or Jones. `NOT Jenkins` also includes Jensen if you're wrong and your table has a fourth entry.

Q **The example data in these exercises seems a little lame. Why would I use a computer to manipulate such small amounts of data?**

A The data-entry requirements for these examples is intentionally kept small for those readers who have to enter the data manually. The principles apply to any data amount—either the tiny examples used in this book or the thousands of records a real college would use. Additionally, the complexity of the data relationships is kept low because this is intended as a book for novices. The data structure shown here would have to be expanded on several levels to operate a real college's student and class system.

Q **What if I want an `OR` criteria for a single field?**

A Just enter the two criteria separated by the word OR. For example, if you want to modify the Temp query to return records only for those students with the first name Jacob or Greg, edit the first criteria row under the FirstName column to read `Jacob OR Greg`, then run the query.

Workshop

Here's where you can test and apply what you have learned today.

Quiz

Possible answers to these questions are provided in Appendix A.

1. What special character do you need to enter to tell Access the criteria you're entering is a date?

2. Will the criterion `Like "[A-E]*"` find Daniels?

3. Will the criterion in question 2 find Enders?

4. Does using an `AND` criterion expand, narrow, or not alter what Access will return compared to an `OR` operative?

5. Can you query an existing query?

6. Do edits made to a query's data alter the underlying data residing in the table the query is based on?

Put Access into Action

1. Open the Temp query you saved at the end of Chapter 10.

2. Review how the data's presented.

3. Switch to Design View.

4. Alter the presentation of data so the query is ordered according to a student's last name. Run the query to see if you've succeeded.

5. Return to Design View. Add the StudentID field back into the query. Hint: You can just drag this from Student Personal to the first column on the left. Access shifts all the columns to the right when you do this.

6. Without displaying the StudentID field, change the order of the query to be in descending order based on the contents of the StudentID field. Run the query to see if your changes worked as you thought they should.

7. Close the query, discarding changes.

M T W

S

11

Basic Reports

This morning's lesson covers the following:

☐ What reports are

☐ Using a Report Wizard for quick results

☐ Customizing reports

Report Concepts

Reports are very similar to forms. The main application difference between them is that reports work much better for data output, especially to printers. Forms have as their primary mission data entry and display. Reports have as their main mission data output.

As with forms, you bind reports to underlying tables or queries. While Access can do much with unbound forms, there's little sense to an unbound report, although Access enables you to create one through the Blank Report option when you tell Access you want to create a new report.

To get a feel for reports, you'll make a sample one in Exercise 11.1 using the Student Personal table. This report prints out students' names and addresses. Later, we'll run through the report again to illustrate how easy it is for Access to create the same data, but on mailing labels.

Exercise 11.1. The basic report.

1. If necessary, launch Access and open the College database. Click on the Report tab. Click on New. Pull down the combo box and click on the Student Personal table to choose it as the basis of this report. This step is called binding the table to this report.

2. Click on the Report Wizards button. Your screen should resemble Figure 11.1.

3. Click on OK to tell Access you'll accept the default single column report.

4. Access opens up the Student Personal table and examines it, determining what fields are available. Click on the field names, then click on the > button for the following fields: FirstName, MiddleName, LastName, Address, City, State, and Zip. This operation tells Access that these are the fields you want for this report. Your screen should resemble Figure 11.2.

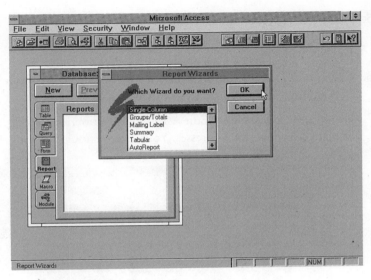

Figure 11.1. *The Report Wizard just starting out.*

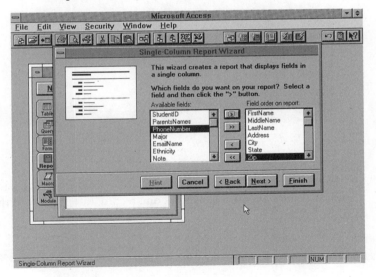

Figure 11.2. *Including fields in a Report Wizard.*

5. Click on the Next > button. Highlight the LastName field by clicking on it. Then click on the > button to tell Access you want to sort, or order on, the LastName field.

6. Click on the Next > button. Click on the Presentation option button and click on the Next > button to move on.

7. You're almost done now. Edit Access's suggestion for a report title to read: Student's Names and Addresses. Your screen should resemble Figure 11.3.

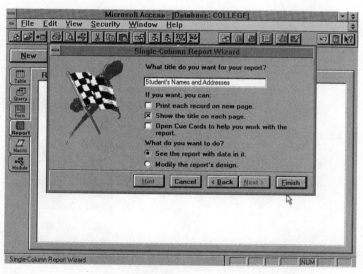

Figure 11.3. *The last wizard screen.*

8. Click on the Finish button. Access grinds away and ends up displaying the finished report. Figure 11.4 shows one record and part of another from the finished report.

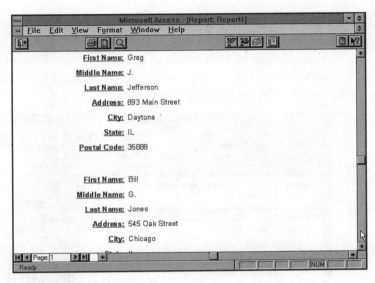

Figure 11.4. *The finished report from a wizard.*

Scroll through this report. If you like, click on the Print button in the toolbar to see a printed version of it. All the data is included. There's nothing wrong with this report, but nothing particularly right with it, either.

Altering the Wizard's Output

For example, there's little reason to identify the address so explicitly. Here's how this report treats a sample address:

Address	23 Elm Street
City	Skokie
State	IL
Postal Code	38766

This same address would be more readable presented conventionally: 23 Elm Street, Skokie, IL 38766. The reason Access relentlessly labels each field is it has no way to know the data in these fields is an address. It might well be part numbers, vendor numbers, and part descriptions as far as Access knows. So Access plays it safe and includes field labels for all wizard-created reports, but you have the option of deleting and rearranging these fields.

Exercise 11.2. Modifying a report.

1. Click on the Close Window button in the toolbar. This is the button on the far left. It corresponds in function to the Design View buttons in other Access modules. Your screen should resemble Figure 11.5, showing the wizard-created report in Design View.

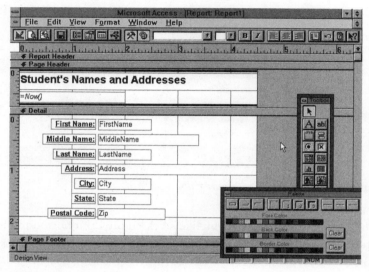

Figure 11.5. *Report Design View.*

The view you have now is very similar to form Design View. Operating in it is also very similar. You rearrange fields by selecting them and dragging them about just as you did in form design. This report is a bit more complex than a simple form because the wizard has left both the report header and footer and the page header and footer sections open.

The Access Way

A *page header* is a section printed at the top of each page. *Page footers* appear at the bottom of each page. Access also can have headers or footers for groups and whole reports. A band is the place in report design where you enter what's to be placed in a header, footer, or the detail section of a report.

In the example shown in Figure 11.5, the words Student's Names and Addresses are in the page header band. These words appear at the top of each page printed or shown by this report. The report header band is a place you put things you want to appear at the top of an entire report. Footers, both page and report, appear at the bottom of each page and report respectively.

This page header band also has the entry Now() in a text box. This is an Access built-in function that prints the current date or time. The advantage of using a function like Now() in this place is the report picks up the computer's date and time whenever you run this report and places it in the page header.

If you entered a date such as June 1, 1995 for the date field, you'd have to edit the report design each time you ran the report to get the right date in this field. Using the Now() function performs this automatically. You can tell Now() is a function because it ends in the open and closed parentheses (). You'll learn more about functions, both built-in and of your own design, later in *Teach Yourself Access 2 in 14 Days*. Built-in functions are discussed in several chapters. Chapter 28, "Programming made Easy with Access Basic," shows you how to create custom functions. Don't be concerned if the operation and meaning of Now() isn't fully clear to you at this point.

2. Since the contents for all these fields are obvious, the field labels aren't necessary. Delete the labels for all these fields by first clicking on them (labels ONLY!) and then pressing the Del or Delete key.

If you feel nimble, you can marquee select all the field labels and then mass delete them with one keystroke. Figure 11.6 shows all the fields selected after a marquee operation. A third alternative is to select each label while holding down the shift key. Remember the shift key operates as an expand selection key in Access. Any way you choose is the right way if it's comfortable to you. However you do the selection, delete the field labels.

Figure 11.7 shows the same screen as 11.6, but with the field labels deleted. The next thing to do is alter the size and shape of the fields.

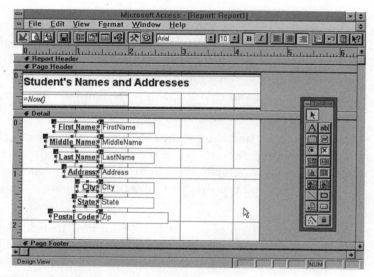

Figure 11.6. *Deleting all labels at once.*

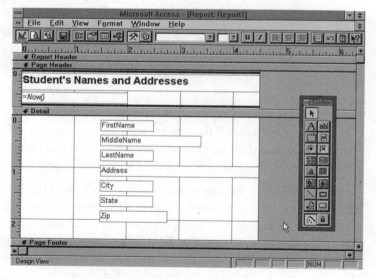

Figure 11.7. *A report without labels.*

3. Click in the MiddleName field. Move to a sizing square and decrease the size of this field until it's roughly an inch long. Figure 11.8 shows the MiddleName field being resized.

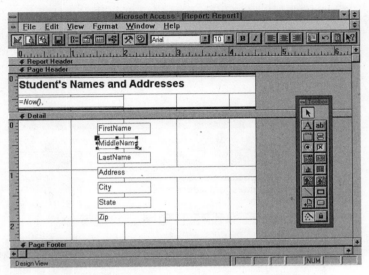

Figure 11.8. *Resizing a report field.*

Remember you can resize a field when the cursor changes to look like a double arrow. You move a field when the cursor looks like a hand. These operations work in report design just as they did in form design.

4. Move the fields around until they look like the example shown in Figure 11.9. This example also shortened the State field to about one-half inch. Move your cursor down to a place right above the strip labeled Page Footer. It changes to a bar with an up and down facing arrow. Click and drag up until you've shortened the detail section of the form to look like Figure 11.9.

The Access Way

You might find it easier to align your report's fields to look like the example's if you alter the default grid and keep Snap to Grid on. This exercise used the Snap to Grid with a grid set at 10 x 12.

To change the default grid spacing from 20 x 24 to a more practical 10 x 12, pull down the menu Edit and choose Select Report. This makes the whole report the selection rather than just one object or section.

Click on the Properties button in the toolbar. Locate the Grid X and Grid Y properties in the Properties list box. Enter 10 for Grid X and 12 for Grid Y. Close the Properties list box by clicking on its button. That's all there is to it.

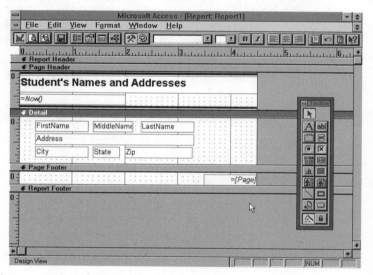

Figure 11.9. *The modified report.*

5. Click on the Print Preview button in the toolbar. It's the one second from the left. Your screen should resemble Figure 11.10.

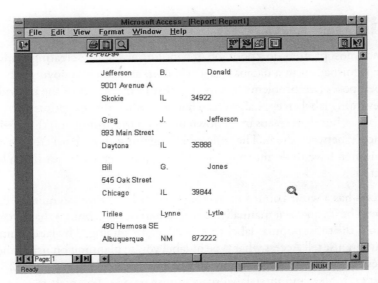

Figure 11.10. *The modified report in Print Preview mode.*

This is serviceable, but still a bit away from what you'd want to give your bosses or clients. We'll come back to this report later and spiff it up even more. For now, pull down the File menu and click on Save As. Name the report Student Names and Addresses when Access prompts you for a name.

DO	**DON'T**

DO use Report Wizards to rough out your reports.

DON'T be disappointed if the wizard's output isn't exactly what you desire. That's what manual design is for. In many cases a report should be laid out according to the qualitative content of your database. Access wizards, at least in the current version, aren't capable of making value judgments on your data, so they use general rules to lay out your reports. General rules applied to a specific case often come close, but very rarely hit a bull's-eye.

Click on File|Close to close this report for now.

11

Mailing Labels

Since most printers do a poor job of handling envelopes, creating mailing labels from the information in a database is a common and often annoying job. Making these labels poses two problems: getting the text in the center of the individual labels and preventing label creep. Label creep happens when the text prints right on the first set of labels, but then creeps up or down until it starts printing off the labels and onto the space in between them. The truly annoying thing about label creep is when it occurs, you often have to do much of the printing job over again, wasting a lot of time and materials.

Access has a wizard aimed at making the label printing job quite a bit easier than it would be if you did it manually. The best part of the wizard is that it has programmed into it the most popular label sizes and layouts cataloged by label number. This way you can just tell Access what type of label you're planning on using and the program does the proper layout. No more do you have to calculate how many 2 3/8" labels plus header, footer, and inter-label spaces fit on a page. The makers of the Label Report Wizard have done all the tedious work for you.

Another difference between the Label Wizard and the standard Report Wizards is the former creates report expressions as you supply it field and punctuation information. That doesn't sound obvious now perhaps, but the next exercise shows how well this works.

Exercise 11.3. Making mailing labels.

1. You should be at the Database View with the report tab clicked. If you're not, navigate back to that place. Click on the New button to start a new report.

2. Click on the pull-down list to select Student Personal as the bound table for this set of mailing labels.

3. Click on the Report Wizards button, then click on Mailing Label as the type of report. Click OK.

   Refer to Figure 11.11. This is where you not only tell Access what fields to include in your mailing labels, but format the labels as you see fit. Note the caption on the top of the right-hand box. It says Label appearance,

indicating you do more than include fields in this place—you do the layout. Look below the box on the left. You'll see a miniature keyboard. This is how you tell Access where to include such mailing label necessities as spaces, colons, dots, and so forth in the layout.

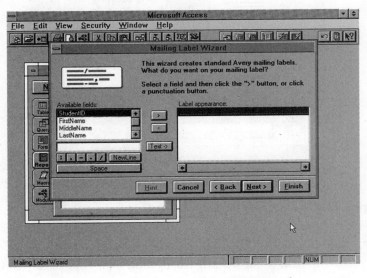

Figure 11.11. *The design section of the Mailing Label Wizard.*

4. Click on the FirstName field in the left-hand box. Click on the > button to insert this field in the label. The next thing you want is a space between the first and the middle names. Click the space bar in the miniature keyboard section to insert a space. Now highlight the MiddleName field and click the > button. Similarly, insert a space and the LastName field to finish the first row. Your screen should resemble Figure 11.12.

5. You're ready to move on to the next line, so click the NewLine button. Access moves the focus down to the second line of your label template.

6. Scroll down the left-hand box until the Address, City, State, and Zip fields come into view. Add the Address field to the second line of the label. Since this is the only entry on the second line, click the NewLine button to move down.

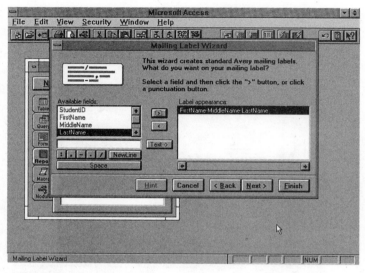

Figure 11.12. *Designing the mailing label.*

7. Add the City field, a comma, a space, the State field, a space, and finally the Zip field to the mailing label's third line. Your screen should resemble Figure 11.13.

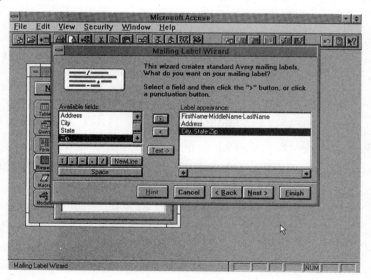

Figure 11.13. *The mailing label formatting finished.*

The Access Way

Note the empty field just below the field list box on the left-hand side of the dialog box shown in Figure 11.13. This is to enter text you want on the label but not in the database. If you want such an entry, such as the word ATTN:, enter it here. Then click the Text button to move your text into the label.

8. Click on the Next > button and choose the LastName field to sort or order this label report on. Your screen should resemble Figure 11.14.

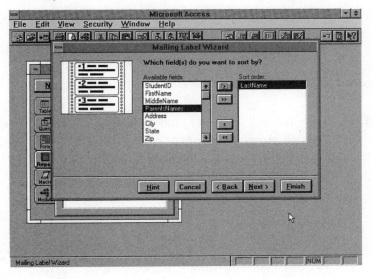

Figure 11.14. *Specifying a sort field.*

9. Click on the Next > button. Here's where you choose your label size either by the Avery catalog number or by the size. This example uses the 3" x 4" Avery 5384 label. Locate and click on that label if Access hasn't anticipated you. Your screen should resemble Figure 11.15.

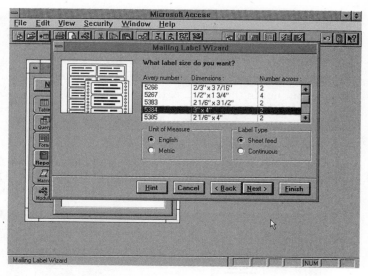

Figure 11.15. *Telling Access which label size to use.*

10. Click on the Next > button to move on to the label formatting dialog box. Here you tell Access what font to use for your labels. This example uses Arial font of 10 point bold-italic in black, as shown in Figure 11.16. Your screen might vary depending upon what fonts you have installed in your Windows setup.

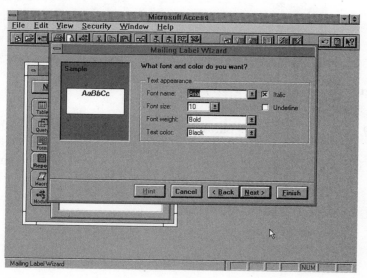

Figure 11.16. *The formatting dialog box for mailing labels.*

11. Click the Next > button to move to the last screen. Make sure the option button "See the mailing labels as they look printed" is your choice. Click on the finish button to look at your label layout without actually doing any printing.

Figure 11.17 shows the Print Preview view of the Mailing Label Wizard's work. If you wanted to print these labels for a mailing, you'd only need to tell Access to print this report and feed Avery 5384 or equivalent labels to your printer. Access makes the tedious and often frustrating job of printing mailing labels as simple as using a wizard.

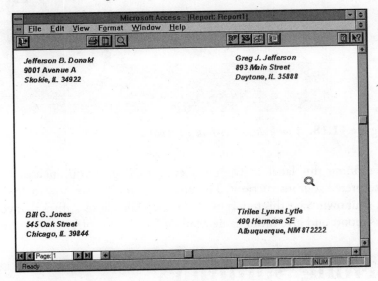

Figure 11.17. *The finished mailing label report.*

A Look Ahead

Before closing up shop for this morning, take a preview of what's to come later on in this day. Click on the Close Window button in the toolbar to move to Design View. Figure 11.18 shows this label in Design View.

Everything included in this label is an expression. You made these expressions when you instructed wizard during the label appearance dialog box, as shown in Figure 11.11.

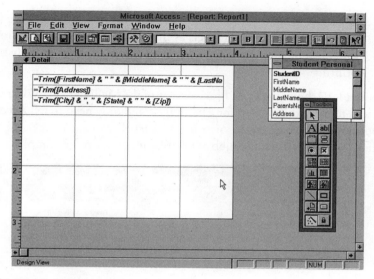

Figure 11.18. *A look at expressions in reports.*

Examining this label in Design View should give you an idea how the wizard interpreted your instructions. This afternoon you'll learn how to do this wizard trick on your own. Save this report by clicking on File|Close. Affirm that you want to save this report and give it the name Mailing Label Example.

Morning Summary

This morning you learned how to use the general Report Wizard and how to modify some aspects of the wizard's output. You also got a good run at designing mailing or other labels by using the Mailing Label Wizard. Keep in mind that the Label Wizard is good not only for mailing labels, but other labels such as folder, record, and book labels as well. The Mailing Label Wizard can be an enormous time and mood saver. Use it whenever you need to put data precisely on standard size labels or cards.

12

Intermediate
Reports

This afternoon you'll learn how to

☐ Create expressions in reports

☐ Group report data

Looking at Report Expressions

This morning you saw how you can include fields in reports. While the first exercise used a Report Wizard, you can also drag fields into reports from a Field list box just as you can drag fields into a form. The procedure in reports is identical to that in forms.

Fields dropped in forms work well, but as you saw, the finished report designed this way leaves a bit to be desired. While the report at the end of Exercise 11.2 was serviceable, it wasn't attractive or professional looking. One of the reasons for this is the fields included in the report take up a fixed space in the report. The fields in the report from Exercise 11.2 must be large enough to show all the data possibly entered in them, but this causes them to be too large for most of the entries. If you were to shrink down the fields so small entries looked good, the longer entries would be truncated, or chopped off.

Fields large enough to show the entire name Constance Jacqueline Fortesque show the name Tom J. Doe like this:

```
Tom        J        Doe
```

Size the fields to fit Tom J. Doe correctly, and Constance Jacqueline Fortesque looks like:

```
Con J For
```

Neither situation is entirely satisfactory. Expressions based on the fields instead of the fields themselves solves the field size dilemma in this type of report. In this case, an expression is a series of fields, punctuation marks, and spaces optionally including some Access-specific instructions. You saw an example of expressions in the Mailing Label Wizard's output. The following exercise shows how to modify the report from Exercise 11.2 to include field expressions.

> ### The Access Way
>
> Field expressions are only one type of expression you can use in Access. You've already seen some Access expressions in queries and in tables. The expressions used in Exercise 12.1 show only a few tricks you can do with expressions.

Exercise 12.1. Field expressions in reports.

This exercise replaces the first and third lines of the report's detail area with expressions that automatically size to fit the field's data.

1. Launch Access if necessary and load the College database. Click on the report tab. Highlight the Student Names and Addresses report and click on the Design button to open this report in Design View. Your screen should resemble Figure 12.1.

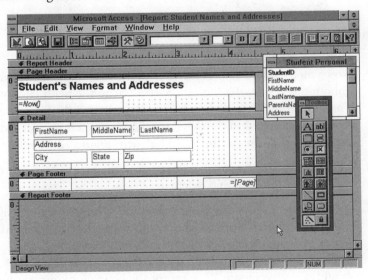

Figure 12.1. *The report in Design View.*

2. Delete the FirstName, MiddleName, and LastName fields from the first line of the detail band of the report design grid. This example used a marquee selection to first highlight all the fields, then the Del key to cut them from

12

the report. Use this technique or one you prefer. After you've cut the fields from your report, your screen should resemble Figure 12.2.

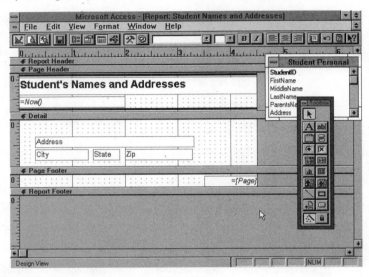

Figure 12.2. *The report with the first line blank.*

3. Now you need a container for your expression. This will be an initially unbound text box. We'll bind the text box to the fields later on. Click in the Toolbox on the Text Box tool. This is the tool with ab| on it. Click in the report's design grid in the detail band and drag a text box field to be roughly the same size as the Address field below it. Figure 12.3 shows this operation.

4. Click away from the new field to remove the highlight. Click only on the label part of this field and delete it.

5. It's now time to bind this field to the underlying table by using an expression. Click on the Properties button in the toolbar. Click on the new text box to bring up its properties in the Properties list box. If necessary, scroll through the list box until you see the Control Source property. Your screen should resemble Figure 12.4, except the Name for your text box will likely be different from that shown in Figure 12.4. The text box's name is unimportant for the purposes of this example.

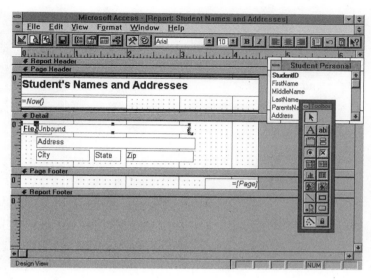

Figure 12.3. *Inserting an unbound text field.*

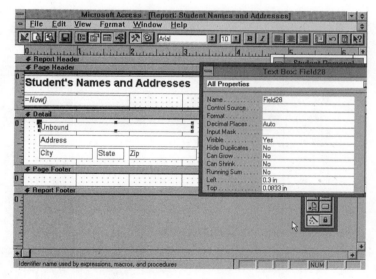

Figure 12.4. *The Control Source property controls what's in a text box.*

6. Click in the empty row to the right of the Control Source label. Press Shift+F2 to zoom into an editing box. This last step isn't necessary to entering an expression, but makes your job much easier. Your screen should resemble Figure 12.5.

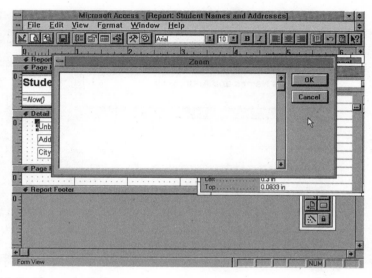
Figure 12.5. *Zoom mode for entering expressions.*

7. Enter the expression: =Trim([FirstName]&" "&[MiddleName]&"
   "&[LastName]) in the Zoom box. Your screen should resemble Figure 12.6.

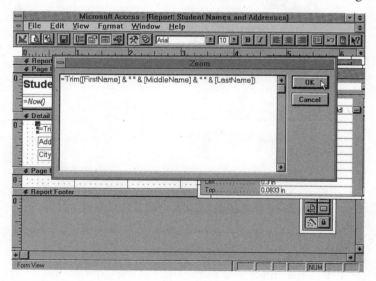

Figure 12.6. *The expression for student name.*

8. Click on OK to close the Zoom box. Click on the Print Preview button to see your results. The first line of your report detail should look like the first lines of the entries in Figure 12.7. Your screen won't match Figure 12.7 exactly until you complete step 9.

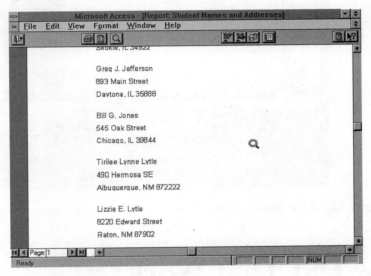

Figure 12.7. *The output of the expression.*

9. Return to Design mode. Delete the third line of the report detail. Insert an unbound text box just as you did for the first line of this report. Delete its label. Highlight the now unbound control. Locate the Control Source entry area for this text box and press Shift+F2. Enter the expression shown in Figure 12.8 for this text box.

10. Click on the Print Preview button in the toolbar. Access runs the report and if you've made no typing errors, you'll see your report now automatically sizes the first and third lines to fit the data. The second line has only one field so it doesn't need this treatment.

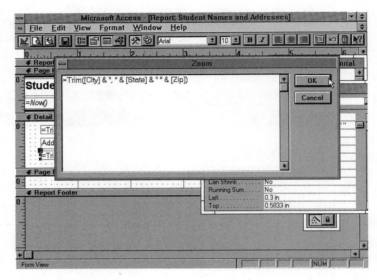

Figure 12.8. *The third line expression.*

How Did That Work?

Back when you started this report, you told Access to bind the Student Personal table to it. This is a key element in how these expressions worked. Return to Design View for this report if you're not there now. Click on the Address field to give it the highlight. Look in the Properties list box to see the control source property for this control. It's set to Address.

A control source is the source of what appears as contents for that control when outside of Design View. In the case of the Address control, the contents of the Address field in the Student Personal table is what appears when you print or preview this report. Access knows to look in Student Personal for the Address field because you told Access that Student Personal is the table bound to this report.

When you enter an equal sign (=) at the beginning of a control source, you're telling Access you'll be entering an expression. You could edit the control source for the Address text box to read =[Address], which gives you the same results as you have now with this control, but it would serve no practical purpose.

The expressions you added to the unbound text controls in lines 1 and 3 are more complex than that. They contain not only the field contents for more than one field, but spaces and a comma.

The Access Way

Access, like many computer programs, interprets the space character as the end of a string of characters. It is unusual in that it'll let you enter field names containing spaces. These are a problem in expressions since Access has no way of knowing when it hits a space if you mean that as an end to the name or a part of the field name.

You can use field names containing spaces by enclosing them in square brackets ([ ]) within expressions.

Look at the expression in the first row of this report's detail band. It reads

```
=Trim([FirstName] & " " & [MiddleName] & " " & [LastName])
```

Let's take it apart to see how it ticks. The first character is the equal sign =. This signals to Access that what follows is an expression.

The second element is the word Trim. Trim() is a built-in Access function that strips white spaces from the right and left side of a string of characters. Access has two related functions, Ltrim() and Rtrim(), which only strip spaces from the left and right of a character string, respectively. Since nothing appears to the right or left of the strings on the first or third line, the Trim here is somewhat unnecessary. It is vital to include Trim for proper layout if you have other fields to the right or left of your expression. It is included in this example more to show general good practice than any necessity.

The parentheses that functions come with and are identified by are for function parameters. Parameters are things the functions operate on. In this case, Trim()'s parameters are the whole expression. This tells Trim() that you want the spaces stripped from the right and left of the whole expression.

The third element is the field FirstName in square brackets [FirstName]. Since the Student Personal table's field names don't contain spaces, there's no requirement to include the field name in brackets, but like using Trim, it's good practice. There's no penalty to using brackets for field names and two advantages to always doing so: You'll never have an expression with a space misfire due to lack of brackets, and you'll be able to differentiate field names from other elements in expressions.

After [FirstName] comes the &, or ampersand operator. This tells Access to concatenate, or join, two elements in a string expression. This first & joins the [FirstName] field to the " ", which is an open quote, a space, and a close quote. If you didn't include

12

this space in the string at this place, the FirstName field would be jammed up against the MiddleName field. The spaces here and after MiddleName prevent Greg J. Jefferson from looking like GregJ.Jefferson.

The rest of the expression follows the first part. The last element is the closed parentheses, indicating the end of what the `Trim()` function is to be applied to.

The third line is almost identical to the first except the first space also has a comma ',' inserted. This gives us the comma after the City field in the third line. Anything enclosed in double quotation marks in an Access expression appears as literals. So if you modified the first row to read:

```
=Trim([FirstName] & " Hi! " & [MiddleName] & " " & [LastName])
```

the report would come out:

```
Greg Hi! J. Jefferson
...
...
Bill Hi! G. Jones
...
...
```

and so forth.

DO   DON'T

DO use expressions liberally in your reports. In many cases, they look much better than just fields.

DON'T neglect to enclose all your field names in square brackets even if Access enables you to get away with skipping this step. Good programming practice always pays off.

Groups

Think back to the query done in Exercise 10.3. This showed students' names and courses sorted or ordered by course number. One logical thing you can derive from this query is a report creating student enrollment cards showing all the courses a student is signed up to take for a semester.

Close the report created in Exercise 12.1, saving any changes. The point of this exercise is to create a report showing all the courses all the students are signed up for, plus add up the course load to see the total credit hours for each student. This is a lot simpler to do than to say, as you'll soon see.

Exercise 12.2. A grouped and totaled report.

1. At the Database View, click on the New button to start a new report. Scroll through the list of queries and tables Access gives you to locate the three-table query done in Chapter 10. This should be called Temp if you followed the book's examples exactly. Click on the query's name, then click on the Report Wizards button.

2. Click on Groups/Totals choice for the type of wizard you want Access to use. Your screen should resemble Figure 12.9.

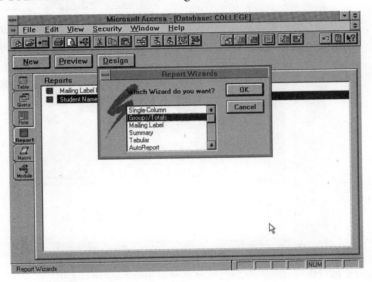

Figure 12.9. *Starting the Groups/Totals Wizard.*

3. Click on OK to move on. Include all the fields from this query into the report by clicking on the >> button.

4. Click on Next >. Click to highlight the LastName as the field you want to group on. Click the > button to move this field to the right-hand box. Click on the Next > button.

The Access Way

LastName works for this example because our tiny database hasn't any duplication of names. In a live application, you wouldn't want to group on the LastName field because duplicate names can easily exist in your data. Instead you'd use the key field for the Student Personal table, which is StudentID. While this report and query works with the sample data, grouping on a field that might contain duplicate entries isn't good practice.

5. Leave the next screen at the default. Your screen should resemble Figure 12.10.

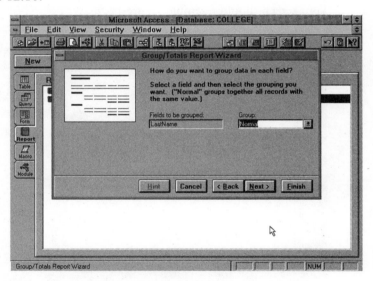

Figure 12.10. *Telling Access what type of grouping to use.*

6. Click on the Next > button to move on to the sorting dialog box.

7. Click on Course Number as the field you want to sort in within each particular group. Click on the > button to move it right. This lists each student's courses in numerical order. Click on the Next > button.

8. Click on the Executive option for the look of the report. The Orientation option should default to Landscape. If it isn't set to do so, click on this option. Click on the Next > button.

9. Enter the name Student Class Cards for a report name. If Access has offered to calculate percentages for you, uncheck this box. Your screen should resemble Figure 12.11.

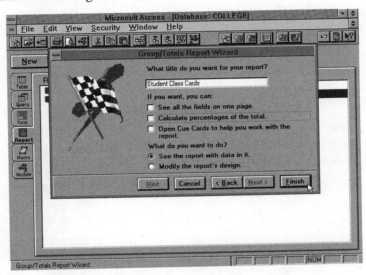

Figure 12.11. *Finishing the Groups/Totals Wizard.*

10. Click on Finish.

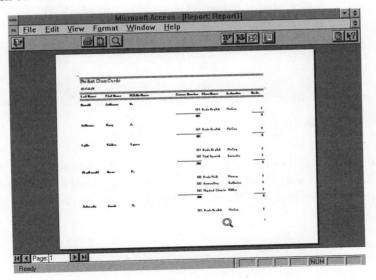

Figure 12.12. *A report with groups and totals.*

If you zoom in on this report, you'll note that Access got excessively zealous to the point of adding up anything even vaguely numerical, such as course numbers. This is silly, but does show another example of how a wizard can't possibly evaluate your data qualitatively. Access has no way of knowing that adding up credit hours is a good thing, but adding up course numbers is meaningless.

Click on the Close Window button on the far left of the toolbar. Access takes you to a very complex-looking Design View. Here you can see the enormous benefit of a wizard. You could have created this report manually, but look at all the work the wizard saved.

Highlight the expression field =Sum([Course Number]) and the line or lines directly above it from both the LastName footer and Report footer bands of the report. Your screen should resemble Figure 12.13.

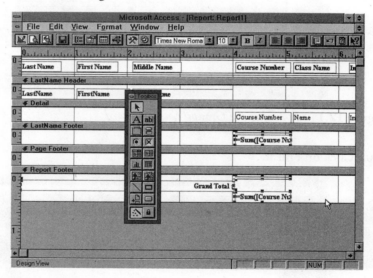

Figure 12.13. *Design View of a complex report.*

Click on the Del or Delete key to cut these fields from our report. Return to Print Preview to see if your edits worked. You now have a quite serviceable report. Save this report as Class Cards. We'll come back to it later to do further modifications, but that's all for today.

Summary

Reports present data much as forms do. The biggest difference between forms and reports is that forms work best on the screen while reports work best printed. You can view report data on the screen and you can print forms, but neither is optimal.

Access contains Report Wizards that work much like Form Wizards. Two extremely handy Report Wizards are the Mailing Label and Groups/Totals ones. Both save you a great deal of time. Since the Mailing Label Wizard has memorized the dimensions of just about all the labels you're likely to encounter, it'll save you a great deal of layout frustration too.

Q&A

Q How do you show the report and page header and footer bands? I need to open these bands before I can enter data into them.

A In report Design View, click on the Format menu, then select either the Report Header/Footer or Page Header/Footer selections.

Q Why can't Access be smart enough to know when field names end and begin without me bothering with square brackets?

A Look at the following: Last Name Street Address. What are the field names? They might be Last Name and Street Address, or there might be three fields here, Last Name, Street and Address. Placing brackets [Last Name][Street Address] removes any ambiguity.

Q I tried printing a mailing label report. The report seems to work all right, but the labels came off in my laser printer. This could have caused real damage. Luckily, none was done. What good is making a mailing label report if I can't use my printer to do output?

A You need to buy mailing labels specifically made for laser printers. These work much better than general-purpose labels. Also, if your printer has the option of using a straight paper path, opt for doing the printing this way even if you have to position a tray to catch the output.

12

Q **Why not just apply the** `Trim()` **function to the fields themselves rather than construct an expression?**

A Following your idea, you'd need three `Trim()`'s, and while Access allows this, you won't get your desired result. Look at the Mailing Label Example report's second line. It reads =`Trim([Address])`. The reason your idea won't work is fields start and end at specific places. If the fields could shift around to make room for nonspace characters and squeeze back for trimmed spaces, your technique would be all right. You wouldn't want to do it anyway. It'd actually be more effort than just making an expression because you'd need to edit three fields.

Q **Can I embed graphics such as my company logo in a report?**

A Yes. Embedding graphics in reports and forms is a subject that we'll come to shortly.

Workshop

Here's where you can test and apply what you have learned today.

Quiz

Possible answers to these questions are provided in Appendix A.

1. What character tells Access an entry in the Control Source property list box is an expression?

2. Why bother with brackets (`[ ]`) for field names?

3. What function does Access have built-in to total number fields in a group or a report? Hint: Look at the Class Cards report in Design View.

4. What properties control the grid spacing in the report design grid? The same properties control the grid spacing in the form design grid.

5. Can you bind a report to another report? To a table? To a query?

Put Access into Action

1. Use the Groups/Totals report wizard to create a report similar to the Class Cards report, but bind it to the Available Classes table. Have the report include all the fields from the table grouped on Department and totaled on hours only.

You'll need to delete some useless sums. Overall, your report creation should go similarly to Exercise 12.2. You can keep this report for later experimentation or delete it because *Teach Yourself Access 2 in 14 Days* won't refer back to it.

2. Examine the Class Cards report in Design View. Look at the page footer band. Note the entry =[page]. What do you suppose that does? Run the report in Print Preview and see if your supposition was right. Will this entry work similarly in the page header band?

3. If you have a printer, print the first page of the Class Cards report. (When you go to print, Access gives you a dialog box where you can instruct it to only print one page.)

4. Return to Design View. Open the Palette and color the Detail section of the report dark gray. Print page one of this report again. Did you like the effect?

5. Close this report, discarding changes.

12

Day

7

13

M T W R F S S

Intermediate Forms

This morning's material covers these topics:

☐ Using list or combo boxes in forms

☐ Binding combo boxes to lists

☐ Dynamic indexing in combo boxes

Using List or Combo Boxes in Forms

Think about the data entered in the Student's Current Courses table. It contains information related to two additional tables: Student Personal, which holds the StudentID; and Available Classes, which holds course number information. You wouldn't want even the possibility of data entered into this form having a wrong StudentID or a wrong course number.

The Student's Current Courses table is linked to both Available Classes and Student Personal and in both cases Access has been told to enforce referential integrity in these links. Referential integrity means that when you enter, for example, a StudentID in the Student's Current Courses, Access will look in Student Personal to make sure that StudentID really exists. The same rule exists for entering a Course Number in Student's Current Courses.

This referential integrity enforcement does prevent entry of wrong or nonexistent StudentID's or Course Numbers. It does nothing to assist the data entry person in finding the right values for these fields.

Primitive data entry systems gave entry people a paper list of valid entries as a reference. This works, but isn't particularly efficient. What would be much better is to have Access look up correct values from within a data entry form bound to Student's Current Courses. This eliminates the need for paper references and greatly speeds up the data entry process. It also goes a long way toward preventing data entry people from entering a valid, but wrong, value for either of these fields.

Like so many things in personal computers, getting a feeling for how this works is easier when seen than explained. The exercises that follow create a form for entering data into Student's Current Courses. Two of the controls on this form will look up existing values from previously entered data.

All the controls on the forms shown so far in this book have been text boxes. You can do data entry and basic editing within them. List and combo boxes are also handy

controls for data entry. A list box shows a list of values you can scroll through. A combo box, a combination of a list box and a text box, has a place to enter data and a drop-down list that works exactly like the list box. Exercise 13.1 shows you how to create a form with a combo box.

Exercise 13.1. A form with combo boxes.

1. If necessary, launch Access and open the College database. Click on the Form tab and click on the New button to create a new form. Pull down the combo box; scroll to the Student's Current Courses table and click on it. Your screen should resemble Figure 13.1.

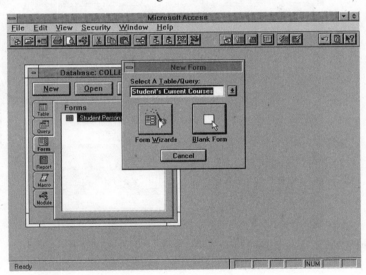

Figure 13.1. *Binding a table to a new form.*

2. Click on the Blank Form button to bypass the wizard.

The Access Way

This will be a simple form with some fancy controls—combo boxes for two fields. There's no way to tell Access to use combo boxes rather than text boxes during a simple wizard form operation. In this case, using the wizard, then undoing what the wizard left us, is more work than just going directly to manual design.

13

3. After clicking on the Blank Form button, your screen should resemble Figure 13.2. Note that in this figure, the Toolbox has been reshaped to a horizontal orientation and the screen maximized. Your actual screen might vary from this figure. If your screen doesn't show the Student's Current Courses list box, click on the Field List button in the toolbar. If your screen is more complex than shown because it has, for example, the Properties list box or the Palette showing, you can optionally keep them or close them by clicking on the appropriate button in the toolbar.

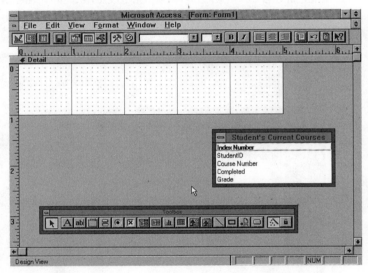

Figure 13.2. *The form design grid.*

4. The Student's Current Courses table has a key field of the Counter data type. Since Access increments this field automatically when you enter records, you don't need to include that in this form. The only fields you need to include on a form are those you enter data into or those that have information you need to view. You can safely skip Index Number because it meets neither of these criteria. Click on the StudentID field to select it for placing on the form.

DO — DON'T

DO include only those fields on your forms you need to view, edit, or make entries into.

DON'T litter up your forms with unnecessary fields. Doing so serves no useful purpose and only confuses the form's users.

5. Examine the Toolbox in Figure 13.2. Note that the magic wand-like tool is selected, indicating Control Wizards are on. Click on your Control Wizard toggle, if necessary, to turn it on too.

6. The first field you'll place on this form is StudentID. You'll use a combo box for this and let a wizard do most of the work. Click on the Combo Box tool in the Toolbox. This tells Access that you want to use this control type for the previously selected StudentID field. Click on the StudentID field in the Student's Current Courses list box. Hold down the mouse button and drag the StudentID field to the form design grid. Release the mouse button. Access will automatically start up the Combo Box Wizard. Your screen should resemble Figure 13.3.

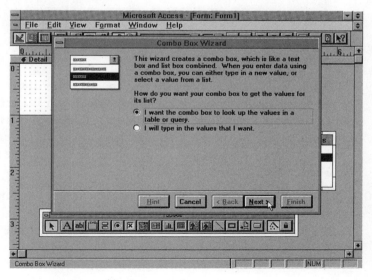

Figure 13.3. *Inserting a combo box in a form.*

13

7. Of course you want the combo box to look up values for you, so leave the top option box checked and click on the Next > button.

8. The values for the StudentID field you want to look up are located in the Student Personal table. Highlight this table in the next list box. Your screen should resemble Figure 13.4. Click on the Next > button.

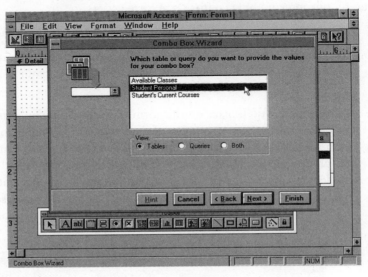

Figure 13.4. *Binding a combo box to a table.*

9. You could have just the StudentID field appear in this combo box, but most people find it easier to search a list for text values such as a person's name than to look for an arbitrary set of numbers and letters such as the StudentID. Click on the > button four times to include not only the StudentID, but the FirstName, MiddleName, and LastName fields too. Your screen should resemble Figure 13.5.

10. Click on the Next > button to move to a dialog where you can adjust the field widths that are shown in this combo box. This example left the field widths at their defaults as shown in Figure 13.6. Click on the Next > button.

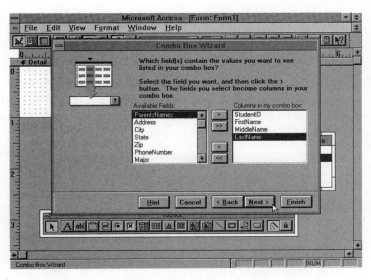

Figure 13.5. *Including fields in a combo box.*

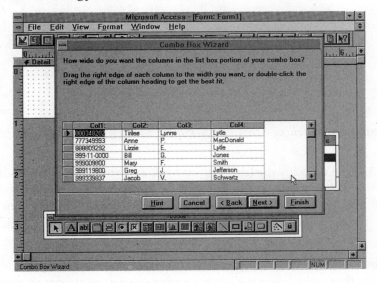

Figure 13.6. *Adjusting the field widths in a combo box.*

11. This screen is vital. Access can look up a value in a table but record an offset value in the receiving table. In this case, we want to both look up and return the StudentID value; but in other cases you might want, for example, to

look up the StudentID value but record the data in the LastName field in your receiving table. Since this isn't the case here, click on the Next > button to move on.

12. The next dialog box lets you tell Access what to do with the value looked up. Because we want to enter the value in the StudentID field of the bound table, Student's Current Courses, leave the default option button selected as in Figure 13.7. Click the Next > button.

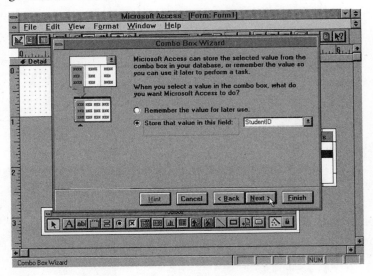

Figure 13.7. *Telling Access how to handle a looked-up value.*

13. Don't modify the label for this field, as is your option in this dialog box. Click on the Finish button to see your results. Access grinds around a bit and ends up placing the now programmed combo box on your form. Click on the Form View button to see how this control works. Click on the down arrow for this combo box. Your screen should resemble Figure 13.8.

Now entering correct values in this form for the StudentID field is as simple as pulling down the combo box and clicking on the value you want from the supplied list. This list has the added advantage of showing not only the StudentID field, but the FirstName, MiddleName, and LastName fields so a data entry person can locate a record on these values, not just StudentID.

The idea of a multicolumn combo box can be an important one if you create applications that serve the public. Have you ever been annoyed that someone you're

doing business with required you to remember your customer identification number before they could locate you in their records? A multicolumn combo box enables you to locate people by various fields in their records.

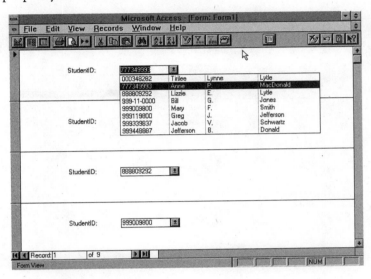

Figure 13.8. *The programmed combo box.*

Auto Indexing

Access will try to locate values already in a combo box list as you make an entry into the text portion of the combo box. Move to a new record by clicking on the New button in the toolbar, then try this: pull down the combo box to show the list portion of the combo box. Press the backspace key to clear any text in the text portion of the combo box. Enter the number 8. Access immediately knows that there's only one value in the list that begins with the number 8, and it not only goes to that value in the list portion, but fills in the text section of the combo box with this value for you. The results of entering an 8 in the text portion of this combo box are shown in Figure 13.9.

Try the same procedure, but enter a 9 instead of an 8. Access immediately moves to the top of the section where StudentIDs start with a 9 and fill the text portion of the combo box with the value located there. Enter two more 9's. This still doesn't give Access any more limiting information because all the StudentID's starting with a

single 9 also start with three 9's. Now enter a 0. Access immediately knows you must mean the StudentID 999009800 because that's the only one that starts with three 9's followed by a 0.

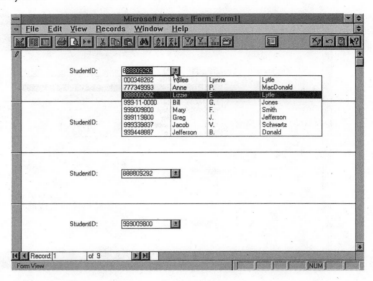

Figure 13.9. *Auto find in action in a combo box.*

Combo box Auto Find or Auto Indexing works the same with text as with numbers. If you have the values Tom, Thomas, and Tirilee in your combo box's list section, entering *T* takes you to the top of the T's and fills in the value Tirilee in the text portion of the combo box. Then entering an *o* or an *h* lets Access move your selection to the single right one if it's not Tirilee.

The Access Way

If you set the Limit to List property to Yes, you're telling Access to limit the entries in a field to those entries already entered in the field specified as a Row Source.

Return to Design View after you're satisfied you are familiar with combo box operation.

The Access Way

If you alter the data in the StudentID field on this form for an existing record, you'll also alter data in the Student's Current Courses. If after experimenting with this control you find your actual data is out of sync with the book, it's likely that you modified existing data rather than experimenting with a new record. You can continue on with slightly modified data or edit your data back to the book's by comparing your data with the unmodified sample data.

Manual Combo or List Box Programming

The wizard works fine for programming list or combo boxes, but the why of the wizard's actions is important to learn also. Like using a calculator only after you know how to add, you should know what a wizard is doing with these controls before you use it. Exercise 13.2 shows how to manually program a combo or list box.

The same method is used for programming a combo box and a list box. Whether you use a list or combo box depends upon your aesthetic sense and your specific application. You can't enter values in a text box that's in a list box—you must choose from what already exists in it. Also, list boxes remain full size—there's no pulling them down. List boxes work well when you want to show a value selection all the time or when you don't want a pull-down control. Figure 13.10 shows the Course Number field as it would appear on this form in a list box.

13

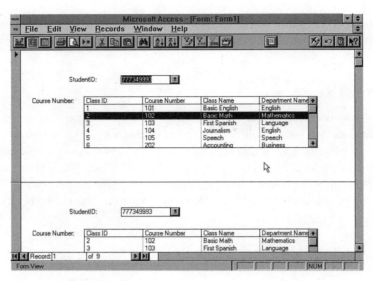

Figure 13.10. *A list box on a form.*

Exercise 13.2 uses a combo box for the Course Number field. If you prefer the list box, you could use that for this application as well.

Exercise 13.2. Manual combo box programming.

1. Return to Design View for the form started in Exercise 13.1. Click on the Control Wizards button in the Toolbox to turn off Control Wizards. Move your cursor to the bottom of the form design grid until it's on the border. Your cursor changes to a bar with an up- and down-facing arrow. Click and drag the form down to resize it to resemble the form in Figure 13.11.

2. Click on the combo box control in the Toolbox. Then click on the Course Number field in the field list box and drag the Course Number field onto the form just under the StudentID field. Your screen should resemble Figure 13.12.

   Note that this time Access didn't start up a Combo Box Wizard. This is because you turned off these wizards by toggling the Wizard control in the Toolbox earlier in the exercise. If you failed to do this and the wizard started anyway, just click on the Cancel button to end the wizard's participation in this exercise.

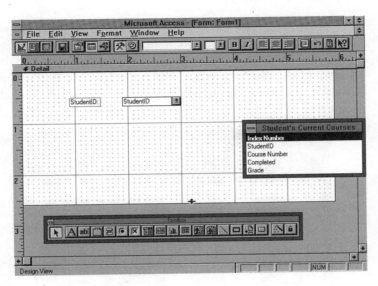

Figure 13.11. *Resizing a form.*

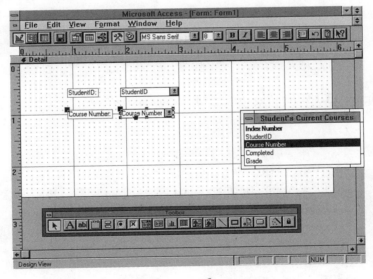

Figure 13.12. *Placing a new combo box on a form.*

13

3. Programming this combo box amounts to setting certain properties for it in the Properties list box. Open this list box by clicking on the appropriate button in the toolbar. Locate the Row Source property and click on its row.

Pull down this property's combo box and click on the Available Classes table. Remember, the values we want to look up for this field reside in the Available Classes table. Setting the Row Source property for the Course Number field effectively binds the Course Number field in this form to the ClassID field in the Available Classes table. Your screen should resemble Figure 13.13.

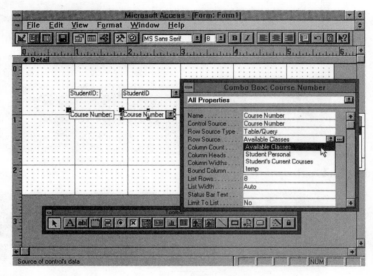

Figure 13.13. *Binding the combo box to a server table.*

The Access Way

Access always binds the first column of a table or query specified in the Row Source property of a list or combo box. In this case, the Course Number field binds to the ClassID rather than the Course Number field in Available Classes. This is right for our purposes. It's not that Access has suddenly grown able to read our minds, but rather that the ClassID field is first in the Available Classes table.

4. Modify the combo box's properties to read like the list box in Figure 13.14.

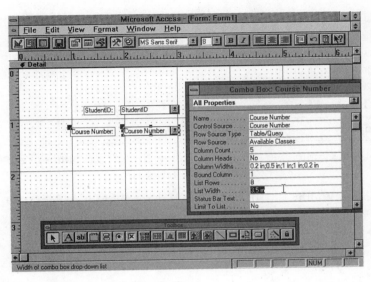

Figure 13.14. *Programming the combo box.*

5. Click on the Form View button to see the operation of this control. Your screen should resemble Figure 13.15.

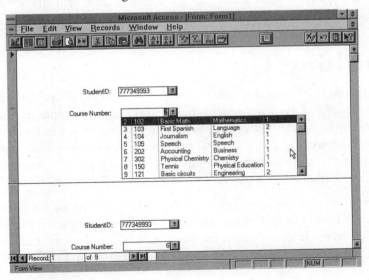

Figure 13.15. *The finished combo box.*

How It Worked

Here are the control's properties you altered with an explanation of what the modifications did.

Table 13.1. The Course Number Combo Box.

Property	Value	Meaning
Column Count	5	Show the first 5 columns of the Available Classes table.
Column Widths	0.2 in; 0.5 in; 1 in; 1 in; 0.2 in	Set these widths for columns 1 to 5 respectively.
List Width	3.5 in	Make the entire list portion of the combo box 3.5 inches.

In use, you'd also probably set the Limit to List Property to Yes to limit the information you can enter into the field.

Finishing Up

Finishing this form takes little more effort. Return to Design View. Locate the check box control in the Toolbox and click on it. Drag the Completed field to the form so it occupies a place on the form similar that to that shown in Figure 13.16. Click on the text control and drag the Grade field to the form so it occupies a place on the form similar that to that shown in Figure 13.16. You'll probably have to rearrange your fields somewhat to make your form identical to Figure 13.16.

The only thing left is to enter a label for this form. Click on the Format menu. Click on the Form Header/Footer selection to show this section of the form design grid. Click on the label control in the Toolbox. Click in the form header band and enter the label: Student Enrollment Form. Your screen should resemble Figure 13.17.

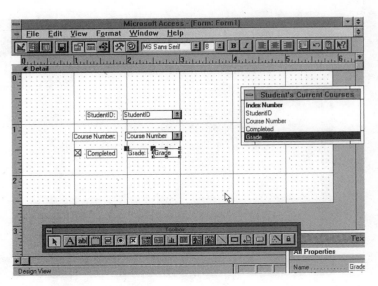

Figure 13.16. *Finishing up the form.*

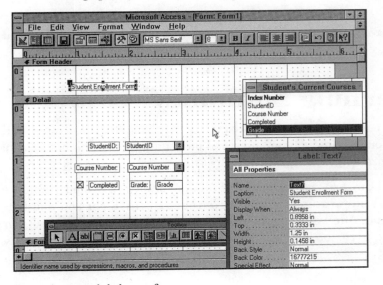

Figure 13.17. *Placing a label on a form.*

Pull down the font size combo box and select 14 as the point size for this label. Click on the Bold button to change the font to bold. Resize the label box to accommodate the new size and style font. Click on the Form View button. Your screen should resemble Figure 13.18.

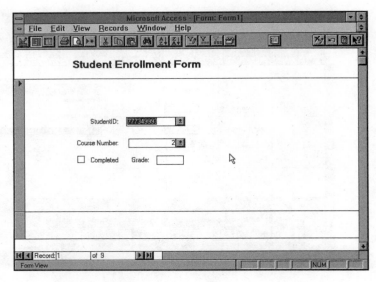

Figure 13.18. *A functionally finished form.*

Save this form as Student Enrollment by clicking on File|Close and agreeing with Access that you do want to save the form.

Morning Summary

The topic of combo and list boxes is somewhat complex and can be initially confusing. You saw how you can insert and program these controls both manually and with a wizard.

The trick to making these controls work properly is to bind their row source property to a proper source. This source can be an entered list or a previously existing query or table. After you've set this property to point to the right source, all that remains of the list or combo box programming is to improve its aesthetics or its ease of use.

14

More Intermediate Forms

The material this afternoon combines the fairly complex topic of option groups with the simple and fun placement of graphic objects in forms. You'll learn the following:

☐ What an option group is

☐ How to modify a table to accept the option group's output

☐ How to place an option group in a form

☐ How to embed an OLE graphic object in a form

The Option Group

An option group is a set of option buttons, toggle buttons, or check boxes in which one control must be selected and no more than one control in a group can be selected.

To quickly get a feel for option groups, start a new form. When Access asks you for a binding table or query, leave the combo box blank and click on the Blank Form button. Your screen should resemble Figure 14.1.

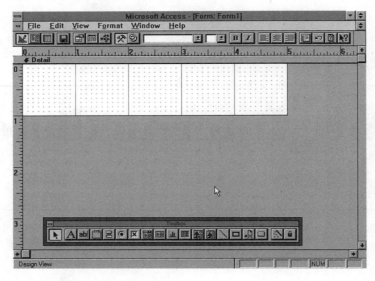

Figure 14.1. *The option group demo form.*

Locate these two controls in the Toolbox: the Option button and the Option Group. Click on the Option Group and click somewhere on the form to place an option group on it. Click on the Lock button in the Toolbox to let you select several Option buttons in a row.

Click on the Option button tool, then click in the option group box. Repeat until you have two or three option buttons in the option group and two or three option buttons outside of the group. Your screen should resemble Figure 14.2. Note that the form in Figure 14.2 has been saved with the name "demo," as you can see in the title bar. Don't be concerned if your form objects have different label numbers than the ones shown here.

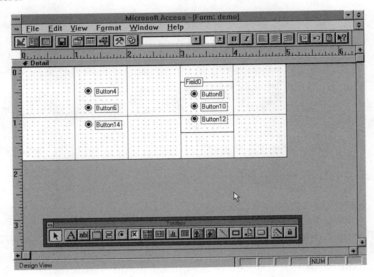

Figure 14.2. *The option group demo form with buttons added.*

Click on the Form View button. Try choosing more than one option button in the option group. Try making no button in the option group selected. Now try the same thing with the buttons outside of the group.

Your form might open with no option group buttons selected, but the minute you do select one you won't be able to return the group to having none selected. The option buttons outside of an option group can toggle on and off unrelated to their neighbors.

What's It Good For?

In many cases you'll want to give your applications a choice from several options. Option buttons work well for this. If you want to force a choice of one from a group of selections, the option group is the easiest way. Take a look at Figure 14.3. This shows the form from Figure 14.2 with labels showing how you might use option buttons in and out of an option group.

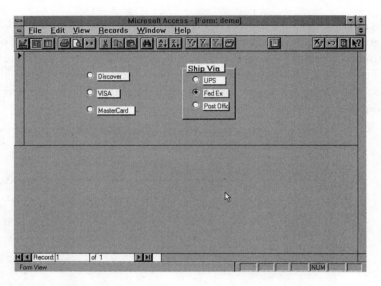

Figure 14.3. *An option group.*

This is another fictional example—for a mail order company where management wants to track people who pay by credit card only. Customers might also pay by COD or check, in which case the management doesn't need an entry. So the option buttons for credit cards exist outside of an option group. However, all orders need to be shipped via some carrier, so the Ship Via option buttons are in an option group.

Our fictional college has three types of student status: full-time, part-time, and visiting scholar. Each student must be one of these, and none can be more than one. This is a great application for an option group.

The value for student status will be held in Student Personal table. The first thing you need to do is modify the table to accept this new data. Exercise 14.1 simply adds a new field to Student Personal to hold either a 1, 2, or 3 to correspond to a student status.

Exercise 14.1. Modifying an existing table.

1. Close the Option group demo form, discarding changes.

2. Back at the Database View, click on the Table tab. Highlight the Student Personal table and click on the Design button to enter Design View for this table.

3. Locate the Note field and click just to the left of it to give the entire row the highlight. Press the Ins or Insert button on your keyboard to insert a blank row just above the Note field. Your screen should resemble Figure 14.4.

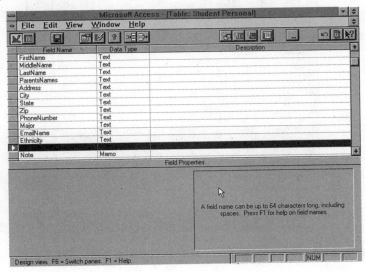

Figure 14.4. *Inserting a new row in a table's design grid.*

4. Click in the Field Name column of the blank row and enter StudentStatus as a field name. Move to the Data Type column and enter Number as a data type. Move to the Field Properties section of the table design grid and change the field size to byte. Finally, change the Default Value property to 1. Your screen should resemble Figure 14.5.

The Access Way

The values in the StudentStatus field will be limited to 1, 2, or 3, as you'll soon see. The Number data type with field size byte is a very efficient way to store information in Access; however, entries in this type of field are limited to positive integers no higher than 255. This fits our projected data perfectly.

The general rule of using a Text data type field unless you're sure you'll be doing math on a field's contents was overridden here for the sake of efficiency and in the sure knowledge that no text will ever be entered in this field.

14

5. Close this table, saving changes.

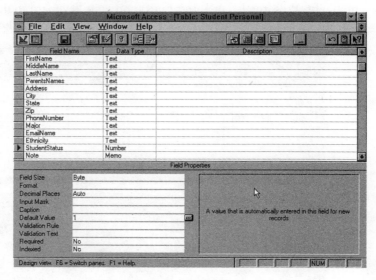

Figure 14.5. *The new field for Student Personal.*

We need a form to place the option group in. As luck would have it, we did save the Student Personal Data form earlier on.

Exercise 14.2 makes room on the Student Personal Data form for the new option group and then installs the option group on it.

Exercise 14.2. Creating and programming the option group.

1. At the Database View, click on the Form tab. Click on the Student Personal Data form, then click on the Design button to open this form in Design View. Your screen should resemble Figure 14.6. Note: Figure 14.6 has a restructured Toolbox to accommodate this new form.

2. Resize and rearrange the fields until your form resembles Figure 14.7. Don't worry if your form doesn't look identical to Figure 14.7. Close is good enough here.

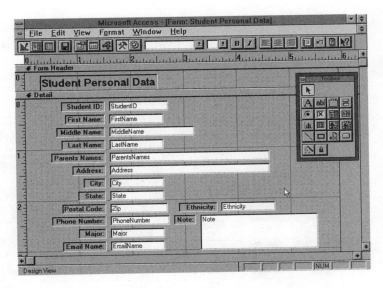

Figure 14.6. *The form Design View.*

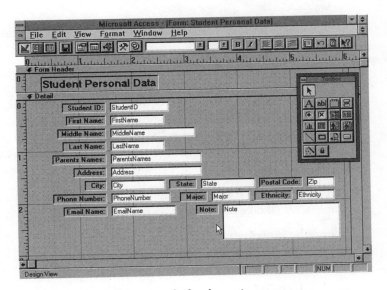

Figure 14.7. *The rearranged form ready for the option group.*

3. Click on the Option Group button in the Toolbox. Click in the lower-left portion of the form to insert the option group there. Your screen should resemble Figure 14.8. You will need to resize and manipulate the default option group's shape to get your screen to resemble Figure 14.8.

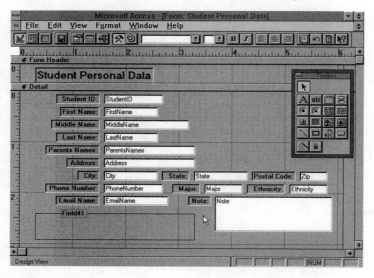

Figure 14.8. *The inserted option group.*

4. Click on the Lock button in the Toolbox, if necessary, to make it active. Insert three option buttons in the option group box as shown in Figure 14.9. Remember, you can drag a control and its label separately by dragging on the large square in the upper-left corner of the control or label when the control has the highlight.

   Don't be concerned if your controls are numbered differently than the example's. We'll take care of this next.

5. Click on the Properties button in the toolbar to open up the Properties list box. Click on the option button at the far left of your screen. Make sure the option button and not its label has the highlight.

6. Locate and edit the Option Value property for this control to 1. If this is the first option button you added to the form it should already have this value. Figure 14.10 shows this control and its Properties list box with the proper value entered for the Option Value.

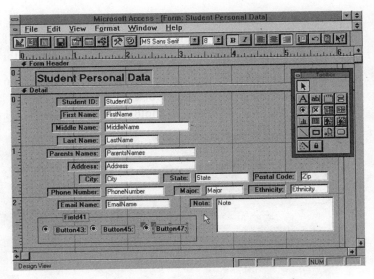

Figure 14.9. *The option buttons placed in the Option group box.*

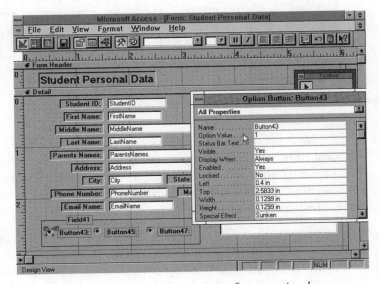

Figure 14.10. *Setting the Option Value property for an option button.*

7. Highlight the label for this option button and enter F/T for its Caption property. This labels this option button as F/T for full-time. If you want to, you can resize the label box to accommodate this new value for its caption.

8. Similarly, set the Option Value property for the middle option button at 2 and the right one at 3. Set their labels' caption properties to P/T and Visiting, respectively. Your screen should resemble Figure 14.11.

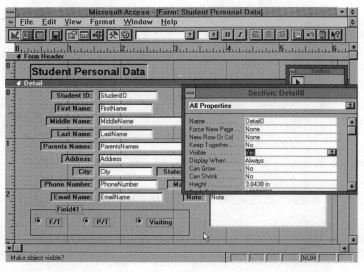

Figure 14.11. *Finishing up the option group.*

9. Finally, bind this option group to the StudentStatus field in the Student Personal table. Click on the option group itself. Look in the Properties list box for the Control Source property. Either pull down the combo box and click on StudentStatus or enter StudentStatus for this property. Your screen should resemble Figure 14.12.

10. Switch to Form View. The current record showing should be Tirilee Lytle. Click on the F/T option button for this student. Scroll through the records one by one, clicking on the F/T option button until you hit Mary Smith. Click on P/T for her record and the next. Move to the next record and set Visiting for the last and next to last records.

11. Close the form, saving changes. Click on the Table tab and open the Student Personal table in Datasheet View. Scroll to the StudentStatus column and note the values you entered at the option group are reflected here.

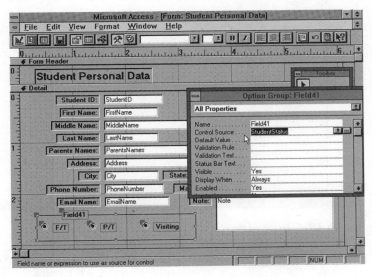

Figure 14.12. *Binding the option group.*

What Good Are Numbers?

Option values must be numbers. Since you want to know if a student's full-time, part-time or visiting, not what the number is, you have to do a final step. Construct a table with two fields: StudentStatus Number and StudentStatus. This table, StudentStatus Lookup, is shown in Figure 14.13 and is part of the sample data.

The next thing to do is construct a simple query linking the StudentStatus field's data in Student Personal with the StudentStatus Lookup table. The design of this demonstration query is shown in Figure 14.14. Figure 14.15 shows this query in action. This query is called Show StudentStatus and is part of the sample data.

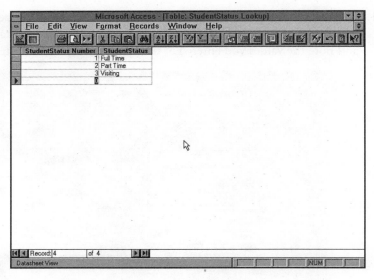

Figure 14.13. *The StudentStatus Lookup table.*

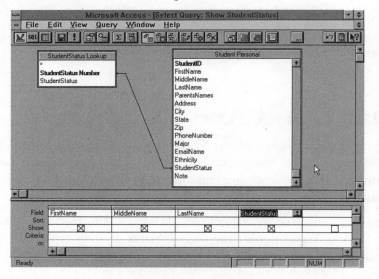

Figure 14.14. *The Design View of the Show StudentStatus query.*

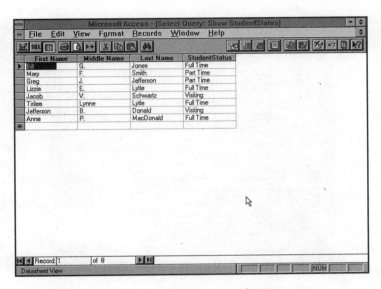

Figure 14.15. *The results of running the Show StudentStatus query.*

Art in Databases

The last thing to cover this afternoon is embedding graphic images in forms and reports. Access can include graphic objects, such as photographs of students, as part of its data set. Such data are called bound OLE objects. The next exercise addresses the other form of graphic embedding—unbound—and shows how to embed decorative objects in your form.

Our fictional college doesn't yet have a logo. Exercise 14.3 creates one and embeds it in the Student Personal Data form.

Exercise 14.3. Embedding a graphic in a form.

1. Return to the Database View and click on the Form tab. Highlight Student Personal Data and click on the Design button to open this form in Design View. Your screen should resemble Figure 14.16.

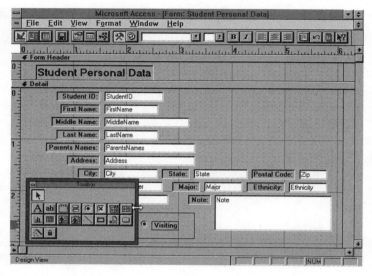

Figure 14.16. *The form ready for a graphic.*

2. Click on the Object Frame button in the Toolbox.

3. Click on the form in the upper-right area. Access responds with the dialog box shown in Figure 14.17.

DO / DON'T

DO use OLE to use other applications' tools in your Access databases if you have these other applications such as Excel 5 or Word 6.

DON'T try using OLE on a marginal system—that is, a computer with less than 16MB. While this works, you'll be disappointed in the performance.

4. Scroll down until you see the entry Paintbrush Picture. Click on this to give it the highlight, then click on OK. Access will launch the Paintbrush program.

5. Create a logo of your choosing. Figure 14.18 is the one done for this book. Use it or one of your own design. You should be able to do better than this example!

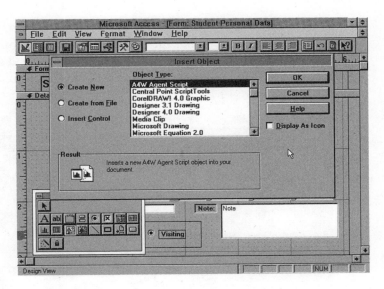

Figure 14.17. *The OLE dialog box.*

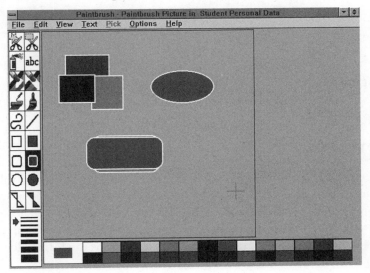

Figure 14.18. *The newly constructed logo.*

6. In Paintbrush, click on File|Exit. Note the Exit command is modified to indicate Paintbrush is acting as a server application for Access. Windows will ask you if you're sure you want to do this. Click on OK.

7. Click on the sizing handles for the logo and size it appropriately. If necessary, open the Properties list box for this control and set the Size Mode property to Stretch. This example also opened the Palette and set the control's format to a raised look. The finished form with logo is shown in Form View in Figure 14.19.

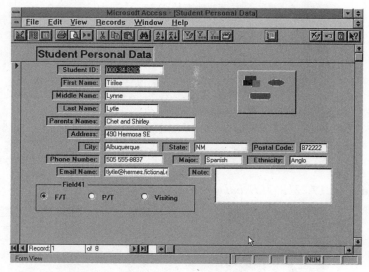

Figure 14.19. *The finished logo in a form.*

Summary

You can use list and combo boxes in forms to look up validation values from tables, queries, or lists other than the table or query you've bound to your form. You use combo or list boxes by first creating a lookup list of some sort. Then place the combo box on your form and bind its Row Source property to the lookup source. In one of the exercises today, for example, you set a combo box in a form to look up valid values for StudentIDs.

Option groups are boxes containing check boxes, option buttons, or toggle buttons. The distinguishing characteristics of an option group are that only one control in the group can be selected and one must be selected. If you wish to use many unrelated option buttons, check boxes, or toggle buttons on your form, you can do so, but don't place them within an option group.

Access stores graphics, sounds, or other OLE type objects as data in a database. These objects are called bound objects. You can show unbound objects in forms and reports as decorative items. With Access you can either create objects at the time you insert them into a form or report, as the exercise this afternoon demonstrated, or use a preexisting file such as a .BMP Paintbrush file you created using a paint program. To use a preexisting file, refer to Figure 14.17. The three option buttons on the left side of the dialog box are an option group. Choose the second button to insert a preexisting file.

Q&A

Q What's an OLE object?

A Certain Windows applications support OLE, which stands for Object Linking and Embedding. Applications that allow objects they create to be used by another application are called OLE server programs. Access 2 is an OLE client application. It can use objects created by an OLE server but cannot share objects it creates with another OLE client. In this example, Paintbrush is an OLE server program and Access the OLE client, so Access can use an object created in Paintbrush for its own use. However, Paintbrush cannot use objects created by Access in its applications, in part because Access isn't an OLE server.

Q What other kinds of OLE objects are there?

A There are as many OLE objects as application programs that can act as an OLE server. For example, Word for Windows 6 and Excel 5 are both OLE servers, so you can embed Word documents and Excel spreadsheets in your Access database. This gives you all the financial and numerical analysis powers of Excel or the editing power of Word in Access. The downside of this is you must own either Word or Excel to use this tool.

Windows comes with all the tools you need to play .wav (WAV) sound files if your computer is sound capable. Using the same techniques as shown in this chapter, you can embed WAV sound files in forms or tables to give your databases some real flair.

Additionally, OLE is resource demanding. A 386/33 with 8MB of RAM works fine for Access alone. Using OLE on this machine would be slow going indeed.

14

Q **I created a combo box and set the Column Widths property to 1 in; 1 in; 2 in; yet the combo box just stays small showing part of only one column. Why?**

A A combo box will stay the size it is during Design View unless you set the List Width property to the total of what's in your Column Widths property. The List Width property can be as wide as you want, but cannot be smaller than the combo box is during Design View.

Q **What's the difference between Row Source and Control Source in a combo box?**

A Row Source is the source for the data in the list portion of a combo or list box. Control Source is where the data entered in this form will end up in the bound table or query.

Q **Why create an unbound form?**

A You'll see the use for this later on. Unbound forms work very well for such things as button menu forms.

Workshop

Here's where you can test and apply what you have learned today.

Quiz

Possible answers to these questions are provided in Appendix A.

1. What property binds an option group to a table field?

2. You have a form MyForm bound to the table MyTable. You want to enter a combo box, MyCombo, on this form that will look up values in a table called MyLookup. Do you enter MyLookup as the control source or row source for MyCombo?

3. Refer to Figure 13.15. What do you suppose the List Rows property does?

4. What property must be set to Yes to limit the possible entries to those already entered as a row source for the combo box?

5. A combo box is a combination of what two other control types?

Put Access into Action

1. Launch Access and open the College database if necessary.

2. Open the Student Personal Data in Design View.

3. Add a new option button to the option group. Label this button N/Degree. You might have to adjust the position of the existing buttons, resize the group, or both.

4. Set the Option Value property for this new control to 4.

5. Format the option group to look like the rest of the form. Change the label for the option group to read Student Status. Switch to Form View. Your screen should resemble Figure 14.20.

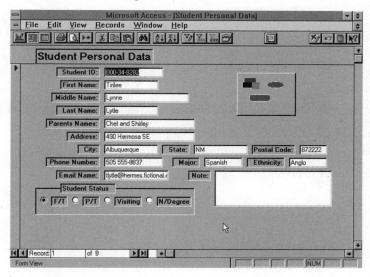

Figure 14.20. *Formatted and edited option group.*

 Tip: You can change the label for a control by either directly editing the label or altering its Caption property from within the Properties list box.

6. Close the form, saving changes. Edit the StudentStatus Lookup table to add a number 4 for StudentStatus Number and Non-Degree for Student Status. Your screen should resemble Figure 14.21.

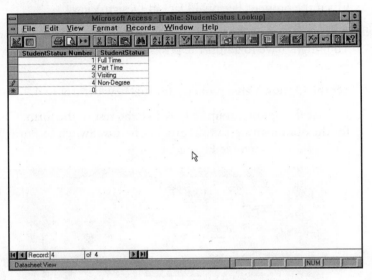

Figure 14.21. *Adding a new value in a lookup table.*

7. Close the table.

Day

8

15

Dates and Artificial Fields

This morning's material covers the following topics:

☐ Artificial fields in queries

☐ How Access handles date information

☐ Date formats

☐ Date arithmetic

In many ways, queries form the heart of Access or any other relational database system. Access can take information from one or more query fields, operate on that information, and then create a new field for the output of the operation.

Dates are an important part of most databases. Think of all you could do with an information system, even if you could only query it by date. Here are a few examples of questions you could find answers to:

How many and which customers of yours have ordered in the past month?

How many customers of yours haven't bought anything in the past year?

What patients haven't been in for their yearly checkup?

How old are your accounts receivable?

How many of your employees have been here long enough to be vested?

What was your sales volume for each month in 1994?

What products sold the greatest quantity in each month of 1994?

You can imagine that extracting such information from a paper-based filing system would be a great chore. With Access, however, each of those questions could be answered in a few minutes by using queries.

Before moving on to dates in queries, this chapter shows you how Access records dates in databases, how it displays dates, and what underlying magic it has to let it perform date-based queries.

One item still missing from the Student Personal table is a place for date of birth. Exercise 15.1 adds a Date field to the Student Personal table and examines how Access can present date information.

Exercise 15.1. Adding a Date field to a table.

1. Launch Access and open the College database if necessary. Click on the Student Personal table to give it the highlight and click on the Design button to open this table in Design View. Locate the StudentStatus field; click just to the left of it to highlight the entire StudentStatus row. Press the Ins or Insert key on your keyboard. Your screen should resemble Figure 15.1.

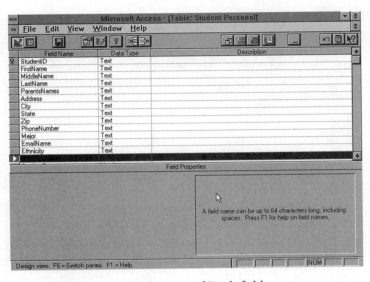

Figure 15.1. *Making room for the Date of Birth field.*

2. Click in the Field Name column. Enter Date of Birth as a label for this field. Tab to the Data Type column and enter a d. Date's the only data type beginning with a d, so Access auto fills in the rest of the column's entry. Your screen should resemble Figure 15.2.

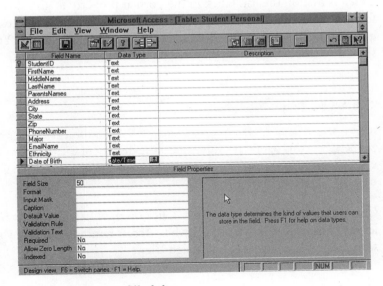

Figure 15.2. *Access's auto fill ability.*

3. Tab away from this field. Access changes the Field Properties section to one appropriate for Date data types. Your screen should resemble Figure 15.3.

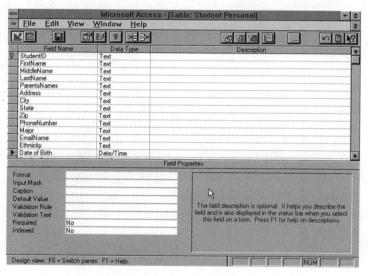

Figure 15.3. *Field properties for the Date data type.*

4. Most of these properties are old friends. The one new property is Format, which is first on the list. Click in the Format property to give this field the focus. Press F4 to drop down the list box for this combo box. Pressing F4 in a combo box has the same effect as clicking on the down arrow. Your screen should resemble Figure 15.4.

The Access Way

Access stores data in Date/Time data type fields uniformly. The Format property for this data type only affects the display of the data, not its value.

5. Choose Long Date for the Format. Click on the Datasheet View button to leave Design View. Click on OK when Access reminds you that you must save your table before leaving Design View.

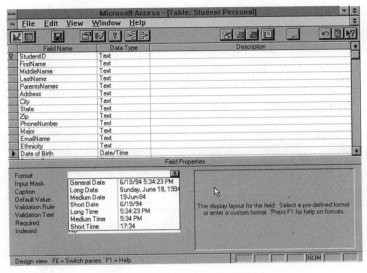

Figure 15.4. *The types of formats for the Date/Time data type.*

Figure 15.5 shows the newly designed table with the Date of Birth field temporarily moved next to the LastName field.

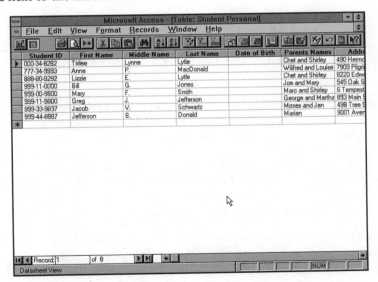

Figure 15.5. *The new field moved next to the LastName field.*

Remember, the way to move a column in Datasheet View is to first click on its header, the place in the column showing its field name. This gives the column a highlight. Release the mouse button, and click on the header again. Access responds by showing a rectangle at the base of the cursor arrow. This signifies you're in move mode. You can now drag the column to any new position you want.

Enter a Date of Birth 12/1/74 for Lytle, as shown in Figure 15.6.

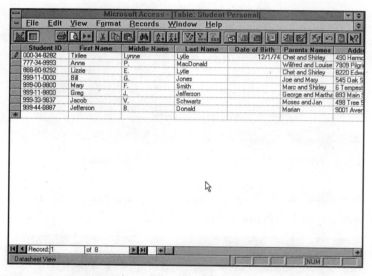

Figure 15.6. *Entering a date in Access.*

Tab out of this field. As soon as you do, Access changes this field to the Long Date format as shown in Figure 15.7. Note that the Date of Birth column in this figure has been slightly widened to show all the detail of this field.

Even though you didn't enter the day of week information, Access was able to return the right day of the week for Lytle's birth. Move down to the next record in the Date of Birth column, the one for MacDonald. Enter 2/30/75 for Anne's birthday. Press Tab. Your screen should resemble Figure 15.8.

Access is smart enough to know that there is no February 30 in 1975, or any other year for that matter. It won't accept dates that make no sense in date fields. You are free to enter wrong dates that are valid, but not obviously invalid entries such as 2/30/75. Click on OK to clear the message box. Edit MacDonald's date of birth to 2/3/75. Access will now accept your entry, as shown in Figure 15.9.

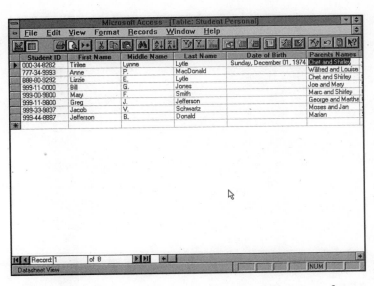

Figure 15.7. *Access automatically changes the date to Long Date format.*

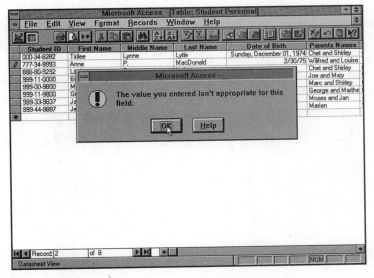

Figure 15.8. *Access refuses to accept incorrect date information.*

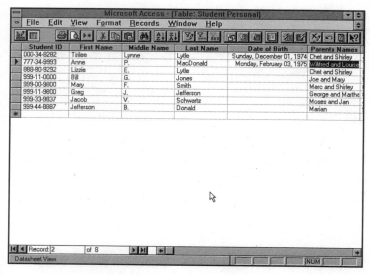

Figure 15.9. *Corrected Date field for date of birth.*

Within certain limits, Access doesn't care how you enter dates. The next student, Lizzie Lytle, was born July 8, 1974. You can enter that date as you've done before, 7/8/74, or in its full format, July 8, 1974. This date is a Monday, but Access won't accept day of week data. It insists on supplying that itself. Finish entering the dates for the students in this table according to Figure 15.10.

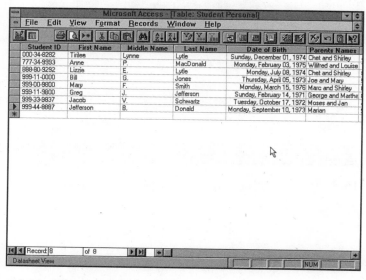

Figure 15.10. *The rest of the birth dates.*

If you want, experiment entering dates in different formats. Access gladly accepts 7 Jul 74, July 7, 1974, and Jul 7, 74, to give you an idea.

Return to Design View. Click in the Date of Birth field to show the field properties for this field. Change the Format property from Long Date to Medium Date. Return to Datasheet View. Click on OK when Access asks you if you want to save your changes. Your screen should resemble Figure 15.11.

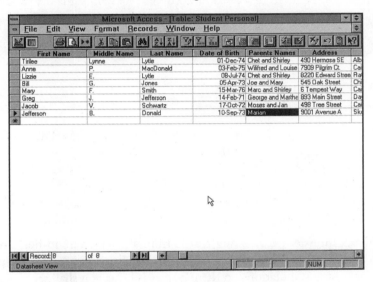

Figure 15.11. *The effect of changing the Date Format property.*

The Access Way

Changing the format of a date doesn't change the value of the date. If you changed the Format property for the Date of Birth field to a time format, Access would have changed all Date of Birth displays to 12:00 A.M., but would still have kept the right data for each record stored in the field Date of Birth.

Close this table. Tell Access you don't want to save layout changes if you rearranged your columns like the book did after Exercise 15.1.

> **The Access Way**
>
> Even though you told Access to discard changes to the table's layout, Access kept the edits you did to this table. That is, discarding layout changes did not cause you to lose the data you entered for date of birth for the students.
>
> Access writes data to disk as soon as you leave a field if the data's valid and in a valid record. Discarding layout changes has nothing to do with the data entered in the table.

Dates in Queries

Internally, Access stores dates as a double precision number. The whole part of the number, the part to the left of the decimal place, is for the date. The fractional part of the number is the time. Access dates start with the number 1 for December 31, 1899, and go up to the year 9999. Dates prior to December 31, 1899, are negative. Thus, the number 2.0000 represents January 1, 1900, in Access's method; January 11, 1900, is day 12.0000; and so forth. Each date is really a number.

In human expression, subtracting 1/2/31 from 4/5/65 is a mind-boggling job. Since these dates are reduced to simple numbers internally within Access, the program can do all sorts of manipulations on them quite easily, as you shall see.

Exercise 15.2 simply shows how you can use dates as criteria for queries.

Exercise 15.2. Date criteria.

1. From the Database View, click on the Query tab. Click on New. Click on the New Query button to bypass the wizard. Click on the Student Personal table from the Add Table list box. Click on Add to add this table to the new query. Your screen should resemble Figure 15.12.

2. Click on Close to close the Add Table list box. If you want to, adjust your screen to resemble the layout in Figure 15.13.

3. Click and drag the FirstName, MiddleName, LastName, and Date of Birth fields from the Field list box to columns 1–4 in the query design grid. Your screen should resemble Figure 15.13.

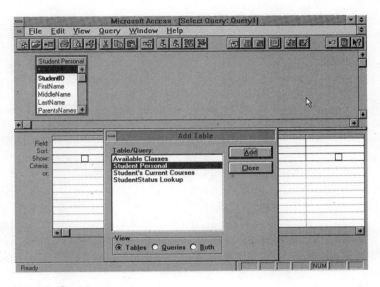

Figure 15.12. *Starting a new query.*

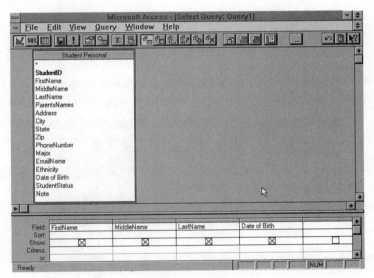

Figure 15.13. *The new query without criteria.*

4. Click on the Run button in the toolbar. Your screen should resemble Figure 15.14.

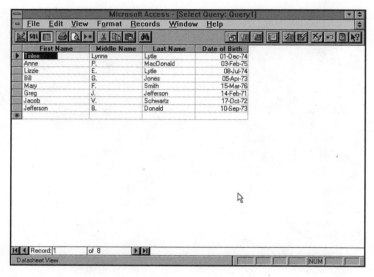

Figure 15.14. *The new query running.*

5. No surprises here. This query just extracts all the records for the selected
   fields. Return to Design View. Enter <1/1/74 in the criteria row for the Date
   of Birth column. Press Tab to move away from this column. Your screen
   should resemble Figure 15.15. Note that Access understands you mean
   1/1/74 to be a date and surrounds your criteria with the needed # marks.

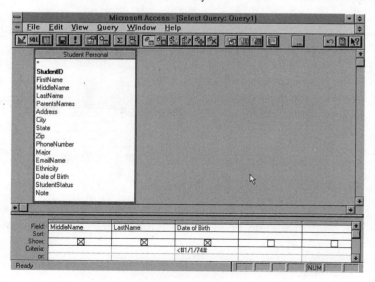

Figure 15.15. *Creating a date criteria.*

6. Again run the query. Access now only returns those records with birthdays earlier than January 1, 1974.

Access can use dates for query criteria the same as it uses text values or numbers. Operators like = (equals), < (less than), > (greater than) work alike with dates, times, and numbers. You can even combine these operators to read <= (less than or equal to), >= (greater than or equal to), and <> (not equal to: literally less than and greater than).

DO	DON'T

DO feel free to use expressions to extract your information in creative ways.

DON'T rely on your query criteria returning what you expect they will. Be sure to try your queries with known data that will yield results in which you can easily spot errors. Don't rely on complex queries until you're absolutely sure they're working correctly.

Date Arithmetic and Artificial Fields

So far, this morning's material has been rather tame and obvious. Things are about to pick up speed. Exercise 15.3 shows how to use date math. It dynamically calculates the age of each student in years. Dynamic calculation means the computer fetches the current date and does the age calculation based on that date and the fixed value of the student's birthday.

Exercise 15.3. Date math and artificial fields.

1. Return to Design View for the query you did in Exercise 15.2. Drag your cursor over the criteria for the Date of Birth field to highlight the entire criteria expression. Press the Del or Delete key on your keyboard to delete this criteria expression.

2. Click on the Field row for the column just to the right of the Date of Birth column. Press Shift+F2 to enter Zoom mode. Enter

```
Age in Years: DateDiff("yyyy",[Date of Birth],Date())
```

in the Zoom box. Your screen should resemble Figure 15.16.

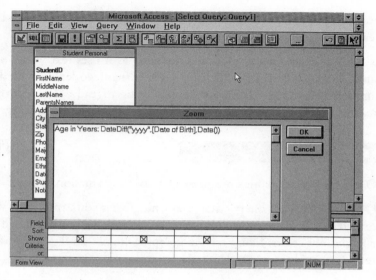

Figure 15.16. *Entering an expression in the Zoom box.*

3. Click on OK to leave Zoom mode. Click on the Run button in the toolbar. Your screen should resemble Figure 15.17.

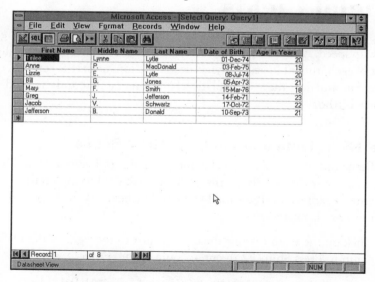

Figure 15.17. *An artificial field with a date calculation.*

The entire operation of this query depends upon the expression

```
Age in Years: DateDiff("yyyy",[Date of Birth],Date())
```

The first part of this expression is the label for this artificial field. Access knows that from the colon at its right side. Anything to the left of the colon in an artificial field is interpreted by Access as a label for the column.

The second part of this expression is its heart: `Datediff`. `Datediff()` is another built-in function that calculates the difference between two dates. It takes parameters between its parentheses `()`. The parameters for `Datediff` read as follows:

```
interval, date1, date2[,firstweekday][,firstweek]
```

The last two parameters in the square brackets (`[]`) are optional. The interval is how you want the date differences to be expressed. You can enter "ww" for weeks, "d" for days, "m" for month. This example used "yyyy" for year interval. Figure 15.18 is the same query edited to return students' ages in months. Figure 15.19 shows the expression that returned the screen in 15.18.

The second element is the first, or earlier, date to figure in the date math expression. In this case you told Access to fetch the data entered into the Date of Birth field to use as the `date1` parameter. You had to enter the field Date of Birth in square brackets because it's a field name with spaces. It's always a good idea to enclose field names in square brackets even if they don't contain spaces. Not only do the brackets act as insurance in case your field names do contain spaces, but they show you at a glance that the entry Date of Birth is a field name and not a function.

The last element of the parameter is the function `date()`. This merely tells Access to use the current system date as `date2`. The two optional functions `[,firstweekday]` and `[,firstweek]` aren't used in this query. You can set the optional parameters `[,firstweekday]` and `[,firstweek]` to count the specific days or weeks in the interval.

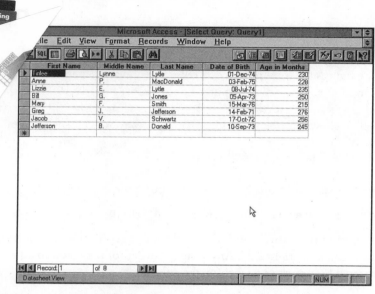

Figure 15.18. *The* `datediff()` *function returning month intervals.*

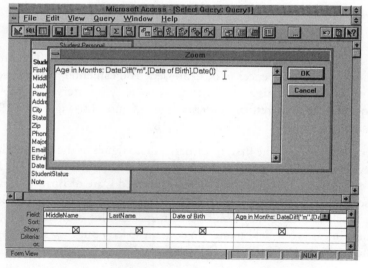

Figure 15.19. *The expression edit box that returns month intervals.*

That's about enough for this morning. Close this query and save it using the name
`Chapter 15`.

Morning Summary

This morning you learned how to include dates in tables, how to format those dates, and how Access stores date information internally. Queries can use dates for criteria, as you saw in Exercise 15.2. Finally, you saw how to create a complex expression to calculate the difference between today's date and the students' dates of birth and return the values in years. Further, you learned how to place the results of this calculation in an artificial field called Age in Years.

16

Parameter Queries

This afternoon you'll learn how to

☐ Construct a parameter query

☐ Use wildcard searches in parameters

☐ Construct a range parameter query

☐ Create a Make Table action query

Parameter Queries

So far all the queries you've done set the query criteria at the Design View. This isn't always desirable for two reasons. First, you might not know what criteria you will need when you run the query or you might want to quickly change criteria for the same query. The second reason for not setting criteria at the Design View is security. You might want a user to be able to establish a query criterion without getting to the Design View for the query.

The way to enter criteria at the time a query is run rather than when it's designed is to convert your query to a parameter query. Access is rather loose when using the words criteria and parameter. If it makes it easier for you to grasp, think of query parameters as criteria entered outside of the Design View.

The first full exercise this afternoon, 16.2, shows the construction of a simple parameter query. Before trying it, go over Exercise 16.1 to see how the parameter works at the familiar Design View. This exercise shows the parallels between criteria and parameters in queries.

Exercise 16.1. A different criteria demonstration.

1. Launch Access and open the College database if necessary. From the Database View, click on the Query tab. Highlight the Chapter 15, "Dates and Artificial Fields," query by clicking on it. Click on Design to open this query in Design View.

2. Locate the Age in Years artificial field. Enter: >=21 on the first criteria row for this field. Your screen should resemble Figure 16.1.

3. Click on the Run button in the toolbar. Access will run the query and return a screen similar to Figure 16.2.

4. Return to Design View and delete the criteria from this query.

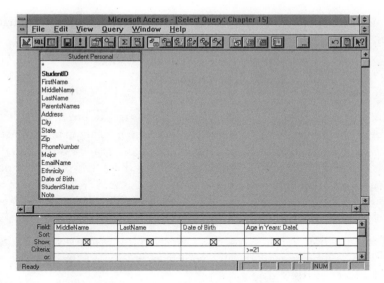

Figure 16.1. *Entering a criterion for an artificial field.*

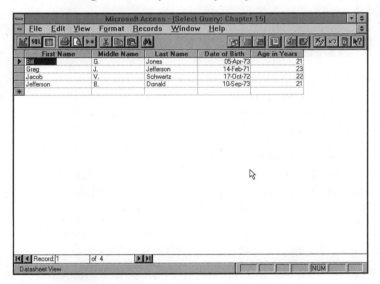

Figure 16.2. *The criteria query running.*

That didn't pack much of a surprise. Access had no problems figuring out that you wanted to select people older than or equal to 21 years old. The query might have taken a little longer to run than other queries because Access had a two-step problem; first it had to do the Datediff() calculation, then it had to apply your criteria to filter out

the unwanted records. The more you ask an Access query to do, the longer it'll take to run.

> **The Access Way**
>
> The query in Exercise 16.1 might seem almost trivial, but it's one that's widely used in databases. Imagine you're creating an aging of your accounts receivable and you want to find out which accounts are less than 30 days old, which are between 31 and 60 days old, and finally which are more than 60 days old. One way to do this is to use the Datediff() function in three columns, then enter these criteria for the three columns: <=30; Between 31 and 60; and >60.
>
> The beauty of using the Datediff() function is that any time you run this query, you'll be up-to-date aging your receivables since the query's partially based on the current date.

The Parameter Query

Exercise 16.2 shows how to construct a simple parameter query. This query will extract information similar to that extracted in Exercise 16.1, but you'll be able to alter your query criteria without entering Design View.

Exercise 16.2. The parameter query.

1. If you're still in Datasheet View from Exercise 16.1, return to Design View. Drag your cursor over the criteria in the Age in Years column and press the Del or Delete key on your keyboard to delete these criteria.

2. Enter [Enter Last Name:] on the Criteria row for the LastName column. Your screen should resemble Figure 16.3.

3. Click on the Run button to run this query. Access responds with the screen shown in Figure 16.4.

4. Enter Lytle in the dialog box and click on OK. Your screen should resemble Figure 16.5.

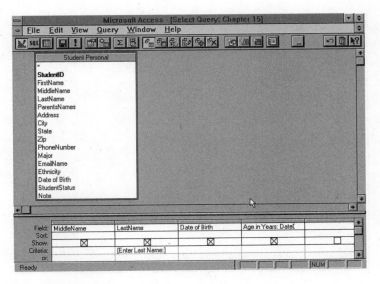

Figure 16.3. *Starting the parameter query.*

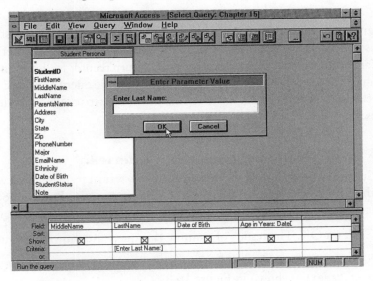

Figure 16.4. *The parameter dialog box.*

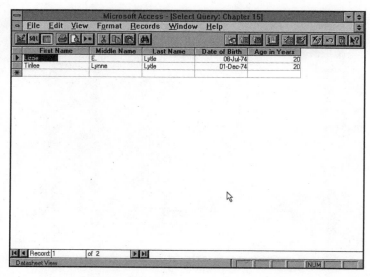

Figure 16.5. *Running with a parameter.*

You can't enter wildcards in parameter dialog boxes with the query constructed as in Exercise 16.2. The expression Like "J*" entered as a straight criterion for the LastName column will, when the query's run, return records for Jones and Jefferson. Entering J* or Like "J*" in the query dialog box for the query done in Exercise 16.2 will yield no records returned. Exercise 16.3 shows how to use wildcards in parameter queries.

Exercise 16.3. Wildcard parameter queries.

1. Starting where you left off in Exercise 16.2, return to Design View. Click on the Run button in the toolbar to run this query again. Enter J* for a parameter in the parameter dialog box. Your screen should resemble Figure 16.6.

   Click on OK. The results of running this query are shown in Figure 16.7.

2. Return to Design View. Edit the parameter criterion to read Like [Enter Last Name:] as shown in Figure 16.8.

3. Run the query again, this time again entering J* for the parameter, as shown in Figure 16.9. Click on OK.

   This time things work like you might have anticipated they'd work earlier. Your screen should resemble Figure 16.10.

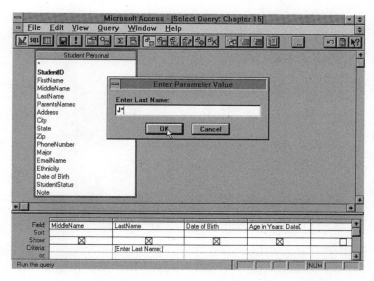

Figure 16.6. *Entering a wildcard in a conventional parameter dialog box.*

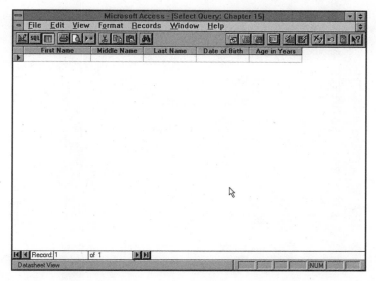

Figure 16.7. *The wildcard parameter surprisingly results in no matched records.*

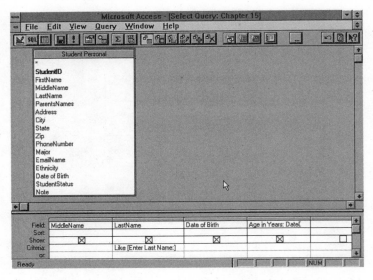

Figure 16.8. *Modifying the parameter criteria to accept wildcards.*

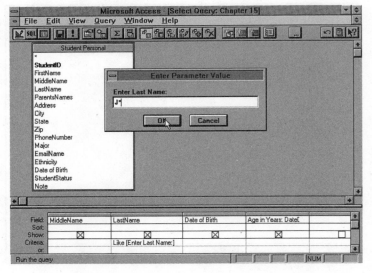

Figure 16.9. *Trying a wildcard parameter in the new query.*

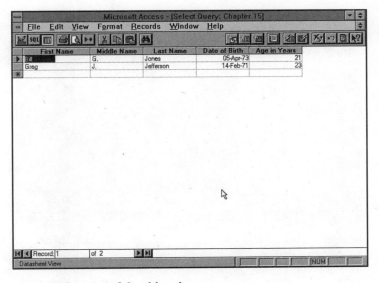

Figure 16.10. *The successful wildcard parameter query.*

Range Parameter Queries

Sometimes you'll want your query to extract information from a table based on a range of information. Look at Figure 16.11. The criterion for the Date of Birth field reads `Between #1/1/73# AND #12/31/73#`.

This query looks as if it'll return all records with student birthdays in 1973. When run, it does just that, as shown in Figure 16.12.

This is a rather stilted query. Sure it's useful, but in many cases you'll want to enter the beginning and ending dates at the time you run the query to ask Access to fetch, for example, all your sales for a particular span of time. Access has, built in, the capacity to do just this. Exercise 16.4 shows you how to construct a parameter query that returns a range of values.

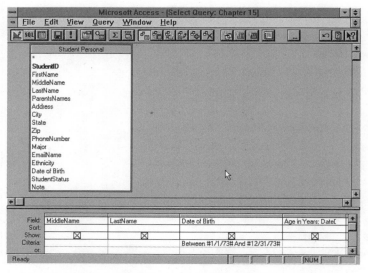

Figure 16.11. *A criteria expression to return all records from 1973.*

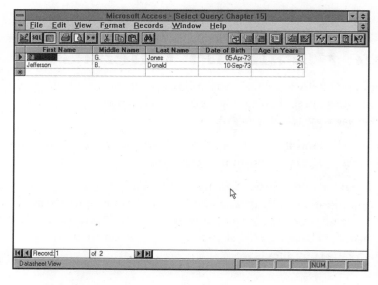

Figure 16.12. *The results of the 1973 query.*

Exercise 16.4. The range parameter query.

1. Return to Design View for the query you constructed in Exercise 16.3. Delete any criteria you might have entered either in the exercise or through your own experimentation. Enter the following on the criteria row for the Date of Birth column:

```
Between [Enter Earliest Date:] AND [Enter Latest Date:]
```

Your screen should resemble Figure 16.13.

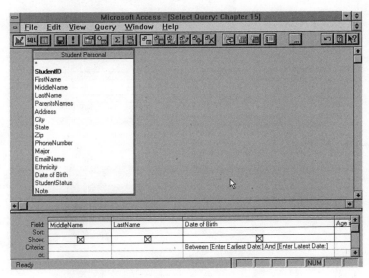

Figure 16.13. *The range parameter query criterion.*

2. You've just told Access that you want two parameter prompts when this query's run. First, Access prompts you with a dialog box saying Enter Earliest Date:. When you enter a value and click on OK, Access will bring up a second dialog box prompting you with Enter Latest Date:.

3. Click on the Run button on the toolbar. Access responds with a screen like the one in Figure 16.14. Note that the field in Figure 16.14 has been expanded to show the entire field's contents.

4. Enter 1/1/73 and click on OK. Access responds with the dialog box shown in Figure 16.15.

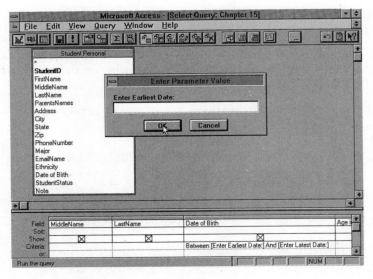

Figure 16.14. *The first range dialog box.*

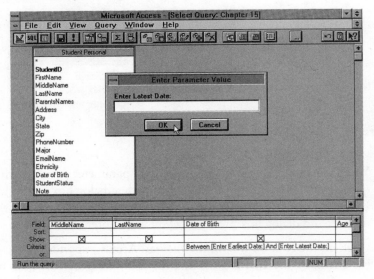

Figure 16.15. *The second range dialog box.*

5. Enter 12/31/73 and click on OK. Access runs the query with these parameters and gives you the screen shown in Figure 16.16.

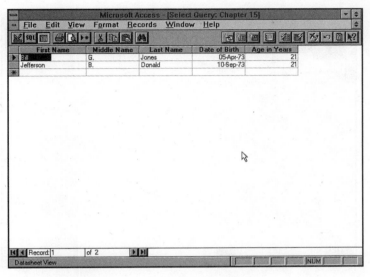

Figure 16.16. *The range parameter query running.*

Although the results of this run are identical to those of the query shown running in Figure 16.11, the difference is that you can now choose your range of values for the parameters at the query's runtime rather than in its Design View. Try running this query again, but enter 1/3/72 and 12/31/73 as criteria. This time you'll also pick up the record for Jacob Schwartz, who was born in October 1972, as shown in Figure 16.17.

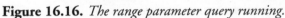

DO   DON'T

DO use parameter queries when you don't want to alter the design of a query to change its criteria.

DON'T use a parameter query to construct queries with unchanging criteria such as "older than 30 days." This works technically, but it slows down the flow of work, as you'll have to enter the same criteria over and over again.

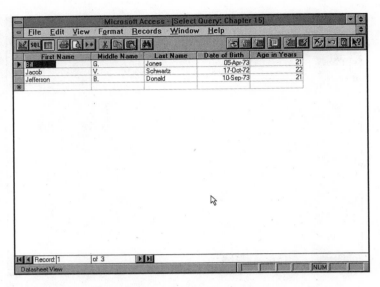

Figure 16.17. *Expanding the parameter query's range.*

Action Queries

One of Access's most powerful features is the ability to take the results of a query and do something with them. Exercise 16.5 shows how you can take the output of a query and have Access automatically create and enter data into a new table. In this exercise, you convert a select query to a simple action query that creates a new table containing the query's output.

Exercise 16.5. The Make Table action query.

1. The default type of query Access creates is called a select query, because it selects records and fields from a table or another query. To make an action query, first construct a select query in the normal way. While this is optional, it's highly recommended that you run the query in Select mode to make sure it's running as you think it should.

2. Pull down the Query menu and choose the type of action query you'd like to construct.

3. Return to Design mode from running the query as in either Figure 16.16 or Figure 16.17. Click on the Query menu. Locate the entry Make Table and

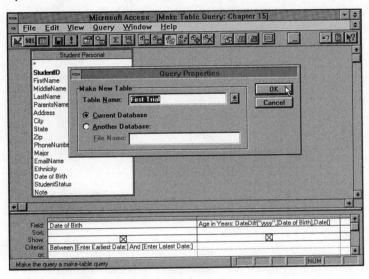

click on it. Access responds with a dialog box. Enter First Trial as a name for your new table. Your screen should resemble Figure 16.18.

Figure 16.18. *Creating the Make Table query.*

4. Make sure the Current Database option button is selected. Click on OK. That's all there is to it. After confirmation from you, Access runs the query and places the contents of it into a new table, First Trial.

Run the query by clicking on the Run button in the toolbar. Access prompts you for two dates. Enter 8/1/72 as the earliest date and 12/31/73 as the latest date, as in Figures 16.19 and 16.20.

Access will crank around a while and respond with a confirmation message box, as shown in Figure 16.21.

Click on OK to run this query. Nothing apparently occurs. Close this query, saving changes. Back at the Database View note that this query now has a new icon next to its name in the Database list box, as shown in Figure 16.22. This visually tells you that this query is an action query that will make a new table.

Did it work? Click on the Table tab. Your screen should resemble Figure 16.23.

Click on the Open button for the First Trial table. Your screen should resemble Figure 16.24.

16

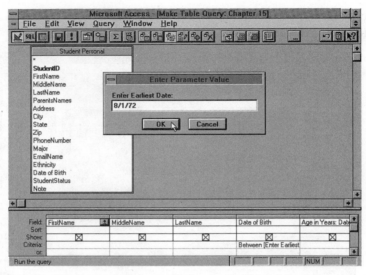

Figure 16.19. *The low end of the range for the Make Table parameter query.*

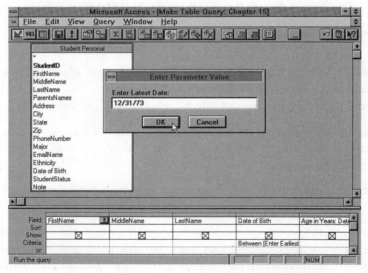

Figure 16.20. *The high end of the range for the Make Table parameter query.*

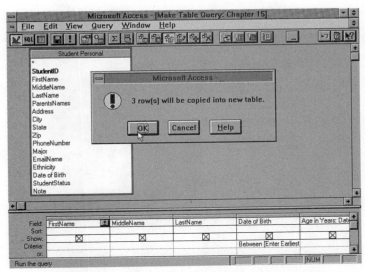

Figure 16.21. *The confirmation message box for the Make Table query.*

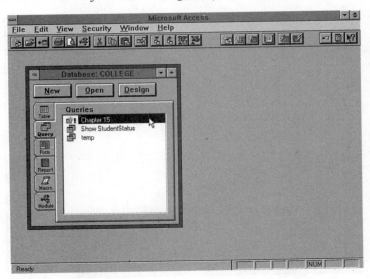

Figure 16.22. *The Database View showing different kinds of queries.*

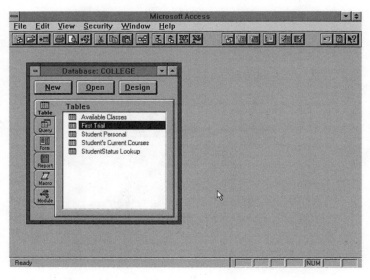

Figure 16.23. *The new table at the Database View.*

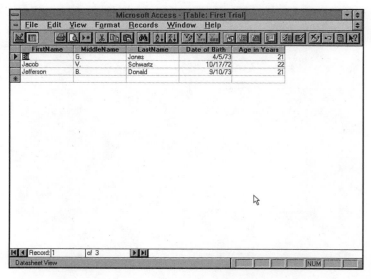

Figure 16.24. *The newly made table showing the records automatically entered.*

DO	DON'T

DO make as many action queries as your application requires. This is a very useful Access capability.

DON'T use these queries as action queries until you've reviewed their output as safe select queries.

It's been a long afternoon, but one covering a lot of new and important territory.

Summary

Today's lesson covers how Access handles dates. Access stores dates serially as double precision numbers. The whole part of the number is the date, while the fractional part is the time. Access can display date information in a variety of formats, but formats are just for show. The underlying value of a Date field remains constant no matter what the format.

Access can create artificial fields based on an expression, using one or more fields in a query. Two special kinds of queries Access can perform are the straight parameter query and the range parameter query. A parameter query will prompt you for a value for a field when run. You can make this value include a wildcard by using the Like operator on the criteria line just to the left of the parameter prompt.

Access can prompt for a range of values to extract data. This is called the range parameter query. You use the Between...AND operators to construct such a query.

Access can use the output of a query to perform some action. To have Access create a table using a query's output, change the query type from Select to Make Table and tell Access what the new query's name is to be.

Q&A

Q Can I enter two parameters on the criteria row to create an AND query?

A Yes. Access will first prompt you for the parameter on the left, but the query will function just like a standard AND query.

Q What about using parameters to create an OR query?

A It works the same as the AND query. Just enter the parameters on two different rows. Access will prompt for the parameter on the topmost row first. Figure 16.25 shows the Chapter 15 query modified to be an OR parameter query. Figure 16.26 is the same query run with Lytle as the Last Name and F. as the Middle criterion.

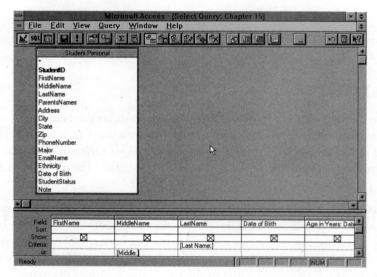

Figure 16.25. *Constructing the* OR *parameter query.*

Q Can I enter a parameter criterion for an artificial field constructed from an expression?

A No, because Access first applies the parameter, then performs the expression. You can effectively do this by creating a Make Table query and then running a parameter query based on that table.

Q Can I use the DateDiff() function to perform time math?

A Yes, it does so whether you ask it to or not. The trick to seeing time intervals between dates is to use *h*, *n*, or *s* for hours, minutes, or seconds. (The *n* for minutes isn't an error. The *m* is reserved for months.)

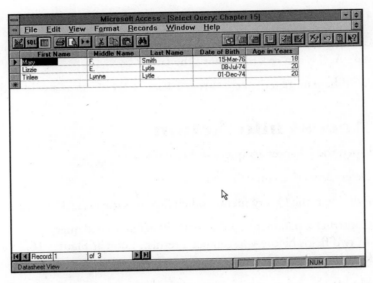

Figure 16.26. *Running the* OR *parameter query.*

Q If I know a date is, say, a Sunday, should I enter the date like this: Sunday, [the date] where [the date] is the date that's a Sunday?

A No. Format the field as Long Date to show days of the week. Access won't permit you to make entries looking identical to its Long Date format. It's funny that way.

Workshop

Here's where you can test and apply the lessons you learned today.

Quiz

Possible answers to these questions are provided in Appendix A.

1. What does >#1/31/95# mean as a criterion?

2. When you change a Date field's Format property, how does that affect the way Access stores the date internally?

3. How can you show days of the week as part of a Date field?

4. Search the Help system for the following information: What's the earliest date Access can record? What's the latest?

5. Will the parameter `Like [Enter a Name:]` accept `U*` as a wildcard criterion?

Put Access into Action

1. Open the Chapter 15 query in Design View.

2. Delete any criteria for this query.

3. Pull down the Query menu and change this query back to a select one.

4. Construct a parameter query that will act as an `AND` query requiring a match on two fields before you can get a return. Look at Figures 16.25 and 16.26 for a hint if you get stuck.

5. Modify the query so both parts of the `AND` query accept wildcards.

6. Modify the query to keep the same parameters, but make it an `OR` query.

7. Close the query, discarding changes.

Day

9

17

Append and Delete Action Queries

This morning you'll learn

☐ What append action queries are

☐ What delete action queries are

☐ How to construct and run these two action queries

☐ Why to compact databases

The Use of Delete and Append Queries

Deleting a single record from a table is quite easy. Just open the table in Datasheet View, locate the record you want to eliminate, and click to the left of the row containing the record to be deleted. This will highlight the row. Press the Del or Delete key on your keyboard to eliminate the record.

What do you do if you want to eliminate many records, such as all those records older than a particular date? You could go through your table record by record to locate, then delete, these records. You could also create a query, extract on the target date range, then delete the records by highlighting them and pressing the Del key.

The second method might sound ingenious, but it's more cumbersome than just doing a delete query. Take a look at Figure 17.1.

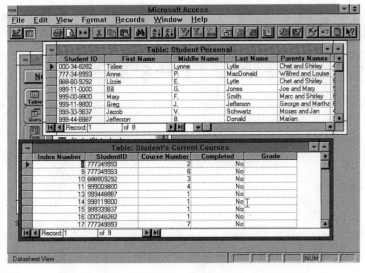

Figure 17.1. *Two tables showing existing records in each.*

Note that the Student's Current Courses table has several entries for Anne MacDonald who's StudentID is 777-34-9993. Student's Current Courses also has no entries for Bill Jones, StudentID 999-11-0000. Exercise 17.1, which demonstrates the delete action query, deletes all of MacDonald's records and Exercise 17.2 adds them back along with some for Jones.

Exercise 17.1. The delete query.

1. Launch Access and open the College database if necessary. Click on the Query tab. Click on the New button to start a new query. Bypass the wizard by clicking on the New Query button. Add the Student's Current Courses table to the query. Close the Add Table list box. Your screen should resemble Figure 17.2.

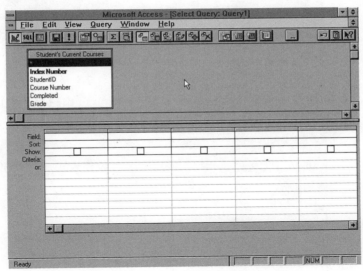

Figure 17.2. *Adding a table to a new query.*

2. Drag the StudentID field from the Field list box to the first column of the query design grid. Add the parameter [Enter StudentID:] to the first criteria row for this query. Your screen should resemble Figure 17.3.

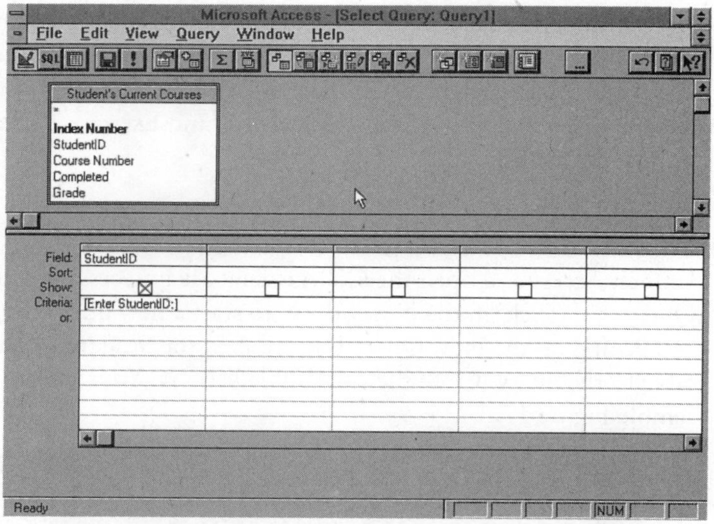

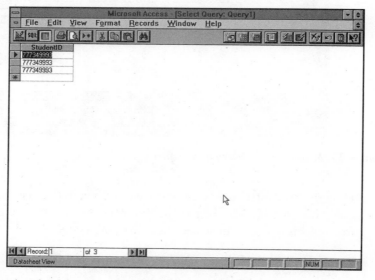

Figure 17.3. *Entering a criteria parameter.*

3. Run the query by clicking on the Run button in the toolbar. Enter
   777349993 as a query parameter. Your screen should resemble Figure 17.4.

Figure 17.4. *The delete query running as a select query.*

The point of running this query first as a select query is to make sure it's running right, extracting all the records you want and none that you don't want. This query is working right, so it's time to alter it to a delete action query.

4. Return to Design View. Click on the Query menu and click on Delete. Your title bar changes to reflect the new type of query this is. Your screen should resemble Figure 17.5.

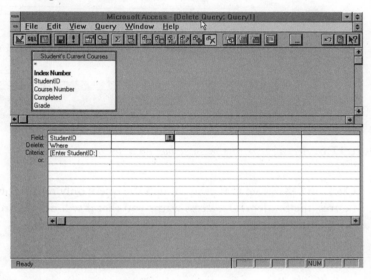

Figure 17.5. *The title bar indicates the type of query.*

Note also that the Delete query button on the toolbar is now selected. You could have altered this query to a delete one by clicking on this button also. There's no qualitative difference between choosing an action query from the menu or toolbar.

5. Click on the Run button in the toolbar. Access again prompts you for a parameter, just as it did when this query was a select one. Enter 777349993 to choose MacDonald's StudentID. Click on OK. Your screen should resemble Figure 17.6.

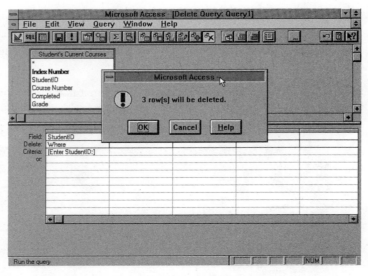

Figure 17.6. *Access's warning message box on a delete action query.*

Click on OK. Note that even though the query only returns one column of figures, the StudentID, Access warns you that it will delete three rows or three entire records.

The Access Way

Action queries work on entire rows or records even if the same query running as a select query returns only part of a row or record.

6. Click on OK. Change the query back to a select one by clicking on the Select query button in the toolbar as shown in Figure 17.7.

7. Run the query. Enter 777349993 again as a StudentID parameter. This time Access returns no records, as shown in Figure 17.8, indicating that there are no longer any records for MacDonald in the Student's Current Courses table.

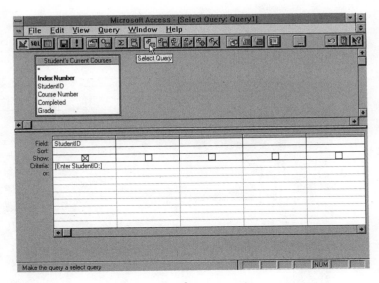

Figure 17.7. *Changing to a select query from an action query.*

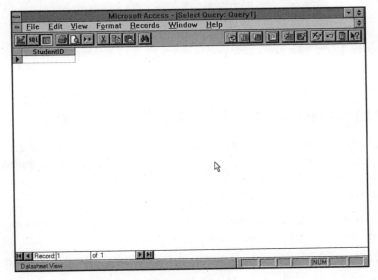

Figure 17.8. *The results of the delete query.*

8. Return to Design View and change this query back to a delete action query by making either the menu or toolbar selections. Close this query, saving it

as Deleter. Figure 17.9 shows the Database View with the new query Deleter as part of the query group. Note the special icon Access assigned to this query, which visually clues you that this is a delete type query.

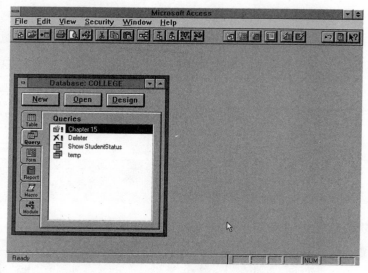

Figure 17.9. *The new delete action query in the Database View.*

Compacting the Database

In many operations, Access leaves "holes" in its databases. For example, when you add a table or query to Access, Access will enlarge the .mdb file to accommodate this new object. However, if you later delete these objects, Access won't dynamically shrink the .mdb file down to its initial size.

After running the action query from Exercise 17.1, Access continues to hold open room for the deleted records, even though they aren't included in the table.

Compacting a database gets rid of these empty spaces or holes Access leaves in its data structure. Exercise 17.2 shows how to compact a database and the results of doing so.

Exercise 17.2. Compacting a database.

1. Return to Database View. Close the College database. Pull down the File menu and choose Compact Database. Access returns with a standard or common dialog box as shown in Figure 17.10.

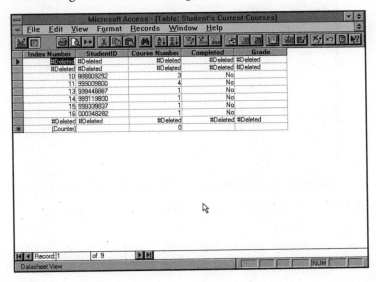

Figure 17.10. *The common dialog box.*

2. Click on the college.mdb file or enter that in the text part of the dialog box. Click on OK. Access will prompt you for a new name for the database to compact into. Enter college1.mdb for a name. Click on OK.

    Access will grind around a while and should finish with no errors. You've extracted all the valid records from college.mdb and dumped them into the idealized database structure college1.mdb.

3. Using DOS or File Manager or whatever tool you prefer, delete the old college.mdb file and rename college1.mdb to college.mdb.

Take a look at Figure 17.11. This is a File Manager-type look at the two databases: college.mdb and college1.mdb. Note that the compacting routine squeezed the database College down from approximately 492,000 bytes to approximately 328,000 bytes—a substantial improvement.

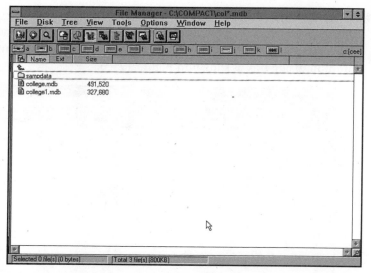

Figure 17.11. *The College database before and after compacting.*

Now look at Figure 17.12. This is the Student's Current Courses table after compacting. The empty spaces have been squeezed out with the rest of the useless space-eaters from the old operations.

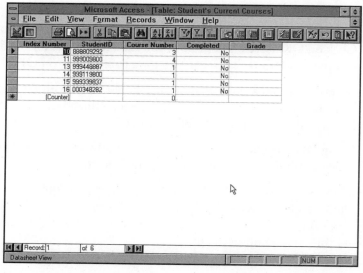

Figure 17.12. *Table after compacting.*

Note: The actual before-and-after sizes of your College database will vary from the example shown here. How much your databases grow and shrink depends upon the actions you take in them. The example shown in Figure 17.11 is typical, but it can't be identical to similar situations.

The Append Action Query

The append action query extracts data from one table or query and appends, or attaches, it to another table. The target table therefore grows to include all the records it had initially plus those records extracted by the query. Exercise 17.3 takes the records from the Append Me table included in the sample data and appends those records to the Student's Current Courses table.

Before doing this query, you need to set the stage. Figure 17.13 shows the Temp query rerun to list the students now signed up for some classes. If you haven't saved this query, look at Figure 17.14, which shows a query in Design View that will help you to follow along with this exercise. If you haven't saved Temp, create the query shown in Figure 17.14.

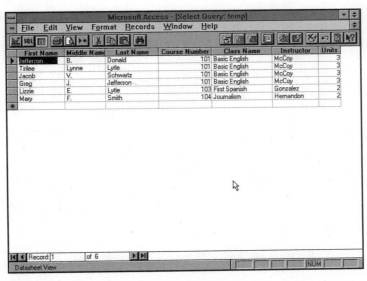

Figure 17.13. *The Temp query run with current data.*

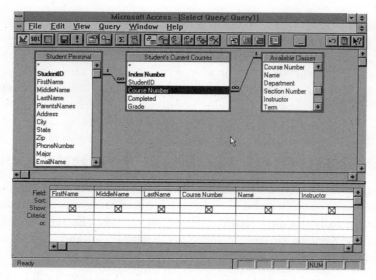

Figure 17.14. *A query to illustrate the effect of an append query.*

Refer to the Temp query shown in Figure 17.13 or the new query shown in Design View in Figure 17.14 and running in Figure 17.15.

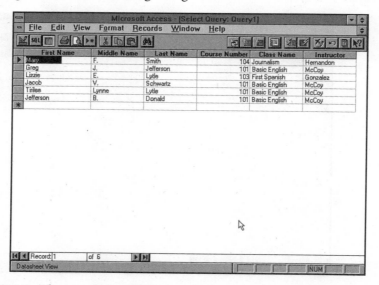

Figure 17.15. *The new three-table query running.*

Note that neither Jones nor MacDonald appears as having taken any courses at this time. Close the Temp query if you have it. Close the new query shown in Figure 17.15 if you constructed this and accept Access's default name for it: Query1.

The purpose of the query created in Exercise 17.3 is to extract records from the Append Me table and append them to the Student's Current Courses table. You will need the Append Me table from the sample data to complete this exercise. If it currently doesn't exist as part of your data, either enter the table's data now or include this table from the sample set you acquired following the directions in Appendix A.

Exercise 17.3. The append query.

1. Close all open tables and queries to clear the work area. Start a new query by moving to the Database View, clicking on the Query tab and clicking on the New button. Choose the New Query button to bypass the wizards.

2. Double-click on the Append Me table in the Add Table list box. Click on Add to add this table to the new query. Click on Close. Your screen should resemble Figure 17.16.

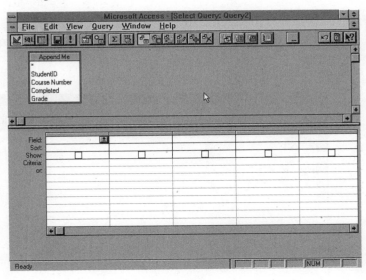

Figure 17.16. *Starting the append action query.*

3. Locate and drag the asterisk from the Field list box to the Field row of the first column of the query design grid. Your screen should resemble Figure 17.17.

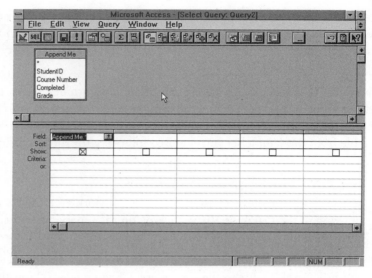

Figure 17.17. *Including the asterisk from the Field list box in the query.*

4. Access changes the asterisk to Append Me.*, which is Access jargon for "include all the fields from Append Me in this query." Click on the Run button in the toolbar to see how this query runs. Your screen should resemble Figure 17.18.

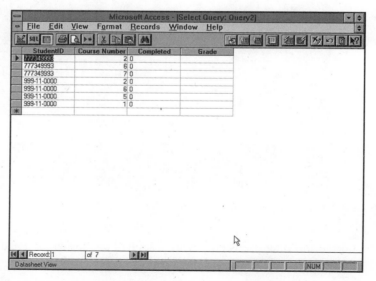

Figure 17.18. *The effect of the Append Me.* field in a query.*

The Access Way

When you include the * from the Field list box into a query, Access will automatically include all the fields from that table in the query.

17

This particular query includes all the records from the Append Me table, since you've entered no restricting criteria.

5. Return to Design View and click on the Append query button in the button bar. The Append query button is the one with the green cross. Alternately, you can choose the menu selections Query|Append.... Your screen should resemble Figure 17.19.

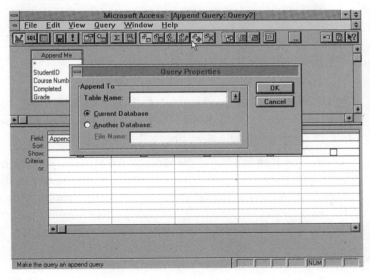

Figure 17.19. *The results of changing the select query to an append query.*

6. Pull down the combo box and choose the Student's Current Courses as a table to append to. Your screen should resemble Figure 17.20.

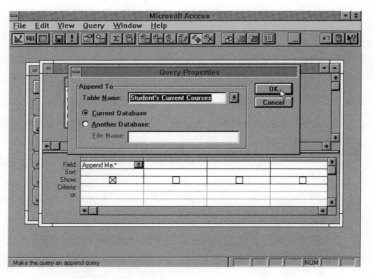

Figure 17.20. *Telling Access what table to append to.*

7. Click on OK. Look how the query design grid has changed. Not only does the title bar change to indicate this is an append query, but the design grid itself changes to include rows needed by append queries.

8. Click on the Run button in the toolbar. Access gives you the message box shown in Figure 17.21, warning you that continuing to run this query will append seven rows to the target table, Student's Current Courses. Click on OK. As with the Delete and Make Table queries, nothing seems to occur.

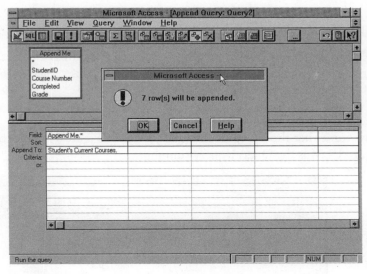

Figure 17.21. *Access warns you of the consequences of this query.*

9. Close this query, saving it as Appender. Figure 17.22 shows how this query appears in the Database View.

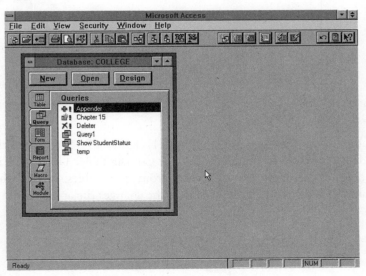

Figure 17.22. *The saved append query.*

The Access Way

Access is a tightly integrated program. The icons shown for the various query types in the Database View are the same as the icons shown in the toolbar for these same queries.

Now run either the Temp or the Query1 query. Figure 17.23 is the Temp query, Figure 17.24 is the Query1 query running.

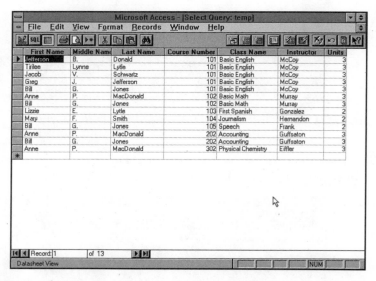

Figure 17.23. *The Temp query showing the results of the append operation.*

Compare Figures 17.22 and 17.23 with 17.13 and 17.15 to see how the append query added records to the Student's Current Courses table. The queries in 17.13, 17.15, 17.22, and 17.23 all extract records from three tables, one of which is Student's Current Courses; therefore, it reflects the changes the append did to that table.

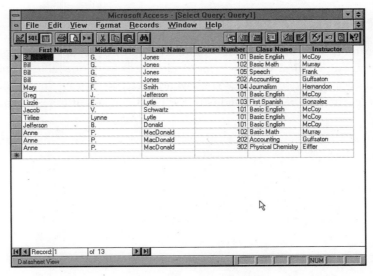

Figure 17.24. *The Query1 query showing the results of the append operation.*

DO	**DON'T**

DO use action queries regularly. An append query combined with a delete query on the same records can act as a powerful archiving tool.

DON'T fail to keep well backed up. Access will always follow your criteria for action queries perfectly. Sometimes, unless you're very careful, you'll enter defective criteria that will extract incorrect data targeted for deletion. The best defense is a solid backup system that's used regularly.

Whichever query you chose to run, Temp or Query1, you can see that now records exist for Jones and MacDonald in the Student's Current Courses table. Close all queries.

If you didn't save the Temp query, rename Query1 Temp by highlighting it at the Database View, then clicking on the File|Rename menu selections. Access will prompt you to supply a new name for Query1. Enter Temp.

Morning Summary

This morning you learned how to delete records in groups by using a delete action query. You also learned how to append records from one table to another using an append action query. Finally, you saw how Access can leave "holes" or dead space in its files that can be eliminated with the File-Compact utility built into Access.

18

Forms with Subforms

This afternoon you'll learn about the following:

- ☐ The need for forms with subforms
- ☐ The steps to create a form with a subform
- ☐ Creating the subform
- ☐ Creating the host or container form
- ☐ Embedding the subform in a form
- ☐ Using the form with a subform

Why You Need Forms with Subforms

Access is a relational database system. In any system such as Access there are relationships between records in various tables; in other words, one record in a table is related to many other records in other tables. Here are some examples:

One customer has many orders.

One order has many line items.

One student has many classes.

In a hospital, one doctor has many patients.

In that same hospital, one patient has many medicines required to be given daily.

One salesman has many sales.

One company has many salesmen and saleswomen.

One department has many sales items.

One store has many departments.

In each of the above examples, and many more you can likely think of, there are one and many sides to a relationship. The link, or common field in both tables, has one occurrence in the one table and potentially an unlimited number of occurrences in the other table.

How do you enter a series of occurrences on the many side of the relationship? For example, you want to enter a series of sales for a particular salesman. The combo box exercise in Chapter 13, "Intermediate Forms," showed how you can look up a StudentID to make sure the value you added to the StudentID field in Student's Current Courses was correct.

The technique shown in Chapter 13 works, but it's slightly cumbersome. It has two drawbacks. First, you can't just enter a series of occurrences for a particular student, but must look up the right StudentID for each record (or use Ctrl+'). Also, you can't see a student's personal information along with his current classes at the same time without making a query and a form to host the query.

Forms with subforms are a very convenient and aesthetically pleasing way to show or enter occurrences on the many side of a one-to-many relationship. There's no reason the same form can't be used to create new records on the one side of the relationship, but that's not the most common use of this technique.

You can easily get lost in Exercise 18.1 unless you have a good idea of the goal shown in Figure 18.15. Take a look at Figure 18.15 to see the finished form with a subform. Here's a list of how you're going to get there. The list is also a good reference list about how to manually create forms with subforms. Like so much else, the job goes much faster with a wizard.

1. Determine the one and the many sides of the relationship to see if the two tables or queries you wish to include are right for the form with subform technique. If necessary, construct the needed queries or tables.

2. Design the subform. This is where the many table or query will appear. In most cases the subform will be a form using the Datasheet View, but it doesn't have to be.

3. Save the subform, giving it a distinctive name. Access users and developers have adopted an informal set of naming conventions for objects in their databases. Using these conventions, if a form is to be named Class Entry, the subform is generally called subClass Entry.

4. Design the container form, leaving room for the subform in your design.

5. Drag the subform into the container form.

6. Test the new form with subform with known data to make sure it's working right.

Preparing for the Form

The subform part of this form enables people to enter, edit, or display a series of classes for an individual student. The first thing to do is set up a query to bind the subform to. Exercise 18.1 shows you how.

> **The Access Way**
>
> Exercise 18.1 uses a query for this subform with a criterion to return or display only those records for which the completed field is equal to No. The exercise uses a query instead of the original table because if this form was bound to the table, it'd show all the classes ever taken by this student, completed or not. This isn't a fatal error, but it would make for an inconveniently long scroll through irrelevant records in the case of students who've enrolled in many classes.
>
> Because this form with subform is only supposed to address current and future classes, we want to restrict it from also displaying complete classes. The best way to do this is to use a query. The way a query can confirm data is another reason to use one for binding to the subform.

Exercise 18.1. Making the subform's query.

1. Launch Access and open the College database if necessary. Click on the Query tab. Click on the New button. Click on the New Query button to bypass the wizards. Click on Student's Current Courses. Click on Add. Click on the Available Classes table. Click on Add. Click on Close. Your screen should resemble Figure 18.1.

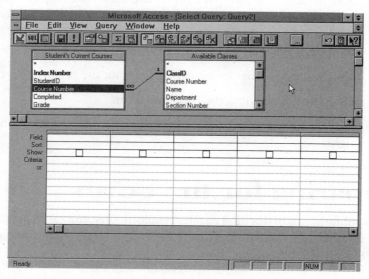

Figure 18.1. *Starting the new subform query.*

2. Drag the fields StudentID, Course Number, and Completed from the Field list box to the query design grid's columns 1–3. Uncheck the display check box for Completed and enter No for this field's criteria on the first criteria row. Your screen should resemble Figure 18.2.

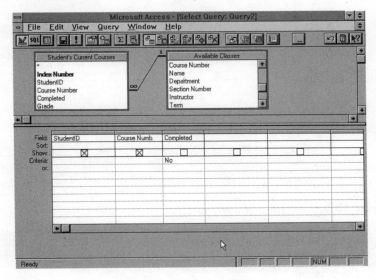

Figure 18.2. *Including the fields from the first table.*

3. Drag the Course Number, Name, and Section Number fields from the Available Classes table to columns 4–6 of the query design grid. Edit the Course Number field from the Available Courses, so that it reads: Course:[Course Number]. Your screen should resemble Figure 18.3.

4. Click on the Run button in the toolbar. Your screen should resemble Figure 18.4.

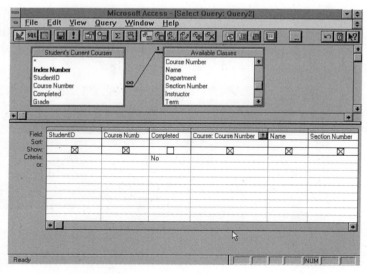

Figure 18.3. *Finishing the query design.*

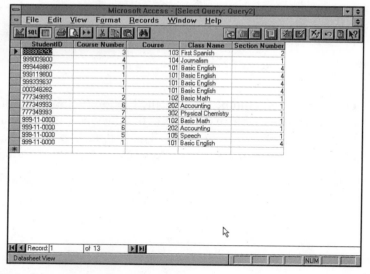

Figure 18.4. *Running the new query.*

5. Now for something way cool. Click in the last row for this query. Press
Ctrl+' (that's the Control key combined with the single quote key). This
combination is the Access repeat key. Access will copy the StudentID data

from the record immediately above the current record. Press Tab. Enter 3 for the Course Number. Your screen should resemble Figure 18.5.

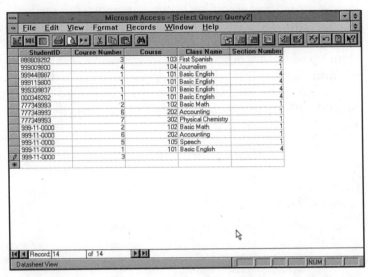

Figure 18.5. *Adding a record in a query.*

6. Now press Tab. Your screen should resemble Figure 18.6.

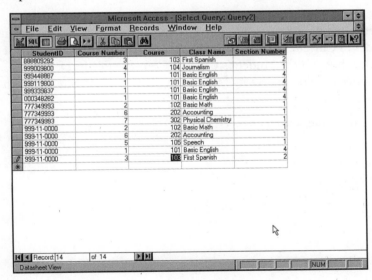

Figure 18.6. *Access automatically looks up and fills in values.*

There's a neat trick queries can do that tables can't! Access fills in the information for you. This happens because the courses at the fictional college are indexed according to course number, but the fictional registrar people demanded a system that would show the human-oriented nonindexed course number, the course name, and the section number to show up when they entered the index course number. This way they could confirm that a student wanted to sign up for such and such a course. In this case, the registrar would ask the student if he wanted to sign up for First Spanish 103 Section 2 when the student put down 3 in the class sign-up form.

7. Close the query, saving it and using the name subClass Entry.

The Access Way

Just as Exercise 18.1 showed how you can use a query to look up confirmation information for classes, you can use this same technique to look up item descriptions from item numbers, employees from employee numbers, customers from their phone numbers, and so forth.

Queries are the heart of any relational database system, including Access. Use them to make your applications better.

There's only one loose end. The Default property for the Completed field of the Student's Current Courses should be set to No. From the Database View, click on the Table tab, open the Student's Current Courses table in Design View, click on the Completed field, and set its Default property to No. Your screen should resemble Figure 18.7.

Close the table, saving changes.

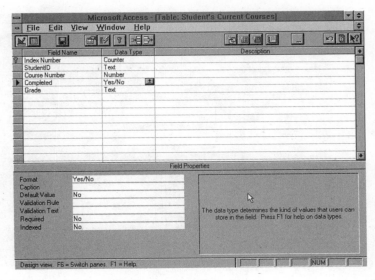

Figure 18.7. *Altering the Default property of a table.*

The Form with Subform

All's ready now to create the main form with a contained subform. There are two ways to do this—the easy way and the hard way. You've probably guessed by now that the easy way is to use a wizard, so that's the way to proceed. After creating this form with a subform and seeing it in action, you'll learn the secret of the magic acts the wizard performed so you can manually design the same thing if the need arises. This comes in a later chapter. For today, just concentrate on making and using the form with subform. Exercise 18.2 uses a wizard to create a form with a subform.

Exercise 18.2. The form with subform.

1. From the Database View, click on the Form tab, then click on the New button. Pull down the combo box and choose Student Personal for the bound table or query. Click on the Form Wizards button to call up a wizard. Highlight the Main/Subform choice in the wizard selection box. Your screen should resemble Figure 18.8.

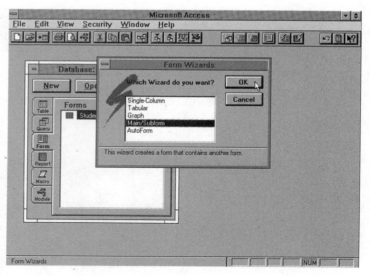

Figure 18.8. *Starting the Main/Subform Wizard.*

The Access Way

When planning a form with a subform, you must know ahead of time which form will contain the other. The container, or main form, is the form you initially bind to the new form even before choosing the Main/Subform Wizard as shown in Figure 18.8.

2. Click on OK to move ahead. Look toward the bottom of the dialog box on your screen now, the one shown in Figure 18.9. Here's where you choose what table or query will be bound to the form that will be contained in the main form. Be sure to have the Queries or Both button checked. The figure shows the Queries option selected to narrow down the list of tables and queries. Locate the subClass Entry query you created in Exercise 18.1. Click on it to give it the highlight. Your screen should resemble Figure 18.9.

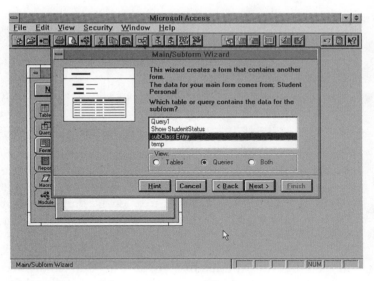

Figure 18.9. *Binding a table or query to a subform.*

3. Click on the Next > button to move on. Click on the > button four times to include the StudentID, FirstName, MiddleName, and LastName fields in the main part of this form. Click on the Major field farther down in the list and click on the > button to move the Major field also onto this form. Your screen should resemble Figure 18.10.

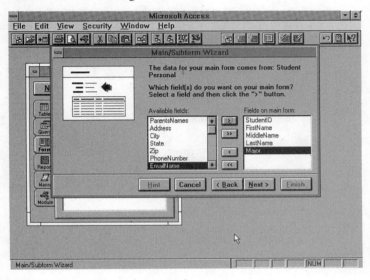

Figure 18.10. *Adding fields to the main form.*

The Access Way

The main, or container, form needs only a few fields from Student Personal—the table it's bound to. These fields—StudentID, FirstName, MiddleName, LastName, and Major—are all that's required to locate a student from Student Personal. The inclusion of the Major field was the result of a request from Student Advisement, who also uses this form.

The balance of the fields in Student Personal don't interest us for the purposes of this form. Remember, the fictional college won't be using this form to create new records in Student Personal—only looking up existing records. If this form were also going to do double duty as a new record-creating form, it would have to contain all the fields from Student Personal.

4. Click on the Next > button to move on. Here you tell the wizard what fields from the query bound to the subform to include in the subform. This form requires them all, so click on the >> button. Your screen should resemble Figure 18.11.

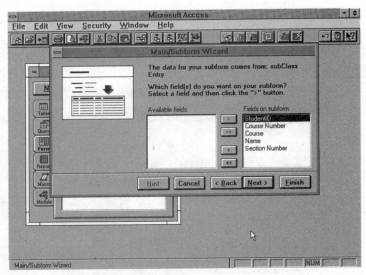

Figure 18.11. *Including fields for the subform.*

5. Click on the Next> button to move on. This screen is the now-familiar layout screen for the wizard forms. Give this form an embossed look by clicking on that option button in the option group. Your screen should resemble Figure 18.12.

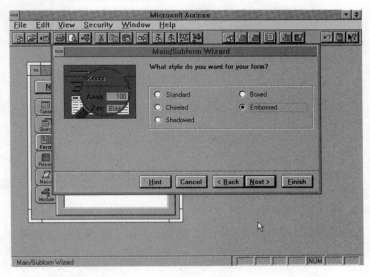

Figure 18.12. *Giving the form an embossed look.*

6. Click on the Next > button. Give this form the name Class Entry. Your screen should resemble Figure 18.13. The process is now done, so click on the Finish button. Access advises you that you must save the subform before it can finish its work. Click on OK and in the next dialog box give the subform the name subClass Entry. Your screen should resemble Figure 18.14. Click on OK to let the wizard finish its work.

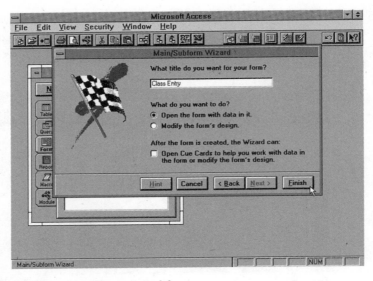

Figure 18.13. *Finishing the main/subform.*

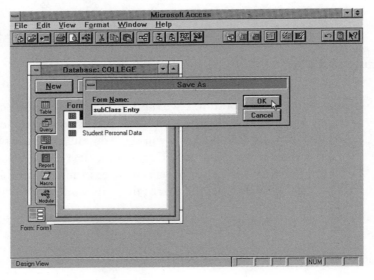

Figure 18.14. *Saving the subform.*

The Main/Subform Wizard creates two forms during its run. The main form is the one you initially bound even before calling on the wizard. The contained, or subform, is the form you told the wizard to bind to the subform in the middle part of the wizard's run. After finishing its run, the wizard called on for Exercise 18.2 should leave you with a form much like the one shown in Figure 18.15.

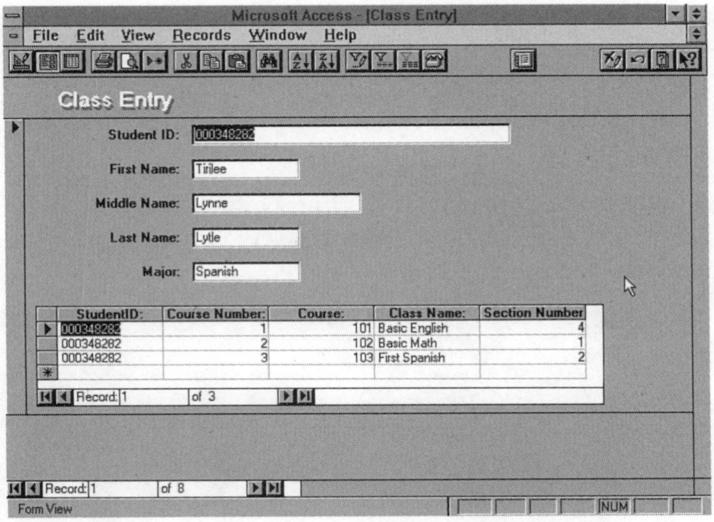

Figure 18.15. *The finished main/subform.*

Refer to the Chapter 18 Demo query, which is shown in Figure 18.16 and included in the sample data set. This is a query constructed to help you understand the relationship of a main form to its subform in a properly constructed form/subform, as in Exercise 18.2.

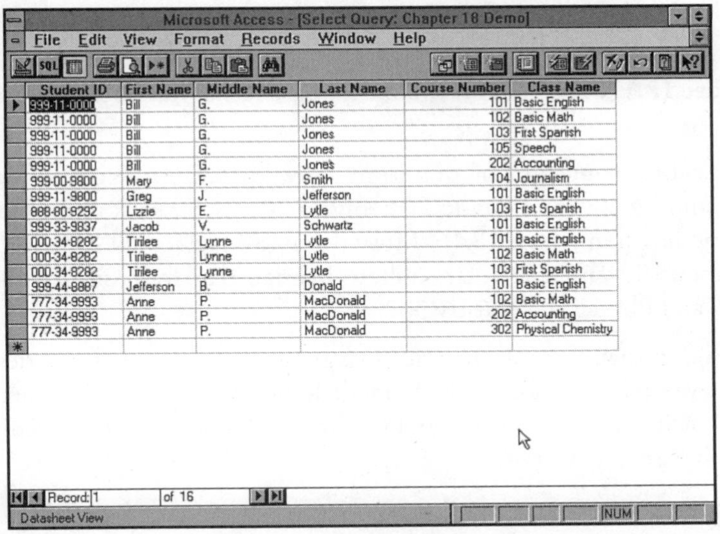

Student ID	First Name	Middle Name	Last Name	Course Number	Class Name
999-11-0000	Bill	G.	Jones	101	Basic English
999-11-0000	Bill	G.	Jones	102	Basic Math
999-11-0000	Bill	G.	Jones	103	First Spanish
999-11-0000	Bill	G.	Jones	105	Speech
999-11-0000	Bill	G.	Jones	202	Accounting
999-00-9800	Mary	F.	Smith	104	Journalism
999-11-9800	Greg	J.	Jefferson	101	Basic English
888-80-9292	Lizzie	E.	Lytle	103	First Spanish
999-33-9837	Jacob	V.	Schwartz	101	Basic English
000-34-8282	Tirilee	Lynne	Lytle	101	Basic English
000-34-8282	Tirilee	Lynne	Lytle	102	Basic Math
000-34-8282	Tirilee	Lynne	Lytle	103	First Spanish
999-44-8887	Jefferson	B.	Donald	101	Basic English
777-34-9993	Anne	P.	MacDonald	102	Basic Math
777-34-9993	Anne	P.	MacDonald	202	Accounting
777-34-9993	Anne	P.	MacDonald	302	Physical Chemistry

Figure 18.16. *A query supplied to clarify the main/subform concept.*

Look at Tirilee Lytle's records in Figure 18.16. She's signed up for three courses: Basic English 101, Basic Math 102, and First Spanish 103. Now look at her record as shown in Figure 18.15, the form with a subform you created in Exercise 18.2. This shows Lytle's record from Student Personal along with those courses she's signed up for—no more and no less.

Move to the next record in the Class Entry form, the one for Anne MacDonald, by clicking on the right-facing arrow at the very bottom of your screen. Your screen should resemble Figure 18.17.

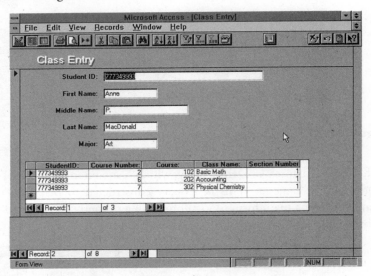

Figure 18.17. *Each form record has a distinct set of records shown in the subform.*

The subform portion of this form shows MacDonald taking Basic Math 102, Accounting 202, and Physical Chemistry 302. Refer back to the Chapter 18 Demo query shown in Figure 18.16. Move down to MacDonald's records as shown in the Chapter 18 Demo query. It also shows her signed up for Basic Math 102, Accounting 202, and Physical Chemistry 302.

The query that the subform is tied to is an Access query. These queries are so powerful that even the inclusion of the StudentID field in this form isn't necessary. Exercise 18.2 included it only so you could see how the StudentID fields remain coordinated in the main and subform.

Try entering a new class for MacDonald. Click in the subform portion of the form in the first empty row of the Course Number column. Enter a 4. As soon as you do, the query bound to the subform supplies the right StudentID for MacDonald. Your screen should resemble Figure 18.18.

The Access Way

A properly constructed main/subform makes entering uncoordinated data into the subform impossible.

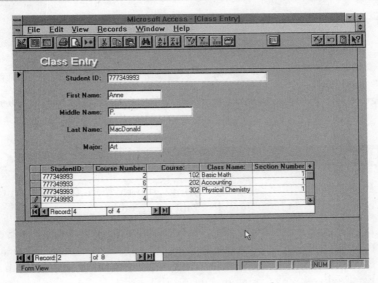

18

Figure 18.18. *Access will not enter uncoordinated data if you construct your forms correctly.*

Access isn't done with its magic yet. Press the Tab key to move away from the Course Number field. Access knows that course 4 is Journalism 104, Section 1, so it obligingly fills in the rest of the information for you as shown in Figure 18.19.

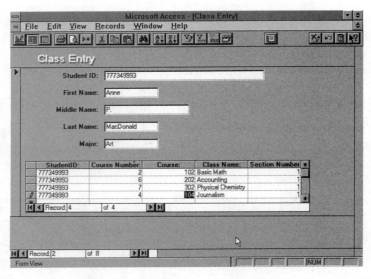

Figure 18.19. *Access can automatically fill in information for you when told to do so.*

DO	**DON'T**

DO generally plan on binding your forms to queries rather than to tables because queries have more flexibility than tables.

DON'T forget that you can't violate table properties by entering data through a query. If your table has a user-supplied primary key field, such as Student Personal does, constructing a query without including the primary key field will make data entry impossible.

Close this form, giving it the name Class Entry. If you have the Chapter 18 Demo query, run it. You'll see that your entry in MacDonald's form/subform is reflected as a change in this database's data. The running Chapter 18 Demo query is shown in Figure 18.20.

Close the Chapter 18 Demo query if it's open.

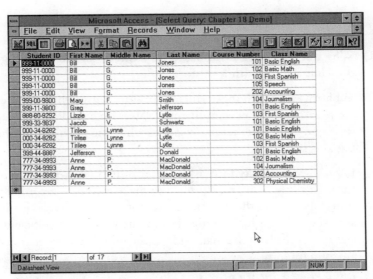

Figure 18.20. *If done right, all data presentations in Access can be of live data.*

Summary

Append queries extract data from a table or query and append, or attach, it to records in a receiving table. Delete queries select and then delete records from the same table that they run from. If you run first an append query then a delete one using the same criteria, you will have moved records from one table to another. Many people do this as a way to archive their records. This gets the records out of the active database, but they're still available in case the need arises.

Forms with subforms, called main and subforms in the terminology of wizards, are forms with other forms embedded in them. Generally speaking, this construction is useful for embedding a form bound to a table or query on the many side of a one-to-many relationship in a form bound to a table or query on the one side. You can construct such a form with subform by starting a new form bound to the table on the one side of the relationship then invoking the Form Wizard of the Main/Subform type.

You don't have to include the common or link fields for the two tables or queries in a form with a subform to keep the forms in synchronization. Access is smart enough to do this even without the inclusion of these fields on either or both forms.

Q&A

Q **Why not just use a form based on a query, as shown in Figure 18.16, to do what a form with a subform does?**

A Subforms are much more efficient in situations such as those outlined for Exercise 18.2. If you want to enter classes for a student using the form/subform, you just enter many classes while the main part of the form remains static.

If you used a unitary form based on the query, you'd have to navigate through all the fields on the form to make each new record. There are shortcuts making that last statement not precisely true, but that doesn't alter the fact that forms and subforms are much more efficient for entering records to the many side of the one-to-many relationship than any unitary form.

Q **I didn't understand how Access knows what records in the subform belong to the main form. That part wasn't made clear to me.**

A It was glossed over. There is a property for the wizard to set for both the main and subform that keeps them in sync. This property, as well as other form with subform subjects, is covered in tomorrow's chapters.

Q **Can I customize a form with a subform or must I accept what the wizard created?**

A You can customize forms with subforms just as you can any other forms. This too is covered in tomorrow's chapters.

Q **Can I use a delete action query to eliminate data from only certain fields in a record?**

A No. Delete queries work on whole rows at a time. You can modify individual fields within a row using an update query, however.

Q **Is there any time when I should not use delete queries?**

A Delete queries are a time-saver if you can identify groups of records by a certain criterion and be sure you want to eliminate all those records. Delete queries will not let you review and confirm deletion of individual records. This type of query only asks for confirmation by warning you how many records you'll lose.

If you can't identify a group of records by a criterion for certain deletion, don't use a delete query. Remember, you can always use a Make Table or append query to extract records, review what you've extracted, and then if you see fit, alter the query to a delete one to eliminate the ones you've reviewed from the append or Make Table query.

Q Can I append records to a table that doesn't yet exist?

A That function is called the Make Table query. It first makes the table's structure, then adds the records. Once the table exists, use the append query to add to it.

Workshop

Here's where you can test and apply the lessons you learned today.

Quiz

Possible answers to these questions are provided in Appendix A.

1. Generally speaking, which would you say are more flexible: queries or tables?

2. Can you bypass table property settings such as primary key entry by entering data through a query?

3. After append queries extract data, do they then append it to the table they extracted it from or to a different table?

4. Do delete queries act on the table or tables they select from, or on different tables?

5. How can you confirm that the delete or append queries are extracting records according to your plans?

Put Access into Action

1. Construct a small query based on the Student Personal table and include the same fields as the main form in Exercise 18.2. Call this query Class Sign Up.

2. Create a form with a subform using a wizard. Make this form similar to the one done in Exercise 18.2, except use the subClass Sign Up query for the main form and don't include the StudentID field in the subform. Use the subClass Entry query for the subform.

3. Name the form Class Sign Up both as a label in the wizard and as a name for the form in the Database View. Name the subform subClass Sign Up— the same as the query it's bound to. Access will give you a warning box saying it couldn't find link fields. Click on OK to acknowledge the message and to indicate that you want to move on.

4. Run the form. Does it run well? Consider how useful it is compared to the form with a subform created in Exercise 18.2. Which do you suppose would be the better form for people in the registration office? Which do you suppose would be the better form for Student Advisement people?

5. Close the form, saving changes. If you want your records to remain in synchronization with the book's, delete any new records you might have made while experimenting with this form, either by deleting manually or by constructing a delete query. Figure 18.21 shows how your finished form with a subform should look.

6. *Teach Yourself Access 2 in 14 Days* does come back to this form in an optional exercise. It serves as solid review of today's topic and an introduction to some of tomorrow's material. You can keep it and the other objects for your own experimentation and use in the next chapter, or if you want to clean up your Database View, highlight the Class Sign Up form in the Database View, then press the Del or Delete key on your keyboard. Give Access the OK to delete the highlighted item. Repeat this for each of the objects you made during this exercise.

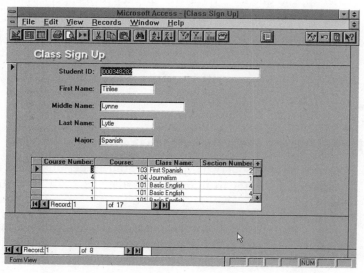

Figure 18.21. *A finished form based on two queries.*

Day

10

19

Form Control Properties

This morning's lesson explains the following:

☐ What a form control property is

☐ How to synchronize main and subforms with control properties

☐ A better way to find records

☐ Filtering records

Control Properties

To a great extent, using Access depends upon understanding and setting properties. You can use the program successfully for minor applications such as simple list management even if you hardly know a thing about properties, but when your needs grow even slightly complex, your time spent learning about this subject will pay off big time.

> **The Access Way**
>
> Much of what applies to form control property settings also applies to reports. Form and report design are very similar subjects, only diverging where the applications of forms and reports divide. For example, you make no data entry on forms, so there's no sense in having combo boxes there.

Many of the basic property settings can be handled, and should be handled, by wizards. Why reinvent the wheel? Let wizards do what they do so well. However, there's a huge world of ability in Access that the wizards don't even try to address. In some cases, venturing into these worlds will call up other wizards or Access helpers so you don't need to do it all yourself. For example, the Form Wizard wasn't sharp enough to know when a combo box made sense for a form's field, but as soon as you put one on the form, you called up the Combo Box Wizard, which made the combo box programming job much easier.

Take a look at Figure 19.1. This is a Property list box for a form control (or field, if you prefer) with the combo box at the top pulled down to show the types of properties a control has. The form in the background is the one generated by the exercise at the end of Chapter 18, "Forms with Subforms."

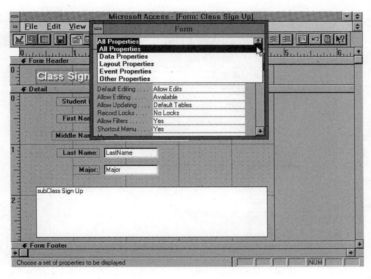

Figure 19.1. *The various types of properties for a control.*

Here are the selections available in the Property list box, with a short explanation of what each does:

All Properties means that all properties from all classifications are shown.

Data Properties determine what can be done with the data that is bound to the control.

Layout Properties control the appearance of the data on the form or report.

Event Properties determine how a control behaves in response to an event. Examples of events in Access are when the cursor's over the control, when a control's clicked on, when the control gets the focus, and when the control loses the focus.

Other Properties are all properties that don't fit in any of the normal classifications. Don't think just because these are classed as "other" they are unimportant. Some of the most used and needed properties are in Other.

A Working Example

Refer to Figure 19.2. This is the form done as an exercise at the end of Chapter 18. It's called Class Sign Up. If you created this form, open it now in Form View so your screen resembles Figure 19.2.

Figure 19.2. *The Class Sign Up form.*

Notice that the subform section of this form isn't particularly useful because it shows more classes than Tirilee Lytle's signed up for. Refer back to the form shown in Figure 18.15 and the query shown in Figure 18.16 to see how this form should work. For some reason, this form can't filter out unrelated records in the subform. Scroll down one record by clicking on the record selector VCR-style buttons at the bottom of the screen. The results of this are shown in Figure 19.3.

The same wrong information is shown in the subform now as is in Figure 19.2. Unlike the form done in Exercise 18.2, this form just shows all the records for all the classes everybody's signed up for in its subform section. This form malfunctions because two inconspicuous form controls are set incorrectly.

If you have this form on your screen, switch to Design View and open the Properties list box. If you elected not to make this form, you should be able to follow along well by looking at the illustrations.

If you do have this form, click on the subform section to give it the highlight and move to Data Properties in the list box. Your screen should resemble Figure 19.4.

The two properties, Link Child Fields and Link Master Fields, are blank. These properties tell the Access form what fields the main and subform have in common. Enter StudentID for both of these properties, as shown in Figure 19.5.

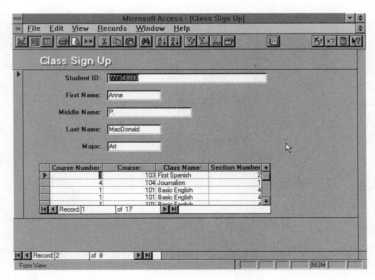

Figure 19.3. *Moving through records has no effect on the subform.*

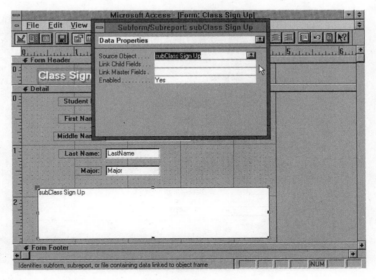

Figure 19.4. *The data properties for a subform control.*

Return to Form View. Now the main and subform are in synchronization the same as in the form done in Exercise 18.2. The correctly running Class Sign Up form is shown in Figure 19.6.

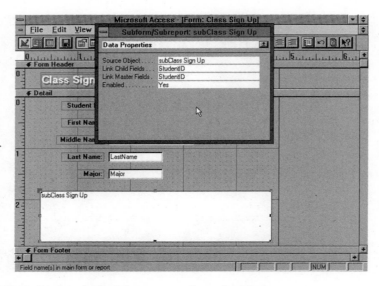

Figure 19.5. *Setting the link between main and subform.*

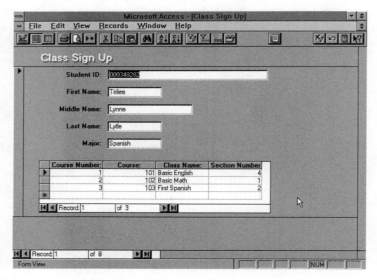

Figure 19.6. *The two-query form running correctly.*

Close the Class Sign Up form if you have it open, saving changes. Exercise 19.1 reviews the Link field control properties.

Exercise 19.1. Field control properties.

1. Launch Access and open the College database if necessary. Open in Design View the Class Entry form done in Exercise 18.2. Your screen should resemble Figure 19.7.

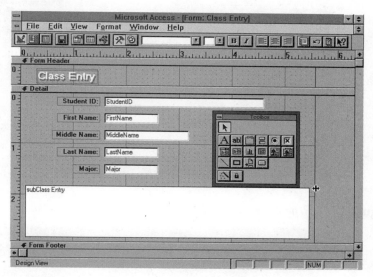

Figure 19.7. *Preparing to alter control properties.*

2. Open the Properties list box by clicking on its button in the toolbar. Click anywhere in the subform subClass Entry section to give it the highlight. Pull down the combo box as shown in Figure 19.1. Click on Data Properties. Your screen should resemble Figure 19.8.

3. Delete the entries for Link Child Fields and Link Master Fields by highlighting them with the mouse cursor then pressing the Del or Delete key on your keyboard. Alternatively, you can press Ctrl+X or choose Edit|Cut to cut the last selection to the clipboard. Switch to Form View. Your screen should resemble Figure 19.9.

The effect of the link breakage is even more apparent in this form than in the Class Sign Up form shown before. Look at Figure 19.9's subform section. You can see that all the classes for all the students are dumped here rather than just the ones that are associated with the record in the master, or main, form.

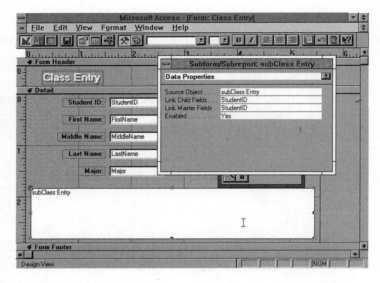

Figure 19.8. *Restricting the number and type of properties shown.*

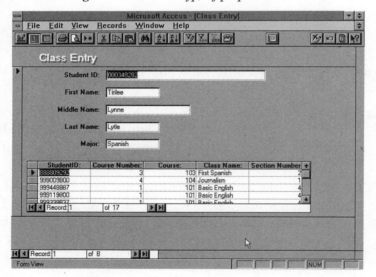

Figure 19.9. *The effect of breaking the link.*

4. Return to Design View and restore StudentID as the entry for the Link Child Fields and Link Master Fields properties. If you cut the entry to the Clipboard, click in a field then press Ctrl+V to paste from the Clipboard. Do this for both fields. Switch back to Form View. Your screen should resemble Figure 19.10.

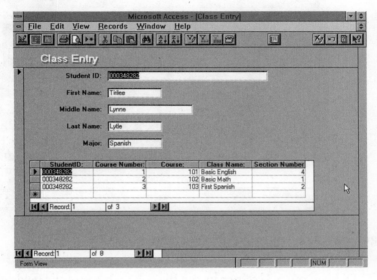

Figure 19.10. *The link restored.*

Enabled and Locked

In many situations you'll want to protect your data from being altered. The people doing the class entry at the registrar's or Student Advisement offices not only need to enter data in the subform, but they also need to be able to view data in the main form. Exercise 19.2, which demonstrates the use and limitations of the Locked and Enabled properties, addresses this need.

Exercise 19.2. Locked and Enabled properties.

1. Starting where you left off in Exercise 19.1, return to Design View. Using the marquee or the Shift+click method, select all the fields in the main form. If your Properties list box isn't on Data, change that to make it so. Locate

the Enabled property in the list box. Click in the Enabled field. Pull down the combo box and choose No. Your screen should resemble Figure 19.11.

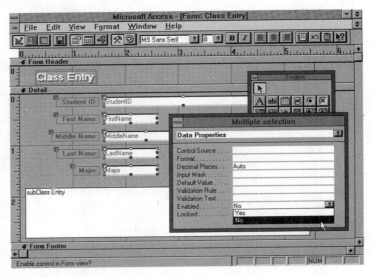

Figure 19.11. *Changing the Enabled property to No.*

Did you catch Access changing the color scheme of the fields in the main form when you clicked on No? This is Access's visual clue that these fields aren't Enabled. Return to Form View. Your screen should resemble Figure 19.12.

The Access Way

Access enables you to set the common properties for many controls at the same time. Just select as many controls as you want to set the same property to, and let Access do the rest.

Try clicking in any of the main form's fields. You can't get your cursor in them at all. In fact, with all the main form's fields disabled this way, you can't leave the subform. In some applications this would be quite efficient. Setting a control's or set of controls' property to Enabled No prevents not only data entry into the field, but any entry.

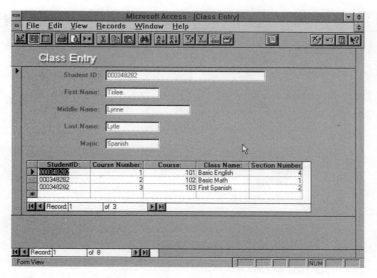

Figure 19.12. *All fields in the main form disabled.*

19

However, there's a drawback to using this form with all the main form's controls disabled. How do you find the record for a particular student? The only way is to scroll through the records until you hit the one you want. You can click in the record selector section and enter the particular record you want, but that won't work unless you know the record number for a particular student in the Student Personal table. If you supplied the registrar and Student Advisement offices with such a list, they could look up the student number, but this would slow each office down considerably.

Setting the Enabled property to No did safeguard the data, but at too great a cost. It would be better to let people enter the main form's fields so they can use Access's search capacity, but prevent them from altering data. The answer is the Locked property.

2. Return to Design mode. Again select all the fields on the main form either by using a marquee or by the Shift+click method. Change the Enabled property back to Yes. Locate the Locked property, right below Enabled. Set that property to Yes. Your screen should resemble Figure 19.13.

DO   **DON'T**

DO use the marquee or Shift+click method to set the properties all for the form's fields.

DON'T choose the Edit|Select All menu selections. That chooses not only just the field, but everything associated with this form.

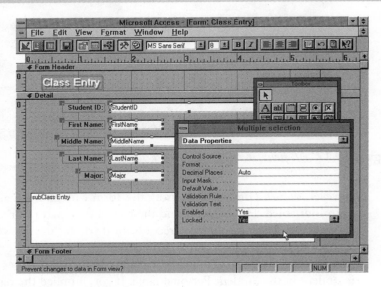

Figure 19.13. *Setting the Locked property.*

3. Return to Form View. Try editing any field in the main form part. You can't edit the fields, but you can enter them.

Searching About

Keep the form from Exercise 19.2 open. Click on the VCR-style record selector button to move to the first record, the one for Tirilee Lytle, if it's not already current. Click in the LastName field, then click on the Find button in the toolbar. This is the button with the binocular icon. Access will bring up the Find in field dialog box. Your screen should resemble Figure 19.14.

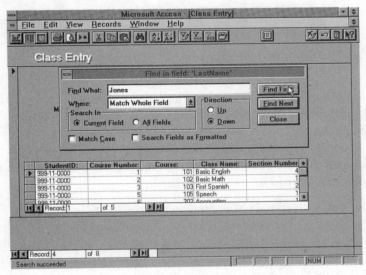

Figure 19.14. *Finding records in a form.*

Enter Jones for a LastName to search for. Click on the Find First button. Not much will seem to occur, but look carefully at the bottom of your screen toward the left of the status bar. Access quietly tells you that your search was successful. Your screen should resemble Figure 19.15.

Figure 19.15. *A successful search for a single record.*

That worked, but because Access obscured our view of the main part of the form, it was a pretty subtle success. Try this as a better way to search. Close the Find in field dialog box and again move to the first record by clicking on the VCR-style record button at the bottom of the screen. If you prefer, you can choose Records|Go To|First from the menus. Again click on the Find button in the toolbar. This time click on the title bar of the Find in field dialog box and drag it to the bottom of your screen. Your screen should resemble Figure 19.16. Now run the Find by clicking on the Find First button. Access should remember the last find you tried, and it should have left Jones in the Find field. Your screen should look like Figure 19.17.

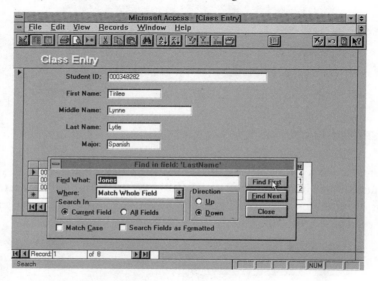

Figure 19.16. *Moving the dialog box out of the way.*

Close the Find in field dialog box. The added advantage of moving the Find in field dialog box so you can see your search results is that you can see if you've hit the right Jones. Access will always bring up the first Jones in the dataset when you click on the Find First button. If the Jones you want is down farther, you have the option of clicking on the Find Next button or closing the Find in field dialog box and scrolling down to the right Jones.

If you have many Joneses, you can start a subsearch by clicking on the FirstName field and entering a Find in field criteria for that. Because you are already in the Joneses records, if you have the right first name for a Jones, the search will find the Jones with the first name of your new criterion. Obviously, in a dataset with many duplicate items such as many Tom Joneses, searching by the unique identifier is much simpler. In this case, the unique identifier is the StudentID number.

Figure 19.17. *The new location makes finds much easier.*

Filtering Records

Sometimes you'll only want to see a subset of your data. You learned how to do this by entering criteria in queries, but what if you have a form you wish to switch subsets of data with? You could create a series of identical forms, each tied to a query with a different criteria set, but that's wasteful, cumbersome, and confusing. Access lets you set filters for records shown in forms. Exercise 19.3 demonstrates this ability. It shows how to design and apply data filters. Keep in mind that you can design and change filters when a form's running. This isn't a task done at design time.

Exercise 19.3. Data filters.

1. If the form Class Entry isn't running in Form View, make it so. Click on the Edit Filter/Sort button on the toolbar. This is the button that is the farthest left of the three buttons with the funnel icon. Your screen should resemble Figure 19.18.

357

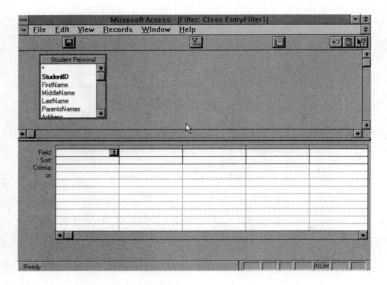

Figure 19.18. *The filter/sort design grid.*

This looks just like the query design grid, and it acts almost the same, too. There is more you can do from the query grid, but as far as setting criteria and sorting, the two act the same. Access is even smart enough to know that the Student Personal table is bound to this form, so it brings up a list box filled with the fields from Student Personal.

2. Drag the LastName field from the list box to the first column of the grid. Enter "Lytle" as a criteria in this column. Your screen should resemble Figure 19.19.

3. Click on the Apply Filter/Sort button. It's the only one with a funnel on it right now. Access will grind away a while and result in a screen similar to Figure 19.20.

   Look down at the bottom of the screen at the record selectors area. Access now shows only two records because only two meet your filter criteria. Also notice the boxes at the bottom right of your screen. One now has the word FLTR in it, signifying that a filter's in action.

4. Click on the Show All Records button in the toolbar. That's the rightmost button in the funnel group. Access clears your filter for the time being and

again shows all the records. Confirm this by examining the record selector area to see that, in fact, all your records are now available, as in Figure 19.21.

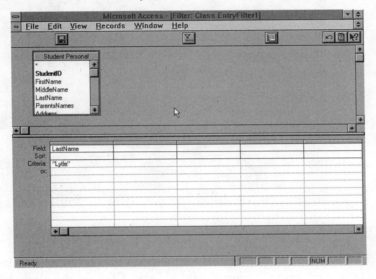

Figure 19.19. *Creating a filter criterion.*

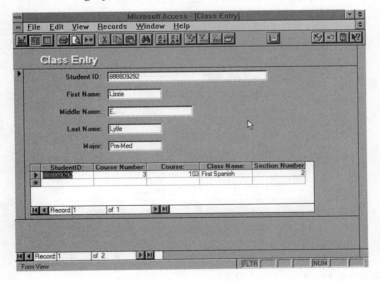

Figure 19.20. *The results of applying a filter.*

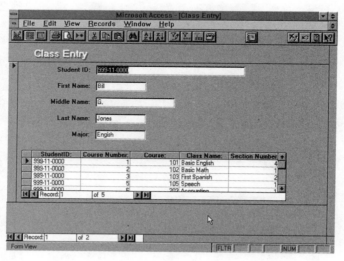

Figure 19.21. *Clearing the filter.*

5. Click on the Edit Filter/Sort button again to enter Filter Design View. Enter
   `Like "J*"` for a criterion instead of Lytle. Click on the Apply Filter/Sort
   button. Your screen should resemble Figure 19.22.

Figure 19.22. *A wildcard filter.*

Access returns all records where the last name begins with J. In this record set,
there are two such records: Jones and Jefferson. Access caught them both.

You can apply any criteria or any sort order here, just as you can in queries. The operation is identical for both. You can save as many filters as you want by choosing the menu items File|Save as Query. You can later recall those saved filters by choosing File|Load Query.

Morning Summary

Access controls have many different classes of properties. These properties can be set during the design phase, and in many cases during runtime. These properties affect how a control behaves, reacts, or looks, and where a control gets its data from or outputs it to. It's fair to say a control is the sum of its properties.

Four important properties are Link Child Fields, Link Master Fields, Enabled, and Locked. The first two from that list apply to which fields in the main form and subform are in common, or linked. The last two properties control entry and editing of the fields and data.

You can filter or sort the underlying data shown in a form or report by clicking on the Edit Filter/Sort button and editing the filter design grid, similar to the way you created criteria and sorts in queries. You can quickly apply and clear the filter from your data by clicking on the Apply Filter/Sort and Clear Filter/Sort buttons on the Form View toolbar.

20

Instantly Smarter Forms

This afternoon you'll learn

☐ What an event is

☐ How to place event-only controls on a form

☐ How to use a wizard to program those controls to respond to certain events

You might have heard that programming computers is a job for brilliant social misfits. For some programming tasks that's still true, but you can do quite a bit of programming in Access with little effort and without losing your social skills. This afternoon's lesson shows you how. If you're a user-designer, much of what you need to do in Access is simplicity itself. If you plan to use Access as a professional development tool, the program has the power. Thousands of professional applications demonstrate this to anybody's satisfaction. However, using the more esoteric Access areas does take at least a little work. You can still learn all of it while retaining your knowledge of what fork to use for a salad.

The First Programmed Command Button

So far you've made use of Access's excellent design to create static forms and reports. Using supplied controls you can open and display data, and when using forms you can edit data. However, to open, close, or scroll through records on them you need to use Access's supplied tools. This chapter starts you on the path of being able to design your own tools.

Exercise 20.1 shows you how to make controls that scroll through records.

Exercise 20.1. Record manipulation.

1. Launch Access and open the College database if necessary. Open the Class Entry form in Design View. If you're picking up where Chapter 19, "Form Control Properties," left off, clear any filters and return to Design mode for the Class Entry form. Your screen should resemble Figure 20.1.

2. Rearrange and resize the controls on your form to resemble Figure 20.2.

   Refer to Figure 20.2 and note that the Control Wizards toggle button is selected in the Toolbox. Make sure your Control Wizards button is similarly selected, or the following steps in this exercise won't work the same for you as they do in the book's example.

3. Click on the Command button control in the Toolbox. It's the one directly to the left of the Control Wizards button in Figure 20.2. Move your cursor on the form and click just below and toward the left of the subform section. Your screen should resemble Figure 20.3, except the number on your Command button is probably different from the figure's.

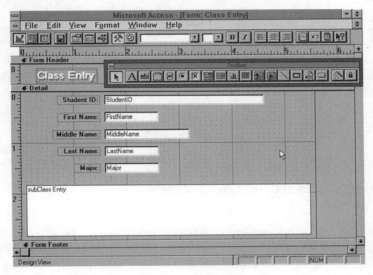

Figure 20.1. *Getting ready to add event-only controls to the form.*

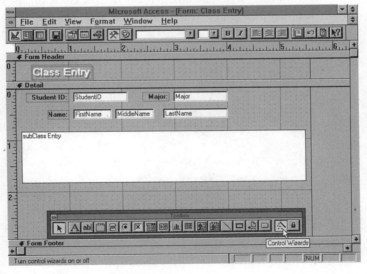

Figure 20.2. *The rearranged form.*

20

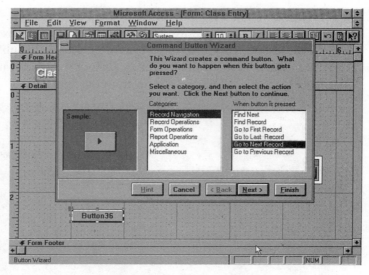

Figure 20.3. *Starting the Command Button Wizard.*

4. Your selection from the Categories list should be Record Navigation and your selection from the "When button is pressed" list should be Go to Next Record, as shown in Figure 20.3. If not, make it so by clicking on the Record Navigation selection in Categories and then selecting Go to Next Record from the "When button is pressed" list. Click on the Next > button when you're done. Your screen should resemble Figure 20.4.

The Access Way

As you'll see later on, you can manually program command buttons, but it makes little sense to do so if what you want is available from this wizard. Look over the lists to get a feel for what's available. When you need a service available from these lists, invoke the wizard. Unlike some things, the way the wizard handles programming command buttons is better than most programmers' methods.

5. The standard left- and right-facing VCR-style controls Access uses for record navigation make sense as analogs for tape operation when the movement is horizontal, but most people think of moving up and down in a record set for navigating records. To give these people an icon on this button that fits their

conceptions, click on the first entry in the Picture list box—the down-facing arrow. Your screen should resemble Figure 20.5.

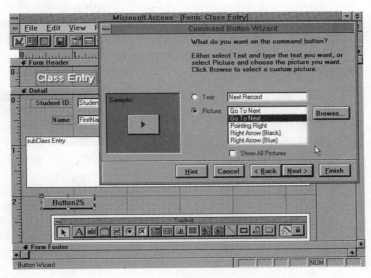

Figure 20.4. *The layout section of the Command Button Wizard.*

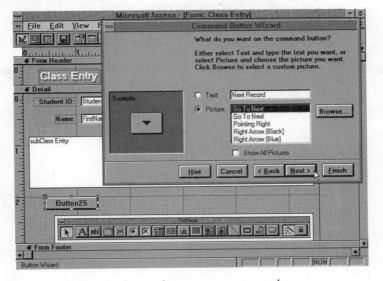

Figure 20.5. *Using an icon that makes sense to most people.*

6. Click on the Next > button. Use conventional Access nomenclature to name this button `cmdNextRecord`. The standard Access naming convention is to start the name of a control with a three-letter description of what type of control it is, followed by a short description of what the control does. The name `cmdNextRecord`, therefore, tells the world that this is a command button (`cmd`) that moves to the next record (`NextRecord`). Your screen should resemble Figure 20.6.

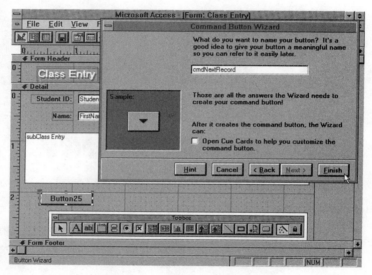

Figure 20.6. *Using standard naming conventions for this command button.*

7. Click on the Finish button. Your screen should resemble Figure 20.7.

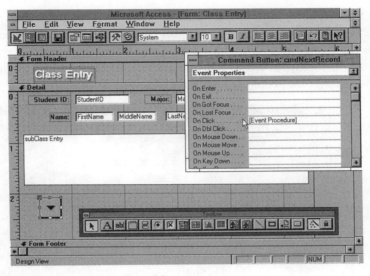

Figure 20.7. *The finished command button.*

Switch to Form View to try out the new command button. Your screen should resemble Figure 20.8.

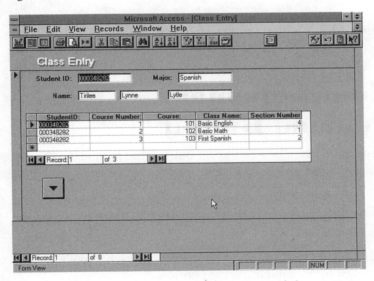

Figure 20.8. *The new command button awaiting a command.*

Click on the new button twice. Access scrolls down through the Records until record 3 shows up. Your screen should resemble Figure 20.9. Your button works to navigate through the records. While this button duplicates the Record Navigation button down at the record selector's area of the screen, the size and icon on the button make it much easier for people to understand and use.

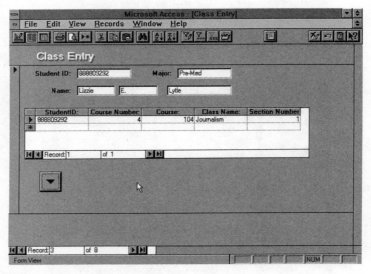

Figure 20.9. *The new command button in use.*

A Complementary Command Button

Exercise 20.2 creates a command button that is similar to the one Exercise 20.1 creates. This second button complements the first one.

Exercise 20.2. Another command button.

1. Return to Design View.

2. Click on the Command button control in the Toolbox. Click on the form next to the cmdNextRecord button.

3. Choose Record Navigation and Go to Previous Record from the wizard's list boxes. Click on the Next > button.

4. Select the up-facing arrow from the layout section of the wizard. Click on the Next > button.

5. Give the button the name `cmdPreviousRecord`.

6. Click on Finish. Your screen should resemble Figure 20.10.

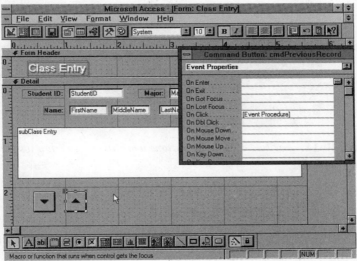

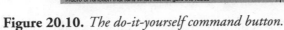

Figure 20.10. *The do-it-yourself command button.*

Return to Form View. Your screen should resemble Figure 20.11. Try using your new command buttons to navigate around your records. They work just fine. Congratulations—you're a computer programmer.

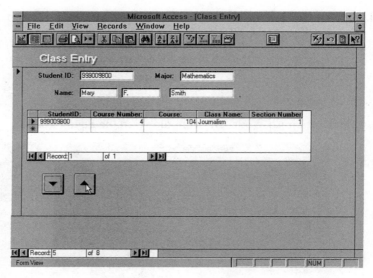

Figure 20.11. *The two command buttons work in conjunction with each other.*

Event Properties

The Command Button Wizard from Exercises 20.1 and 20.2 actually wrote Access Basic code. This section takes a look at what that code is.

Return to Design View and open the Properties list box if it's not already open. Pull down the combo box in the Properties list box and choose Event Properties. Click on the first command button you made, the one that moves down one record at a time. Your screen should resemble Figure 20.12.

The On Click property has been set to [Event Procedure]. This was done by the wizard. It means that the wizard has created some Access Basic Code (or ABC) that will be called into action whenever the control is clicked on.

Examine the other event properties for command buttons. These controls can react to such events as Got Focus, On Mouse Move, On Enter, and other such odd-sounding events. The vast majority of things you program a command button to do are in response to the On Click event. The wizard you used in Exercises 20.1 and 20.2 programs the On Click event for a command button.

Take a look at Figure 20.13. This shows the events a form can react to. This is only a partial list. The screen isn't large enough to hold them all.

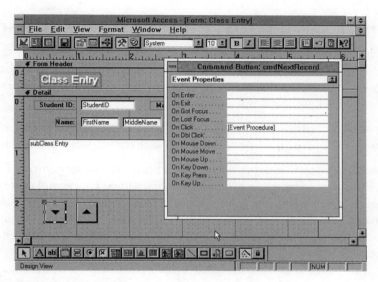

Figure 20.12. *The list box showing Event Properties.*

Keep in mind that Figure 20.13 only shows the event properties associated with a form. There are also Layout, Data, and Other properties. Don't be concerned if some of these properties' behaviors aren't obvious to you by their names. Especially don't be concerned that you need to memorize all of these properties. The online help system in Access has all of these memorized for you.

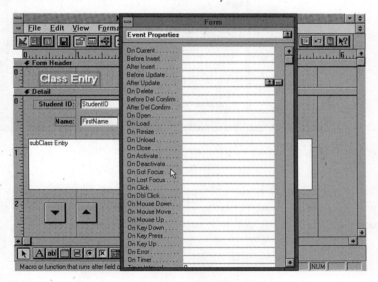

Figure 20.13. *A partial list of Event Properties for a form.*

Context-Sensitive Help to the Rescue

Here's how to get help about one of the more obscure properties shown in Figure 20.12. Click in the entry area next to the Mouse Down property. What could Mouse Down mean? Does that mean the event of moving the mouse cursor south, or could it mean clicking the mouse button?

Press F1 to find out. Pressing F1 calls up context-sensitive help if appropriate, and it's surely appropriate now. Access responds with the help screen shown in Figure 20.14.

Reading this section doesn't help all that much. It only seems to confirm that you set this property to react to a Mouse Down or a Mouse Up event. Locate the underlined words Mouse Down or Mouse Up and move your mouse cursor to be over these words. Your cursor will change to look like a hand, as shown in Figure 20.14. Click once. Access Help jumps to the entry specifically defining these events, as shown in Figure 20.15.

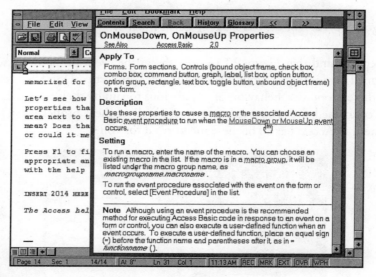

Figure 20.14. *The Access Help system working in context.*

Here in plain English is the explanation you needed. The Mouse Down event is when a person clicks the mouse button. The help system also explains how this event differs from the On Click event that it superficially resembles.

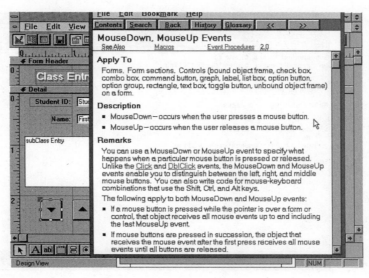

Figure 20.15. *The specific help you needed.*

Back to the Event Procedure

Close the help system for now, and see what an event procedure is like. With your screen like Figure 20.12, click in the entry area that now contains [Event Procedure], next to the On Click property. Access responds by showing two icons at the right side of the line—a combo box down arrow and an ellipsis (...). Click on the ellipsis. This action calls up the Access Basic code that runs when you click on this button. Your screen should resemble Figure 20.16.

The Access Way

Clicking on the ellipsis in this context brings up the code builder, where you can enter your own code or edit code already associated with the Event property. Access also has an expression builder that helps you build complex expressions.

At first blush this looks like some arcane and imposing foreign language. Although you obviously didn't need to know what this code does to create it, below is the same code, taken line by line with a short nontechnical explanation for each line. Like so many things that look complex at first, it's really quite simple when it's taken apart.

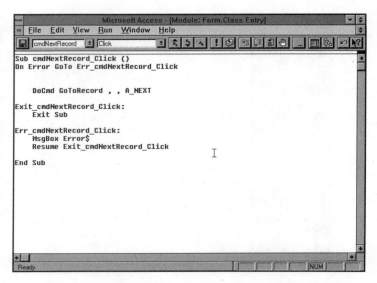

Figure 20.16. *The code attached to the On Click event of a command button.*

1. `Sub cmdNextRecord_Click ()`

   This line declares the start of a new sub or routine that's going to run when
   the cmdNextRecord control is clicked. Remember that you named your control
   cmdNextRecord at the end of the wizard process. Had you named your
   control cmdHelloThere, this line would read `Sub cmdHelloThere_Click ()`.

2. `On Error GoTo Err_cmdNextRecord_Click`

   This instructs the computer in the case of an error condition—which means
   something unforeseen has occurred—to jump down to the line
   `Err_cmdNextRecord_Click:` (line 6) and continue execution from there.

3. `DoCmd GoToRecord , , A_NEXT`

   DoCmd is the Access Basic code call to action. There are many actions, such as
   changing cursors, moving through records, opening and closing forms, and
   dozens of others. The two commas are placeholders for options unneeded by
   this On Click sub. The A_NEXT tells the GoToRecord command to go to the
   next record.

4. `Exit_cmdNextRecord_Click:`

   This is a label used as a location for code to jump to in case of errors. You can tell at a glance that it's a label since it ends with a colon (:). In this code fragment, line 8 will jump here if it does run.

5. `Exit Sub`

   Exit this routine.

6. `Err_cmdNextRecord_Click:`

   Another label. This is the place where line 2 jumps to if something goes awry. This entire section of code runs only in the case of an error condition.

7. `MsgBox Error$`

   Display the standard error message box.

8. `Resume Exit_cmdNextRecord_Click`

   After the message box closes, jump to line 4.

9. `End Sub`

   This signals Access that this code segment ends here.

Don't Worry

Don't be concerned if even with an explanation you don't feel confident about your understanding of this code. Remember, you programmed the cmdNextRecord command button without ever knowing a line of code. You did it once, you can do it again.

DO   DON'T

DO feel free to experiment with this code to see what changes you can make.

DON'T feel bad if what you do results in obscure complaints from Access. Just remember what you did so you can undo it. If things get totally out of hand, deleting the offending control from the form and then using the wizard to re-create it will put all things right again.

For now, close the code window if it's open and close the Class Entry form, saving changes.

Summary

Access controls have many different properties. Each item in Access has its own set of control properties. For example, the form itself has an On Resize property that makes sense for it, but doesn't apply or appear for the command button control.

Event properties describe how controls respond to certain events, such as being clicked or double-clicked over. One class of Event properties is the Event procedure. Event procedures are Access Basic code that activates when the Event property it's attached to occurs.

Control Wizards can save you a lot of programming headaches and, equally important, won't make any typographic errors when writing Access Basic code. Use the wizard if one exists for your purposes, to save a lot of time and possible grief.

Q&A

Q Can I attach more than one DoCmd action to an event?

A Yes. You can attach as many as you like.

Q If my common (or link) fields don't have the same name, can I still synchronize main and subforms?

A Yes. This is why the two properties Link Child Fields and Link Master Fields exist. You tell Access what the names of the link fields are here. Remember to use the field names as those names appear in the Properties list box. Don't use the caption or label for the fields in place of the name.

Q Can I use greater- or lesser-than operatives as filter criteria?

A Yes. The < and > operators, just like all the rest, work the same in filters as in queries. For example, Not "IL" returns all those records that don't have IL as their data.

Q Is there a list of all the actions I can do with DoCmd?

A Access's online help has all these actions grouped both by name and by function. Search on DoCmd.

Q How do I apply a sort without a filter to records shown in a form?

A Click on the Edit Filter/Sort button. Drag the field you want to sort on into the query design grid from the Field list box. Click on the Sort row in the column you dragged the field to. Pull down the combo box and choose Ascending or Descending from the short list.

Q Can I use my own pictures on button faces?

A Yes. You can use any program that can create an .ico (icon) or .bmp (Windows Paintbrush bitmap) file. Create your artwork, save it, then use the Browse button in the wizard to set the button's face with your creation. You can also set the button face by directly entering your file name in the Picture property of the button's Layout properties.

Workshop

Here's where you can test and apply the lessons you learned today.

Quiz

Possible answers to these questions are provided in Appendix A.

1. Are the types of control properties the same no matter what type the control?

2. How do you display only Data properties from the Properties list box?

3. You have a main and subform with a link field SSN. How do you tell Access to synchronize the main and subform using the SSN field?

4. How would the code line `Sub cmdNextRecord_Click ()` change if the event you wanted the sub for was called Clack?

5. Will the filter `Like "Ka"` let the name Kaplan through? What about Kramer? Will the filter `Like "Ka*"` let the name Kaplan through? What about Kramer?

Put Access into Action

1. Open the Class Entry form in Design View.

2. Make sure the Wizard button is selected in the Toolbox.

3. Place a command button on the Class Entry form at the right side, under the subform section.

4. Use the wizard to set this button's On Click property to an event procedure that will, when clicked, close the form. Hint: Look under Form Operations in the wizard.

5. Give the button a stop sign icon and name it `cmdExit`. Switch to Form View. Your screen should resemble Figure 20.17.

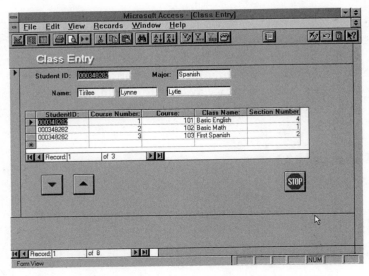

Figure 20.17. *The form with an Exit button added.*

6. Save the form by selecting the menu choices File|Save Form. Click on the button to see if it works.

11

M T R S

Morning

21 Fancy Form Layout

Afternoon

22 Expressions in Reports and Queries

21

Fancy Form Layout

This morning you'll learn

☐ How to clean up a form's look

☐ What tab order is and how to change it

☐ How to alter a subform's design

☐ How to use graphic elements in form design

☐ About form page layout considerations

Your Own Tools

Having record navigation tools both on the form and below it uses up extra space and makes little sense. The first exercise this morning extends the subject of control properties to eliminate this redundancy.

To review where you left off, glance at the Put Access into Action section of last chapter's Workshop. Exercise 21.1 uses the form Class Entry as modified by the exercise at the end of Chapter 20, "Instantly Smarter Forms," which added an Exit button to the form. If you want your screens to closely resemble those shown in *Teach Yourself Access 2 in 14 Days* and you haven't done the end exercise from Chapter 20, take time now to do it. The presence or lack of the Exit button on the form won't make any functional difference for the following exercises, but your screens won't look like the ones in the book if you don't add the button.

Exercise 21.1 demonstrates the use of record selectors and scroll bars in forms.

Exercise 21.1. Record selectors and navigation buttons.

1. Launch Access and open the College database if necessary. Click on the Form tab and open the Class Entry form in Design View. Your screen should resemble Figure 21.1.

   Look at the Property list box. The default view for this form is Single Form. This means that by default Access will only show one record at a time. This makes sense for this form because it includes a subform. There's no practical way to show many records bound to the main form and also show the records bound to the subform.

2. Click on the Datasheet View button in the toolbar. That's the one that is third from the left—just to the right of the Form View button. Your screen should resemble Figure 21.2.

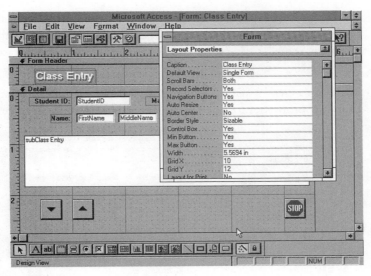

Figure 21.1. *A form ready for modification.*

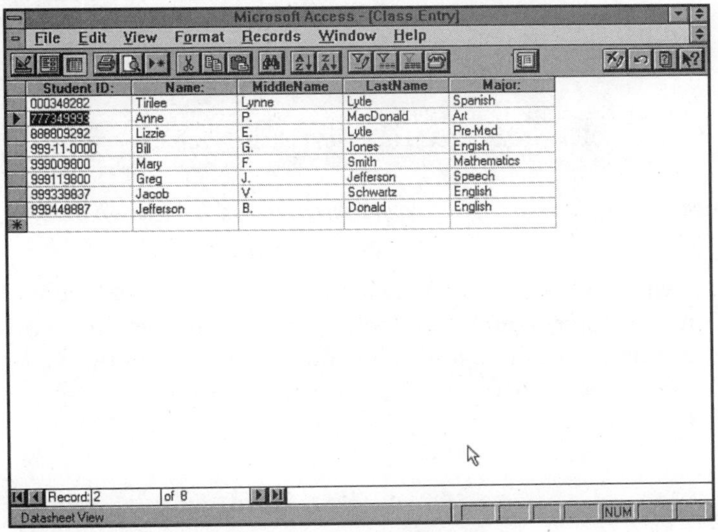

Figure 21.2. *The Class Entry form in Datasheet View.*

Viewing Class Entry in Datasheet View worked, but because all the class information is lost in this view, it doesn't make any sense to allow it. Additionally, it makes little sense to have record selectors for this form as only one record's ever going to show at one time.

3. Return to Design View. Change both the Record Selectors and Navigation Buttons properties to No. Your screen should resemble Figure 21.3.

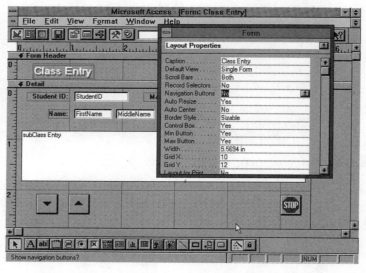

Figure 21.3. *Eliminating the record selectors and navigation buttons from a form.*

4. Switch to Form View. Your screen should resemble Figure 21.4. Notice how much cleaner your screen looks without record selectors or navigation buttons. There's no loss in function because the buttons added through the wizard yesterday replace the navigation buttons.

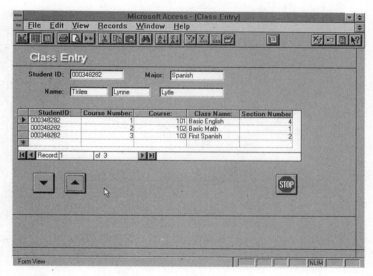

Figure 21.4. *The new, cleaner look for this form.*

Tab Order

Click in the StudentID control and press Tab four times. Normally, when you tab through a form you expect to move from left to right and then back to the far left and down. This is the way we read, and users expect forms to behave the same way. However in this case, the tab moves from the StudentID control to the FirstName, then to MiddleName, then to LastName, and then makes a disconcerting jump up to Major. Tab action such as this is sure to annoy users, so get ready to change it to a more intuitive pattern.

Exercise 21.2 shows how to alter the tab order in a form and eliminate controls from being in the tab order.

Exercise 21.2. Changing the tab order.

1. Starting where Exercise 21.1 ended, return to Design View. Click on the menu selections Edit|Tab Order. Your screen should resemble Figure 21.5.

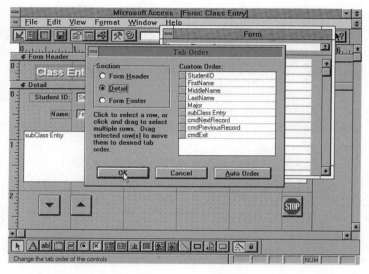

Figure 21.5. *The Tab Order list box.*

Figure 21.5 shows the Tab Order list box. This list box shows the order in which controls get focus when you tab through a form. By default Access places the first inserted control at the top of the Tab Order list box. The wizard that made this form placed the StudentID field first and the subform last. The work you did yesterday added three button controls to the end of the tab order. The only change needed at this point is to move the Major field to second in the tab order rather than its current place of fourth.

2. Click just to the left of the Major entry in the list box, on the gray area that looks like a record selector. Your screen should resemble Figure 21.6.

3. Click again on the now-pressed gray square. Your cursor should change to gain a box at its end, indicating that the cursor's in move mode. Continue to press your mouse button and drag the Major field up until it's just below the StudentID field. Release the mouse button. Your screen should resemble Figure 21.7. Click on OK to close the Tab Order list box and save your changes.

The Access Way

The technique for changing the order of controls in the Tab Order list box is the same as changing the order of almost anything in Access. It is a

bit tricky at first, but once you have the hang of it for any function (such as changing column order in a query), you have it made for them all.

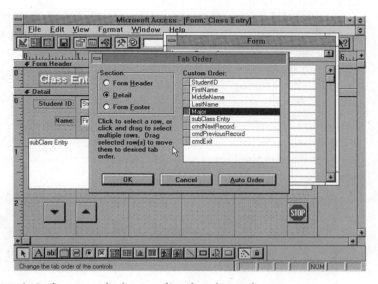

Figure 21.6. *Indicating which control's tab order to change.*

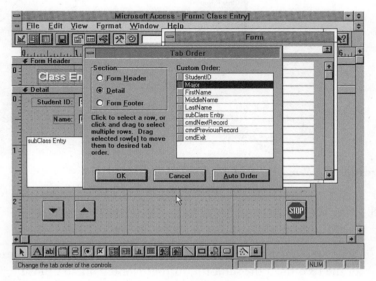

Figure 21.7. *Moving a field to change the tab order.*

4. Return to Form View and again click in the StudentID field. Again press Tab four times. Due to your efforts, the cursor now behaves like people expect it should.

   There's another important tab characteristic called Tab Stop. This property determines if a control ever gets focus when a form is tabbed through. The three command buttons should only need to be clicked by using the mouse, rather than tabbing to them and pressing Enter—the alternate way to activate the On Click property of a command button. Also, having these buttons in the tab order is inconvenient because they must be passed through when tabbing. In the case of the Exit button, you don't want your users accidentally tabbing to and pressing it.

5. Return to Design View. Select all the command buttons either through a marquee selection or by using the Shift+click method. Select Other for property types in the Property list box. Your screen should resemble Figure 21.8.

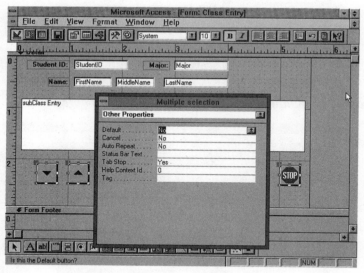

Figure 21.8. *Removing controls from the tab order.*

6. Alter the Tab Stop property to No. Return to Form View. Locate a record without many class entries, as shown in Figure 21.9.

   Start tabbing anywhere on the form. As soon as your cursor reaches the end of the records in the subform, further tabbing doesn't move it at all. There's no way to tab to the command buttons.

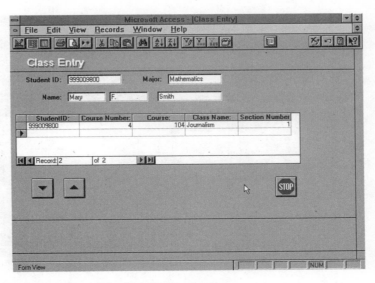

Figure 21.9. *The effect of the Tab Stop property.*

Take a look at how the Tab Stop property acts when set to No. Click on the cmdNextRecord button and press Tab. Instead of jumping to the cmdPreviousRecord button, Access jumped to the StudentID field in the next record. Access will not tab to any control with the Tab Stop property set to No.

7. Close this form, saving changes.

Modifying Subforms

While the main form is open in Design View, the subform's only available as a white rectangle. You can click on it to give it the highlight, but there's no way to alter the subform's properties other than those that relate to its functioning as a control in the main form. Additionally, there's no way to get to the subform's separate controls.

Exercise 21.3 shows how to alter the internal characteristics of a subform.

Exercise 21.3. Altering a subform.

1. From the Database View, locate the form subClass Entry. Open it in Design View. Your screen should resemble Figure 21.10.

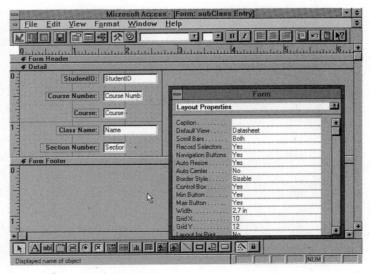

Figure 21.10. *The subform opened in Design View.*

You might be disconcerted to see that this form, which appears like a grid within the main form, has its fields stacked in the subform itself. Access changed the default view of this form to Datasheet View. Look at the Properties list box in Figure 21.10 and locate the Default View property. This property sets how the form appears when its host or main form is in Form View. It's now set to Datasheet View, which is a logical choice because the records bound to this form are on the many side of the one-to-many relationship.

2. Change the Navigation Buttons property to No and the Border Style property to Thin. Click in the form detail section on the StudentID field. This field is unnecessary and doesn't need to be displayed, so press the Del or Delete key on your keyboard to erase it from the subform.

3. Use a marquee or the Shift+click method to highlight all the remaining controls in the detail section of the form. Center them vertically in the detail section of the form. Move your cursor to just above the Form Footer bar until it changes to a bar with up- and down-facing arrows. Click and drag the detail section of the form until it's just large enough to accommodate the remaining fields. Your screen should resemble Figure 21.11.

4. Close this form, saving changes.

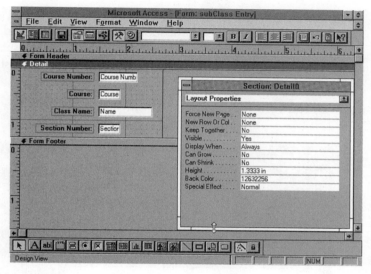

Figure 21.11. *Finishing up the changes to the subform.*

Your form now has a cleaner look after the elimination of the unnecessary controls.
From the Database View open the Class Entry form. Your screen should resemble
Figure 21.12.

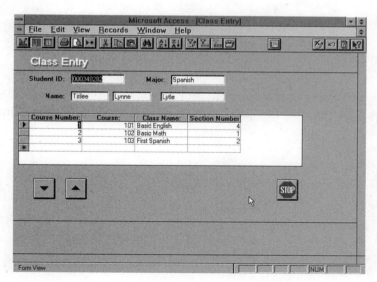

Figure 21.12. *The main form reflects the changes made in the subform.*

Right now there's too much white space surrounding the subform. This is the result of having shrunk the effective area of the subform by deleting the StudentID control. The main form has a container that was sized correctly for the subform when it included the StudentID control. This container wasn't automatically shrunk to fit the new needs of the subform.

Change to Design View and resize the subform's container. This operation is shown in Figure 21.13.

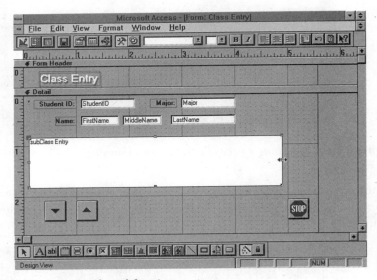

Figure 21.13. *Resizing the subform's container.*

Size the subform's container and move the main form's controls around until they look right given the new proportion of the subform. The finished form for this step is shown in Figure 21.14.

The Access Way

The easiest way to size a main form's subform container is to switch Snap to Grid off in the Layout menu. Then alternate small changes with many switches back and forth between Form and Design Views until you have the look you want.

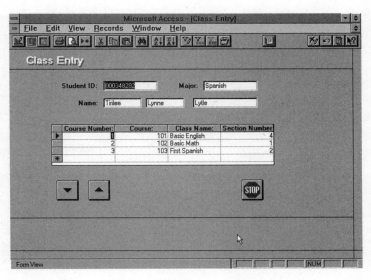

Figure 21.14. *The form reorganized for the new subform's size.*

Graphic Elements in Forms

Access gives you two graphic elements you can use to spruce up your forms—lines and rectangles. By changing the properties of these elements, you can radically alter their looks. Use these elements to isolate form controls into logical groupings, to enhance the aesthetic appeal of your forms, and to break your forms into sections.

The following exercise takes the rather barren-looking Class Entry form and gives it some fancy elements. It's up to you how ornate to make your forms. Remember, because you can embed any graphic in your form, you have no effective limit as to how elaborate you can be. The problem with forms containing too much frou-frou is that they might appear frivolous. Also, keep in mind your target audience. What's overly baroque for financial analysts might be overly stark for children.

Exercise 21.4 shows some uses for graphic elements in forms and how their properties affect their appearance.

Exercise 21.4. Graphic elements in forms.

1. Open the Class Entry form in Design View, or if it's already open, switch to Design View. Your screen should resemble Figure 21.15. Locate the Rectangle tool in the Toolbox. Refer to Figure 21.15 for help finding this tool.

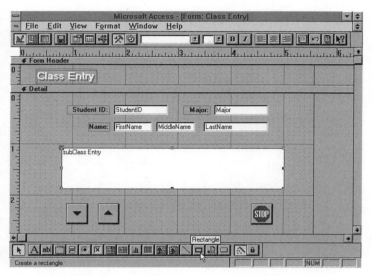

Figure 21.15. *Getting ready to add graphic elements to a form.*

2. Click on the Rectangle tool, then move your cursor to slightly above and left of the StudentID field label. Click and drag a rectangle starting above and left of StudentID and ending below and to the right of the LastName control. Your screen should resemble Figure 21.16.

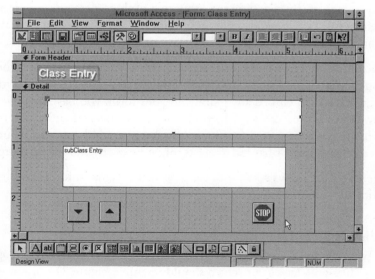

Figure 21.16. *Adding a rectangle to a form.*

Oops! The rectangle Access adds is a solid one. Because of this it covers rather than surrounds the previously incorporated controls. This isn't the desired effect, to say the least. The situation is easily corrected, however.

3. Click on the menu selections Format|Send to Back. This tells Access you want the rectangle in the background rather than the foreground. Your screen should resemble Figure 21.17.

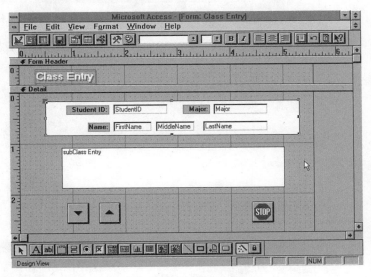

Figure 21.17. *Sending the rectangle to the background.*

4. Open the Palette and click on deep blue for the back color and 2 as the border width. Make sure the Special Effects setting is Normal. Your screen should resemble Figure 21.18.

Because *Teach Yourself Access 2 in 14 Days'* figures are in gray scale, Figures 21.18, 21.19, and 21.20 only approximate the look of the form with its added color.

5. The command button section of this form is separate in function from either of the other two sections, so let's set it apart visually. Locate the Line tool just to the right of the Rectangle tool in the Toolbox. Click on this tool. Move to the form's detail area and draw a horizontal line between the subform and the buttons, spanning the entire width of the form. Widen the form and extend the line so the line extends the entire horizontal length of the screen when in Form View. Getting this right might take some trial and error.

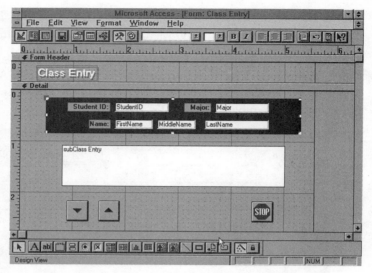

Figure 21.18. *Adding some fancy elements to the rectangle.*

6. In the Palette, click on deep blue as this line's color and 3 as its border width. Your screen should resemble Figure 21.19.

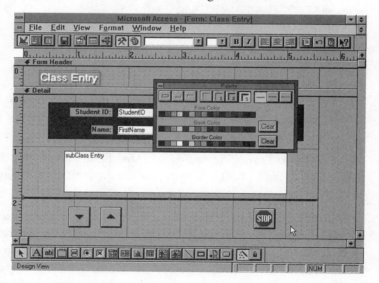

Figure 21.19. *Adding a line to a form.*

7. Switch to Form View. Your screen should resemble Figure 21.20.

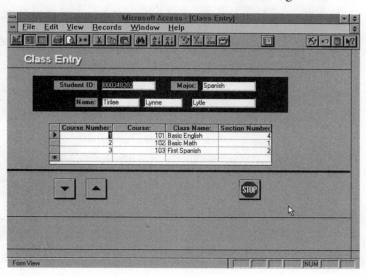

Figure 21.20. *The finished form.*

While hardly a work of art, this form does succeed at many design goals. It contains all the information needed by the registrar and Student Advisement, with nothing extra. People using the form won't be confused over excessive design elements, yet will clearly be able to determine the three separate form areas. Close this form, saving changes.

Page Layout Considerations

This form's only view is Single Form, so it doesn't make any difference where the command buttons appear. If this form were capable of being displayed as a series of continuous forms, each detail section would have its own command buttons, which just take up room with no added function. Figure 21.21 is the form from Figure 21.20, with the subform deleted and the view changed to Continuous Forms. This figure shows the command button duplication in Continuous Forms View.

The safe way to handle controls you want to see only once on a form is to locate them in the form header or footer sections. Figure 21.22 is the form from Figure 21.21, with the command buttons located in the form footer.

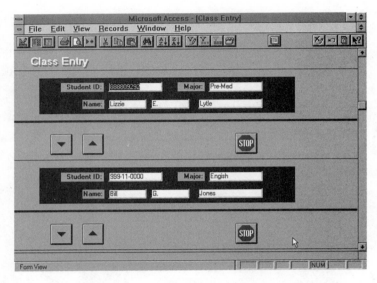

Figure 21.21. *Command buttons in the detail section don't work right in continuous forms.*

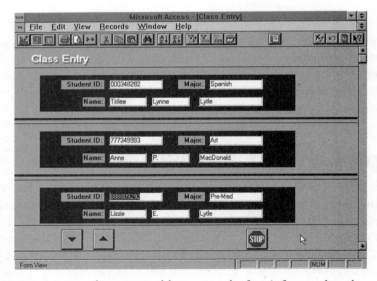

Figure 21.22. *Moving the command buttons to the form's footer solves the problem.*

Locating the command buttons in the form's footer recovers lost room and makes for a better form overall than locating them in the Detail section.

Morning Summary

By default, Access equips forms with a complete set of selectors, scroll bars, and navigation tools. In many cases you can delete one or all of these items. In doing so, you can simplify your forms, making more room for data display (if you're careful), without decreasing your form's functionality.

The tab order is the order in which controls get focus as you tab around your form. Access assigns tab order in the same order in which controls are placed on a form. You can change the tab order to one of your choosing. Additionally, you can leave a control out of the tab order by setting its Tab Stop property to No.

Creative use of lines and rectangles can highlight or separate sections of forms. Remember, you can assign lines and rectangles to be in the foreground or background, according to your needs.

21

22

Expressions in Reports and Queries

This afternoon you'll learn the following methods:

☐ How to create a complex query with an expression

☐ How to add a table to a query

☐ How to manually design a report

☐ How to group records in a report

☐ How to use expressions in reports

The Situation

You might have feared report cards when in school—or perhaps you're still in school and living in fear of report cards. This afternoon you get to design report cards for others.

At the end of each term, the instructors at the fictional college sit down at computers and call up a query that lists all the students that were in their classes the past semester. The instructors check a box indicating if the course was completed and, if so, enter a grade for the student. This information's entered in the Student's Current Courses table.

After the instructors have done their entry chores, the computer folk run a query that extracts those records from the Student's Current Courses table and puts the course information with the grades into a new table, Completed Courses. Figure 22.1 shows the Completed Courses table for the students at the fictional college.

The college tracks students' performances with a numerical scale where the highest grade one can get is 4.5 for an A+. This, times the number of units a course is worth, equals the entire weighted value grade for having taken that course. Figure 22.2 shows the link table, Grade Values, which, when used in a query, assigns a numerical value to the letter grade the instructors assign a student. Both Completed Courses and Grade Values are part of the sample data.

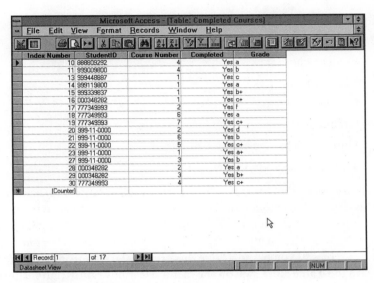

Figure 22.1. *The Completed Courses table.*

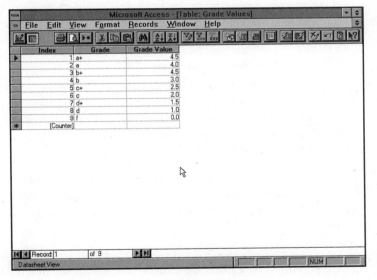

Figure 22.2. *The link table for calculating grade values.*

Before designing the report, you need a table or query to bind it to. No single table now holds all the information you need, which is the following:

Student name

Student address

Classes completed

Grades given

Unit values for the classes completed

Weighted values of grades

The first exercise this afternoon constructs a moderately complex query that contains all this data and a mathematical expression. This is a long exercise, but one that goes over some familiar ground. Prior to starting this exercise, make sure you have established a one-to-many relationship between the Student Personal and Completed Courses tables. If you haven't done this previously, start from the Database View and click on the Table tab. Click on the menu selections Edit|Relationships. Click on the Add Table button on the toolbar. Add the Completed Courses table to the Relationships grid. Drag your mouse from the StudentID field in Student Personal to the StudentID field in Completed Courses. Now you're ready for Exercise 22.1.

Exercise 22.1. Expressions in queries.

1. Launch Access and open the College database if necessary. Click on the Query tab. Click on the New button to start a new query. Click on the New Query button to bypass the wizards. Add the Student Personal, Completed Courses, and Available Classes tables to the query. Click on Close. Your screen should resemble Figure 22.3.

   Access knows there's a link between the Completed Courses and Student Personal because a one-to-many relationship has been established for these tables with Student Personal on the one side. So far, no relationship has been created that tells Access if any link exists between Completed Courses and Available Classes.

   The common or link fields are Course Number in Completed Courses and ClassID in Available Classes. It's up to you to manually tell Access of this link so it can synchronize records from both tables in this query.

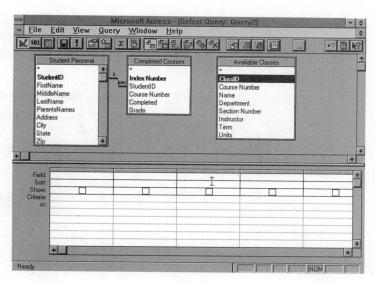

Figure 22.3. *The new query just starting.*

2. Click on the Course Number field in Completed Courses as shown in Figure 22.4.

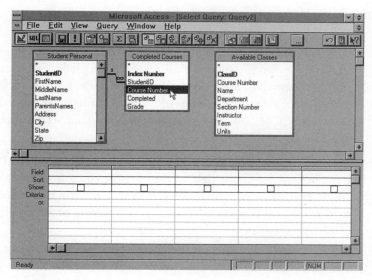

Figure 22.4. *Showing Access one link field.*

3. Click and hold your mouse over the highlighted field. Without letting go of the mouse button, drag your cursor until it's over the ClassID field in the Available Classes list box. Release the mouse button. Your screen should resemble Figure 22.5.

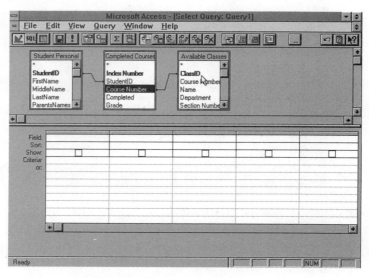

Figure 22.5. *Manually establishing a link.*

4. There's something missing. The Completed Courses table has the grades themselves, but not the numerical value for the grades. That's located in the Grade Values table. Click on the Add Table button in the toolbar to bring up the Add Table list box. The Add Table button is the one with the yellow cross. Click on the Grade Values table. Your screen should resemble Figure 22.6.

5. Click on the Add button to add it to the query. Close the Add Table list box. Click on the Grade field in the Completed Courses list box and drag a link to the Grade field in Grade Values, just like you did in Step 3. To make better sense of this query, rearrange your screen to resemble Figure 22.7.

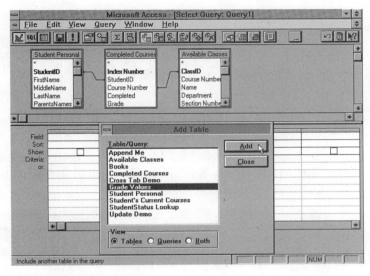

Figure 22.6. *Adding a table to a query.*

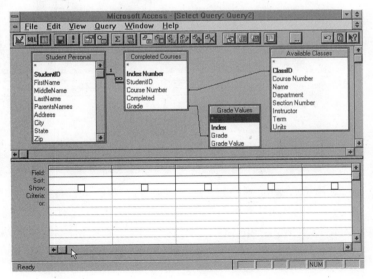

Figure 22.7. *Linking the new table to the query.*

The Access Way

Access can figure out query relationships even if the join lines extend behind table list boxes, but leaving things arranged this way can confuse the humans using Access. When constructing queries, try to arrange your join lines so they don't run behind the table list boxes.

6. Drag the StudentID, FirstName, MiddleName, LastName, Address, City, State, and Zip fields from the Student Personal to the query design grid. Your screen should resemble Figure 22.8.

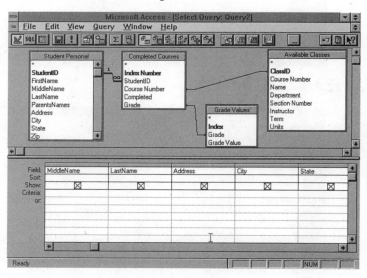

Figure 22.8. *Including the fields from the first table.*

7. Drag the Course Number, Name, and Units fields from the Available Classes table to the next columns in the query design grid. Your screen should resemble Figure 22.9.

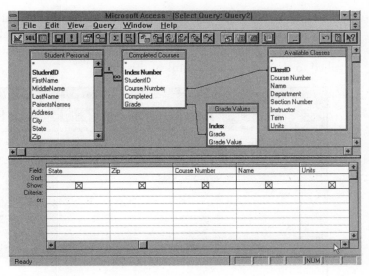

Figure 22.9. *Adding fields from the second table.*

8. Add the Grade field from the Completed Courses table and the Grade Value field from the Grade Values table to the query design grid. Your screen should resemble Figure 22.10.

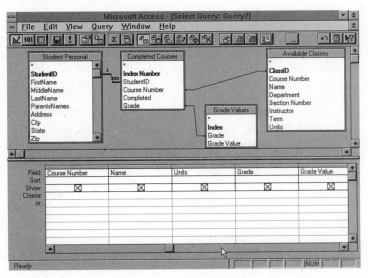

Figure 22.10. *Adding fields from the last two tables into the query.*

9. Scroll back to the StudentID field, click in the sort row for this field, and choose Ascending for a sort order. Run your query now to make sure it's running properly. Figure 22.11, which shows this query running, has been scrolled to show the last columns of this query.

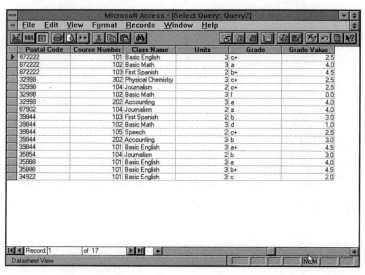

Figure 22.11. *The running query.*

There's one more thing to do. This query shows the unit values for each class finished, the grade, and the grade value, but not the weighted value the student gets credit for. That value is called the Weighted Value and is the Units times the Grade Value. You need to calculate that also.

10. Return to Design View and scroll until you see an empty column to the right of the Grade Value field. Click in that field and press Shift+F2 to enter Zoom. Enter Weighted Value: [Units]*[Grade Value] in the Zoom box. Your screen should resemble Figure 22.12.

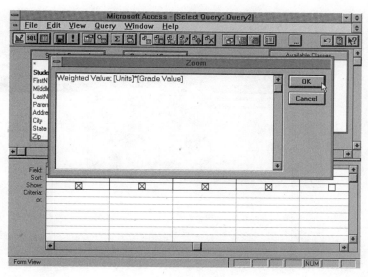

Figure 22.12. *An expression to do calculations in a query.*

11. Click on OK to close Zoom. Run the query again. Close and save this query as `Report Cards`.

After finishing Exercise 22.1, you have a query that report cards can be based on. This is the first step needed for the finished report cards report. Exercise 22.2 picks up where 22.1 left off. Designing the actual report cards report would be easier using a wizard to do some of the work, but Exercise 22.2 doesn't use one, so you can learn some important details about report design. This exercise manually creates a grouped report with several expressions and a secondary sort order.

Exercise 22.2. Grouping and sorting in reports.

1. Click on the Report tab to move to the reports section of your database. Click on the New button to start a new report. Choose Report Cards as the query to bind to this report. Your screen should resemble Figure 22.13.

2. Click on the Blank Report button. Access moves you into the report design grid. Increase the vertical width of the page header area to about 1.5 inches to give you some working room. Click on and drag the StudentID field from the Field list box to the page header area. Your screen should resemble Figure 22.14.

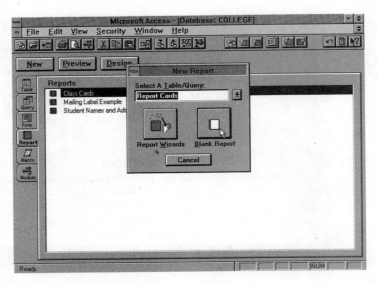

Figure 22.13. *Starting the new report.*

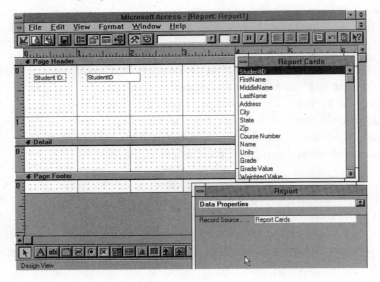

Figure 22.14. *Starting to place fields in a report.*

This report will have a student's ID, name, and address in the page header area, details about courses completed and grades given in the detail area, and, when finished tomorrow, summary information in the group footer area. The page header will also act as an address for windowed envelopes.

3. Create an expression for the student's name by inserting an unbound text box right below the StudentID field. Delete the label for this field. Enter the expression shown in Figure 22.15 for a Control Source for this unbound field. Figure 22.15 shows the Control Source property line in Zoom mode.

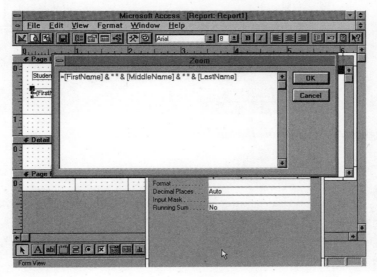

Figure 22.15. *Inserting an expression in a text box.*

4. Add the Address field right below the unbound text field containing the student's name. Delete this field's label. Add another unbound text field below the address and enter the expression shown in Figure 22.16 in it as a control source. Delete this field's label as well.

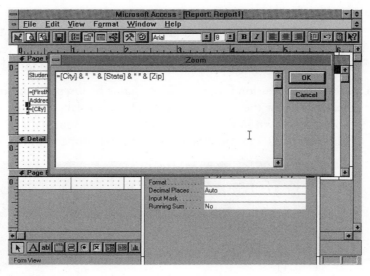

Figure 22.16. *Making the third line of the address.*

Note: Report designing is a skill acquired over time. Rather than finish your report only to find something at the start has gone awry, switch back and forth between Design and Sample or Print Preview Views to see your progress and to catch any misdirection early.

5. These next two steps are a little tricky. You want the course information for each student in the detail section of the form, but the labels for the course information in the page header. This prevents repeating these labels for each course the student has completed. Drag the fields Course Number, Name, and Grade onto the Detail section of the form. Using either a marquee or Shift+click, highlight only the labels for these fields. Your screen should resemble Figure 22.17.

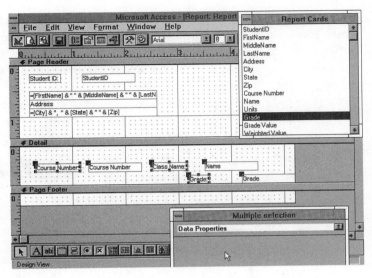

Figure 22.17. *Moving the field labels to the page header.*

6. Press Ctrl+X to cut these fields to the Clipboard. Click in the Page Header section of the report design grid. Press Ctrl+V to paste the label fields into this section of the report. Arrange all the fields so they resemble Figure 22.18.

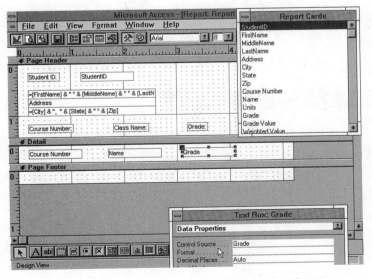

Figure 22.18. *Placing proper elements in the header and detail sections.*

7. You need to tell Access to group the details of the courses completed and grades given according to StudentID. Click on the Sorting and Grouping button in the toolbar. Click in the first column of the list box that pops up and enter or scroll to StudentID as a field to group on. Access will, by default, add the Ascending value to the Sort Order column. Make sure the Group On and Keep Together properties are set to Each Value and Whole Group respectively, as shown in Figure 22.19. Click on the Sorting and Grouping button in the toolbar again to close the list box.

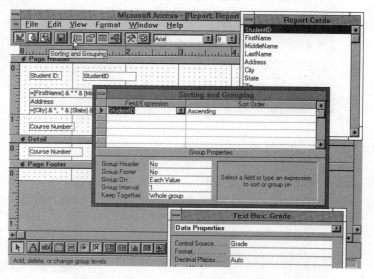

Figure 22.19. *Creating a sorted grouping for the report.*

DO   **DON'T**

DO make sure you group on unique values from your dataset.

DON'T make the mistake of assuming values are unique when they're not. For example, grouping on LastName might seem all right for this dataset, but in fact there are two Lytles in it, making that grouping invalid.

At this point it's a good idea to check the progress of this report. Click on the Sample Preview button to see how the report's coming along. Your screen should resemble Figure 22.20.

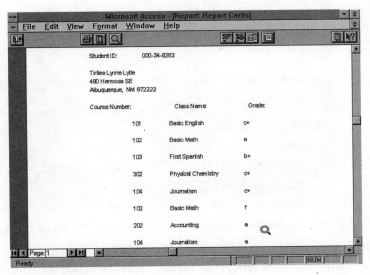

Figure 22.20. *The report still needs some work.*

Well, that's not exactly what we had planned. This report seems to attach all the completed courses to one student, Tirilee Lytle. Actually, this report does have the courses grouped by student, but it lacks the breaks necessary to make that obvious.

8. Return to Design View. Open the Sorting and Grouping list box by clicking on the Sorting and Grouping button in the toolbar. Add a group header and footer section for StudentID. Additionally, add Course Number as the second criterion on the second row of the list box. Your screen should resemble Figure 22.21.

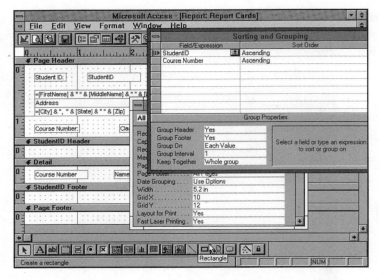

Figure 22.21. *Creating a secondary sort order and adding group headers and footers.*

Try switching to Print Preview View again. Your screen should resemble Figure 22.22.

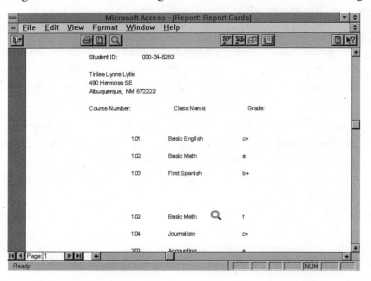

Figure 22.22. *The groups are now visible.*

The only thing necessary to finish this report's basic structure is to break the report's page on each group and add the right header to the groups.

9. Return to Design View. Click in the StudentID Header section to make it current. Open the Properties list box and locate the Force New Page property under Layout Properties. Change this property from None to Before Section. Your screen should resemble Figure 22.23.

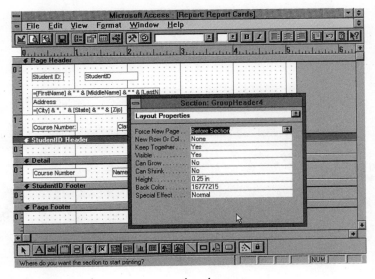

Figure 22.23. *Forcing the report to page break on groups.*

Click on the Print Preview button in the toolbar. Access has it right. The courses completed by each student are grouped with the student's personal information, the courses are sorted according to course number, and each student's personal and course information is contained on a single page.

Close this report, saving it with the name Report Cards. The report's still not quite ready for prime time as it lacks grade point calculations and is a little confusing to read. These problems are addressed in an exercise in Chapter 23.

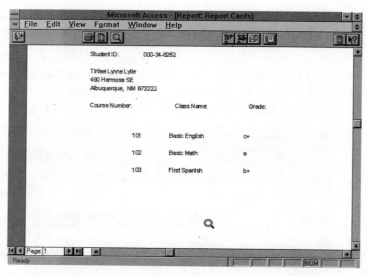

Figure 22.24. *The first record of the grouped report.*

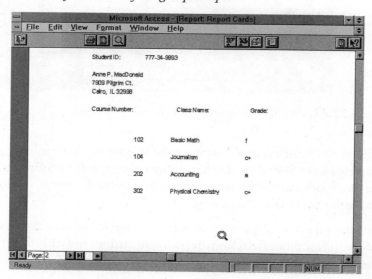

Figure 22.25. *The second record of the grouped report.*

Summary

Access can spruce up a report or a form by using lines and rectangles to highlight and separate report or form sections. Access assigns a tab order to controls based on the order they were placed on a form. You can change the tab order by altering the Tab Order list box and leave controls off the tab order by altering their Tab Stop property.

Access has no trouble creating a query from many tables. The report card query required four to work right and also needed an Expression field. You create Expression fields in a query by adding `Field Name:[Expression]` to an otherwise empty column in the query design grid. Field Name is the name you want to appear at the top of the column and the expression is any valid Access expression. Be sure to end your field name with a colon (:).

The first field placed in the Grouping and Sorting box while in report Design View is the field Access will group on. Subsequent fields placed in this box are fields to sort on within a group. Access's grouping isn't particularly apparent unless you break the groups with a group header, group footer, or both. If you want your groups one to a page, you have to set the group's Force Page Break property to anything other than None, the default.

Q&A

Q How can I set the page size for my reports?

A Use the Print Setup dialog boxes in the File menu to change the defaults. Remember, Access's wizards use these defaults when making a report. If your wizard made reports that seem to be aimed at bizarre paper sizes, the fault's in the Print Setup settings under the File menu selection.

Q Can I calculate on a calculated field in a query?

A Yes. Look at Figure 22.26. This shows a field called Demo added to the Report Cards query that performs a calculation on a calculated field: Weighted Value.

22

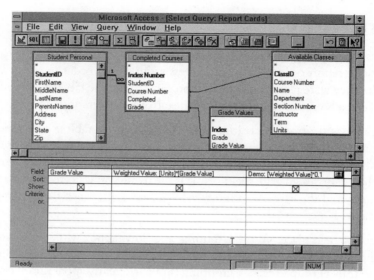

Figure 22.26. *A calculation on another calculation.*

When run, the Demo field calculates and returns 10% of the value calculated in the Weighted Value field. Refer to Figure 22.27 to see the results of running the Report Cards query with the Demo field.

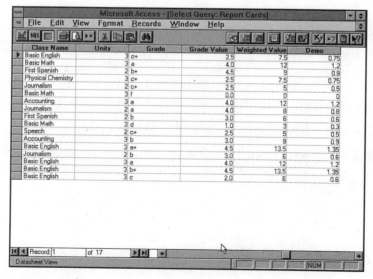

Figure 22.27. *Running the modified query.*

Q Could I have put the labels for Course Number, Name, and Grade in the group header band?

A Yes, and your results would have been effectively identical to those in Exercise 22.2. Your method is actually better, but due to the flow of the exercise, the headers for the detail band were placed in the Page Header band.

Q Can I do calculations in reports?

A Yes. That subject's coming up tomorrow morning.

Q Could I have created a report with a subreport like I did in forms?

A Yes, and the method is almost identical. Access gives you many ways to get to the same place. For example, the calculation done in the Report Cards query could have been done in the report itself.

Workshop

Here's where you can test and apply the lessons you learned today.

Quiz

Possible answers to these questions are provided in Appendix A.

1. What's the significance of the colon in the query column label Weighted Value:?

2. How often will a label in the Report Header band print in a report?

3. Refer to the Report Cards query. If the expression `Name:[FirstName]&" "&[LastName]` were entered in a column's Field row, would it be valid?

4. Does the StudentID field need to appear on a report for the report to group on it?

5. Refer to Figure 22.21. What icon does Access use to distinguish the grouping field from a sort within the group field?

Put Access into Action

1. Use a wizard to create a report that groups on courses and includes all the students signed up for those courses.

2. Add the names of the students' parents to the report.

3. Sort on the students' parents' names within each group.

4. Alter the report to make each class print out on a separate piece of paper.

5. Save this report if you choose to. *Teach Yourself Access 2 in 14 Days* does not come back or refer to it.

Day

12

23

Complex Reports

This morning you'll learn

☐ How to enter calculation expressions in reports

☐ How Access evaluates expressions

☐ How to create better report layouts

☐ How to create dynamic report controls

Calculations in Reports

Yesterday's report saved as Report Cards does several things needed for the fictional college.

Refer to Figure 23.1, which shows the Report Cards report in Print Preview. This report does the following:

Groups the completed classes with the right student

Puts students' personal information and completed courses on discrete pages

Reports the completed courses by name and letter grade

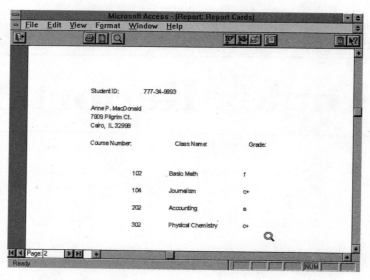

Figure 23.1. *The Report Cards report.*

This is fine, but more information is needed. The first three additional things the college needs from this report are a student's completed course load, a student's unadjusted grade point average (GPA) for this term, and the Weighted Value GPA for the courses taken. The way to have the report show these things is to place an unbound text field where you want these figures to print (or appear) and then enter an expression to calculate these values.

> **The Access Way**
>
> The exercises in this chapter might seem a bit irrelevant to business users of Access, but the principles shown this morning can be applied to calculating order totals, salesperson average sales, or any other calculation not done in a bound table or query.

Exercise 23.1 demonstrates how to create calculations in reports. The technique shown is identical to the technique used for forms. All the material in this exercise applies to forms also.

Exercise 23.1. Calculation expressions in reports.

1. Launch Access and open the College database if necessary. Open the Report Cards report in Design View. Your screen should resemble Figure 23.2.

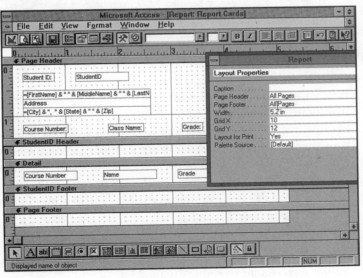

Figure 23.2. *The report in Design View.*

The first thing to do with this report is to calculate the entire course load completed. This is simply the sum of the units from the Report Card query. This and other calculations will appear in the group footer band.

2. Widen the group footer band to give yourself some working room. Refer to Figure 23.3. Add an unbound text box control to the StudentID group footer band. Edit the label for this unbound text control to read Units Completed. Your screen should resemble Figure 23.3.

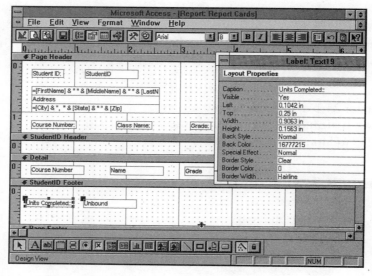

Figure 23.3. *Adding the unbound control.*

Access can do calculations using any field in the bound query or table, not just those showing in the report. In this way reports are similar to queries because queries can filter, sort, or use criteria based on fields not included or showing in the query. The following step uses the Access built-in function SUM() to calculate the sum of units taken. Access knows you want the sum of units for a group based on StudentID and not the entire mass of students because the SUM() expression is in the StudentID group footer band rather than the report footer band.

3. Switch so Data properties are listed in the Properties list box. Edit the Control Source property for the unbound text box to read =sum([Units]). Your screen should resemble Figure 23.4.

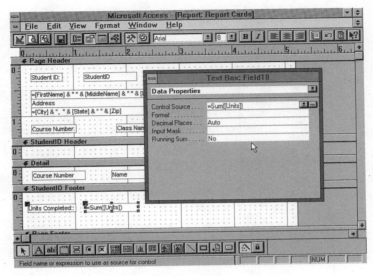

Figure 23.4. *Inserting the built-in function SUM( ).*

4. Edit the Name for this unbound control to read txtTotal. Switch to Print Preview View. Your screen should resemble Figure 23.5.

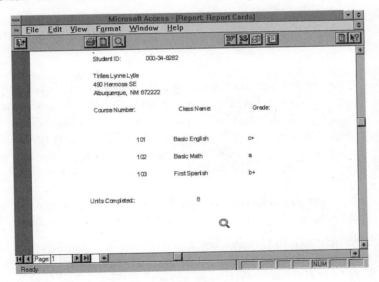

Figure 23.5. *The report now calculates totals.*

Refer to Figure 23.6, which is the query Report Card running with the Units column moved next to the LastName column. Check to make sure Access is calculating the correct number of units for each student. In this case, it is.

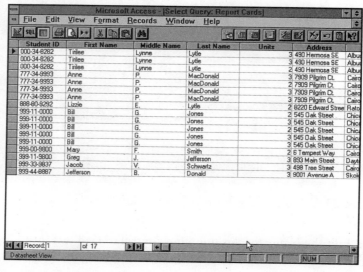

Figure 23.6. *Double-checking for accuracy.*

Note: Access is a computer program. As such, it's incapable of making math errors, but you can enter the wrong expression, which Access will correctly calculate to yield the wrong answer. Always check Access's output against known data before committing critical applications to the computer. This applies to any computer program, not just to Access.

The next step is to calculate the Raw GPA for this term. This is simply the nonweighted average of the Grade Values for courses taken.

5. Switch back to Design View and enter a new unbound text box right below the txtTotal one. Edit its Name to read txtRawGPA, its label to read Raw Term GPA. Enter =Avg([Grade Value]) as the Control Source property for this control. Your screen should resemble Figure 23.7.

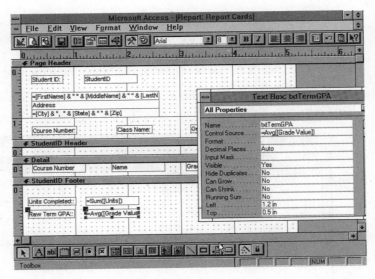

Figure 23.7. *Calculating an average value for a group.*

Again switch back to Print Preview mode to check to see if the report's doing the calculations correctly. Refer to Figure 23.8.

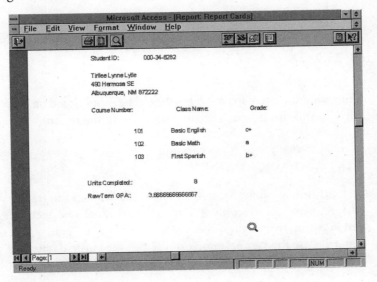

Figure 23.8. *Checking Access's output.*

Things look all right at first glance. However, closer examination reveals a problem. In this example, Tirilee Lytle has a *c*+, an *a*, and a *b*+. This means Access should be calculating the average of 2.5, 4.0, and 3.5. The correct answer is 3.33, but Access has 3.66! Something's awry for sure.

6. Take a look at Figure 23.9. This is the Grade Value table, which serves as a lookup to match the letter grade with the grade value.

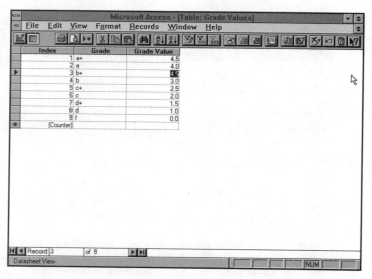

Figure 23.9. *The lookup table.*

Examine the entry for *b*+. This should be 3.5, but a data entry error has it 4.5, and this is what's causing the error in the report.

The Access Way

An error in a foundation table such as this lookup for grade values can have severe repercussions throughout your database. Access has no way of knowing that 4.5 was the wrong entry for a *b*+ grade. Access would merrily use this wrong value throughout the entire database if left unchecked.

7. Open your Grade Values table by pressing F11 to enter the Database View, clicking on the Table tab, and opening the Grade Values table in Datasheet mode. Edit the *b+* entry to include the correct value of 3.5 and close the table. Return to the Report Cards report, still in Print Preview View.

Access updates the queries when they're run or when a form or report bound to them calls them by switching into Print, Sample, or Print Preview mode. Close this report, saving changes if prompted to do so. Open it again in Print Preview mode. Access reruns the query and now the correct value is reported in your report. Your screen should resemble Figure 23.10.

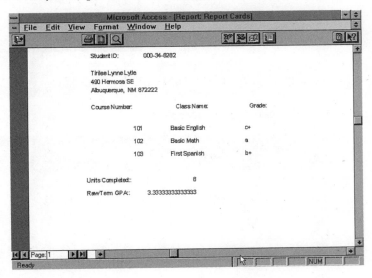

Figure 23.10. *Opening a report updates the bound query.*

The correct value's now in the Raw Term GPA field, but it looks a little long and overly precise for this field.

8. Return to Design View. Locate the Format property in the list box. Click next to this field and pull down the combo box. Locate the Fixed property and click on it. Your screen should resemble Figure 23.11.

9. Return to Print Preview mode to see the effect of altering the Format property. Your screen should resemble Figure 23.12.

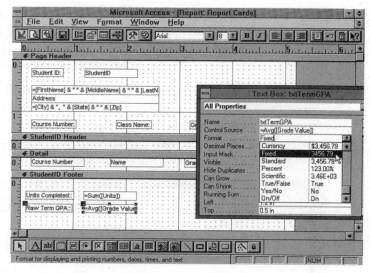

Figure 23.11. *Formatting a number field.*

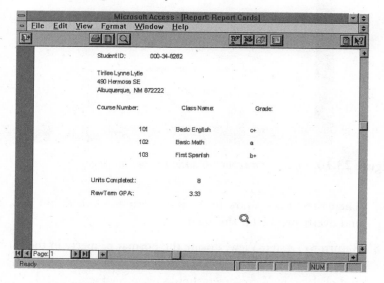

Figure 23.12. *The effect of setting the Format property.*

That's more like it. The final thing to add as a calculation is the Weighted Value GPA. The Weighted Value GPA is the sum of the Weighted Values, divided by the total units completed.

10. Return to Design View. Add a new unbound text box to the StudentID group footer band. Edit its label to read `Weighted Value GPA`. Enter `=(Sum([Weighted Value]))/(Sum([Units]))` for a Control Source for this control. You might want to enter Zoom by pressing Shift+F2 to enter this long expression. Edit the Name to read `txtWeightedGPA` and change the Format property to Fixed. Arrange your fields to resemble Figure 23.13.

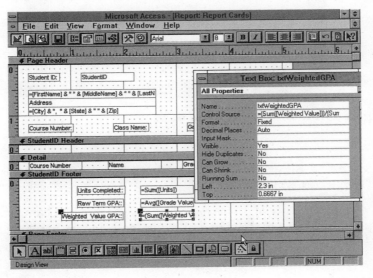

Figure 23.13. *Entering a complex expression.*

Switch to Print Preview mode. Figure 23.14 shows the Report Cards report with the modifications done in this exercise and with the fields slightly adjusted for alignment.

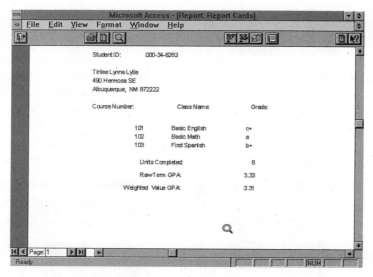

Figure 23.14. *The fully functional report.*

The Access Way

Avoid using circular expressions. This occurs when you have the input of expression B set to the output of expression A and the input of expression A set to the output of expression B. Setting up such references will result in infinite regression—something worth avoiding.

How Access Evaluates Expressions

Access uses the standard algebraic hierarchy to evaluate expressions. Take the following expression:

```
6 + 3 * 4 = ?
```

If you add 6 + 3 and then multiply by 4, the answer is 36. If you multiply 3 * 4 and then add the 6, the answer is 18. Which is right? Well, there is no right answer unless you tell Access what you want. In this case Access does the multiplication first and then the addition because it adheres to the standard algebraic hierarchy, which says do calculations in the following order:

1. Exponential

2. Multiplication

3. Division

4. Addition

5. Subtraction

These words form the acronym EMDAS. The mnemonic for remembering this is "Eeks—My Dear Aunt Sally!" If you want Access to evaluate expressions out of the standard hierarchy, enclose your expressions in parentheses. For example:

```
(6 + 3) * 4 = 36
```

and

```
6 + 3 * 4 = 18
```

Expressions within parentheses are always evaluated first and separately. The expression from Exercise 23.1, `=(Sum([Weighted Value]))/(Sum([Units]))`, uses parentheses to make sure each sum is evaluated first, and only then is the division done. This is, strictly speaking, unnecessary here because these particular expressions aren't sensitive to order. The placing of the parentheses is just a good habit, like enclosing all control names in square brackets.

23

DO	**DON'T**

DO create expressions in queries for values needed in the queries.

DON'T create expressions in queries for values needed only in the bound forms or reports. The Report Cards report violates this rule by including the Weighted Value expression in a query. The reason for the violation was to demonstrate technique, not to show the right way to create a report.

Layouts for Reports

At the end of Exercise 23.1, the Report Cards report is functionally all right, but not very attractive. The method for adding layout elements to a report is identical to that for forms. There is the possibility of more bands in a report, which adds slightly more complexity, but is nothing overwhelming.

Exercise 23.2 adds some graphics to the Report Cards report.

Exercise 23.2. Graphic elements in reports.

1. Starting where Exercise 23.1 leaves off, return to Design View. Rearrange your report controls to resemble Figure 23.15.

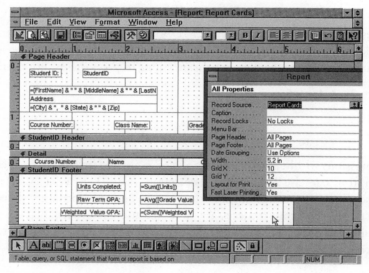

Figure 23.15. *Getting ready to add graphics to a report.*

2. Add a rectangle over the controls in the StudentID group footer area. Send it to the back by clicking on the Format|Send to Back menu selections. Your screen should resemble Figure 23.16.

3. Add underlines to the column titles in the Page Header area. Open the Palette and increase these lines to width 2. Your screen should resemble Figure 23.17.

4. Change the alignment for the Course Number and Grade text boxes to Center. Switch to Print Preview. Your screen should resemble Figure 23.18.

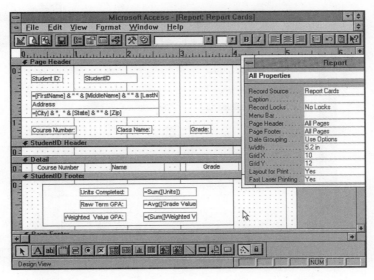

Figure 23.16. *Adding a box to a report.*

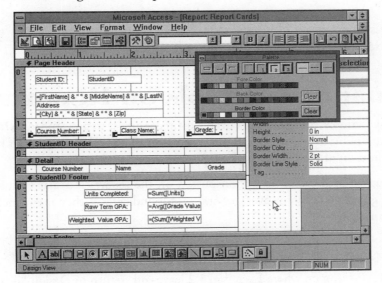

Figure 23.17. *Adding lines to column heads in a report.*

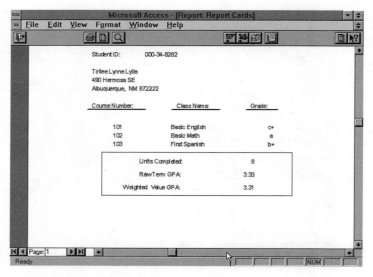

Figure 23.18. *The report with graphic elements.*

This report now is a bit easier to read. It's still not anyone's idea of a work of art, but its sections are at least set off from each other.

Dynamic Controls on Reports

The fictional college awards dean's list recognition to any student with a weighted grade point average over 3.1 for a semester. The registrar wants to have a visible indication of this award on the report card.

Exercise 23.3 places an option button on the report card that evaluates students' weighted grade point averages and visibly indicates if they merit inclusion in the dean's list.

Exercise 23.3. A dynamic control.

1. Picking up where Exercise 23.2 leaves off, return to Design View. Your screen should resemble Figure 23.19.

2. Place an unbound option button control in the StudentID footer rectangle just to the right of the previously placed fields. You might have to enlarge your rectangle to accommodate this new control. Edit the label for the new option button to read `Dean's List`. Orient the control and its label to resemble Figure 23.20.

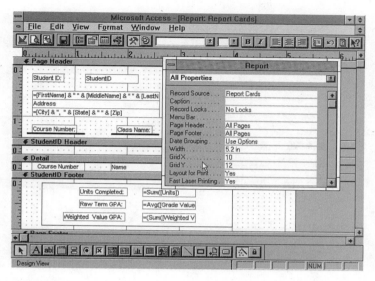

Figure 23.19. *Getting ready to place a dynamic control on the form.*

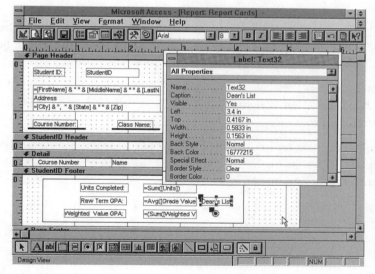

Figure 23.20. *Adding the dynamic control.*

3. Click on the control portion of the new control. Locate the Name field in the Properties list box and name this control `optDeansList`. Locate the Control Source property and enter the expression `=[txtWeightedGPA]>3.1`. Your screen should resemble Figure 23.21.

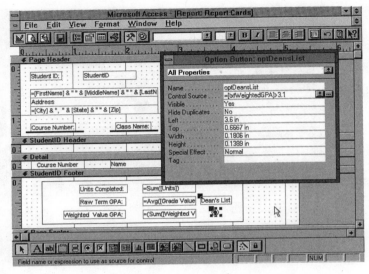

Figure 23.21. *Programming the dynamic control.*

This expression tells Access to examine the txtWeightedGPA field, and if the value of that field exceeds 3.1, change the value of the option button to True. Otherwise the option button's value is False.

Switch to Print Preview. Take a look at Tirilee Lytle's report card, shown in Figure 23.22. Because her Weighted GPA is 3.31, it's above 3.1 and the Dean's List option button is set to True.

Scroll to the next record, the one for Anne MacDonald. Anne didn't do too well this term, as shown in Figure 23.23. Because her Weighted GPA is less than 3.1, her Dean's List option button is set to False.

Close this report, saving changes.

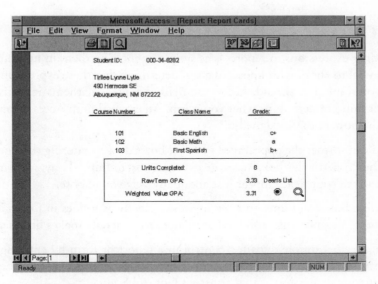

Figure 23.22. *A report card rating dean's list status.*

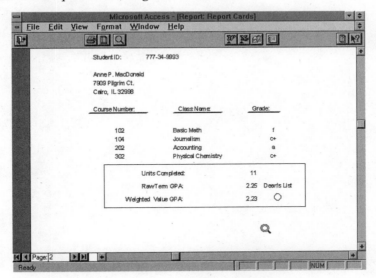

Figure 23.23. *A report card failing to meet dean's list status.*

Morning Summary

Adding expressions to reports is as simple as entering them in unbound text boxes. It's vital to check with known data to determine that these expressions are working as you think they should. Access can neither make a mathematical mistake nor read your mind to determine what you mean. An expression in Access is only as accurate as the human that designed it.

You can format the appearance of a text box's data by altering the Format property in the Properties list box. Access gives you almost unlimited ways to format fields. You can make your fields appear just about any way you choose.

Adding boxes and lines to a report works exactly as it does in forms. Because most printers are gray scale, using color in a report generally makes little sense.

You create a simple dynamic control in a report or form by entering an unbound control to the report—usually a check box or option button—and then entering an evaluating expression as that control's Control Source.

24

Introduction
to Macros

This afternoon you'll learn

- [ ] What a macro is
- [ ] What three programming languages Access supports
- [ ] What Structured Query Language (SQL) is
- [ ] How to use the macro design grid
- [ ] How to make simple macros
- [ ] How to make a switchboard form

Macros

A macro, as far as Access is concerned, is a simple programming language that enables you to automate certain tasks. Fundamentally, a macro is a series of actions executed either linearly in response to an event or upon certain conditions being met after an event. Like so many computer topics, macros are simpler to understand after you've seen one or two in action than in the pure abstraction of text.

You can use macros for many tasks. Some of the more common uses of macros are

- [ ] Programming buttons to do a series of actions such as opening or closing forms
- [ ] Setting or removing filters or sort orders in forms and reports
- [ ] Changing the properties or values of controls during runtime
- [ ] Helping ensure accurate data entry by watching the data entered and advising the data entry people of any errors they're making
- [ ] Automating tasks that you do often

Access's Three Programming Languages

Access supports three programming languages: Access Basic, macros, and Structured Query Language. Structured Query Language, used mostly in queries, is often abbreviated to SQL—pronounced "seekel" or "sequel." Actually, every query you construct by example using the query design grid is "backed up" by SQL. Take a look at Figure 24.1. This is the Report Cards query's SQL code.

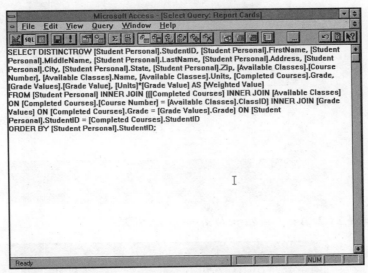

Figure 24.1. *The SQL code from a query.*

To see the SQL code that makes up a query, enter Design View for a query and click on the SQL button in the toolbar. If you chose to, you could construct an Access query using native SQL rather than the query design grid, which uses a technique called QBE (Query By Example). Few people use native SQL within Access since QBE is much easier.

Take a look at the very simple query shown in Design View in Figure 24.2.

This query contains the two fields StudentID and FirstName from Student Personal and returns only the FirstName because the box under StudentID is unchecked. Figure 24.3 is the query running and Figure 24.4 is the SQL that makes up this query.

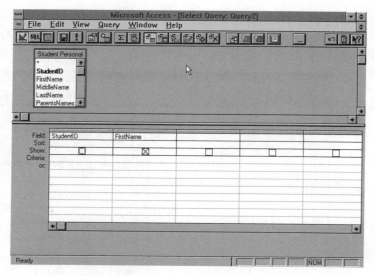

Figure 24.2. *A simple query to demonstrate SQL.*

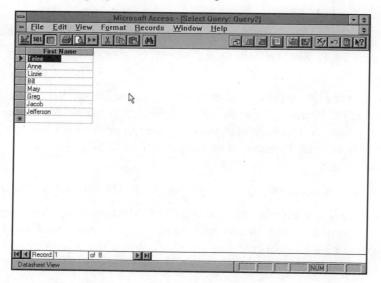

Figure 24.3. *The simple query in action.*

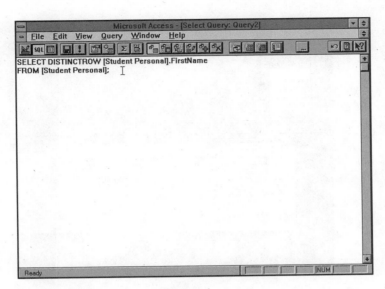

Figure 24.4. *The SQL code behind the simple query.*

If you give it a moment's thought, the SQL code isn't particularly difficult to understand except for that odd construction: SELECT DISTINCTROW. The SELECT part means choose for extraction, which is what queries do. The DISTINCT means not to pull duplicate records from the queried table. The ROW portion means to evaluate the entire row to determine duplicate records. The balance of the SQL code says display the FirstName field in Student Personal from the Student Personal table.

Criteria in SQL comes from the WHERE statement. Look at Figure 24.5, the query design grid with a criterion added. Now look at Figure 24.6, the same query's SQL, and note the change from Figure 24.4.

24

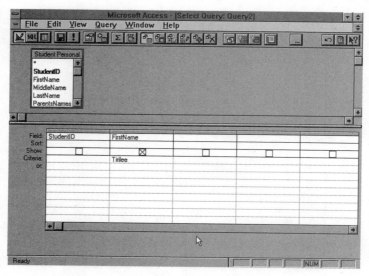

Figure 24.5. *Adding a criterion to Access's QBE.*

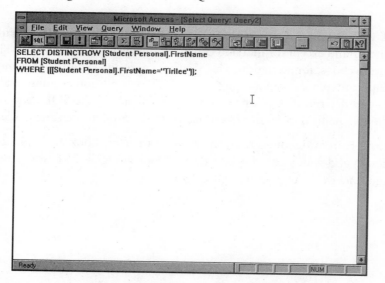

Figure 24.6. *The effect of adding a criterion as seen in SQL.*

Access has added the line WHERE ((([Student Personal].FirstName="Tirilee")); to the query in SQL. When run, the query's return is shown in Figure 24.7.

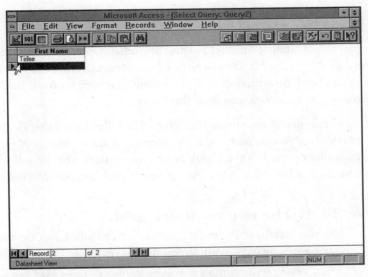

Figure 24.7. *The results of a* WHERE *statement in SQL.*

SQL is a topic that's simple in details yet huge in scope. It has very few operatives, or key words, but by combining these few operatives you can query SQL compliant databases in almost any way imaginable.

Using SQL

There's little reason for most people to use SQL in Access. There's nothing superior in a hand-entered SQL query over a QBE one done using the query design grid. The SQL capability of Access isn't even known to most users. Some database systems require SQL to query them. Access acts as a good front end for those systems. It's also a great training ground for those who want to learn SQL.

One area where some people use SQL natively is in constructing code in Visual Basic to be used querying Access databases. Because this topic is both complex and more one for a Visual Basic text than an Access one, *Teach Yourself Access 2 in 14 Days* ends the SQL discussion here. However, this is a rich topic well-covered in other texts. If you're planning on using Access as a professional developer, it's also a topic you need at least basic familiarity with.

Looking at Macros

Chapter 20, "Instantly Smarter Forms," introduces Access Basic with an exercise that programs a command button to respond to an event. The earlier part of this chapter gives you a brief introduction to SQL, so now's the time for the third Access language, macros—how they look and how they work.

You construct macros in a macro design grid just like many other Access objects. Also, like many other Access parts, much of making macros consists of pulling down lists and choosing options. Take a look at macros yourself now by following along with Exercise 24.1, which shows the macro design grid and constructs a simple macro.

Exercise 24.1. The macro design grid.

1. From the Database View, click on the Macro tab. Click on the New button to start a new macro. Your screen should resemble Figure 24.8.

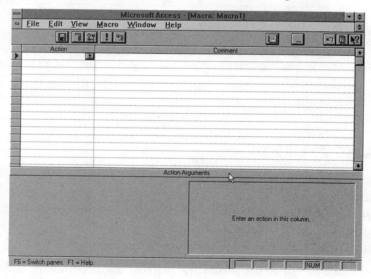

Figure 24.8. *The macro design grid.*

2. Click on the down arrow for the combo box in the Action column. Your screen should resemble Figure 24.9.

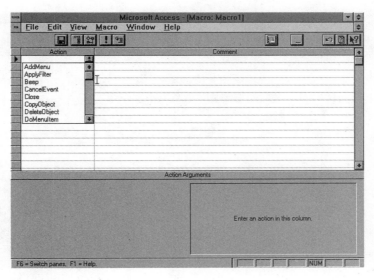

Figure 24.9. *The list of macro actions.*

Macro actions are the heart of the macro. In some cases, macro actions take no arguments or parameters. In other cases, macro actions require rather elaborate and specific parameters or arguments. To start, let's make a simple macro that just causes your computer to beep.

If you have a sound card, make sure the speakers and the amplifier are on so you'll hear the next macro in action.

3. Pull down the Action combo box and click on Beep. Click on the Run button in the toolbar. This is the button with the bang (!) on it just like in the query section of Access.

4. Access beeps and gives you a message box like in Figure 24.10. Click on OK and save the macro, naming it Beeper. After you save it, the macro runs, beeping your system once. Try clicking on the Run button several times to cause Access to beep your computer several times. If you have a special sound assigned to beep in Windows, you'll hear your assigned sound. Congratulations! You've just programmed your first macro.

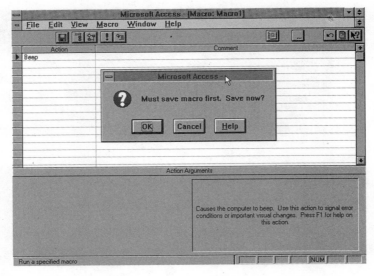

Figure 24.10. *The message box.*

That was awfully easy and so are most macro tasks. There's no real way to run a macro with an error trap like the Event Procedure in Chapter 20. For this reason some professional programmers frown on using a lot of macros in Access applications. If there's no error trap, Access doesn't know what to do in case of an error condition and generally exits rather ungracefully.

The lack of an error trap in macros is a disadvantage. However, error traps are mostly a concern for those distributing applications to others, especially outside the developer's organization. Most internal or for-your-own-use Access applications can do just fine without error traps. The ease of programming macros counteracts the lack of traps in macros for the vast majority of Access users.

DO / DON'T

DO use a wizard to program your command buttons when you have the right wizard. This will give you the best of both worlds: easy button programming and error trapping through Access Basic.

DON'T get overly worried if you find programming in Access Basic to be overwhelming and you choose to use macros for actions where no wizard exists. Most noncommerical Access applications can do just fine even when lacking a few error traps.

Time to give this macro a little more to do.

5. Pull down the combo box in the second row of the Action column. Scroll to and select OpenForm. Access automatically brings up the Action Arguments section at the bottom of the screen. Click next to the Form Name argument section and pull down the combo box. Click on Class Entry as the form to open. Your screen should resemble Figure 24.11.

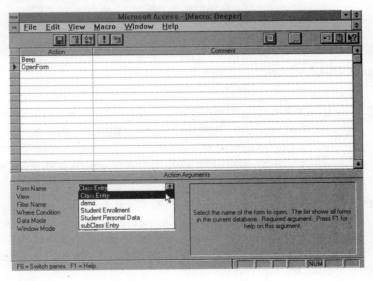

Figure 24.11. *The OpenForm macro.*

459

6. Again click on the Run button in the toolbar. Access again reminds you that you must save the macro, so click on OK. Access lets fly with another beep in response to your programmed Beep line as the first action in this macro, then opens the Class Entry form responding to the second. Your screen should resemble Figure 24.12.

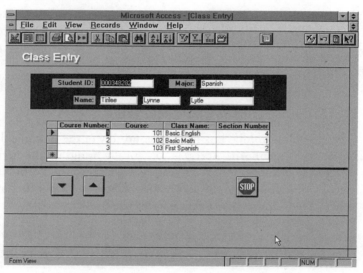

Figure 24.12. *Running an OpenForm macro.*

7. Click on the cmdExit button to exit this form—that's the one with the stop sign on it. If you don't have a cmdExit button on your form, exit the form by double-clicking on its control menu icon or choosing the menu selections File|Close. Access returns you to the macro design grid. Your screen should resemble Figure 24.13.

8. Close the Beeper macro. Back at the Database View, optionally delete it by clicking on it then pressing the Del or Delete key on the keyboard and confirming to Access that you want to delete this macro. *Teach Yourself Access 2 in 14 Days* won't come back to Beeper, but you might want to keep it around for experimentation.

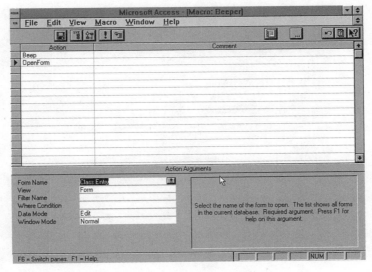

Figure 24.13. *Access closes the form and returns to the design grid.*

A Switchboard Form

You saw how easy it was to create a macro that, when run, opens a form. Doing many other things with macros is equally easy. Exercise 24.2 shows you how to make a switchboard form. This is a specialized unbound form containing command buttons that can act as a menu system for your applications.

Exercise 24.2. The switchboard or menu form.

1. With Access launched and the College database open, click on the Form tab, then click on the New button to start a new form. Your screen should resemble Figure 24.14.

2. Click on the Blank Form button without binding any table or query to the new form. Move your mouse cursor to the bottom right corner of the form design area. When you hit the corner, the cursor will change to a box with four arrows sticking out from it. Click your mouse button and drag the form until it fits the screen. This operation is shown in Figure 24.15.

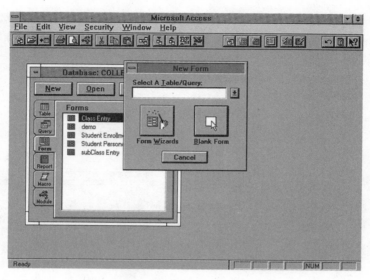

Figure 24.14. *Starting a switchboard form.*

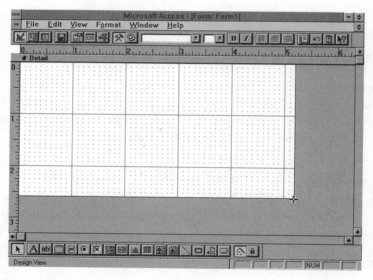

Figure 24.15. *Enlarging the form design grid.*

These next steps give the form its basic design elements.

3. Click on the Label control in the Toolbox and click again in the upper-left corner of the form design grid. Enter `Fictional College` as a label. Change the font size to 18 and the style to bold as shown in Figure 24.16. You will have to resize your label to make the new font fit.

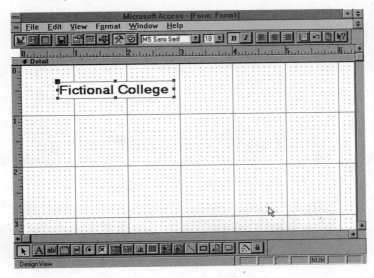

Figure 24.16. *Inserting a label control.*

4. Click on the Lock control in the Toolbox. Make sure the Wizard button in the Toolbox is deselected. Click on the Command button control in the Toolbox and place three command buttons on the form as shown in Figure 24.17.

   The next step is to name and caption the Command button controls.

5. Click on the Lock button to remove the lock. Click on the Select Objects tool in the Toolbox to deselect the Command button tool. Open the Properties list box if necessary. Highlight each button in turn and change their Name property to cmdOpenClassEntry, cmdOpenReportCards, and cmdExit respectively. While in the Properties list box, change the buttons' Caption property to Class Entry, Report Cards, and E&xit, respectively. Figure 24.18 shows how your screen should look after changing the last button's Name and Caption properties.

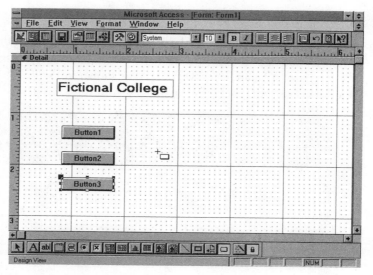

Figure 24.17. *Placing command buttons in the form.*

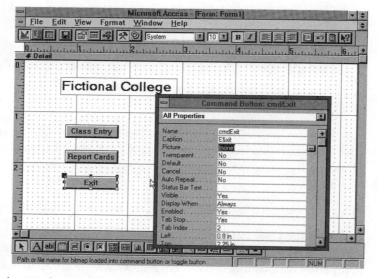

Figure 24.18. *Altering command button's properties.*

6. Click on the menu selections File|Save As and name this form Switchboard.

The Macros

Exercise 24.3 creates a macro for the Switchboard form you made in Exercise 24.2.

Exercise 24.3. The compound macro.

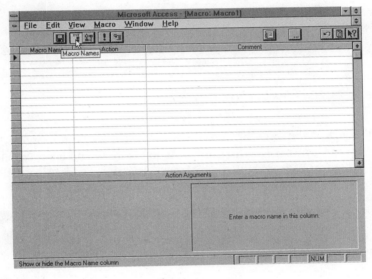

1. If the form from Exercise 24.2 is still open, press the F11 key to enter Database View. If you're in Database View already, you don't need to press F11. Click on the Macro tab. Click on New. Locate the Macro Names button in the toolbar and click on it. Your screen should resemble Figure 24.19.

Figure 24.19. *Starting the compound macro.*

Macros have one overall name that appears at the Database View. Macros can also have subnames that appear in the Macro Names column. When you attach this macro to the switchboard form, you'll see how this works.

2. Click in the first row of the Macro Names column and enter `OpenClassEntry` for a name. Move to the Actions column, pull down the combo box, and click on OpenForm. In the Action Arguments section, specify the Class Entry form as the one to be opened. Your screen should resemble Figure 24.20.

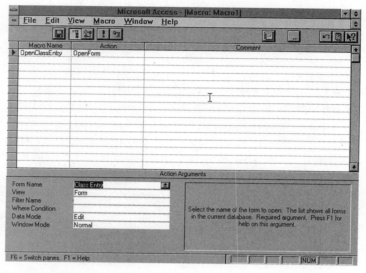

Figure 24.20. *The OpenForm macro.*

3. Click in the second row of the Macro Names column. Enter
   OpenReportCards. Move to the Action column and enter OpenReport. Specify
   Report Cards as the Report Name and make sure the View is Print Preview.
   Your screen should resemble Figure 24.21.

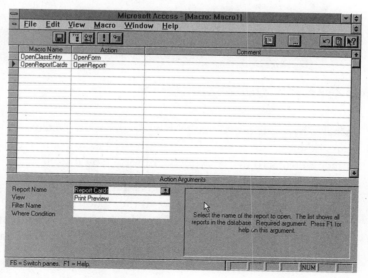

Figure 24.21. *The OpenReport macro.*

4. Click in the third row of the Macro Names column. Enter Exit as a name and move to the Action column. Enter Quit as an action. Your screen should resemble Figure 24.22.

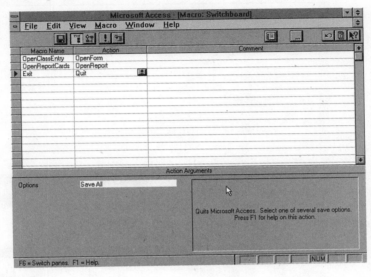

Figure 24.22. *The exit macro.*

5. Exit and save this macro, giving it the name Switchboard.

Putting It All Together

All's ready now to attach the macro from Exercise 24.3 to the form from Exercise 24.2.

Exercise 24.4. Activating the form.

1. Open up the Switchboard form in Design View either by switching to it or clicking on the Form tab and then clicking on Design after giving the Switchboard form the highlight. Your screen should resemble Figure 24.23.

2. Click on the cmdOpenClassEntry command button. Open the Properties list box if necessary. Switch the list box to show only Event Properties. Locate the On Click event in the list box and pull down the combo box. Locate the Switchboard.OpenClassEntry entry and click on it. Your screen should resemble Figure 24.24.

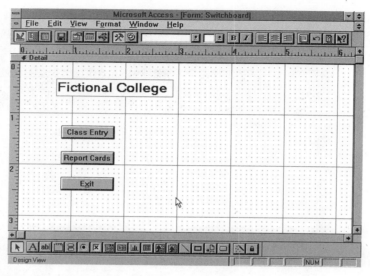

Figure 24.23. *The Switchboard form in Design View.*

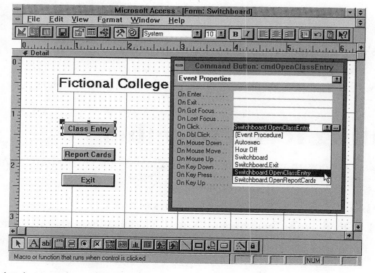

Figure 24.24. *Attaching the macro to the command button.*

3. Click on the cmdOpenReportCards control, and assign the Switchboard.OpenReportCards macro to its On Click property. Your screen should resemble Figure 24.25.

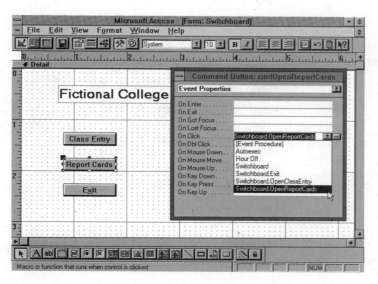

Figure 24.25. *Attaching the next macro to the next command button.*

4. Using the same technique, attach the Switchboard.Exit macro to the cmdExit button. Your screen should resemble Figure 24.26.

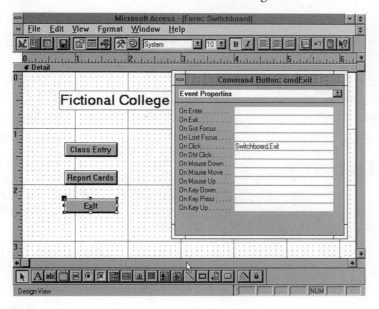

Figure 24.26. *Attaching the last macro.*

5. Click on File|Save to save the form's changes.

Switch to Form View. Your screen should resemble Figure 24.27.

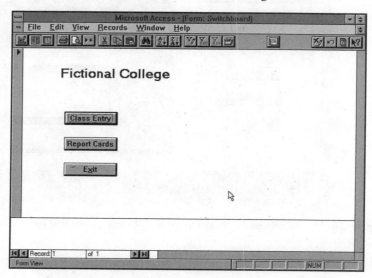

Figure 24.27. *The activated Switchboard form.*

Try clicking on the button labeled Class Entry. You'll switch to the Class Entry form. Click on the button with the stop sign on it within the Class Entry form. You'll return to the Switchboard form.

Experiment with these buttons—starting and ending the Class Entry form and the Report Cards report. One caution: The button labeled Exit will exit you from Access.

Summary

You can add unbound expressions to reports or forms as easily as adding an unbound text box control and then entering the expression as its Control Source property. You control the appearance of text boxes by altering the Format property.

Just as you can add lines and boxes to forms, so too can you add these elements to reports. The big difference between report and form design is, since most printers are gray scale, generally people only use color for their forms.

Access has three languages native to it: Access Basic, SQL, and macros. You can design queries using SQL if you're so inclined, but most people prefer to use the query design grid (QBE) and let Access do the SQL dirty work.

Macros have two parts: Action and Action Arguments. Simple macros, such as the Beep, take no arguments, but most others do. Programming Access macros can be as simple as clicking on the macro action and then clicking on the right arguments. Macros can get more complex as you'll see later, but much can be done by point and click.

Q&A

Q Why bother to learn and use SQL?

A If you'll only be using Access for querying Access tables, there isn't any reason. SQL is a common query language used by professional database managers to query many different databases. Many large system databases require SQL to extract information. Access can provide a very convenient front end for these database systems, but the vast majority of Access users aren't even aware that Access includes an SQL capacity.

Q If a field is in a query, but not showing in the query's return, can I still use it in a report expression?

A Yes. There's no need for a field to show in a query to have it be useful in a report expression. Any field included in the query showing in the query return or not can be in a report (or form) expression.

Q Do main and subreports need to be bound to each other through a common link?

A No. You can include several unbound subreports in a main report.

Q Can I make macros respond when certain conditions are valid?

A Yes. That's a topic coming up tomorrow morning.

Q Can I use the On Click property with controls other than command buttons?

A Yes. Any control having an On Click property can respond to mouse clicks like command buttons. Most people think of command buttons when they think of clicking though.

Workshop

Here's where you can test and apply the lessons you learned today.

Quiz

Possible answers to these questions are provided in Appendix A.

1. Look at the way Exercise 24.2 had you enter the Caption property for the cmdExit button—E&xit—in step 5. Now look at the way the button looks in Design or Form View. What do you suppose the ampersand (&) does?

2. If the View option for the Switchboard.OpenReportCards macro was changed to Print, what do you suppose would happen when you run the macro?

3. Name two ways to change the width of a line or box in reports or forms.

4. What does the dot (.) do in a macro name?

5. The word Not works as a criteria in queries, but won't work in mathematical expressions. How can you specify a Not or Not Equal To operator in an Access expression?

Put Access into Action

1. Start a new macro. Enter Close as a macro action.

2. Click in the Action Arguments section. Pull down the Object Type combo box and enter Form as an object type.

3. Click in the Object Name section and enter Student Personal Data as an object name. Your screen should resemble Figure 24.28.

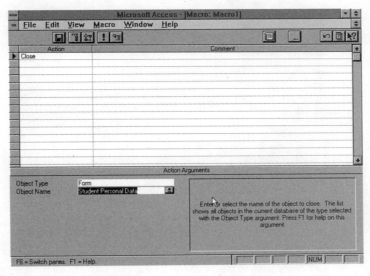

Figure 24.28. *The finished macro.*

4. Close the macro, saving it as Student Personal Data.

5. Open the Student Personal Data form in Design View. Place a command button in the footer section toward the right side of the form. Name the button cmdCloseForm and give it the caption &Close Form.

6. Assign the macro Student Personal Data to the On Click property for this button. Your screen should resemble Figure 24.29.

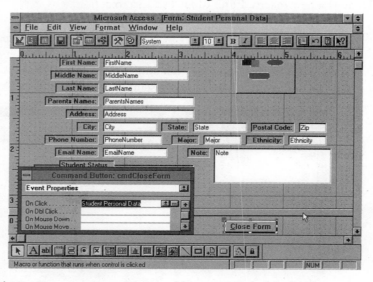

Figure 24.29. *Programming a command button to close a form.*

7. Click on File|Save to save your changes. Switch to Form View. Your screen should resemble Figure 24.30.

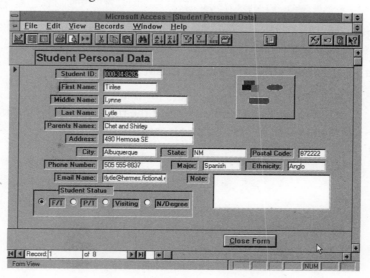

Figure 24.30. *Running the form with the new command button.*

8. Click on the new command button. Did it work like you anticipated?

9. Reopen the form in Form View. Press Alt+C. What happened? Why do you suppose it happened?

24

13

25

More Macro Magic

This morning's lesson covers these topics:

☐ The concept of conditional branching

☐ How to program branching or conditional macros

☐ Practical uses for conditional macros

☐ Macros that change control values

☐ Access identifiers

Conditional Branching in Macros

All but the simplest computer programs rely at least somewhat on evaluating a condition and then taking action based on the results of that evaluation.

You created a program that evaluated a condition and reacted accordingly yesterday morning when you added a dynamic control to the Report Cards report. The optDeansList option button had as a control source an expression that examined the value for the Weighted GPA and set itself to True if it was above 3.1. Otherwise it set itself to False. This is a very simple example of an evaluate-then-branch computer routine. Although simple, as you saw, it was useful too.

The optDeansList option button set itself according to a value for another control. On their own, there are only limited things controls can do, but team them up with macros and the field widens quite a bit. The problem's how to get the macro rather than the control to evaluate a condition and act on what it finds. As you've likely guessed by now, Access provides a simple way to do this evaluation. The second problem to address is how to decide when the macro should do the evaluation.

Take a look at Figure 25.1. This is the macro design grid with all the possible columns showing.

Note that in addition to the Macro Name column, there's also a Condition column. By default, macros execute under any condition when called. If you make an entry in the Condition column, the macro starts, does the evaluation, and executes, depending on the results of the evaluation. In other words, it branches.

One very handy thing a macro can do is flash a message box informing data entry people of just about anything, from a credit overrun to an error condition to a sales suggestion. Exercise 25.1 creates a macro that brings up a message box if certain

conditions are met. It evaluates the contents of the Ethnicity field when a new student is registered and it responds accordingly.

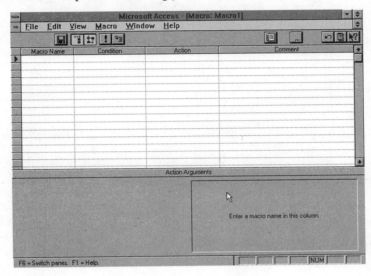

Figure 25.1. *All the columns in the macro design grid.*

Exercise 25.1. Conditional message box macro.

1. Launch Access and open the College database if necessary. Click on the Macro tab, click on the Student Personal Data macro, and click on the Design button to edit this macro. Click on both the Macro Names and the Condition buttons in the toolbar to open both these columns. Your screen should resemble Figure 25.1, but with the Student Personal Data macro loaded in addition to the figure. Figure 25.2 shows the Condition button. The Macro Names button is just to the left of the Condition button.

Generally speaking, the first thing to do with a macro is to give it a name, unless the macro will contain only one routine. It's good practice to group macros according to usage, as this macro demonstrates. This macro has the overall name Student Personal Data because all the macros (or macro names) in it are called from this form. In this specific case the inclusion of the macro in a group is another example of good practice—it is not absolutely necessary.

25

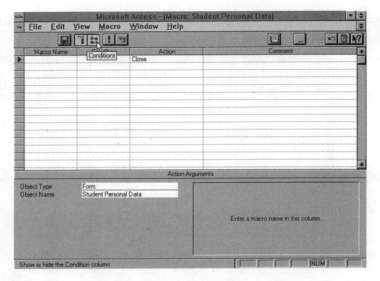

Figure 25.2. *Adding the Condition and Macro Names columns.*

2. Click in the Macro Names field in the first row and enter the new name
   `Exit` for the Close action. Click in the second row of the Macro Names
   column and add the name `Scholarship`. Your screen should resemble
   Figure 25.3.

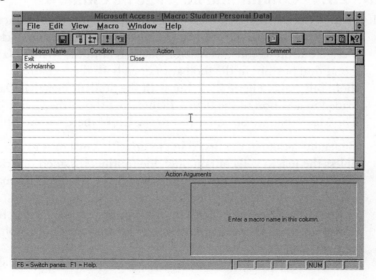

Figure 25.3. *The macro name.*

3. Click in the Condition column and enter [Ethnicity]="Black". This means you want to have the macro evaluate the entry in the Ethnicity field (or control) and take action if the condition's met. In this case the condition the macro looks for is the text in the text box control. Your screen should resemble Figure 25.4.

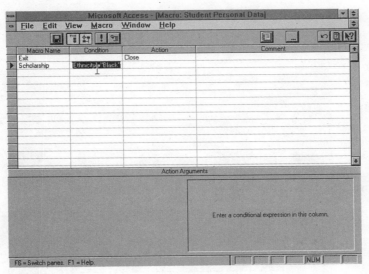

Figure 25.4. *Entering a condition for the macro.*

Now you need to enter the action to be taken in case the condition is met. The fictional college has an equally fictional Roy Wilkens Scholarship for students of African heritage. This macro reminds the data-entry person to tell the student about this scholarship.

4. Click in the Action column of the second row, pull down the action combo box list, and click on MsgBox. Your screen should resemble Figure 25.5.

5. Edit the Title argument to be Scholarship Alert! and the message box type to be Information, and enter the text Is This Student Aware of the Wilkens Scholarship? as the Message argument. Figure 25.6 shows how your screen will look when you're done. In Figure 25.6 the Message argument is being entered in Zoom mode.

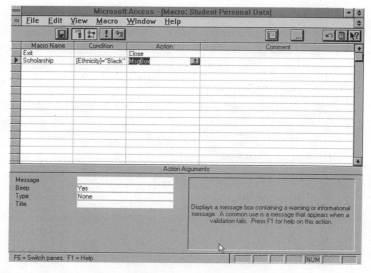

Figure 25.5. *Specifying that the action is to be a message box.*

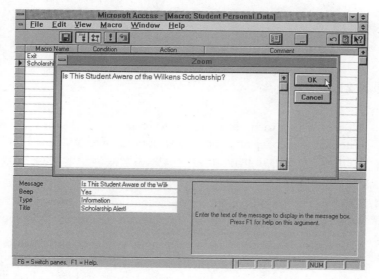

Figure 25.6. *Entering arguments for a message box.*

6. Close this macro, saving changes.

Prepare to Use the Macro

Two more things need to be done at this point. First, the command button cmdCloseForm in Student Personal Data must be alerted that there's a change in the macro attached to it. Second, the Student Personal Data.Scholarship macro must be attached to the form in just the right way to come into action at an appropriate time.

In Exercise 25.2 you edit the On Click property for cmdCloseForm, causing it to point to the right macro, and you attach the Scholarship macro to the proper event.

Exercise 25.2. Attaching macros.

1. Back in Database View, click on the Form tab, highlight the Student Personal Data form, and click on the Design button to open this form in Design View. Your screen should resemble Figure 25.7.

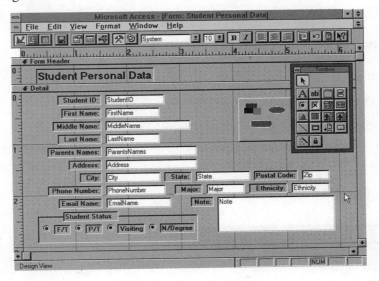

Figure 25.7. *Ready to add macros to a form.*

2. If necessary, scroll down to see the form's footer area—the place where you placed the Exit button. Open the Properties list box by clicking on its button in the toolbar. Tell the list box you only want to examine the Event Properties. Click on the cmdCloseForm button to highlight it. Pull down the On Click combo box, locate the Student Personal Data.Exit macro, and click on it. Your screen should resemble Figure 25.8.

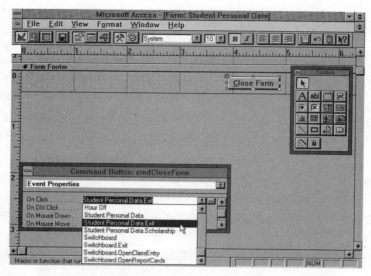

Figure 25.8. *Editing the On Click property.*

Well, that's fixed. Now move on to assign the other macro name to the appropriate event.

3. Scroll back up so the detail portion of the form is showing again. Click on the Ethnicity field to highlight it. Locate the After Update property in the Properties list box. Click on it and pull down its combo box. Locate the Student Personal Data.Scholarship macro and click on it. Your screen should resemble Figure 25.9.

DO　　　　　　　　　　　　　　　　　　　　**DON'T**

DO make sure to have the field itself highlighted when trying to enter event-driven macros.

DON'T highlight the field's label or you won't see the events for the control shown in the list box. There are no events that can occur to a label.

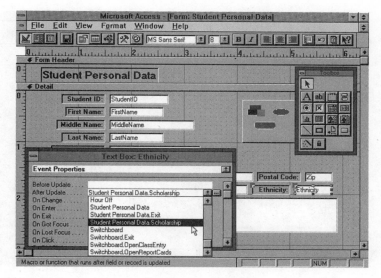

Figure 25.9. *Adding a macro to the After Update property.*

Macros in Action

Let's see how this new macro works. Switch to Form View for the Student Personal Data form. Click on the New button in the toolbar and enter the information for a new student shown in Figure 25.10.

> **Note:** When entering data for this and the next student, you might find your tab order to be wrong for the natural order of this form. If you prefer a different tab order, switch back to Design View and adjust the tab order following the example shown in Day 11.

Now enter the data for the next student, as shown in Figure 25.11, up to but not beyond the point of entering Black as this student's Ethnicity.

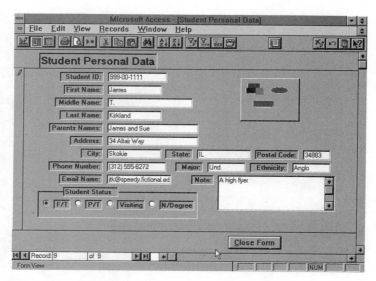

Figure 25.10. *A new non-Black student.*

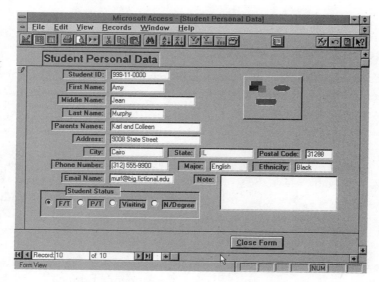

Figure 25.11. *Another record set to call the macro.*

Press Enter or tab out of this field. Access looks at the entry, finds it to be Black, and now that the condition's met, executes the macro. Your screen should resemble Figure 25.12.

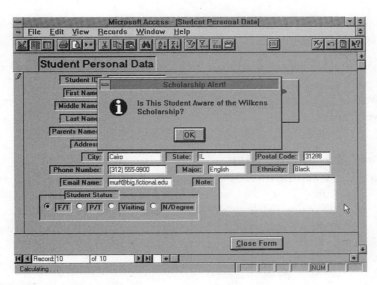

Figure 25.12. *The macro executing.*

It works just as it should. Click on OK to close the message box. Return to the Ethnicity field by clicking on it, and again tab out. The message box doesn't appear because the macro only executes when the field's been updated. That's the meaning of the After Update event property. Click on the Close button to end the session with this form. Save the changes to this form when prompted by Access.

The Access Way

This macro could have been successfully added to the On Exit property of this control. However, the fictional college wanted this macro to be executed only when a new student is registered. If the macro executed each time the field was exited, it would execute every time someone tabbed through this field.

25

Macros That Alter Properties

A macro can have an action that alters control properties. The next two exercises show this in action. The form and the controls that have their properties altered aren't terribly useful, but the technique is. The reasons for the rather hokey example are

simplicity and a desire to focus only on the issues rather than be overwhelmed by many irrelevant details.

Exercise 25.3 creates a very simple form with four controls. Two of the controls respond to events by altering the other two controls' properties with a macro. Each macro in this exercise is a multiline one and represents an increase in complexity in several areas.

Exercise 25.3. The form.

1. If you have any Access objects open, close them, saving changes where indicated. From the Database View, click on the Form tab and click on the New button. Click on the Blank Form button without binding the form to any table or query. Increase the size of the form design grid to give yourself some working room. Your screen should resemble Figure 25.13.

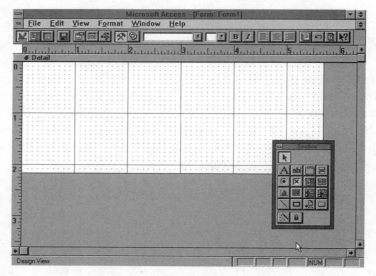

Figure 25.13. *An unbound form in Design View.*

2. Place a label control on the form with the caption I'm Green in 18-point font. Open the Palette and set the background color to green. Your screen should resemble Figure 25.14.

3. Open the Properties list box if necessary. Set it to show All Properties. Locate the Visible property and set this to No. Your screen should resemble Figure 25.15.

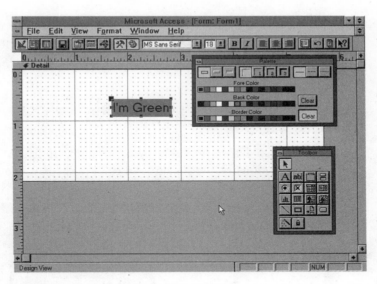

Figure 25.14. *The Green label control.*

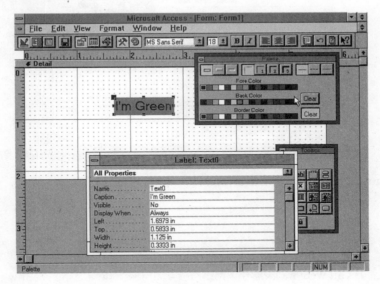

Figure 25.15. *Making the control invisible.*

25

4. Create another label control that is exactly the same size and location as the one done in Step 2. Give this label the caption I'm Red in 18-point font. Set the background color to red and the Visible property to No. Your screen should resemble Figure 25.16.

The Access Way

A shortcut to Step 4 is to choose the menu selections Edit|Duplicate and then edit the caption and the background color of the new control.

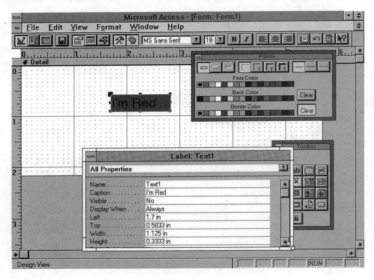

Figure 25.16. *The Red label control.*

The Access Way

If you were making this form for your use, you'd also probably change the Name properties for this and the other controls on this form to conform to a naming convention. This exercise skips these steps to remain focused on the goal—the macro that alters control properties.

5. Switch to Form View. Since both label controls have their Visible properties set to No, the screen looks blank, as shown in Figure 25.17.

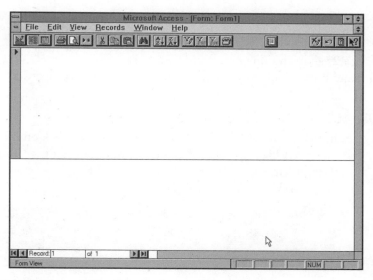

Figure 25.17. *The running form with invisible controls.*

6. Return to Design View and add two command buttons. Edit the caption of one to read Green and the other Red. Your screen should resemble Figure 25.18.

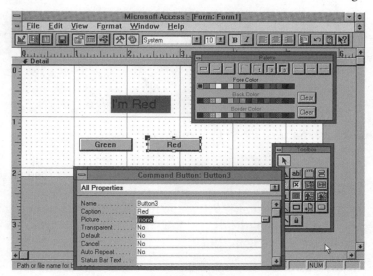

Figure 25.18. *Adding the two command buttons to the form.*

7. Close this form, saving it as Red Green when Access prompts.

25

The next section creates a macro that changes the control properties when called by the command buttons.

Exercise 25.4 creates one macro containing two macro names. When called by its command button, this macro changes the labels' Visible properties.

Exercise 25.4. Control property macros.

1. From the Database View, click on the Macro tab. Click on New to start a new macro. Open the Macro Names column, but not the Condition one. Click on the menu selections File|Save As and name this macro Red Green. Your screen should resemble Figure 25.19.

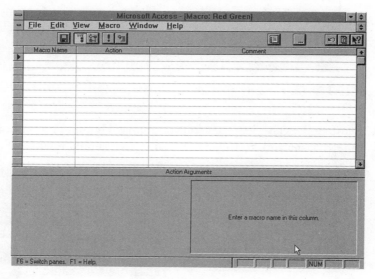

Figure 25.19. *Starting the Red Green macro.*

2. The first part of this macro shows the red label. Enter the macro name ShowRed in the Macro Names column. Tab to the Action column and set SetValue as an action. Click in the Item line of the Action Arguments section to bring up the three-dot (ellipsis;...) build button. Your screen should resemble Figure 25.20.

These macros do the same thing but work in opposition. One positively sets the green label's Visible property to No and the red label's Visible property to Yes. The other sets the red label's Visible property to No and the green label's Visible property to Yes.

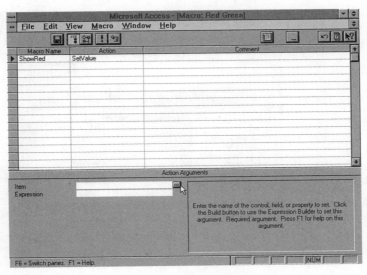

Figure 25.20. *Getting ready to call the expression builder.*

3. Click on the build button (...) on the Item line to bring up the expression builder. Double-click on Forms and All Forms, and then click on Red Green to tell the expression builder you're interested in this form. Locate the Text0 field in the second column and click on that. Scroll to and locate the Visible property in column three. Click on that. Click on the Paste button to paste this argument into the expression builder. Your screen should resemble Figure 25.21.

The Access Way

Access, in this context, might not construct the entire expression shown in Figure 25.21 when you click on the Paste button. If it doesn't, edit the expression to be the same as shown in the figure. You can freely edit expressions pasted into the expression builder's text box.

4. Click on OK to place your expression in the Item line of the Action Arguments. Because Text0 is the Green label, the ShowRed macro should set its Visible property to No. Click on the second line of the Action Arguments section and set the expression to No.

25

495

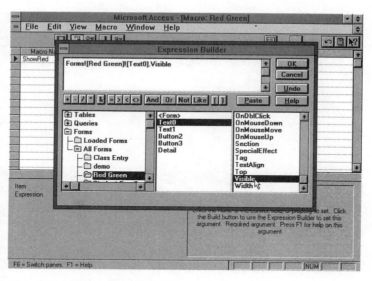

Figure 25.21. *Using the expression builder.*

5. Click in the second line of the Action column and again choose SetValue as an action. Click in the Item section and again bring up the expression builder. This time choose Forms![Red Green]![Text1].Visible by clicking those items as they appear in the columns and then Paste them to the expression builder area. Your screen should resemble Figure 25.22.

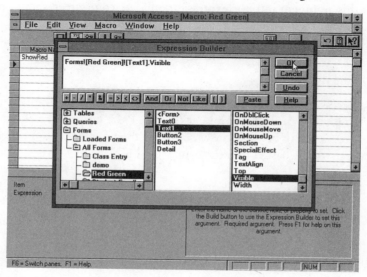

Figure 25.22. *Setting the second* SetValue *argument.*

6. Click on OK. Click on the Expression line of the Action Arguments section and enter Yes. Your screen should resemble Figure 25.23.

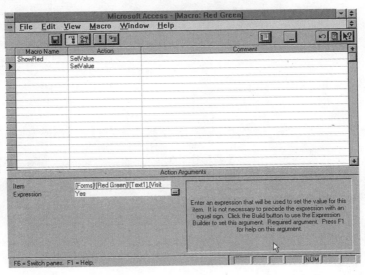

Figure 25.23. *Settings to reveal the Red label.*

7. Create a new macro name ShowGreen on the next line of the Macro Names column. Enter two SetValue actions for this macro, too. This time set them just the opposite to the ShowRed macro.

The Access Way

A shortcut to doing Step 7 is to click in the Item line for the first SetValue, press Shift+F2 to enter Zoom, copy the expression to the Clipboard, close Zoom, click on the new SetValue, and paste the expression into the new Item line. Do this for both SetValues in the ShowGreen macro. Then set the Expressions for each SetValue to opposite those of ShowRed.

Have the Text0 Visible property set to Yes and the Text1 Visible property set to No. After entering these two values, your screen should resemble Figure 25.24.

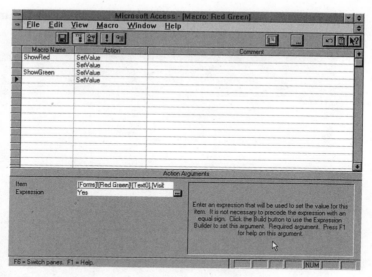

Figure 25.24. *Settings to reveal the Green label.*

8. Close this macro, saving changes.

Placing the Macros on the Form

You now have a demonstration form and the macros that will, when called, change the label control's Visible property. Although this set of exercises focuses on the Visible property, there are many other properties you can change while a form is running.

Exercise 25.5 attaches the macros done in Exercise 25.4 to controls in the Red Green form.

Exercise 25.5. Putting it all together.

1. From the Database View, click on the Form tab and open the Red Green form in Design View. Your screen should resemble Figure 25.25.

2. Open the Properties list box if necessary and limit the display to Event Properties. Click on the Green button to highlight it. Locate the On Click property for this control in the Properties list box. Click on the combo box pull-down arrow to show a list of macros available in this database. Locate and click on the Red Green.ShowGreen macro. Your screen should resemble Figure 25.26.

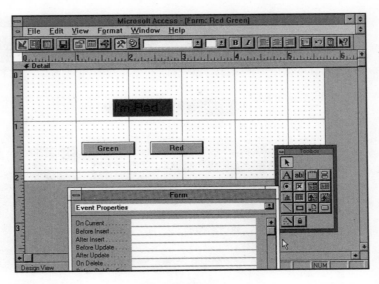

Figure 25.25. *The form open in Design View.*

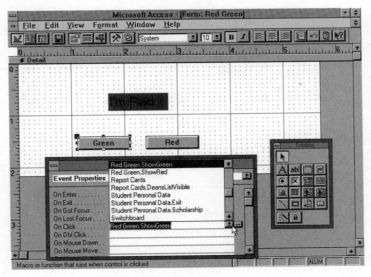

Figure 25.26. *Programming the Green button.*

3. Similarly, click on the Red button to highlight it and set its On Click property to Red Green.ShowRed. Your screen should resemble Figure 25.27.

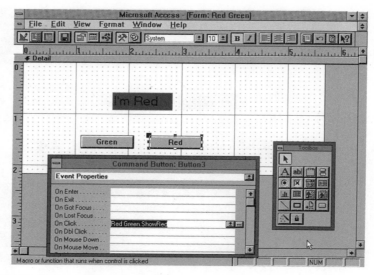

Figure 25.27. *Programming the Red button.*

Switch to Form View. When launched, each label control has its Visible property set to No so you see a screen like in Figure 25.28.

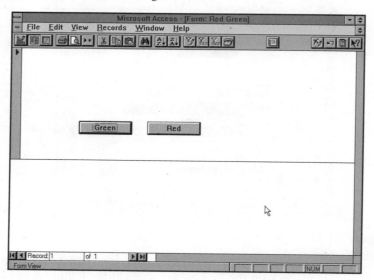

Figure 25.28. *The Red Green form at launch.*

Click on the Green button. This sets the I'm Red label's (Text1) Visible property to No and the I'm Green (Text0) to Yes. Setting a Visible property to No when it's already at No, as with the I'm Red label, has no effect, but it's important, as you'll see later. After clicking on the Green button, your screen should resemble Figure 25.29.

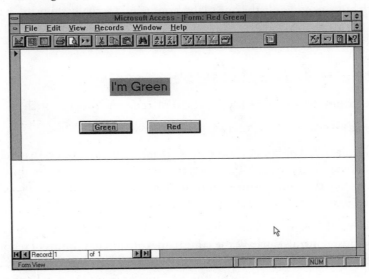

Figure 25.29. *The effect of clicking on the Green button.*

Click on the Red button. Your screen should resemble Figure 25.30.

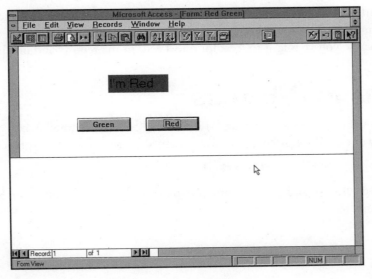

Figure 25.30. *The effect of clicking on the Red button.*

The Red button's ShowRed macro sets the Visible property for the Red label to Yes and the Visible property for the Green label to No. Try clicking on each button. The colors and labels switch, just as you expect them to. If the macros left out switching the "off" label's Visible property to No, both labels would be visible after clicking on both buttons and only the one to the front would actually show up in the form. Close this form, saving changes.

Access Identifiers

The expression builder (or your edits) placed constructions such as

```
[Forms]![Red Green]![Text0].[Visible]
```

in the macros. The bangs (!) and dots (.) are Access identifiers that help Access locate the controls and properties you wish to address. In the expression above, you're telling Access that the control you want to address is named Text0, it's located in something called Red Green, and that something's one of Access's forms.

You must be explicit when telling Access where to find the control you're interested in because controls can have the same names on different forms or reports, and for that matter forms and reports (for example) can have the same names. So the field Text0 might appear on two or more forms and two or more reports. Look at the following expressions:

```
Reports![CaseStudy]![Text0].Visible
Forms![CaseStudy]![Text0].Visible
```

Both expressions refer to discrete controls that have the same name and are on a same-named report and form. Access will have no trouble finding the correct control because you've told it to look for one Text0 in the reports and one in the forms.

Dots and Bangs

Generally speaking, the bang (!) is followed by a user-named Access object, whereas the dot (.) is followed by an Access-named object. So in the expression

```
[Forms]![Red Green]![Text0].[Visible]
```

`[Red Green]` and `[Text0]` are user-named objects, whereas `[Visible]` is Access-named.

Also, generally speaking, you don't need to use full identifiers in macros. Access automatically looks on the current form or report for the named controls. This exercise forced the use of full identifiers to introduce you to them. When using Access Basic, you must use full and syntactically correct identifiers.

Access is intentionally programmed not to need full identifiers in macros so you can construct more macros for very generalized use. That is, the same macro works on [Text0]-named fields on both the report CaseStudy and the form CaseStudy when called from within that form.

Morning Summary

Macros can evaluate a situation, such as a text entry or numeric value, and take action accordingly. This morning's exercise evaluates a text box field when it is updated and responds with a message box if it finds the entry to be "Black."

Macros can also change the properties of a control. This morning you saw how to create a macro that set two controls' properties from Visible = True to Visible = False when called.

You can combine the abilities of macros. For example, you could create a macro that evaluates a condition and alters properties rather than flashing a message box.

Access uses the bang (!) and the dot (.) as identifiers. Bangs precede user-defined objects, whereas, generally speaking, dots precede Access-defined ones. Be sure to use square brackets in your identifying expressions to maintain consistency and to ensure that Access always knows what you're referring to.

25

26

Two Tricky Queries

This afternoon you'll learn

- ☐ What an update query is
- ☐ How to make an update query
- ☐ What a crosstab query is
- ☐ How to make a crosstab query

The morning's lesson went on a little long, so this afternoon's is shorter in length; nevertheless, the subjects it covers are very important in Access. While the importance of the crosstab query varies with the database in question, the update query is one used by most databases on a regular basis.

Update Queries

An update query is a query that, when run, alters the fields of target records. This is the only action query that acts on fields rather than entire records. For example, if you wanted to delete an entire record or set of records, you could perform a delete action query. If you wanted to delete a field or set of fields in a record (change them to blank), the delete query wouldn't work but the update query would.

Open the Update Demo table in Datasheet View. This table is supplied as part of the sample data. Your screen should resemble Figure 26.1.

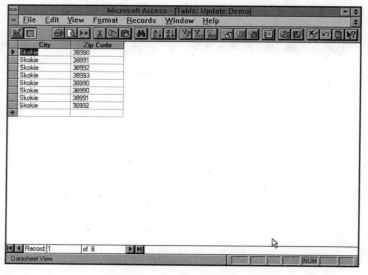

Figure 26.1. *The table to be updated.*

This table is an extract showing the City and Zip Codes from some selected records. The following exercise uses this table rather than the entire dataset so you can more easily see the behavior of the update query.

The fictional college has received word from the U.S. Postal Service that the fictional Skokie Zip Code 38990 will be changed to 38989. Exercise 26.1 shows how to make this change using an update action query in Access.

This exercise creates an update query that looks for any Zip Codes meeting the criteria of 38990 and changes them to 38989.

Exercise 26.1. Update queries.

1. Close the Update Demo table if it's open. Starting from the Database View, click on the Query tab. Click on the New button to start a new query. Skip the Query wizard. Add the Update Demo table to the query design grid. Your screen should resemble Figure 26.2.

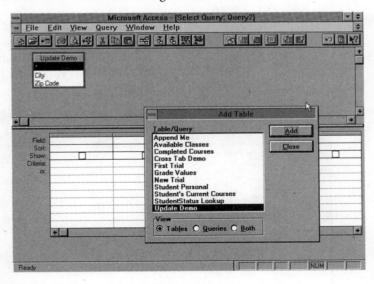

Figure 26.2. *Starting the update action query.*

2. Close the Add Table list box. Click on the menu selections File|Save As and save this query as Updater. Add both of the fields from the list box to the query design grid. Your screen should resemble Figure 26.3.

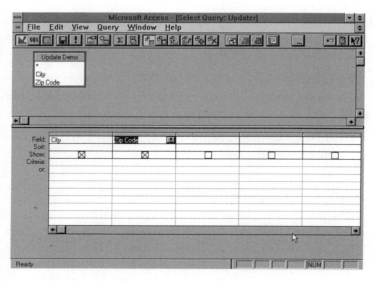

Figure 26.3. *Adding fields to the query design grid.*

3. Run the query. As expected, Access returns all the records from the Update Demo table because no criteria has been specified. Your screen should resemble Figure 26.4.

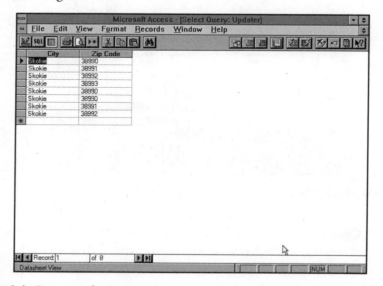

Figure 26.4. *Running the raw query.*

The Access Way

Running this query in Select mode before changing to the action update query might seem like being overly cautious. In this case it is, since the data set's so small. However, in most live cases you can't see an overview of your data as you can here, and running as a select query first is important. This example is the right way to run an action query when your live data is at stake, but it's slightly overdoing it for this dataset.

4. Return to Design View. Add the criterion "38990" to the Zip Code field's criteria row. Your screen should resemble Figure 26.5. When you run the query, Access now extracts only those Skokie addresses with the Zip Code of 38990, as shown in Figure 26.6.

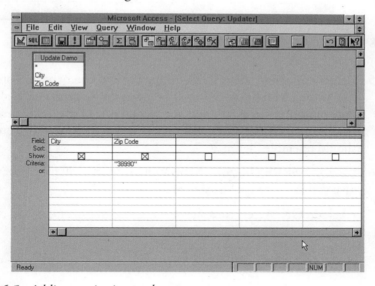

Figure 26.5. *Adding a criterion to the query.*

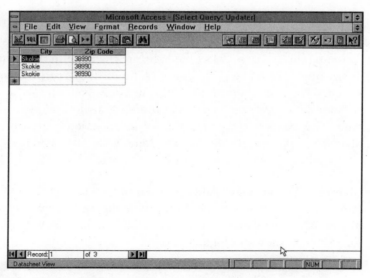

Figure 26.6. *The results of the criteria.*

5. Return to Design View. Click on the Update Query button on the toolbar. It's the one with the pencil on it between the Append and Make-Table query buttons. Access changes the second row of the query design grid to read "Update to." Add "38989" as a criterion to update to. Your screen should resemble Figure 26.7.

6. Click on the Run button on the toolbar. Access will grind away a while and give you the message box shown in Figure 26.8.

7. Click on OK. Access runs the query. Close this query, saving changes.

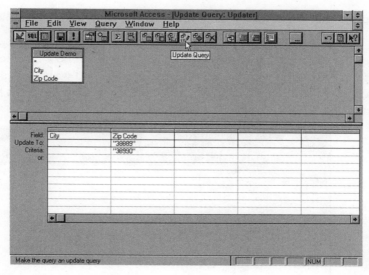

Figure 26.7. *Updating the criteria.*

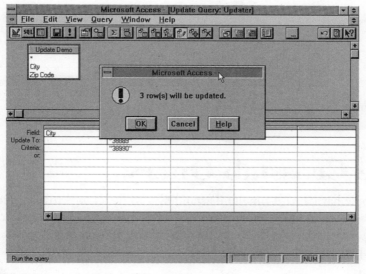

Figure 26.8. *The Update Query message box.*

26

Back at the Database View, notice how the new query Updater has a distinctive icon showing you that not only is it an action query, but an update one.

Click on the Table tab. Open up the Update Demo table in Datasheet View. Your screen should resemble Figure 26.9.

The three records that were formerly "Skokie, 38990" are now "Skokie, 38989." Note that unlike other action queries, nothing in the record was touched except for the specific field you chose to update. Close this table to clear the decks for what comes next.

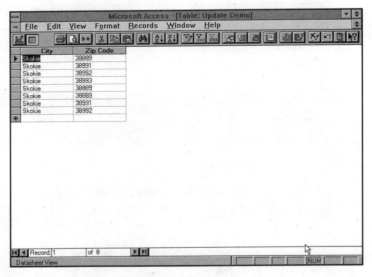

Figure 26.9. *The update query's results.*

The Crosstab Query

People have a hard time understanding and designing crosstab queries. However, these queries can be quite important when analyzing your data. Microsoft has gone to great lengths in both Access 2 and Excel 5 to make the creation of these queries quite simple. The Excel term for a crosstab query is a Pivot Table.

Technically speaking, a crosstab query is a two-dimensional matrix with a mathematical operation performed at each intersection. Once again, a crosstab is much easier to understand in the concrete than in the abstract. Take a look at Figure 26.10. This is the Cross Tab Demo table taken from the sample data. The fictional college has a for-profit subsidiary selling boats of all types, from canoes to yachts. This table is a segment of the sales register for this subsidiary.

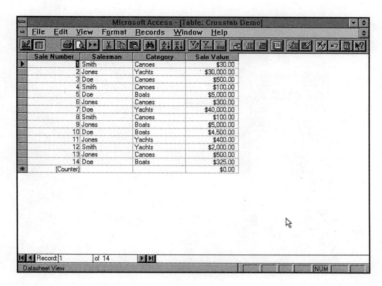

Figure 26.10. *The Cross Tab Demo table.*

Each record has the name of the salesman, the classification the sale fits into, and the amount of the sale. The fictional college wants to analyze this data to determine the dollar amount of sales for each salesman in each category and the sales frequency for each salesman in each category. A crosstab query is just the ticket for both of these tasks.

Exercise 26.2 creates two crosstabs—one showing the sum of the dollars and one showing the frequency of sales.

Exercise 26.2. The crosstab query.

1. Close the Cross Tab Demo table if it's open. Click on the Query tab. Click on the New button. Choose Query Wizards. Click on the Crosstab Query as a wizard type. Your screen should resemble Figure 26.11.

2. Click on OK. Locate the Cross Tab Demo table in the next list box and click on it. Your screen should resemble Figure 26.12.

3. Click on the Next > button. This query lists the salesmen in the rows and the category of sales across the top. Click on the field Salesman to highlight it and click on the > button to move it to the right list box. Your screen should resemble Figure 26.13.

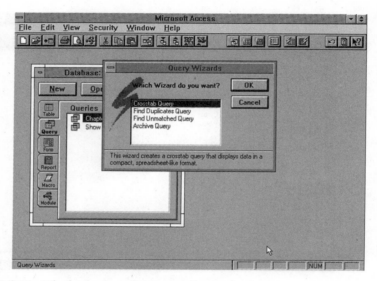

Figure 26.11. *The beginning of the crosstab query.*

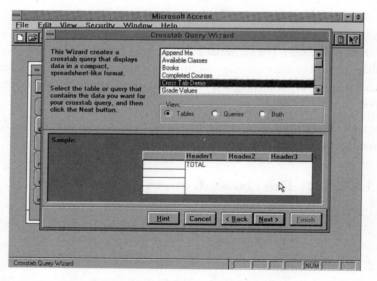

Figure 26.12. *Binding the query to the right table.*

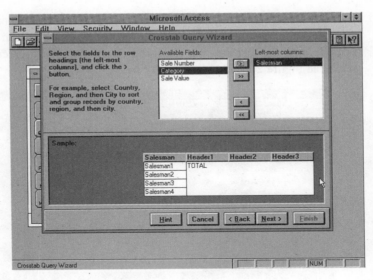

Figure 26.13. *Choosing the rows in a crosstab.*

4. Click on the Next > button. The column heads are the categories of the sales, so highlight Category in the next list box. Your screen should resemble Figure 26.14.

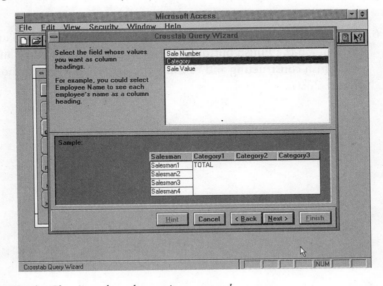

Figure 26.14. *Choosing the columns in a crosstab.*

5. Click on Next >. The figure to calculate for each salesman in each category is the Sale Value, so highlight that in the left list box and Sum in the right list box (because the first crosstab is a summation one). Your screen should resemble Figure 26.15.

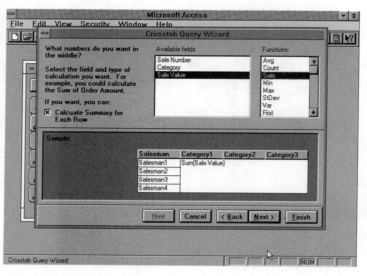

Figure 26.15. *Choosing a field to sum on.*

6. Click on the Next > button to proceed. Accept the Access defaults by clicking on the Finish button. Access will grind away a while and eventually will finish constructing and running the query. Your screen should resemble Figure 26.16.

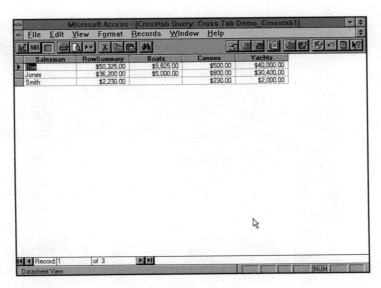

Figure 26.16. *The finished crosstab query running.*

Look how handy the results are. At a glance you can see that Doe outsold everybody else in Boats and Yachts, but Jones was the winner in the Canoes category. Since the dataset was a little small, a trained eye could have seen this by examining the raw data in the table, but what happens when sales occurrences are in the thousands or millions? That's what computers are for.

Switch to Design View. Your screen should resemble Figure 26.17.

The underlying design of a crosstab query isn't very obvious. That's why Microsoft went to the trouble of making a special wizard for it. The heart of this query is in the third and fourth columns. Notice that the Total row has the word Sum in it for the third and fourth columns. This tells Access to sum the Sale Values for the crosstab.

Click on this row, pull down the combo box for the third column, locate the Count function, and click on it. Your screen should resemble Figure 26.18.

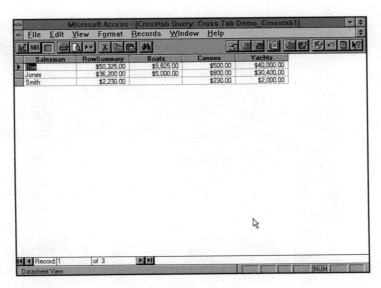

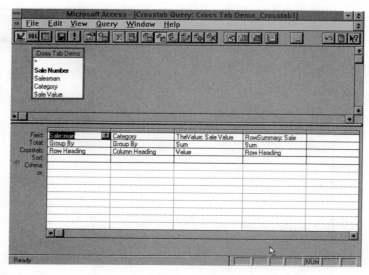

Figure 26.17. *The Design View of a crosstab query.*

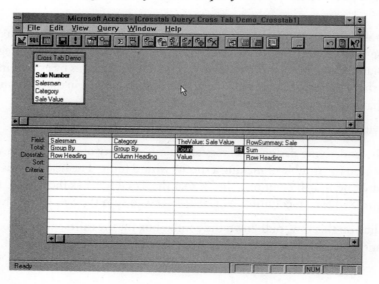

Figure 26.18. *Changing a crosstab's operative.*

Click on the Run button again. Your screen should resemble Figure 26.19.

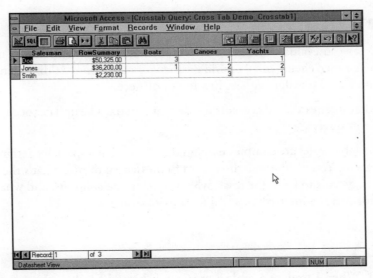

Figure 26.19. *The new crosstab.*

Now you can see at a glance that while Doe and Jones outsold Smith dollarwise, Smith had the greatest number of sales occurrences in the Canoes category. This query demonstrates how useful crosstabs can be. Trying to show this data using most other techniques would have been less clear or more difficult.

The Access Way

Time-saver: You can make one crosstab and then use many operatives in the same frame by changing the operative (count, sum, avg, etc.) and clicking on File|Save As for each operative. This gives you a series of crosstabs showing different aspects of the same data.

Close this query, saving changes.

Don't feel bad if you think you haven't fully grasped crosstabs now. This is a difficult topic for just about everybody. Use the wizard to make your crosstabs. After doing a few, you'll catch on to the magic Access performs behind the scenes.

Summary

Macros can evaluate situations and branch accordingly depending upon how you programmed them. They can do a variety of tasks, from Adding items to a custom menu bar to transferring text in and out of Access.

Update queries alter data according to your criteria. The updates occur to the queried table or query.

Crosstab queries are complex enough that Access has a specially designed wizard just for them. You need to tell the wizard four essential things: what's the source for the query, what's to be in the rows, what's to be in the columns, and what operation to perform at the intersections and for a row summary.

Q&A

Q When I update a table a crosstab is bound to, does the crosstab query get updated too?

A Yes, the next time the query is run. If you have both the Cross Tab Demo table and the Cross Tab Demo_Crosstab1 query open at the same time and you edit the table, the query won't reflect the edits until it's run again (or requeried).

Q Can I base a form on a crosstab query?

A Sure. Look at Figure 26.20. This is a form based on the crosstab query done in Exercise 26.2. The advantage of using a form to view crosstab data is that you have all the form services available to you.

Q Are there many restrictions in the expressions I can use in the Condition column in macro design?

A From Access's standpoint, almost anything goes. You are restricted from using some SQL statements you probably wouldn't want to use here anyway, but that's about it. On the other hand, if you have complex conditions, you're probably much better off using Access Basic to evaluate them because ABC has much better facilities for evaluating conditions than do macros.

If you'd like to see more on this, search online help on topics such as If...Then and Select Case.

Q How do crosstabs differ from subtotals?

A Crosstabs act on two dimensions, across and down. Subtotals only operate on one, either across or down.

Q If I update a field from a table on the one side of a relationship, will Access update the related fields on the many side(s), or will I lose my link(s)?

A If you have the Enforce Referential Integrity box and the Cascading Updates box checked when you establish the link(s), Access will update the many side(s) of the relationships. If you have only Enforce Referential Integrity checked, Access will balk at the update. If you have neither box checked, you really don't have a one-to-many link established.

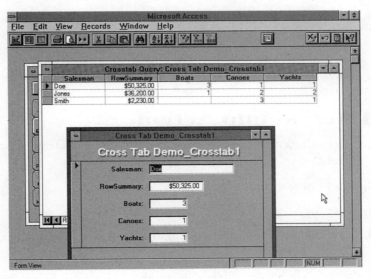

Figure 26.20. *A form based on a crosstab.*

Workshop

Here's where you can test and apply the lessons you learned today.

Quiz

Possible answers to these questions are provided in Appendix A.

1. Can you make a crosstab that finds average values?

2. What usually follows the bang (!) identifier?

3. What usually follows the dot (.) identifier?

4. Can the Update query act on individual fields in a table, or must it work on entire rows, like the delete query?

5. Do you think you could have reworked this morning's macro to alter a single label's color and caption instead of altering the visible property for two labels?

Put Access into Action

1. Start a new crosstab query based on the Cross Tab Demo table that uses the wizard.

2. Place Category in the rows.

3. Place the Salesman fields in the columns.

4. Have the query show the maximum sales in each category for each salesman. Run the query.

   When it's running, your new query should look like Figure 26.21.

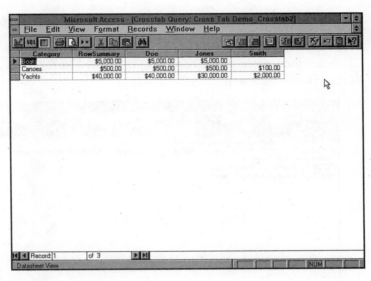

Figure 26.21. *The pivoted query.*

Switch to Design View. Your new query should resemble Figure 26.22 in Design View.

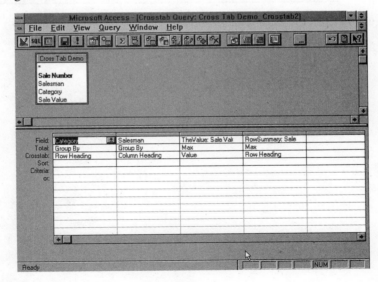

Figure 26.22. *The new query in Design View.*

5. Look at the SQL code for this query, shown in Figure 26.23. Which term do you suppose you'd change to make this a summing crosstab?

6. Close the query when you're done with it. *Teach Yourself Access 2 in 14 Days* does not come back to it.

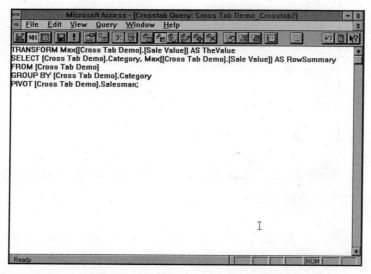

Figure 26.23. *The SQL code behind the crosstab.*

27

Customizing Access

This morning you'll learn how to

☐ Customize a toolbar

☐ Add dialing capability to Access

☐ Create custom buttons for toolbars

☐ Use custom buttons

Customizing Toolbars

You can customize the buttons on Access's standard toolbars, specify when toolbars are displayed, and even make your own toolbars from scratch. Access has a built-in phone dialer called the Autodialer. This dialer is available through using a special button on any toolbar. To use this button, you must first install it on a toolbar, then configure it for your particular use through its Setup routine.

The technique used to install the dialer button on a toolbar is identical to adding or deleting buttons from any toolbar. Exercise 27.1 demonstrates this technique.

Exercise 27.1. Customizing toolbars.

1. Launch Access and load the College database if necessary. Click on the Form tab. Double-click on the Student Personal Data form to open it in Form View. Your screen should resemble Figure 27.1.

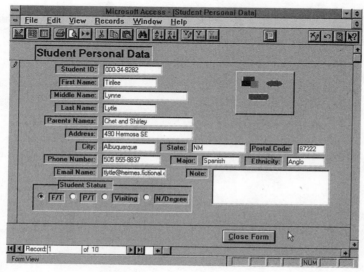

Figure 27.1. *Getting ready to customize the Form View toolbar.*

The easiest way to customize a built-in toolbar is to launch whatever context the toolbar naturally pops up in. Because this exercise will customize the Form View toolbar, it started by loading a form in Form View that brought up the target toolbar.

2. Right-click on the toolbar shown in Figure 27.1 away from any button, then click on Toolbars from the pop-up menu. If you prefer, choose the menu selections View|Toolbars. Either way your screen should resemble Figure 27.2.

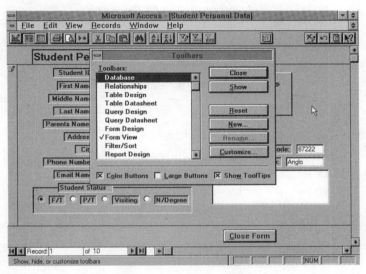

Figure 27.2. *The Toolbars dialog box.*

3. You can change the look of all toolbars from this dialog box. Try clicking on the Large Buttons check box now. Your screen should resemble Figure 27.3.

Changing the size of the buttons makes them easier to see, but they also displace a lot more room this way. Not only is there less room now for the form, but notice that the buttons on the right of the toolbar, including the important help buttons, are now off the screen. Click again on the Large Buttons check box to return to smaller button sizes. If you want to use Large Buttons, you'll have less room for them on a toolbar.

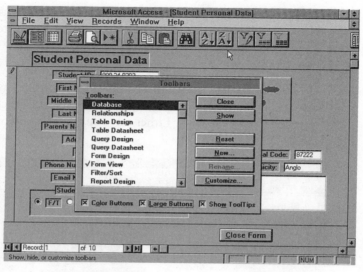

Figure 27.3. *Changing to large buttons.*

Of course, you can always detach a toolbar from the top of the screen, which will reveal the now hidden buttons. Look at Figure 27.4. This is the large button Form View toolbar detached from its anchor spot as it would appear in a typical form. It doesn't seem terribly convenient anywhere.

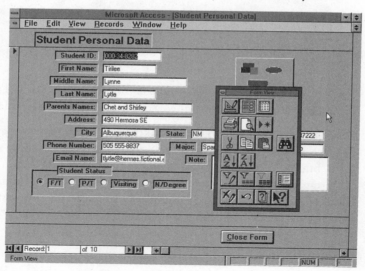

Figure 27.4. *The floating large button toolbar.*

The Access Way

The Large Button option for the toolbar is useful for high screen resolutions, not the standard VGA one. The Large Button option is overwhelming at standard screen resolutions, but almost mandatory at very high ones.

4. From where you left off in Step 3, click on the Customize button. Your screen should resemble Figure 27.5.

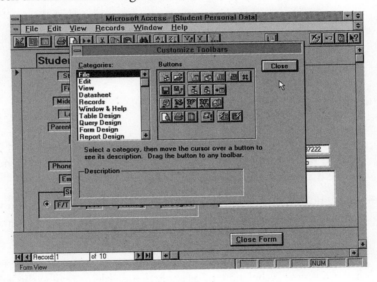

Figure 27.5. *The toolbar customize dialog box.*

The scrolling list box on the left is the categories of buttons Access has supplied. Click on the various categories to see the buttons available to you. You can add any of these buttons to any toolbar even if it doesn't make sense in context. While in this mode, you can also remove or rearrange buttons on any showing toolbar.

5. To find out what each button does, move your mouse cursor over it to see a balloon style help window. Look at Figure 27.6, which shows the Edit category's Find Next button.

27

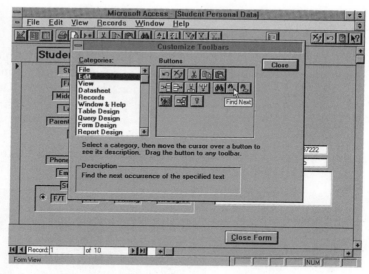

Figure 27.6. *The Edit category of buttons.*

Note that besides the balloon style help, the full description of what this button will do appears in the Description message section at the lower-left of the dialog box.

Add a button at this point by dragging it to the toolbar. If you want to remove a button from the toolbar, now's the time to do it. Removing a button is as simple as dragging it from the toolbar to any place away from the toolbar.

Take the time either now or as soon as possible to review the various pre-programmed buttons you have available to use. For example, right now click on the Form Design category and locate the first four buttons in the third row. The first of these buttons is shown in Figure 27.7.

Wouldn't it be great to have these buttons available to you when you're doing Form Design?

DO   DON'T

DO customize your toolbars to help you.

DON'T forget that buttons will appear where you place them, not where they naturally belong. Look at Figure 27.8, which has the align left button

placed in the Form View toolbar. Access will cheerfully place this button in
this toolbar, but you can't use it there. When placing buttons, remember
context.

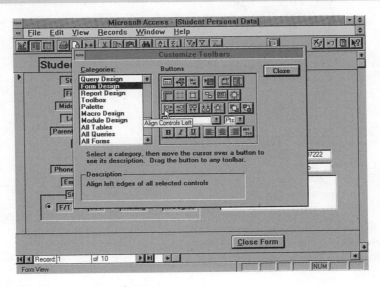

Figure 27.7. *The alignment buttons.*

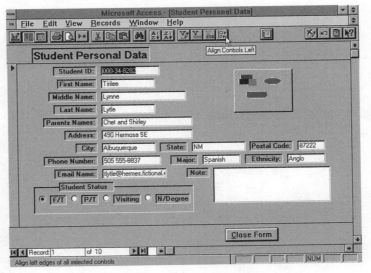

Figure 27.8. *A useful button rendered useless due to context.*

6. Picking up from Step 5, click on the Records category and locate the
   Autodialer button. Refer to Figure 27.9 for direction.

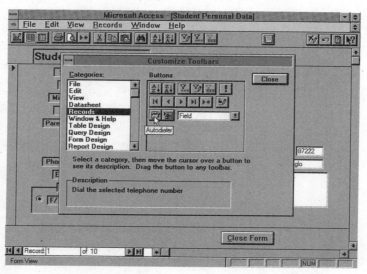

Figure 27.9. *The Autodialer button.*

7. Drag the Autodialer button to the toolbar. Drop it just to the right of the
   Show All Records button. Your screen should resemble Figure 27.10.

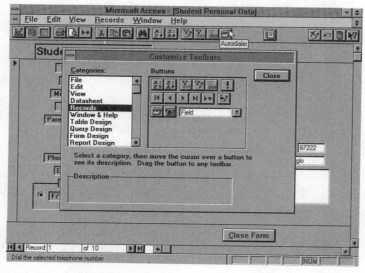

Figure 27.10. *Inserting a new button.*

8. Click on the Close button to end the toolbar customizing session.

You're now able to dial phone numbers from within Access. If you have a modem, you can do the next exercise. If you don't have a modem, you should get an idea of what Exercise 27.2 does by reading along. This short exercise shows the Autodialer in action.

Exercise 27.2. The Autodialer.

1. Click on the Autodialer button. Access will respond with a dialog box as shown in Figure 27.11. Note that Access will insert the contents of whatever field has the focus in the Autodialer's Number field.

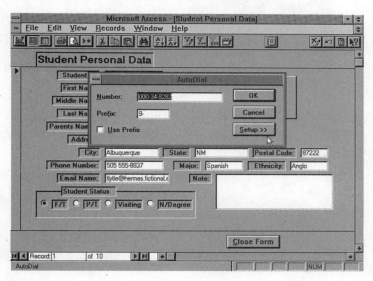

Figure 27.11. *The Autodialer starting.*

2. Click on the Setup>> button. Your screen should resemble Figure 27.12.

   This setup is right for one particular computer. Your options will likely be different.

3. Click on OK. Immediately Click on OK for the next message box to cancel the call in progress.

   Your Autodialer is set up now and ready for action.

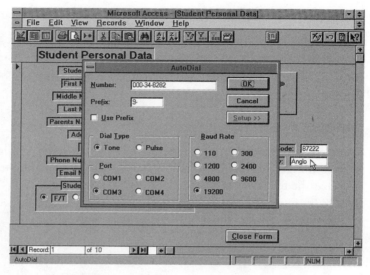

Figure 27.12. *The modem setup dialog box.*

To use the Autodialer, click in a phone number field, then click on the Autodialer button. If you use the sample data's first record, your screen should resemble Figure 27.13.

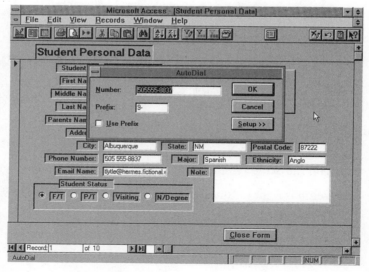

Figure 27.13. *The Autodialer in action.*

Click on the OK button. Access will start to dial your number. Your screen should resemble Figure 27.14. If you click on the OK button now without picking up the phone, you'll cancel the call.

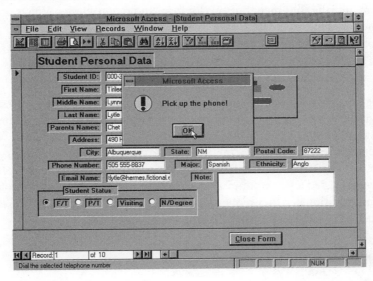

Figure 27.14. *Dialing from Access.*

<table><tr><td>**DO**</td><td>**DON'T**</td></tr></table>

DO use the Autodialer to increase the utility of your programs created using Access.

DON'T forget about prefixes. You probably need a 1 before long distance calls, but you don't want to make this a standard prefix because this will cause Access to dial a 1 before every number. Instead, keep in mind the need of a 1 before long distance calls only and include them in your phone numbers. So, if the call is to the 505 area code shown in Figure 27.13, enter this phone number not as 505 555-8837, but as 1505 555-8837.

Similarly, enter international numbers exactly as you'd dial them.

27

Creating a Custom Button

Access comes with an interesting array of buttons you can assign to toolbars. Some of them, like the alignment buttons for form and report Design Views, are so handy you almost wonder why they aren't standard issue on these toolbars. Even so, your applications will occasionally call for buttons Access doesn't have. In these cases, you can create a custom routine, attach it to a custom button, and include this button on any toolbar. The next two short exercises show how to do these two operations.

The fictional college has found that the registrar's office personnel often have to switch from their current form to the Class Entry form in response to a phone call. As things stand now, this requires closing the current form, entering Database View, and then opening the Class Entry form. Equally bad, the switch back requires similar steps in reverse. These switches are disrupting but necessary. The registrar's office employees have requested a way to immediately switch to the Class Entry form from any other form. Additionally, they request that when the Class Entry form is closed, the program return to where it left off in the other form.

> **The Access Way**
>
> A shortcut to the closing and opening of forms is to press F11 or Alt+F1 to immediately enter Database View from any form. You can then open any other form without closing the current one. The problem is less severe than the registrar's office made it out to be in the preceding paragraph, but still isn't as convenient as having a toolbar shortcut.

Exercise 27.3 creates a macro that opens the Class Entry form.

Exercise 27.3. A custom macro for a toolbar.

1. Return to the Database View. Click on the Macro button. Click on New to create a new macro. Click on File|Save As to save the new macro as Open Class Entry. Your screen should resemble Figure 27.15.

2. Click in the Action column. Pull down the combo box and locate the OpenForm action. Click on it.

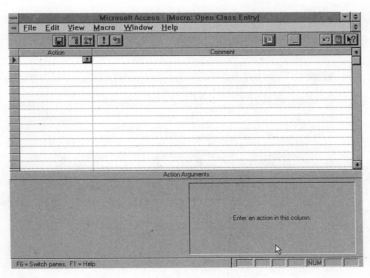

Figure 27.15. *Starting the form open macro.*

3. Click on the Form Name line in the Action Arguments section. Pull down the combo box and click on Class Entry. Your screen should resemble Figure 27.16.

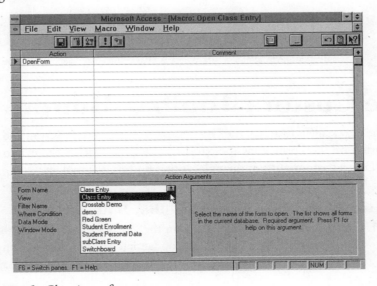

Figure 27.16. *Choosing a form to open.*

4. Click on the menu choices File|Save. Test this macro by clicking on the Run button in the toolbar. This should launch the Class Entry form. Your screen should resemble Figure 27.17.

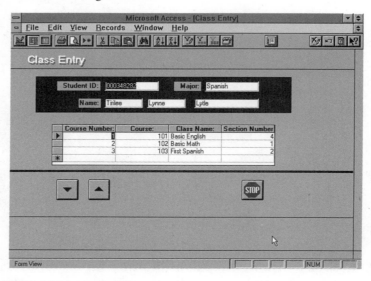

Figure 27.17. *The macro works.*

5. Click on the button with the Stop sign icon to close the form and return to the macro design grid. Close the macro if it's running right. If not, examine your macro and correct any wrong entries.

The Custom Toolbar Button

The next stage is to attach the Open Form macro to a new button and then place the button on the Form View toolbar. Exercise 27.4 attaches the macro from Exercise 27.3 to a custom button, then places that button in a toolbar.

Exercise 27.4. The Custom Toolbar button.

1. From the Database View, click on the Form button. Launch the Red Green form in Form View. The form you launch isn't important—any one will do. If you used the Red Green form, your screen should resemble Figure 27.18.

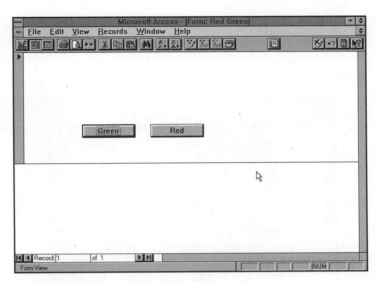

Figure 27.18. *The Red Green form opened.*

2. Right-click on the toolbar at any place where there's no button. Click on the Toolbars selection from the pop-up menu. Your screen should resemble Figure 27.19.

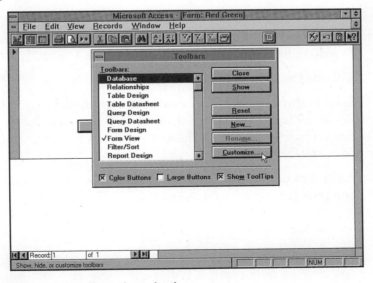

Figure 27.19. *The Toolbars choice list box.*

3. Click on the Customize button. Scroll the left list box down until you see All Macros. Click on that entry. This will bring up a list of all macros. Locate Open Class Entry and click on that. Your screen should resemble Figure 27.20.

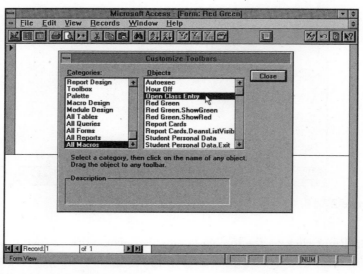

Figure 27.20. *Locating the macro.*

4. Click on and drag Open Class Entry onto the toolbar right next to the Autodialer button. Your screen should resemble Figure 27.21.

5. Click on the Close button.

   Every macro dragged to the toolbar will show the same scroll-like icon. While this is all right if you only have one macro on a toolbar, if you have many, it can be confusing. The next steps show how to customize the icon of any toolbar button.

6. Right-click on the new button. Click on the Customize choice from the pop-up menu. Your screen should resemble Figure 27.22.

The Access Way

You can customize any toolbar during a customize session by choosing the Show button for any highlighted toolbar in the Toolbars list box

shown in Figure 27.19. These exercises skip this step for simplicity, but you should know it's there. Similarly, you can customize a button face without exiting the button placement routine, but this exercise exits then re-enters so you can see each step of this procedure.

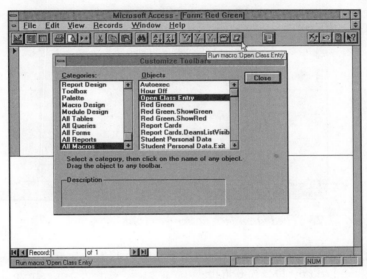

Figure 27.21. *Inserting the macro into the toolbar.*

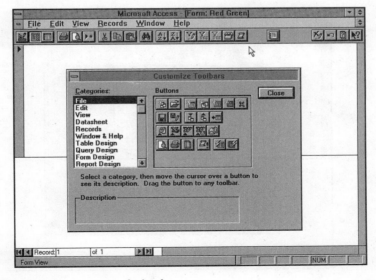

27

Figure 27.22. *The customize dialog box.*

7. Again, right-click on the macro button. Access will pop up a new menu with one entry—Choose Button Face. Your screen should resemble Figure 27.23.

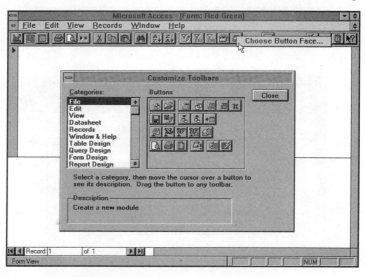

Figure 27.23. *The button face customize menu.*

8. Left-click on the menu selection. Click on the button face that has a face on it and edit the Description line to read `Class Entry`. Your screen should resemble Figure 27.24.

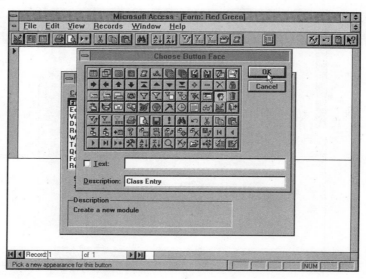

Figure 27.24. *Customizing the button's face and balloon help.*

9. Click on OK, then close. Move your cursor over the button. You'll see your new button icon and new balloon help entry. Your screen should resemble Figure 27.25.

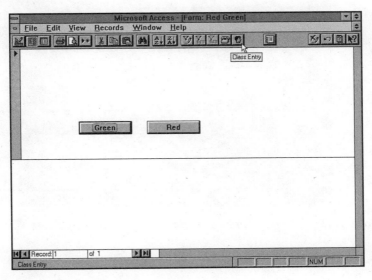

Figure 27.25. *The finished custom button.*

Click on the new button. Access will bring up the Class Entry form. Your screen should resemble Figure 27.26.

Click on the Stop sign button to exit Class Entry. Access switches you back to the Red Green form where you left off.

The Access Way

Access switched back to the Red Green form when Class Entry closed because it never closed Red Green when it launched Class Entry. Had the macro closed the current form before launching Class Entry, exit from Class Entry would have landed you back in the Database View.

If you're running Access on a low RAM computer, you might not be able to open several Access forms at the same time and get satisfactory performance.

27

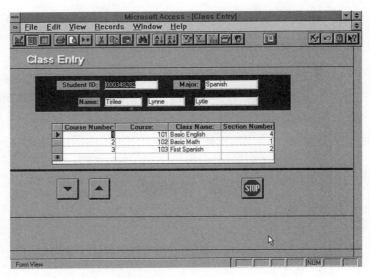

Figure 27.26. *The new button in action.*

Morning Summary

You can add, move, or delete buttons from any toolbar. The simplest way to do this is to launch the view that has the toolbar you want to modify, right-click on it, choose Customize, and navigate to find the button you want to add. Once the customize box is showing, you can freely delete or move any visible toolbar button.

One of the handiest buttons is the Autodialer. Adding the Autodialer to a toolbar gives you the ability to dial from within Access.

You can attach a macro to a button and then place that button on a toolbar. You can also customize the look of a button. While you can't attach Access Basic code directly to a button, you can attach a macro with the RunCode action that will call Access Basic routines.

> **Note:** This chapter is a reworked version of my old book. I felt it was a waste to redo it from scratch since this material applies to both Accesses equally. There are some significant but small changes, especially for continuity with the rest of the book. Please use this version rather than the last.

28

Programming Made Easy with Access Basic

This lesson covers

- ☐ When to use Access Basic
- ☐ Making a custom function
- ☐ Variables, loops, and other programming concepts
- ☐ Identifiers
- ☐ Message Boxes
- ☐ Input Boxes

Access Basic is the fully functional programming language for the Access database program. Using it is significantly more difficult than using Access itself or the macro extensions of Access. Microsoft has made it a design goal that using Access should not require programming in Basic for most database chores. However, there are some tasks that simply require its use.

When To Use Access Basic

Use Access Basic when nothing else will do the job. You need Access Basic when

- ☐ You need to create a custom function not possible through an expression.

- ☐ You need to get complex input from your user. Macros and parameter queries allow simple data input, but these tools are limited to a single input data line with an OK and Cancel button. You need Access Basic for a more complex input.

- ☐ You need to perform a conditional loop. Macros cannot, for example, use loops like the WHILE...WEND loop. WHILE...WEND means WHILE [a certain condition exists perform a certain task and] WEND [end when the condition fails to exist or ends].

- ☐ You need to trap errors; that is, if an error occurs when the macro is running, the results can be unpredictable. Writing Access Basic Code (ABC) makes it possible to determine what to do when an unexpected error occurs. This is something anyone who uses your applications will appreciate.

- ☐ You need to use Dynamic Data Exchange (DDE), allowing data to be exchanged "on the fly" with other Windows-based applications. This means a second application can process your data in realtime.

☐ You need to invoke Windows API (Application Program Interface). The Windows API is a library of functions used to interact with the Windows Environment. This extends the already powerful Access environment.

Custom Functions

You've seen several built-in Access functions such as `Now()` and `sum()` in previous chapters. As you design your forms, you might find yourself repeatedly typing in a long, calculated expression. Rather than continuing to do this, you could create a custom function that does the same thing. In a module, you'd type something like this:

```
Function Repeat(AnyField)
Repeat = That long expression
End Function
```

In this case, the name of the function is `Repeat`. It will apply to some field represented by `AnyField`, and the entry `That long expression` is the long expression you're converting to a custom function.

This is similar to elementary algebra. One of the first things you learn with algebra is to use letter symbols to replace certain numeric quantities. So if in algebra you saw

```
Let A = 2+3+4+5
```

and then saw the expression

```
B = A + 3
```

you'd understand that the quantity B is equal to 17. In the preceding code example, you take the long expression and assign it to the function `Repeat`.

Complex Input

Macros have to work with what they find already entered into Access. You can't poke new information into them when they run. In some cases, you might want to have your user enter information during a database operation or put it into jargon at runtime. You've seen how queries can act on user-entered parameters. Using Access Basic, you can go further. You can develop a program that asks users for information and then executes an action based on what they enter.

28

Conditional Loops

A conditional loop executes, or fails to execute, a particular action until some other condition exists. Using macro conditions you can, in some cases, test to see if a certain thing is true and act accordingly. That's a static test—it checks once to see if something's true and moves on. Say you want to get a user input, test to see if it's between 1 and 35, and then take different actions depending upon whether the input's from 1 to 10, 11 to 21, 22 to 30, or 31 to 35. Doing this in Access Basic is quite easy.

ACCESS JARGON

> **conditional loop:** a feature available in Access Basic that repeats a group of statements as long as a certain condition is true. For example, you might create a conditional loop to keep prompting the user for new records as long as he or she didn't press the Escape key, telling Access that "as long as the Escape key isn't pressed, keep on doing this." This is similar to the Condition section of the macro design grid, but Access Basic allows for the possibility of dynamic conditions.

You might force macros to test these conditions, but the process is rather laborious. However, you can't use a macro to get a runtime user input to test.

The Event-Driven Model

In the past, database programming languages—for example, the one that comes with the dBASE family of products—executed procedurally; that is, from top to bottom. Access Basic, on the other hand, is event-driven, meaning it responds to events usually caused by users. The examples used in this lesson respond to the event of a pushed button. They could just as easily respond to form events such as On Exit, On Enter, On Open, Mouse Over, and so forth.

What's the Difference?

Programs using traditional procedural programming languages like Pascal or dBASE execute outside of the user's ability to control. Once started, a procedural program just

goes, following its own programmed path unless a hard interrupt ends its run and only occasionally stopping to either display a message or get some user-supplied information. The program and programmer are in control.

Windows programs, on the other hand, are all independent processes that can be started and stopped by the user at just about any point. As event-driven programs, they respond to the user's needs or actions. Such things as clicking a mouse, moving a cursor into a field, pressing a button on a form, loading a form, and exiting a field are all events that can trigger any action you care to program into the event.

You've Already Done One

In Chapter 25, "More Macro Magic," you created a routine that responded to the contents of a control. The macro then either posted a message box or didn't. Note, there would never have been a message box if the event of exiting an updated control had occurred.

Identifiers

Access Basic uses the same identifier syntax as Access macros. The line of code

```
If Forms![Test Form]![Test Field] < 10 Then...
```

tests to see if the contents of the control `Test Field`, embedded in the form `Test Form`, equal less than the value of `10`. If so, Access Basic executes the line following the word `Then`.

Annotating Code

Unless you create the simplest functions and subroutines, you should annotate your code using remarks. Remarks or annotations don't execute with your code, but rather enable you or others to know your intentions for what a particular segment of code is supposed to do. Remarks are a nuisance when creating code, but they become invaluable when you need to come back to the code weeks or months later to do some maintenance or alter the code to a slightly different purpose. Remarks also enable others to follow your coding logic.

28

DO	DON'T

DO comment well. If you program Access for others, you have an ethical responsibility to heavily remark your Access Basic and macro code. Not doing so might make the code you write inaccessible, and your customer might later need to modify or rewrite what you've created. As an analogy, your failing to remark your code, thus making it difficult or impossible for someone else to modify, is similar to a car dealer's putting a combination lock on a car's hood so only that dealership can perform maintenance on the engine.

DON'T fall into the trap of not remarking while writing the code using the excuse that you'll come back to it later. That later rarely comes and if it does, you might have, by that time, forgotten what remarking needs to be made.

You insert remarks (usually called "comments") into your code by starting the remark with either the keyword REM or the single quote mark. Look at the following code fragments:

```
REM This example demonstrates remarks in Access Basic
If Sales > Expenses THEN : REM > symbol means greater than
Profit = True 'We made money
...
```

The first line uses the REM statement to tell Access, "Don't execute anything on this line." Line two uses the REM statement after the colon :. The colon in Basic means two or more separate instructions on one line. In this case, the colon separates an instruction with a remark. Another executable instruction could just as easily have followed the colon on this line. Line three uses the single quote to tell Access, "Don't execute anything on this line after the quote mark."

A Question of Style

Its critics say Basic is a difficult-to-maintain programming language, but the problem is more the way people use it than anything inherent in the language itself. Three traps people fall into are cramming too many instructions on one line, not remarking, and using non-descriptive labels. Each trap makes the code much more difficult to understand than if the separate instructions were each given on separate lines, the code

was liberally remarked, and variables had descriptive labels. Basic doesn't care if each instruction gets its own line, if remarks exist, or if variables have long names. Code Example One and Code Example Two execute identically:

Code Example One

```
Dim A As Integer:Dim B(0 To 50):GoSub X1
```

Code Example Two

```
Dim DepartmentNumber As Integer 'Department Number is whole
REM Each Department has 0 to 50 people.
Dim NumberOfEmployees(0 To 50)
GoSub Initialize 'Go to initialization routines
```

In Code Example One, the programmer crams all the code on one line and fails to either remark the code or use descriptive labels. Code Example Two uses separate lines, descriptive labels, and plenty of remarks. Which do you think will be clearer if in three months this or another programmer needs to return to modify this code snippet?

The Access Way

Don't worry if you can't follow these code snippets. They're here only to illustrate principles. Actual instructions for using Access Basic's vocabulary follows this conceptual introduction. In the preceding case, the Dim code word is a holdover from early Basic days. It's short for "dimension" and was first used to tell the computer how much storage space to reserve for a particular array. Array is computer talk for a matrix, so the line

```
Dim NumberOfEmployees(0 To 50)
```

means, "computer, reserve enough space for 51 entries in a matrix under the name NumberOfEmployees." Access Basic uses the Dim statement for more than arrays. It also tells Access the type of variable, as in the line

```
Dim DepartmentNumber As Integer
```

which tells Access DepartmentNumber will be a whole number or an integer.

If you are new to computer programming, you might be having some trouble understanding some of these concepts. Just plow on until you start working the examples later on, and then many of these abstractions will come into focus.

28

Functions, Declarations, and Subs

Access Basic is composed of three building blocks: Function Procedures, Declarations, and Sub Procedures.

The Declarations section of an Access Basic module globally defines constants, variables, and data types for later use in Subs and Functions. A global declaration is valid for the entire scope of the Basic module but not valid across different modules. Access Basic, like many Basics, will allow implicit declarations. This is terrible programming practice and is the prime reason for Basic having a bad reputation among professional programmers. You can force Access Basic to error on implicit declarations by adding the line

```
Option Explicit
```

in the module's Declarations section.

What's This Implicit/Explicit Business All About?

Unless you're an experienced programmer, the preceding section might seem a little difficult to follow. Here's an explanation. When writing programming code, you assign names to variables and constants. Variables are values that can change during the execution of a code. Constants are values that cannot change during code execution. A constant might be the value of an interest rate declared as

```
Const InterestRate = .08750
```

in the Declarations section. Then the code line

```
100 * InterestRate
```

would return the value 8.75.

Variables change depending upon program code or user input. In the preceding example, you don't ask your user for a value of InterestRate, you declare it. In the following example, GotUserNumber is a variable because its value depends upon user input.

Danger in Variable Land

Look at the following code snippet. Here's how it's supposed to work: Access displays a message box with the title Implicit Variable Demo. It then sets zero as the value for the variable Defvalue. It then takes input from the user and triples it in the last line.

This code will not run correctly due to a typo.

```
Prompt = "Enter the number you want to triple" 'sets msg
MTitle = "Implicit Variable Demo" ' Title of msgbox.
Defvalue = 0 : REM set a default value to zero
GotUserNumber = InputBox(Prompt, MTitle, Defvalue)
' Get a 5) number using an input box.
GotUserNnmber = GotUserNumber * 3 'What's wrong here?
```

If you're a very careful reader, you might have spotted the error. The intent of this code is to triple a number specified by a user. The number entered by the user here is given the variable label GotUserNumber by the program in line four. The last line is supposed to change the variable to three times the user-entered amount, but it doesn't. In other words, the intent of this code is for the variable GotUserNumber to be equal to three times the value entered by the user.

There's a minor typo that will throw a giant-sized monkey wrench in this code. The programmer mistyped the variable name, GotUserNumber, as GotUserNnmber in the last line. The result of this error will be that the variable GotUserNumber will contain the original amount inputted by the user, while a new variable, GotUserNnmber, implicitly declared, will contain the triple value of GotUserNumber.

> **Note:** This lesson uses a lot of jargon specific to computer programming. Terms like declarations, variables, constants, code, function, array, and subs will be familiar if you've programmed a computer before but might still be vague concepts at this point if you haven't. Rather than worrying about memorizing the exact definitions now, continue along and, with use, these terms will grow clear. If you forget a definition now, look it up in the glossary.

If the programmer later uses the value of GotUserNumber in a calculation, the calculation will come out wrong. Can you imagine the gravity of this error if this final calculation is critical?

Had the programmer used the Option Explicit instruction in the Declarations section of this module and then declared GotUserNumber as a type of variable, Access Basic would have complained when it hit the GotUserNnmber word.

28

Function Procedures

Procedures create functions for use in Access tables, forms, queries, reports, and macros. These functions are called by other Access objects such as forms. Here's a section of an Access function to determine the commission amount:

```
Function WhatRate(SalesValue)
If SalesValue > 10000 THEN
WhatRate = .05
Else
WhatRate = .025
End If
```

Note the variables `SalesValue` and `CommissionRate` were declared appropriately in the Declarations section of the module holding this function; however, to focus only on the subject, the entire Declarations section isn't shown here.

Sub Procedures

Sub Procedures are identical to Function Procedures except they can only be called by other Subs or Functions and cannot return a value to the caller. In the preceding example, the value `CommissionRate` is returned by the Procedure, and the function itself is called by a form event. Subs are used for housekeeping chores within modules. Most of the time you'll be using Function Procedures rather than Subs.

Use Subs for altering values already contained in calling Functions. Access uses Subs as Event Procedures when you've used a wizard to create a control.

A Simple First Code Example

The first code exercise is simplicity itself, but it demonstrates basic programming concepts and how to tie an Access Basic function to a form object.

Exercise 28.1. Tie an Access Basic function to a form control.

This exercise links a new function to a form control.

1. Launch Access. Open the College database if necessary. Click the Module button. Click New. Access moves you to a screen like the one in Figure 28.1.

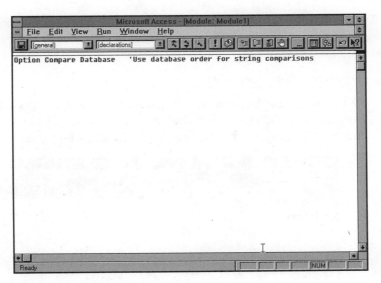

Figure 28.1. *Starting Access Basic.*

Before moving on, take a look at the Button bar. Right in the middle there's a combo box labeled Procedure. This combo box has (declarations) showing. This means we're now in the declarations section of this yet-to-be-named module. Pull down the combo box. Right now, the only entry in it is the (declarations) as you've yet to define a function or a sub.

The Access Way

Access modules can contain many functions or subs. This is similar to macros; one macro at the database level might contain many named macros. You should use it similarly too. If you have a series of related procedures, contain them within a module rather than having a new module for each procedure.

28

Back to the screen. The first two buttons on the left move you to the previous and next procedure, respectively. Right now they do nothing because there are no procedures yet. After this there's a New Procedure button and next is our familiar Run button. At the far right of the toolbar are the Undo and Help buttons.

2. Position the cursor back to where it was in the module by clicking at the cursor's original place. Without moving the cursor at all from where it is, enter

```
Function DisplayMessage()
```

When you press the Enter key, Access scans the line, realizes you're trying to define a new function with the name DisplayMessage, and moves you to a function design area. Your screen should look like Figure 28.2.

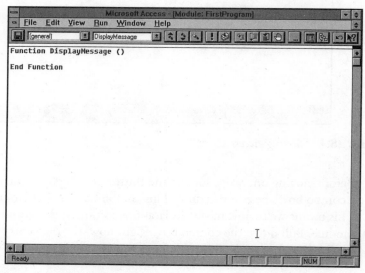

Figure 28.2. *Starting a new function.*

3. Note the Procedure combo box now contains your new function. Pull down the combo box and see the list has now been extended to two entries: (declarations) and DisplayMessage. Click (declarations). Access moves you back to the declarations section of the module. Pull down the combo box again. Click DisplayMessage. Access takes you back to the function design.

4. This function simply displays the message I'm a computer programmer at a button press. Add the following line right below the Function DisplayMessage() line:

```
MsgBox "I'm a computer programmer"
```

Your screen should resemble Figure 28.3.

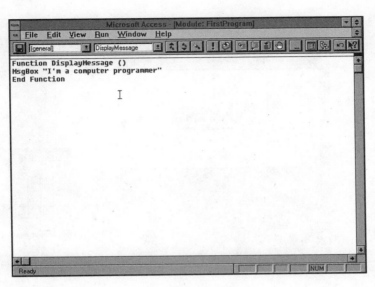

Figure 28.3. *Entering the executing code line.*

5. Pull down the File menu and select Close. When Access asks if you want to save the changes to the module, click Yes and save it under the name `FirstProgram`.

A Place to Show Off

You need a place to demonstrate the new function. Exercise 28.2 puts it into use and also shows you how to vary it.

Exercise 28.2. Using the function.

1. Click the Forms button in the database window and choose New. Don't bind the form to any table or query, and choose Blank Form rather than a wizard. Make sure the Toolbox is showing. Click the command button tool. Draw a command button in the detail section of the form measuring about one-half inch high and one inch long. Your screen should resemble Figure 28.4.

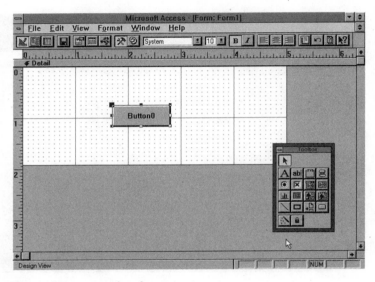

Figure 28.4. *A place to attach a function.*

2. Open the Properties list box if necessary and locate the On Click property.
   Enter =DisplayMessage() on the line next to On Push.

The Access Way

If you were assigning a macro called DisplayMessage to the On Push
property of this command button, you'd enter DisplayMessage at the On
Push property line. Since DisplayMessage is a function written in Access
Basic, you have to indicate this to Access. The syntax of starting the
property with an = and ending with a () tells Access to look for
DisplayMessage as a function in a Basic module.

Your screen should resemble Figure 28.5.

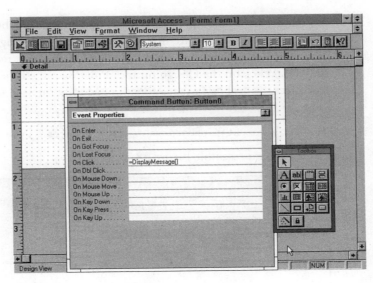

Figure 28.5. *Entering the new function.*

3. Switch to Form View. Click on the button. When you do, the form should bring up the message box as shown in Figure 28.6.

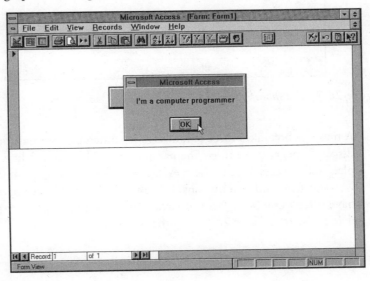

Figure 28.6. *The running function.*

4. Now to modify the function. Click OK to close the message box. Close the form, saving it as `Temp Form`. Return to the module by clicking the Module button in the database window. Highlight the FirstProgram module (if necessary) and click on the Design button. Pull down the Procedure combo box and select the `DisplayMessage` function. Modify the second line to the following:

```
MsgBox "I'm a computer programmer", 65, "Progress in Access"
```

Your screen should resemble Figure 28.7.

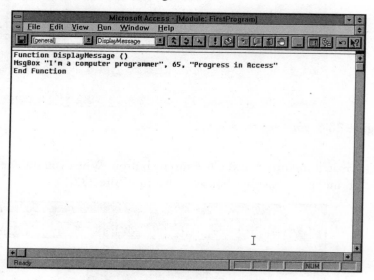

Figure 28.7. *The modified message box.*

A message box takes three parameters separated by commas: the message, the display type, and the title. The parameter 65 added to the line in the second place tells Access to alter the message box to one having an Information Message icon and two buttons, OK and Cancel. Message boxes in Access have three numerically set properties: button count/type, icon type, and default button. Table 28.1 gives these values.

Table 28.1. Message box properties.

Button Type/Number

Value	Meaning
0	Display OK button
1	Display OK and Cancel buttons
2	Display Abort, Retry, Ignore buttons
3	Display Yes, No, and Cancel buttons
4	Display Yes and No buttons
5	Display Retry and Cancel buttons

Icon

Value	Meaning
0	No icon
16	Critical message icon
32	Warning (query) icon
48	Warning (message) icon
64	Information icon

Default

Value	Default Button
0	First button
256	Second button
512	Third button

28

Adding the value 65 as the message box type changes the message box to one having the properties of 64 + 1. Refer to the preceding table and note 64 gives you the Information icon and the 1 gives you two buttons, OK and Cancel. Adding the string `"Progress in Access"` as the final property alters the message box's title to one saying Progress in Access.

5. Close and save this module. Open the Temp Form in Form View. Click on its single button. Your three-parameter message box is done and your screen should resemble Figure 28.8.

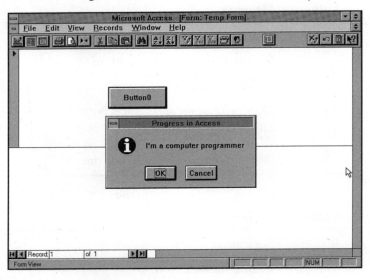

Figure 28.8. *The modified message box.*

Congratulate yourself. You've just entered the ranks of Access Basic programmers. Click OK or Cancel and close this form.

Passing Variable Parameters

Remember, one of the reasons you might need to code in Access Basic is to get user input beyond a parameter query. The following exercise adapts the message box from Exercise 28.2 to accept user-defined criteria for use in a message box display.

The chief tool for getting user input in Access Basic is the Inputbox function. Using Inputbox is very similar to using the Messagebox function. The three significant differences are as follows:

☐ You need to choose the right Inputbox function depending upon if you want a variant or a string returned.

☐ An Inputbox passes its contents to a variable.

☐ You can place an Inputbox anywhere on the screen.

Defining A Global Type

The section titled "Functions, Declarations, and Subs," mentions declaration of variables. The message box example used no variables, so no declarations were necessary. An input box requires an implicit or explicit variable declaration because it's a variable that Access Basic uses to capture the user input and move that input to the message box.

Since you'll be using only one variable in Exercise 28.3, it's slightly overkill to explicitly declare that one variable; however, it's never too early to learn good programming practice.

Exercise 28.3. Declaring variables.

1. From the Database View, click on the Module tab. Click on the FirstProgram module and click on the Design button. Your screen should resemble Figure 28.9.

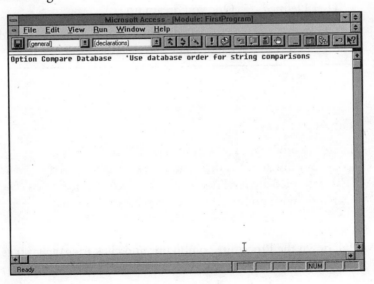

Figure 28.9. *Getting ready to make some declarations.*

28

2. Enter Option Explicit on the first empty line and Dim Response As String on the second line of the declarations section. Option Explicit forces you to declare variables before using them. The line Dim Response As String declares there will be a variable with the name Response and it will be a string. See Table 28.2 for other types of Access Basic variables.

Table 28.2. Access Basic variable types.

Type	Meaning
String	Alphanumeric and non-printing characters.
Long	Whole numbers from –2,147,483,648 to 2,147,483,647.
Integer	Whole numbers from –32,678 to 32,676.
Single	Single precision floating point data type. Uses less storage space than Double.
Currency	A high precision data type optimized for monetary transactions. Use this data type for critical calculations such as accrued interest.
Double	A general-purpose high precision floating point.
User Defined	One you dream up.
Variant	The default Access data type used for undeclared data types.

The Access Way

There are other types of Access objects also. The subject's very wide in scope, but much of the discussion's really an advanced topic not relevant to an intermediate level book such as *Teach Yourself Access 2 in 14 Days*. Search online help for complete coverage of this topic.

3. Pull down the Procedure combo box and click `DisplayMessage` to move to the procedure. Enter

```
Response = InputBox$("Enter a Message", "Input Box Demo", "I choose
nothing")
```

on the second line of the procedure, below the `Function DisplayMessage()` line. Modify the third line to read

```
MsgBox Response, 65, "Progress in Access"
```

Your screen should resemble Figure 28.10.

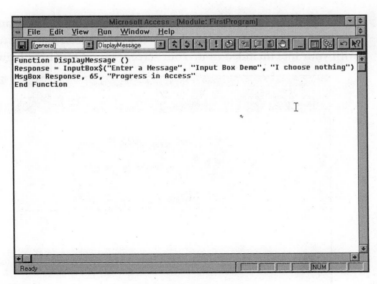

Figure 28.10. *Input box code added to the function.*

4. Close the module, saving changes.

   Open the Temp Form form in Run mode if it's not there already. Click the command button. Access gives you the input box shown in Figure 28.11.

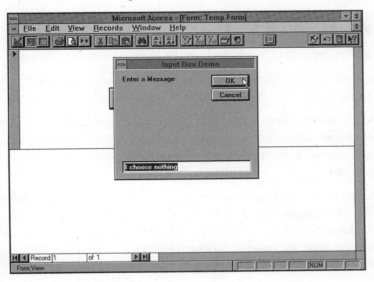

Figure 28.11. *The input box in action.*

5. Enter anything that comes to mind on the input line. The example entered `Programming is Easy After All!` Click OK. Access runs the message box with your line included in it. Your screen should resemble Figure 28.12.

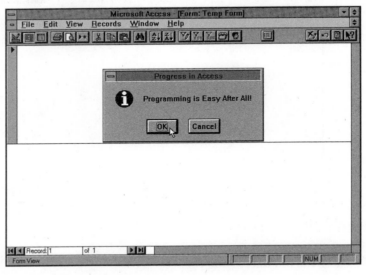

Figure 28.12. *The message box with the input box's contents.*

How It Worked

Examine the second line of code in the `DisplayMessage()` function:

```
Response = InputBox$("Enter a Message", "Input Box Demo", "I choose
nothing")
```

The first word is `Response`, which is the variable you declared as a string type in the declarations section of this module. This part of the line tells Access where to store what you enter in the input box. In this case, Access stores the string in a variable called `Response`.

The rest of the line just defines the input box. The first part, `InputBox$`, tells Access to use an input box. The `$` part of the `InputBox$` statement tells Access the input box will return a string type variable. Had this read `InputBox`, Access would have expected a variant type of variable. Using `InputBox$` here is another example of good programming practice rather than dire necessity.

The next part, `"Enter a Message"`, is the prompt for the input box. `"Input Box Demo"` is the title of the input box, and finally `"I choose nothing"` is the default value for the input box. If you didn't enter a string in the input box but just clicked OK, Access would have displayed `I choose nothing` as the message in the message box. Click on cancel to close the input box.

Additionally, the `InputBox$` parameters could have included x and y positions for the input box. X and y placement parameters are numbers representing how far in twips the coordinate position of the input box should be from the upper left-hand corner of the Access screen. A twip is 1/20 point and a point is 1/72 inch, so there are 1,440 twips to an inch.

Close the form, saving any changes you've made. Return to the module, making it active. Close it, saving changes.

Summary

When the Customize dialog box is visible you can add, move, or delete buttons from any toolbar. Also, through the customize process you can create custom buttons, change the look of new or built-in buttons, and change the balloon help attached to buttons of your making.

Access has been carefully designed so that no programming is necessary in most cases. However, it also includes both macros and Access Basic. Most people find programming Access macros much easier than using Access Basic because Access steps you through the macro process, but there are times you'll need to use Access's supplied Basic programming language.

Basic as a language has been criticized by professional programmers as a sloppy language. However, that's an unfair characterization. Basic has great flexibility that permits sloppiness, whereas more structured languages like Pascal won't. By using good programming practices, you can create good maintainable code in Basic as well as you can in any other language.

An important thing to remember to use when programming in Access Basic is the Option Explicit statement in the declarations section of a module. This forces you to declare variables prior to using them. Using Option Explicit prevents you from inadvertently implicitly declaring variables by making the inevitable typo.

The second thing to remember is to annotate your code using remarks. You define a remark by starting a Basic statement with the REM keyword or the single quote. The

28

examples in this lesson were too simple to require remarks, but if your procedures or declarations grow to above 10 lines or so, or if you feel your programming logic isn't obvious, make sure to use a liberal number of remarks.

These examples created a new function `DisplayMessage()` for use anywhere in the College database. It is a simple function, but it also demonstrates the fundamentals of Access Basic programming.

Q&A

Q **Can I use a function I created in Access Basic in a macro?**

A Yes. The way to do this is to use the `RunCode` macro action and specify the function you want to run along with any parameters the function needs.

Q **I've heard Basic is a bad language to use because it's so full of `GoTo` branches. How true is this? Should I avoid `GoTo`'s when I program?**

A This is a preposterous charge against Basic. Sure, some people misuse `GoTo` statements to create spaghetti-like code that's quite difficult to follow much less maintain, but all programming languages need to have some branching. It's not the use of branching routines, but the misuse of them that's the problem. There are just as many bad practices committed using other languages such as Fortran or C as in Basic.

It is true that Basic is a bit freer though and will let you go much further astray than very tight languages such as Pascal or ModulA. Like any kind of freedom, the freedom Basic allows you must be practiced in conjunction with responsibility.

As soon as you start doing high-power Access Basic programming, you will need some branching, and there's no reason to avoid either `GoSub` or `GoTo` statements. The first thing to keep in mind when creating these structures is to annotate where the jump goes, why it jumps, and where it will jump back to in a remark. The second thing is to clearly label where you are jumping to. The statement

```
Goto A
```

isn't terribly clear. The statement

```
Goto DoSortRoutine
```

is much better.

The third thing to keep in mind is to avoid jumping to another jump. The following is just about impossible to understand after it's written:

```
Goto Animate
...
Animate:
Goto SectionEight
....
SectionEight:
Goto DoItNow
DoItNow:
```

The fourth rule is to jump to labels, which are descriptive words followed by a colon, rather than line numbers. Jumping to line numbers is a practice particularly fraught with danger.

Finally, only use GoTo's when you can't use the following more structured statements:

```
If...Then...Else; For...Next; Select Case; or Do...Loop
```

Q Is there some way to use Access Basic to put pictures on command buttons?

A You can do this, but you don't need Access Basic. With the button highlighted in Design View, open the Properties list box for the tool. Locate the Picture property. Just enter the full path for the bitmap you want to include on the button on this line. For example, if you wanted to place a picture `c:\windows\skylight.bmp` in the button shown in Temp Form, enter `c:\windows\skylight.bmp` on the line to the right of the property Picture. Make sure to include the entire path for your bitmapped picture when trying this trick. You also can click on the ellipsis button and browse for the picture.

Figure 28.13 is a huge command button with a .bmp picture assigned to it.

28

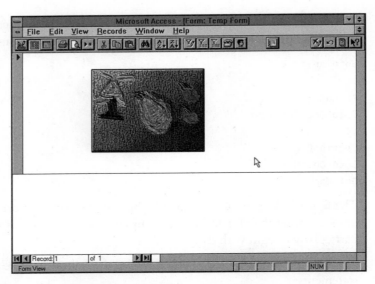

Figure 28.13. *A really large and colorful command button.*

Q What's the button limit for a Toolbar?

A You can place as many buttons as you have room. Don't overdo it because too many buttons will make it difficult to find any.

Workshop

Here's where you can test and apply the lessons you learned today.

Quiz

Possible answers to these questions are provided in Appendix A.

1. Say you have the statement

    ```
    DefStr A-Z
    ```

    in the declarations section of an Access Basic module and

    ```
    Dim Interest As Double
    ```

    in a procedure. Will Interest be a string or a double precision floating-point type when used in the procedure?

2. If you want to execute a loop 10 times, should you use a macro or a module?

3. How would you use Access Basic to create a custom menu on a form?

4. When would you use the Currency data type in Access Basic? What's the disadvantage of using this data type?

5. How do you create a remark in Access Basic code?

Put Access into Action

1. Start a new module.

2. Declare two string and one integer data types. The two strings will be a title and a message in a message box. The integer will be the message box type.

3. Create a new function, `Chapter28()` with three input box lines to give a user an opportunity to enter a message box title, message box message, and a message box type.

4. Add a message box function to the user-defined function that will display a message box using the criteria gotten from the input boxes.

5. Add placement parameters for each of the input boxes. Search online help for the exact syntax to do this. Close the module saving as LastExercise.

6. Open Temp Form in Design View.

7. Attach your custom function to the On Click property of the command button.

8. Test the function by switching to Form View and clicking the button.

9. Close the form and module, discarding changes.

28

Extra Credit

OLE 2,
Menu Building,
and More

This extra credit chapter shows you how to

☐ Attach external data sources

☐ Use Access with a spreadsheet

☐ Use Access tables in a word processor

☐ Take advantage of OLE 2 in Access

☐ Create custom menus

☐ Use custom menus in forms

External Data Sources

Access is carefully designed to be able to work cooperatively with other Windows and non-Windows programs. Sometimes you'll find that your data is in a table created by another program. While you can convert this table and use it in Access, in many instances this isn't desirable.

Consider, for example, a company with a mixed computing environment. Some people use Access, and some people who lack the hardware necessary for a Windows program still use Paradox for DOS, a text-based data manager. There might very well be data in Paradox tables that need to be used both by the Access and Paradox users. While Paradox lacks the ability to use Access tables, Access can use and update Paradox ones.

This example uses Paradox, but it could equally apply to other data managers such as dBASE.

If you have Paradox, you might want to work along with the following exercise, which shows how to attach an external table to an Access database. If you just read the steps you'll get a good idea of what's involved.

First, look at Figure 29.1. This is a fragment of a Paradox for DOS 3.5 table. The purpose of this table is to track fixed assets at the fictional college.

Since some users at the college who need to refer to this table still use Paradox but some use Access, the college's accounting department requested that this table be available from within both Paradox 3.5 and Access. Exercise 29.1 shows how to attach an external table to an Access database.

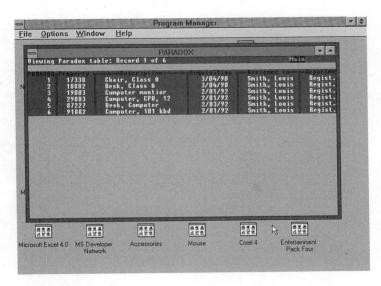

Figure 29.1. *The Paradox table.*

Exercise 29.1. Attaching an external table.

1. Launch Access and open the College database if necessary. Your screen should resemble Figure 29.2.

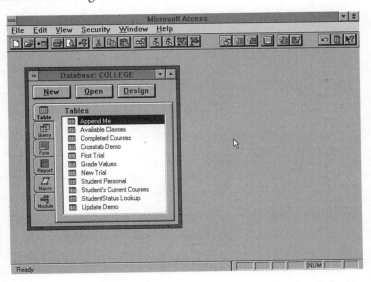

Figure 29.2. *Access ready for action.*

2. Pull down the File menu and select Attach Table. Your screen should resemble Figure 29.3.

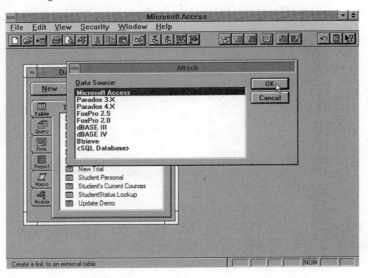

Figure 29.3. *Choose the type of table to attach.*

The Access Way

You need to have told Access's setup that you want to install certain drivers to attach these types of tables. If your File|Attach Table menu selection doesn't have the table type you need in the box shown in Figure 29.3, run Setup again and install the right driver.

3. For this exercise, click on the Paradox 3.X table type since the table was made using Paradox 3.5.

4. Access will respond with a Select File labeled common dialog box as shown in Figure 29.4. Since Paradox tables end in .db, Access filters for this extension file.

5. Click on the Attach button. Access will grind away a while and flash a success message box if all went well. Click on OK to close the message box; close the Select file dialog box. This should leave you with a screen resembling Figure 29.5. Your screen will differ, depending upon the name of the table you attached. This table's name was Paradox.

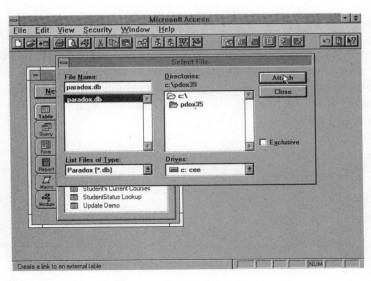

Figure 29.4. *Indicating the right table to attach.*

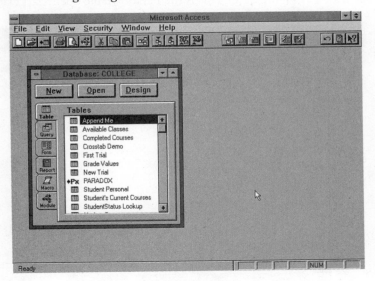

Figure 29.5. *The attached table at the Database View.*

The right-facing arrow next to the table's name indicates this is an attached table. The Px means it's a Paradox one. The name Paradox is the name of the table itself.

How Does It Work?

You can use attached tables just like ones made in your database, except you can't alter their structure in such a way to render them unreadable to the native program. For example, Access can use spaces in table names, but Paradox can't. You can't, therefore, change the name of the table to From Paradox because then the native program couldn't handle it.

> **The Access Way**
>
> Generally speaking, you're better off not even trying to restructure attached tables in Access. Let the native program do this. If you don't want to use the tables with the native program, don't attach them, import them. Then you're free to restructure all you want.

Take a look at Figure 29.6. This is the Paradox table opened in Datasheet View.

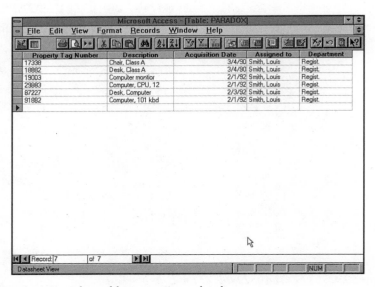

Figure 29.6. *A Paradox table in an Access database.*

Figure 29.7 shows a record added to the Paradox table.

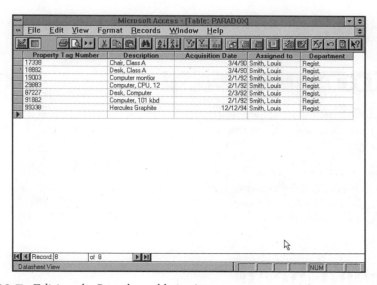

Figure 29.7. *Editing the Paradox table in Access.*

The new record shows the acquisition of a new video board for Louis Smith's computer. Now look at Figure 29.8.

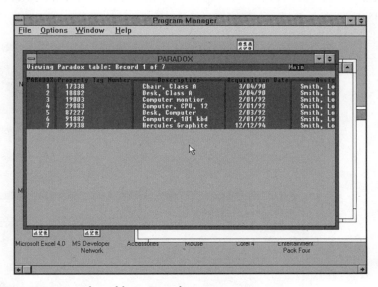

Figure 29.8. *Viewing the table in Paradox.*

Both Paradox and Access can view, edit, and update this table when it's attached to an Access database.

DO	DON'T

DO attach tables when you need to keep them in their native format for those occasions when you want the older programs to view, edit, or add to them.

DON'T expect to be able to open the table for editing simultaneously in Access and the older program unless your operating system can give you the necessary locking support.

Spreadsheets

Access can export to various spreadsheets, but as part of the Microsoft Office package, it naturally works best and easiest with Excel, which is also part of Office. Look at Figure 29.9. This is the College database at the Database View with the Query tab selected and the Report Cards query highlighted. Note the Toolbar button at the cursor.

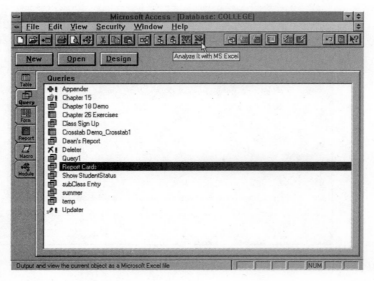

Figure 29.9. *The Analyze It button.*

Click on this button and whatever's highlighted is immediately brought up in Excel 5, as shown in Figure 29.10.

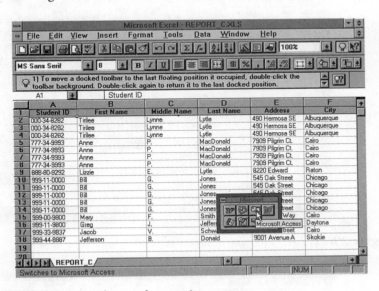

Figure 29.10. *Using Excel to analyze an Access query.*

Take a look at the Microsoft toolbar shown floating in the lower part of the spreadsheet grid. Excel has a link back to Access also. The other icons represent Microsoft programs in the Office plus FoxPro for Windows, which isn't a Microsoft program but is part of Microsoft's productivity offerings.

Once your query or table is in Excel, you naturally have all Excel's outstanding analytical tools available to you. For example, Figure 29.11 shows how a 10-second edit of the query gives the standard deviation for the entire raw grades population.

The Access Way

Access exports the values of formulas or expressions, not the expressions themselves, to Excel. Look at Figure 29.12; the expression that yielded the Weighted GPA has been replaced by the value calculated by that expression.

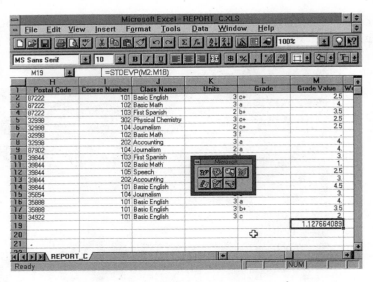

Figure 29.11. *Excel applying a statistical function to Access data.*

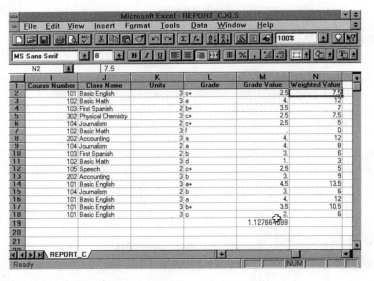

Figure 29.12. *Excel sees the values, not the expressions.*

Using Access Tables in a Word Processor

A common interaction between a word processor and a database is the mail merge. Access 2 has a built-in wizard for doing mail merges with Word for Windows, which makes such merges a snap.

Less well known, but often quite useful, is the use of database objects as a table in a word processor. The interactivity of the Microsoft Office group of programs makes this not only possible, but easy.

Take a look at Figure 29.13.

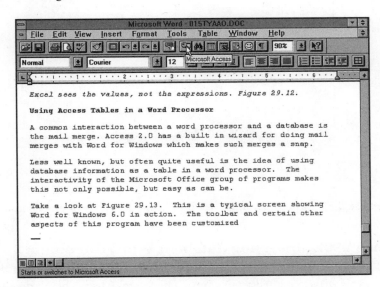

Figure 29.13. *Word for Windows in action showing the Access button.*

This is a typical screen showing Word for Windows 6 in action. The toolbar and certain other aspects of this program have been customized for this user. Take a look at the upper toolbar, the one right below the menu bar. There's a button with an Access icon on it that has Microsoft Access for its balloon help. Using this button, you can launch Access from Word. Embedding an Access table in a Word document takes a step or two more than clicking on a button.

Take a look at Figure 29.14. This is a tiny demonstration table made just for this chapter. It's included in the sample data. Using it, you'll see how easy it is to place this, or any other table, in your word processing document if you're using Word for Windows version 6 or later.

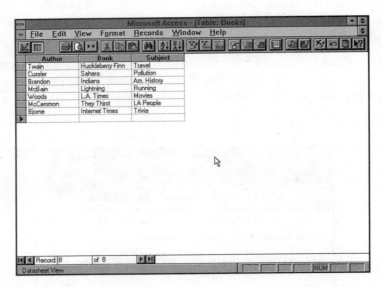

Figure 29.14. *The Books table.*

Exercise 29.2 shows how to embed an Access table in a Word document.

Exercise 29.2. Inserting data in a Word document.

1. Launch Word for Windows version 6 or higher. Have current the document you wish to embed a table into. This exercise uses a blank document called Worddemo. Your screen should resemble Figure 29.15.

2. Click on the menu selections Insert|Database. Your screen should resemble Figure 29.16.

3. Click on the Get Data button and specify the .mdb extension for the database in the bottom combo box of this dialog box. Navigate to where the College database is on your system. Double-click on the database's name. This demonstration uses C:\compact as a location for the database. Your screen should resemble Figure 29.17, except the location of your database will probably be different.

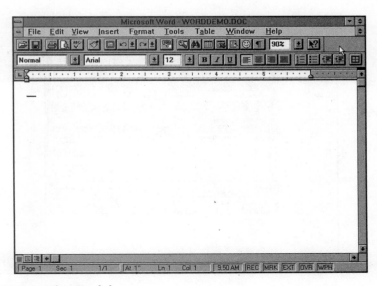

Figure 29.15. *The Word document.*

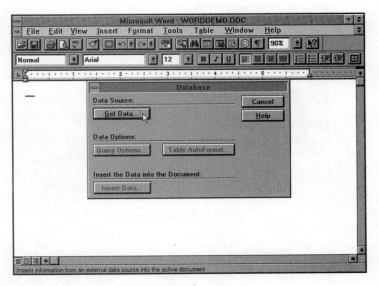

Figure 29.16. *The Database dialog box in Word.*

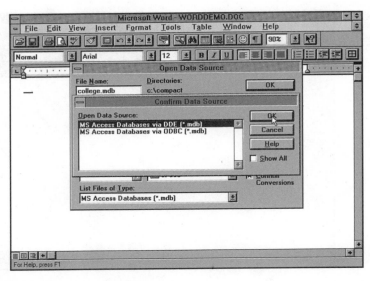

Figure 29.17. *Locating a database.*

4. Accept DDE as a transfer scheme; click on OK. You'll get a tabbed dialog where you get to specify which table or query to embed in your document. Your screen should resemble Figure 29.18.

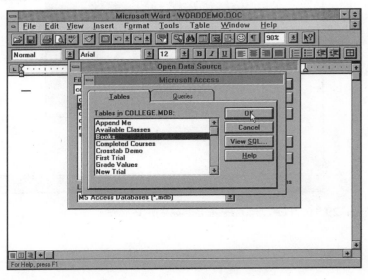

Figure 29.18. *Choose a table or query for embedding.*

5. Highlight the Books table and click on OK. This will bring you back to the first dialog box, as shown in Figure 29.19.

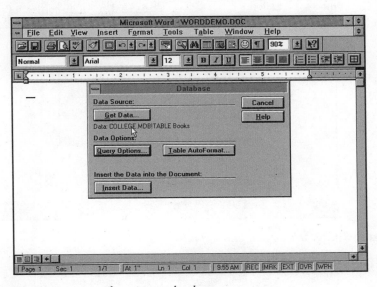

Figure 29.19. *Getting ready to insert the data.*

6. Click on the Insert Data button. Your screen should resemble Figure 29.20. Access gives you a choice of inserting all the data or just some of it. This exercise inserts all the data.

7. Click on OK. Windows will switch you to Access. Switch back to Word. Your screen should resemble Figure 29.21.

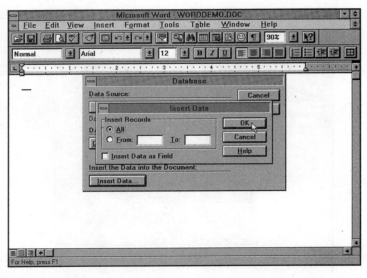

Figure 29.20. *The option to insert all the records or just some.*

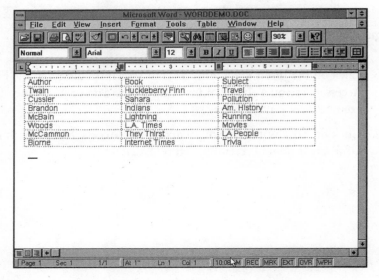

Figure 29.21. *An Access table inserted in a Word document.*

The new table is a standard Word table. You can edit or reformat as you see fit. After this type of insertion, there remains no link between Word and Access. Edits made in Access will not be reflected in the Word table and edits made to the Word table will not appear in the Access database.

OLE 2 Wonders

You can embed an entire application in your Access databases. This will give you the all the tools of an application like Word or Excel from within Access. The magic behind this is OLE 2. OLE means Object Linking and Embedding. You can use OLE compliant programs from within an Access form without ever leaving the form, as the next exercise shows.

Exercise 29.3 creates a Memo field in an otherwise blank form. When in this field, you'll have all of Word's editing tools available to you. To keep a solid focus, this exercise uses a new blank unbound form. You can do the same thing with your bound working forms.

Exercise 29.3. OLE 2 in action.

1. Start a new unbound form. Increase the size of the form design grid to give yourself some working room. Your screen should resemble Figure 29.22.

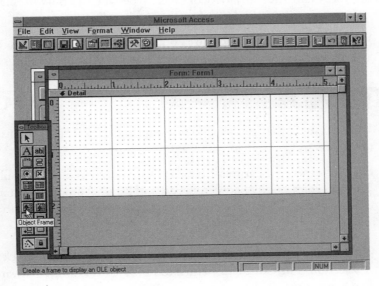

Figure 29.22. *Starting the new form.*

2. Click on the Object Frame tool in the Toolbox and insert a frame in the form design grid. Access will pop up a dialog box, as shown in Figure 29.23.

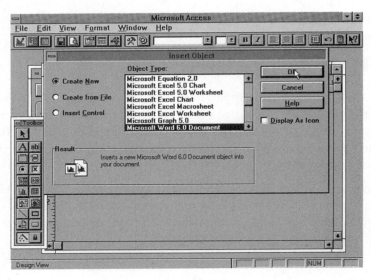

Figure 29.23. *The Insert Object dialog box.*

Note that there is a variety of object types you can bind to this field. Your exact selections will depend upon your installed programs.

3. Locate the Word for Windows 6 Document line, highlight it, and click on OK. Your screen should resemble Figure 29.24.

DO   DON'T

DO remember that you need fully compliant OLE 2 applications to render the results shown in Figure 29.23.

DON'T expect similar results using less than fully compliant applications. The best connectivity between Access and external programs comes from using it with the other programs that make up the Microsoft Office.

4. Enter any phrase such as the one shown in Figure 29.24. Click on the menu selections File|Close and Return to Form. This is located toward the top of the menu list, as shown in Figure 29.25.

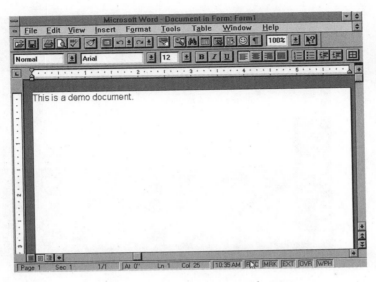

Figure 29.24. *Launching Word as an OLE server application.*

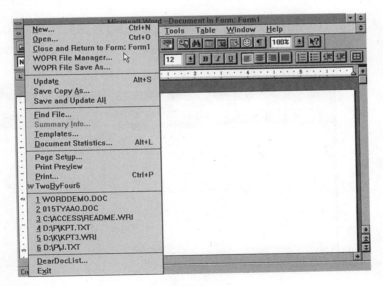

Figure 29.25. *Return with the link established.*

5. After you exit Word, your screen should resemble Figure 29.26.

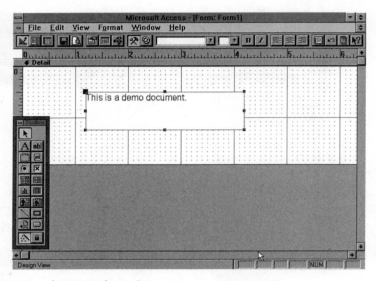

Figure 29.26. *The OLE object shown in Access's Design View.*

6. Open up the Properties list box if necessary. Switch the Enabled property from No, the default, to Yes. Switch to Form View. Your screen should resemble Figure 29.27.

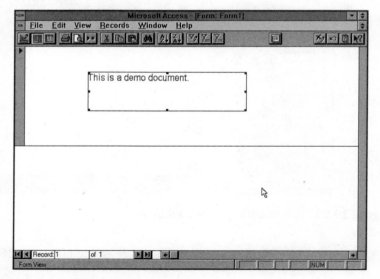

Figure 29.27. *The OLE object in Form View.*

Double-click on the OLE object. Windows brings up the Word toolbars for you to use when editing this object. You can now edit the contents of this object frame just as you would if you were in Word, because for all practical purposes you have a window into Word. Your screen should resemble Figure 29.28.

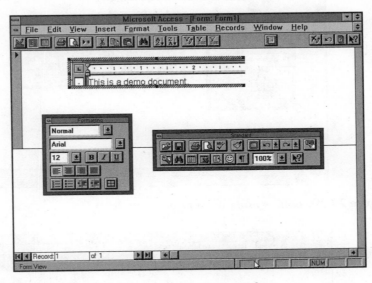

Figure 29.28. *The Word tools in use inside an Access form.*

This example changed the font for the entry from Arial to Braggadocio. The editing is shown in Figure 29.29.

Click anywhere outside of the OLE control and Windows closes the Word tools, leaving your edits intact (see Figure 29.30).

The Access Way

With the advent of OLE 2, you're no longer restricted to using a program's tools within that program alone. As Exercise 29.3 demonstrated, you can use, for example, all of Word's editing, Visio's charting, or Excel's analytical tools in Access without ever leaving the Access program. As long as it's OLE 2 compliant, it's available for use in Access.

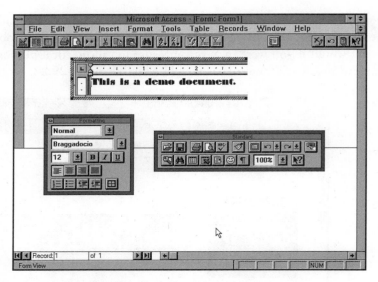

Figure 29.29. *Editing using Word's tools in an Access form.*

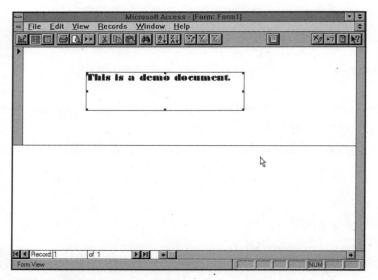

Figure 29.30. *The edits persist.*

Using this technique you can embed any OLE 2 compliant server application within an Access object. Exercise 29.3 could have used an Excel 5 spreadsheet or a Visio chart as easily as a Word document.

DO	DON'T

DO take advantage of OLE 2 in your Access applications. Having Excel's or Word's tools to use within your forms, for example, can extend your applications' scopes enormously.

DON'T expect decent OLE 2 performance on minimally equipped computers. The minimum RAM for OLE 2 to perform adequately is 8 mb; 12 or 16 mb is much better.

Custom Menus

Chapter 27, "Customizing Access," covers how to create custom toolbars. Access can also create custom menus for use with its objects. For the most part, people create custom menus to restrict a user's choices when in Form View. Creating custom menus is simple. Once you've seen a simple example such as Exercise 29.4, making your own more complex menus will be straightforward.

Custom menus are a specialized type of macro. The easiest way to make a menu is with the Menu Builder. Exercise 29.4 shows the Menu Builder in action.

Exercise 29.4. Custom menus.

1. Launch Access and have the College database open. Click on the File menu and choose Add-ins. From the Add-ins flyout, choose Menu Builder. Your screen should resemble Figure 29.31.

2. Click on New to tell the Menu Builder you want to create a new menu system.

The Access Way

You can return to the Menu Builder to edit or delete custom menus.

3. Access enables you to edit existing menus or make a new one from an empty menu bar. Since that's what you want here, click on <Empty Menu Bar>, then click on OK. Your screen should resemble Figure 29.33.

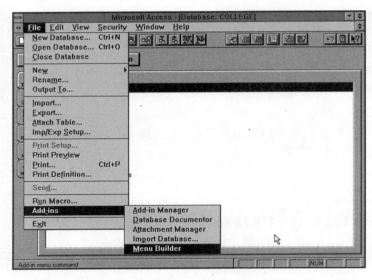

Figure 29.31. *Starting the Menu Builder.*

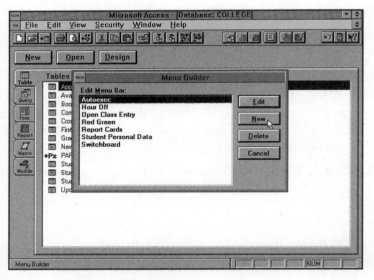

Figure 29.32. *Making a new menu.*

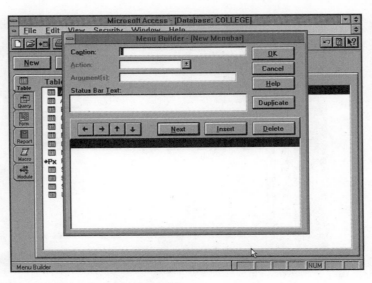

Figure 29.33. *The launched Menu Builder.*

4. Enter &File as a first entry on the menu bar. The first line of the menu bar has no action other than a pull-down for the rest of the menu. The ampersand before the F means the F is the hot letter. Pressing Alt+F will pull down the File menu in this system. If the entry read Fil&e, the e would be the hot letter and Alt+E would activate the File menu. Press tab to move into the Status Bar Text area and enter Open File menu. Your screen should resemble Figure 29.34.

5. Click on Next to move on. Click on the right-facing arrow. This tells Access that the next entry is on the File menu.

The Access Way

Making menus is just like making an outline. Entries on the far left of the details section appear on the menu bar. Entries below and to the right of them appear below them and are sub-entries. Exit is a sub-entry to File in this example. Sub-entries can have sub-entries too, but take it easy when making submenus as you can lose your users quickly. The left- and right-facing arrows control the hierarchic status of a menu entry.

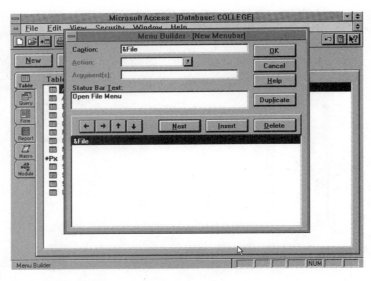

Figure 29.34. *Making an entry for the menu bar.*

6. Click in the Caption box and enter E&xit. Tab to the Action line. Pull down Action combo box, choose DoMenuItem, then tab to the next line, Arguments. Click on the Build icon and locate the menu item Exit from the Command list and click on it. Your screen should resemble Figure 29.35.

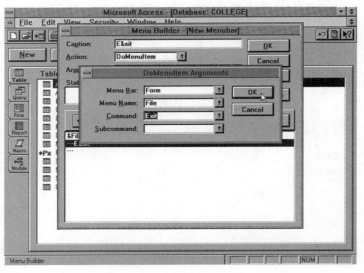

Figure 29.35. *Attaching some action to a menu.*

7. Click on OK. You've just created your first menu system. Your screen should resemble Figure 29.36.

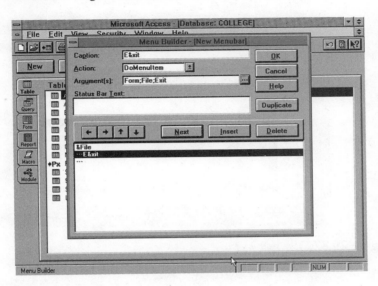

Figure 29.36. *The finished tiny menu system.*

8. Click on Next to move on. Click on the left-facing arrow to move up the menu hierarchy to the menu bar entries level again. Enter &User with a sub-entry &Message. Enter as an Action RunMacro with MenuMessage as an Argument for &Message. Your screen should resemble Figure 29.37.

9. Click on OK. Save the menu as MyNewMenu. Your screen should resemble Figure 29.38.

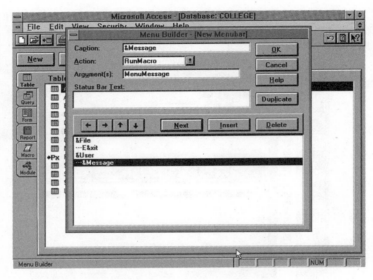

Figure 29.37. *The user menu.*

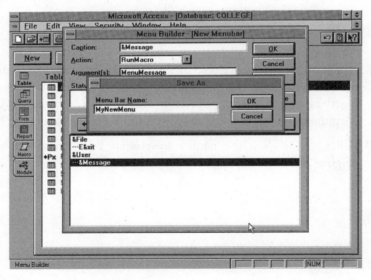

Figure 29.38. *The completed menu.*

Using Custom Menus

Before moving on, create a new macro named MenuMessage. Have the new macro show a message box with the message I Can Make Custom Menus. This macro is shown in Figure 29.39.

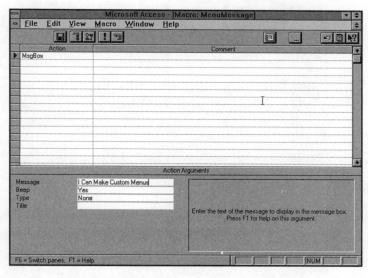

Figure 29.39. *The MenuMessage macro.*

Open the Class Entry form in Design View. Make sure the form itself is selected. Open the Properties list box and locate the Menu Bar property. Pull down the combo box for this entry, locate the macro MyNewMenu, and click on it. Your screen should resemble Figure 29.40.

Switch to Form View. Your screen should resemble Figure 29.41.

Pull down the User menu and click on the only entry, Message. Your screen should resemble Figure 29.42.

Close the message box by clicking on OK. Pull down the File menu and choose Exit. Save changes if you want to. The form will close.

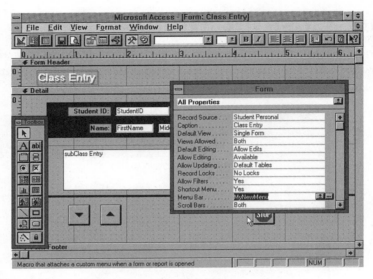

Figure 29.40. *Placing a custom menu on a form.*

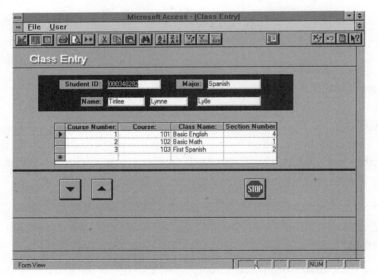

Figure 29.41. *The new menu attached to the Class Entry form.*

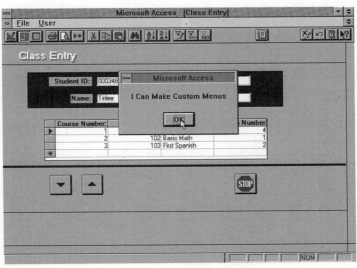

Figure 29.42. *Running a macro from a custom menu.*

Summary

When you need to use Access along with other programs to manipulate or view data, you can, in many cases, attach a table from the other program to an Access database. While you can edit and update this attached information fully, you're limited to how much you can restructure an attached table.

Clicking the Excel button in Access brings up the Excel spreadsheet with the Access object loaded. Since the Access object is converted to a new Excel file when the spreadsheet's called, you can edit the object and use Excel's analytical tools freely.

Access and Word work well together. You can export a special mail merge report from Access to Word by using the Mail Merge report wizard. By using Word's Insert capacity, you can add an Access table or query to a Word document.

Access can embed any OLE 2 compliant server's tools as an unbound object. When these tools are embedded, you can use edit-in-place to call them up from within Access.

Custom menus are specialized macros most easily made using the Menu Builder, which is an Access add-in. Menu items can execute standard menu actions as well as macros or Access Basic Code. You attach your custom menus to an Access object by editing the object's Menu Bar property.

A

Quiz Answers

Answers for Day 1

1. Laptop installs don't give you wizards or cue cards.

2. A double-pointed arrow.

3. Double-click on its icon.

4. No.

Answers for Day 2

1. Click on the Table tab, then click on the New button.

2. Customers.

3. It saves time and effort.

4. 255.

5. 64 characters and spaces.

6. Its name will be shortened (truncated).

Answers for Day 3

1. In both cases, it changes into a bar with two opposite pointing arrows.

2. No.

3. Yes.

4. Yes, you can override default properties without special considerations.

5. No.

6. To help users enter and read field data.

Answers for Day 4

1. The field changes its color scheme to the opposite of normal. For example, if normal is black on white, highlighted fields will be white on black.

2. The hand cursor.

3. A thin, double-faced arrow.

4. No.

5. Click on one, then press shift and click on the other.

6. Use a marquee selection. That is click and drag to surround the fields.

Answers for Day 5

1. The #'s surrounding the date. Usually Access is smart enough to supply these for you, so you don't always need to enter them manually.

2. Yes.

3. Yes.

4. Narrow.

5. Yes.

6. Yes.

Answers for Day 6

1. The equals (=) sign.

2. To positively indicate to Access that you mean a field. Also, to be able to include white spaces in a field name when used in an expression.

3. Sum().

4. Grid X and Grid Y properties.

5. You can bind reports only to tables or queries.

Answers for Day 7

1. Control Source.

2. Row Source.

3. Tells Access the maximum number of rows of the Row Source to display when the combo box is pulled down.

4. Limit to List.

5. Text box and list box.

Answers for Day 8

1. After January 31, 1995.

2. It has no effect.

3. Use the Long Date format.

4. January 1, 100, to December 31, 9999.

5. Yes.

Answers for Day 9

1. Queries.

2. No.

3. A different table.

4. The same table.

5. Run them as select queries first.

Answers for Day 10

1. No. Many vary depending upon control types.

2. Drop down the combo box in the Properties list box and click on Data Properties.

3. By setting the Link Child Fields and Link Master Fields properties to the link fields.

4. `Sub cmdNextRecord_Clack ()`

5. `Like "Ka"` won't let either Kaplan or Kramer through. `Like "Ka*"` will allow Kaplan but not Kramer.

Answers for Day 11

1. The phrase to the left of the colon will be the column's title or label.

2. Once, at the start or top of the report.

3. Yes.

4. No.

5. Group fields have the same icon in the Sorting and Grouping list box as the Sorting and Grouping toolbar button.

Answers for Day 12

1. The & in a caption tells Access that the character which follows, in this case the x, is the hot key for this control. Entering Alt+hot key when the form is active will give this control the focus, or in this case, exit the form.

2. The report Report Cards would print to the printer rather than show on the screen.

3. Change the width through the Properties list box settings or by clicking in the Palette when the line or rectangle has the focus.

4. Separate the macro name from the macro itself.

5. Use the greater-than and lesser-than symbols in combination: <>.

Answers for Day 13

1. Yes.

2. The bang (!) is always followed by a user-defined object.

3. The dot (.) is usually followed by an Access-defined object or a property name.

4. Update queries can act on individual fields within a record.

5. Yes, you could have taken this approach.

Answers for Day 14

1. A double-precision number.

2. A module. You can call the module from a macro, however.

3. You wouldn't. You'd use either a macro or a macro built using the menu builder. Note: You can alter menu characteristics through Access Basic.

4. When you need precise floating-point calculations such as interest computations. The currency data type takes up more storage space than less precise field sizes.

5. Start the remark with REM or the single quote mark (').

B

Exercise Guide/ Quick Reference

Exercise 2.1. Introduction to cue cards.

Like so many things in a visual tool like Access, you can learn how to use Cue Cards best by trying one out. This exercise serves as an introduction to Cue Cards.

Exercise 2.2. Creating a new database.

This exercise teaches you how to create a new database.

Exercise 2.3. Using a wizard to make a new table.

This exercise shows how to make a table using a wizard.

Exercise 2.4. Help with Help.

Sometimes the help you need can't be found through Cue Cards or by using wizards. In those cases, such as how to use a particular function, you'll likely use Access's online help system. This exercise steps you through some parts of Access's online help.

Exercise 3.1. Creating the new database.

Before you can start any database project, you need a new database to store database objects. This exercise gets you moving in the right direction.

Exercise 3.2. Creating the Student Personal table.

This exercise creates the first table for the book's sample database.

Exercise 4.1. Modifying a table.

Nobody plans perfectly. Many times you'll design a table only to realize that either a particular field's data type is wrong, or you included a field you shouldn't have, or left one out you need. In all these cases, you'll need to modify an existing table design, the purpose of this exercise.

Exercise 4.2. Adding a field to an existing table.

You can easily add a field to an existing Access database. This exercise shows you how to go about adding the field Ethnicity to the Student Personal table.

Exercise 4.3. Creating a table without a wizard.

As valuable as the wizards are, it's important for you to know how to accomplish these tasks on your own. This exercise teaches you how to create a table without a wizard.

Exercise 4.4. Creating a one-to-many link.

Often, you want to be sure you can enter many records that correspond to another single record. A relationship where one record can be linked to many is called, not surprisingly, a one-to-many relationship. Making sure a

record exists in the table on the one side before any records can be entered in the many side is called referential integrity. This exercise demonstrates how to create a one-to-many link.

Exercise 5.1. Entering data directly into a table.

Tables in and of themselves do nothing. It's the data they can store that's the heart of your database project. Entering data into a table is as simple as typing it in. The exercise shows how you create your first record using Access.

Exercise 5.2. Adding an input mask.

This exercise demonstrates a level of data accuracy by creating an input mask for data entry.

Exercise 5.3. Changing the field order of a table.

Sometimes you aren't happy with the field order you've created. This exercise shows you how to move fields to different positions.

Exercise 5.4. Changing the apparent field order.

When you change the field order in the field design grid, you also change the order the fields appear in the Datasheet View. You can make changes in the Datasheet View that won't change the field order in the Database Design View, however, as this exercise shows.

Exercise 5.5. Changing apparent field widths and heights.

The Field Size property for text fields determines the capacity of the fields, but doesn't affect how wide they're shown in the Datasheet View. Naturally that leaves some fields appearing too small while others are too wide in the Default Datasheet View. As this exercise demonstrates, changing apparent field sizes from Access's default in the Datasheet View is quite simple.

Exercise 6.1. Setting a Default field property.

Our fictional college is in northern Illinois, and most of the students are from Illinois. Therefore, it makes sense for us to set a default value to IL for the state field in our Student Personal table. This exercise shows how it's done.

Exercise 6.2. Setting the Data Validation field property.

In many cases you'll want to limit field entries to one or a certain array of selections. One way to do this in Access is to set the Data-Validation field property. This exercise isn't an optimal use of the Data-Validation property, but working through this and reviewing the table of data-validation examples will give you a good idea of this field property's use.

Exercise 6.3. Making a data validation error message.

This exercise teaches you how to change the default data message.

Exercise 7.1. An instant form.

This exercise demonstrates how easily Access handles the job of making a simple data-entry form.

Exercise 7.2. Using a wizard to make a form.

This exercise teaches you how to use Access's built-in wizard capabilities to create a form.

Exercise 8.1. Resizing a form control.

To make all the fields or form controls fit on one screen conveniently, you need to both alter the size of some overly wide ones and then move some of them up from the bottom of the form. Keep in mind that the terms field control and form control, or just control, refer to the same thing. This exercise demonstrates how to manipulate these controls.

Exercise 8.2. Moving form controls.

This exercise moves two controls with their labels so the entire form fits on one screen.

Exercise 8.3. Marquee selections.

Often you'll want to act on several controls at once. This exercise teaches you how to choose several controls quickly and easily by using a marquee selection.

Exercise 8.4. Using the palette.

This exercise covers how to alter the appearance of form elements with the palette.

Exercise 9.1. The simple query.

This exercise constructs a simple query in Access.

Exercise 9.2. Sorting in a query.

This exercise demonstrates how to make your queries more effective by sorting the data they retrieve.

Exercise 9.3. A criteria query.

Access queries also perform the very important function of extracting subsets of your data. This exercise shows how to convert the general query made in Exercises 9.1 and 9.2 into one with a criterion.

Exercise 9.4. Variations of criteria.

Access has a wide variety of criteria you can enter into a query. Using a little imagination and some knowledge, you can extract your data in almost any manner you can think of. This exercise goes into some variations on the criteria theme.

Exercise 9.5. ORs and ANDs in criteria.

This exercise illustrates the distinction between logical ORs and ANDs in queries.

Exercise 10.1. A two-table query.

This exercise shows how you construct a simple two-table query.

Exercise 10.2. The three-table query.

This exercise refines the query from Exercise 10.1, including information about course title and credit hours.

Exercise 11.1. The basic report.

This exercise creates a report that prints out students' names and addresses.

Exercise 11.2. Modifying a report.

This exercise covers deleting and rearranging fields in a report.

Exercise 11.3. Making mailing labels.

This exercise demonstrates the Label Wizard.

Exercise 12.1. Field expressions in reports.

This exercise will replace the first and third lines of the report's detail area with expressions that automatically size to fit the field's data.

Exercise 12.2. A grouped and totaled report.

This exercise creates a report showing all the courses all the students are signed up for, plus it adds up the course load to show the total credit hours for each student.

Exercise 13.1. A form with combo boxes.

All the controls on your previously made forms have been text boxes. These allow data entry and basic editing within them. List and combo boxes are two handy controls for data entry. A list box shows a list of values you can scroll through. A combo box is a combination of a list box and a text box. It has a place to enter data and a drop-down list that works identically to the list box.

Exercise 13.2. Manual combo box programming.

This exercise uses a combo box for the Course Number field. If you prefer the list box, you could use that for this application as well.

Exercise 14.1. Modifying an existing table.

This short exercise just adds a new field to the Student Personal table to hold either a 1, 2, or 3 that will correspond with a student status.

Exercise 14.2. Creating and programming the option group.

The purpose of this exercise is to make room on the Student Personal Data form for the new option group and then to install the option group on it.

Exercise 14.3. Embedding a graphic in a form.

This exercise creates a logo for the fictional college and embeds it in the Student Personal Data form.

Exercise 15.1. Adding a Date field to a table.

This exercise adds a Date field to the Student Personal table and examines how Access can present date information.

Exercise 15.2. Date criteria.

The exercise simply shows how you can use dates as criteria for queries.

Exercise 15.3. Date math and artificial fields.

This exercise dynamically calculates the age of each student in years. Dynamic calculation means the computer fetches the current date and does the age calculation based on that date and the fixed value of the student's birthday.

Exercise 16.1. A different criteria demonstration.

This exercise shows the parallels between criteria and parameters in queries.

Exercise 16.2. The parameter query.

This exercise constructs a simple parameter query and demonstrates its operation.

Exercise 16.3. Wildcard parameter queries.

This exercise shows how to use wildcards in parameter queries.

Exercise 16.4. The range parameter query.

This exercise shows how to create a parameter query that will return a range of values.

Exercise 16.5. The Make Table action query.

This exercise shows how to convert a query from a select query to a simple action query. This action query creates a new table containing the query's output.

Exercise 17.1. The delete query.

This exercise demonstrates the delete action query.

Exercise 17.2. Compacting a database.

This exercise shows how to compact a database and the results of doing so.

Exercise 17.3. The append query.

This query extracts records from the Append Me table and appends them to the Student's Current Classes table. You will need the Append Me table from the sample data to complete this exercise. If it currently doesn't exist as part of your data, either enter the table's data now or include this table from the sample set you acquired following the directions in Appendix A.

Exercise 18.1. Making the subform's query.

This short exercise creates a query to bind to the new subform.

Exercise 18.2. The form with subform.

This exercise uses a wizard to create a form with a subform.

Exercise 19.1. Field control properties.

This exercise fully demonstrates Link field control properties.

Exercise 19.2. Locked and Enabled properties.

This exercise demonstrates the use and limitations of the Locked and Enabled properties.

Exercise 19.3. Data filters.

The exercise shows how to design and apply data filters. Keep in mind that you can design and change filters when a form's running. This isn't a task done at design time.

Exercise 20.1. Record manipulation.

This exercise shows you how you can make controls that scroll through records.

Exercise 20.2. Another command button.

This exercise creates a command button that moves up one record at a time.

Exercise 21.1. Record selectors and navigation buttons.

The purpose of this exercise is to demonstrate the use of record selectors and scroll bars in forms.

Exercise 21.2. Changing the tab order.

This exercise shows how to alter the tab order in a form and eliminate controls from being in the tab order.

Exercise 21.3. Altering a subform.

This exercise shows how to alter the properties of a subform.

Exercise 21.4. Graphic elements in forms.

The purpose of this exercise is to show some uses for graphic elements in forms and how their properties affect their appearance.

Exercise 22.1. Expressions in queries.

This exercise shows how to construct a moderately complex query containing a mathematical expression.

Exercise 22.2. Grouping and sorting in reports.

This exercise manually creates a grouped report with several expressions and a secondary sort order.

Exercise 23.1. Calculation expressions in reports.

This exercise demonstrates how to create calculations in reports. The technique shown is identical to the technique used for forms. All the material in this exercise applies to forms also.

Exercise 23.2. Graphic elements in reports.

This exercise adds some graphics to the Report Cards report.

Exercise 23.3. A dynamic control.

This exercise places an option button on the report card that evaluates a student's weighted grade point average and visibly indicates if it merits inclusion on the dean's list.

Exercise 24.1. The macro design grid.

This exercise shows the macro design grid and constructs a simple macro.

Exercise 24.2. The switchboard or menu form.

This exercise constructs a simple unbound form that acts as a switchboard for the College database.

Exercise 24.3. The compound macro.

This exercise designs a compound macro for use in the Switchboard form.

Exercise 24.4. Activating the form.

This exercise attaches the macros to the command buttons.

Exercise 25.1. Conditional message box macro.

This macro evaluates the contents of the Ethnicity field when a new student's registered and responds accordingly.

Exercise 25.2. Attaching macros.

This exercise edits the On Click property for cmdCloseForm, causing it to point to the right macro, and attaches the Scholarship macro to the proper event.

Exercise 25.3. The form.

This exercise creates a very simple form with four controls. Two of the controls respond to events by altering the other two's control properties by a macro. Each macro in this exercise is a multiline one and represents an increase in complexity in several areas.

Exercise 25.4. Control property macros.

This exercise creates one macro containing two macro names. When called by its command button, this macro changes the labels' Visible properties.

Exercise 25.5. Putting it all together.

This exercise attaches the macros done in Exercise 25.4 to controls in the Red Green form.

Exercise 26.1. Update queries.

This exercise creates an update query that looks for any Zip Codes meeting the criterion of 38990 and changes them to 38989.

Exercise 26.2. The crosstab query.

This exercise creates two crosstabs—one showing the sum of the dollars and one showing the frequency of sales.

Exercise 27.1. Customizing toolbars.

This exercise installs a dialer button in the Form View toolbar.

Exercise 27.2. The Autodialer.

This short exercise shows the Autodialer in action.

Exercise 27.3. A custom macro for a toolbar.

This exercise creates a macro that opens the Class Entry form.

Exercise 27.4. The Custom Toolbar button.

This exercise attaches the macro from Exercise 27.3 to a custom button, then places that button in a toolbar.

Exercise 28.1. Tie an Access Basic function to a form control.

This exercise links a new function to a form control.

Exercise 28.2. Using the function.

This exercise attaches the new function to a form control.

Exercise 28.3. Declaring variables.

This exercise demonstrates use of variables.

Exercise 29.1. Attaching an external table.

This exercise shows how to attach an external table to an Access database.

Exercise 29.2. Inserting data in a Word document.

This exercise shows how to embed an Access table in a Word document.

Exercise 29.3. OLE 2 in action.

This exercise creates a Memo field in an otherwise blank form. When in this field, you'll have all of Word's editing tools available to you. To keep a solid focus, this exercise uses a new blank unbound form. You can do the same thing with your bound working forms.

Exercise 29.4. Custom menus.

This exercise creates a very simple menu system for use with the Class Entry form.

C

The Toolbox
Illustrated

Microsoft Access uses a Toolbox as a place to store the tools, or controls, you'll use to design forms and reports. This appendix offers an explanation of each tool and an illustration of the Toolbox for easy reference.

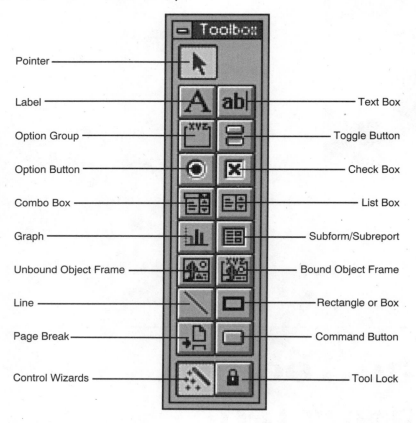

Pointer: Click this to return to the pointer cursor. The pointer cursor is used to make selections either on the design grid or from menus, the Toolbox, or the Button bar.

Label: Use this tool to create a label. Use labels for decoration, instructions, or to identify fields.

Text Box: The Text Box tool or control holds text. This is one of the most flexible tools in Access. Text boxes can be used for data entry or display, or to hold calculated fields.

Option Group: An option group holds other tools, such as option buttons, check boxes, or toggle buttons, in a group. Only one control at a time can be chosen within an option group.

Toggle Button: A toggle button toggles between being selected and unselected at the click of a mouse button. It's a good control for Yes/No fields.

Option Button: Also called radio buttons, option buttons are similar in function to check boxes and toggle buttons. An option button is selected and deselected at the click of the mouse button.

Check Box: Another toggle type tool that's changed from selected to deselected with a mouse click.

Combo Box: A combo box is a text box grafted to the top of a list box and tied to the list. Using a combo box, you can choose from a list as you can with a list box, or enter a value not on the list as you can in a text box.

List Box: A list box presents a list of entries from a field in a table or query. You cannot enter your own value or edit values from the list.

Graph: Summons up the GraphWizard to insert graphs in Access.

Subform/Subreport: Used to insert a subform or subreport in a form or report.

Unbound Object Frame: Displays an OLE object that's not stored in an Access database.

Bound Object Frame: Displays an OLE object stored in an Access database.

Line: Used to draw lines on a form or report.

Rectangle or Box: Used to create squares or rectangles on a form or report.

Page Break: This tool inserts a page break.

Command Button: A command button carries out a set of programmed instructions when clicked. The most common use for command buttons in Access is to execute macros.

Control Wizards: With control wizards on, any control you create will automatically be created with a wizard. With control wizards off, you can create the control without the help of a wizard.

Tool Lock: This tool is a toggle to keep a currently selected tool current until you click a different tool or click the lock tool again.

D

Access Toolbars

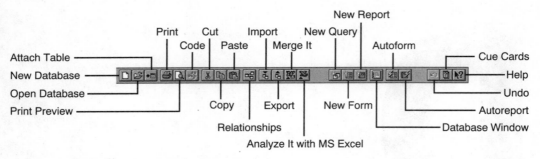

Figure D.1. *The Database toolbar.*

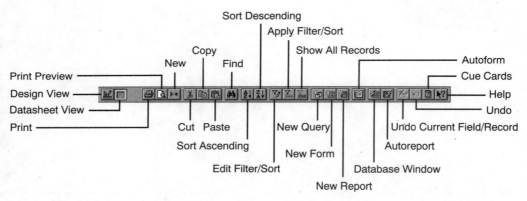

Figure D.2. *The Table Datasheet toolbar.*

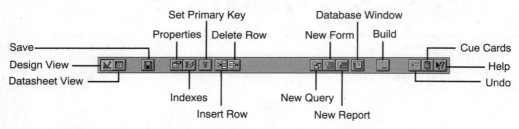

Figure D.3. *The Table Design toolbar.*

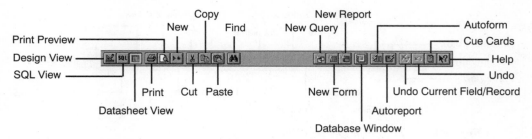

Figure D.4. *The Query Datasheet toolbar.*

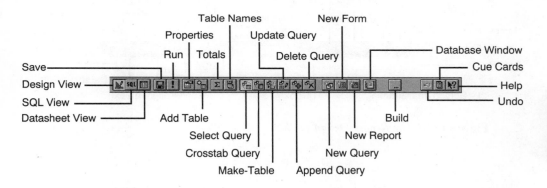

Figure D.5. *The Query Design toolbar.*

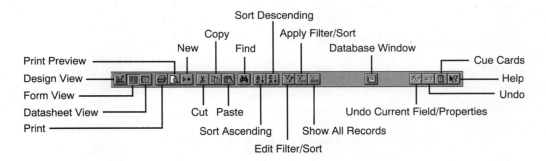

Figure D.6. *The Form View toolbar.*

D

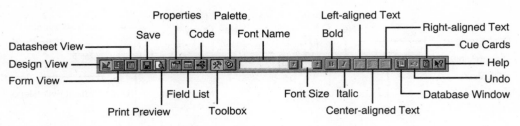

Figure D.7. *The Form Design toolbar.*

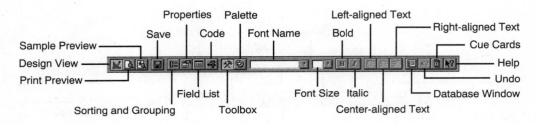

Figure D.8. *The Report Design toolbar.*

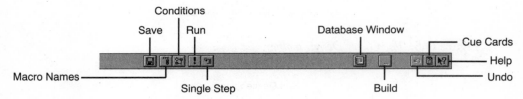

Figure D.9. *The Macro toolbar.*

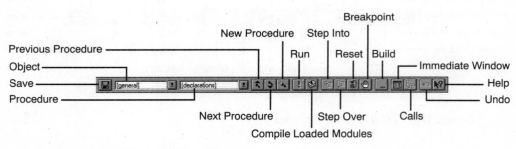

Figure D.10. *The Module toolbar.*

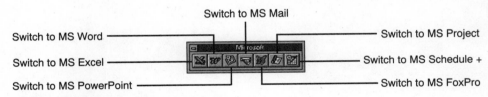

Figure D.11. *The Microsoft toolbar.*

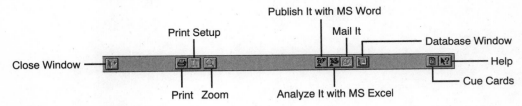

Figure D.12. *The Print Preview toolbar.*

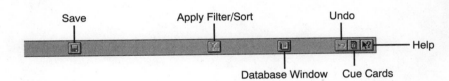

Figure D.13. *The Filter/Sort toolbar.*

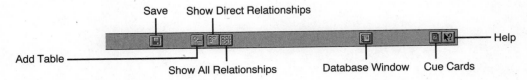

Figure D.14. *The Relationships toolbar.*

E

The Sample Data

One of the easiest methods to teach is to have you follow along with a real-world example. In this book I develop a database for a fictitious college. The following appendix lists all the data you need to follow the exercises in the book. You can save hours of typing, however. This entire database is available on CompuServe. Type go sams and then search Library 4, Databases, for file TYA14.EXE.

Append Me

StudentID:	777349993
Course Number:	2
Completed:	0
Grade:	
StudentID:	777349993
Course Number:	6
Completed:	0
Grade:	
StudentID:	777349993
Course Number:	7
Completed:	0
Grade:	
StudentID:	999-11-0000
Course Number:	2
Completed:	0
Grade:	
StudentID:	999-11-0000
Course Number:	6
Completed:	0
Grade:	
StudentID:	999-11-0000
Course Number:	5
Completed:	0
Grade:	
StudentID:	999-11-0000
Course Number:	1
Completed:	0
Grade:	

Available Classes

Class ID:	1
Course Number:	101
Class Name:	Basic English
Department Name:	English
Section Number:	4
Instructor:	McCoy
Term:	2-94
Units:	3
Class ID:	2
Course Number:	102
Class Name:	Basic Math
Department Name:	Mathematics
Section Number:	1
Instructor:	Murray
Term:	2-94
Units:	3
Class ID:	3
Course Number:	103
Class Name:	First Spanish
Department Name:	Language
Section Number:	2
Instructor:	Gonzalez
Term:	2-94
Units:	2
Class ID:	4
Course Number:	104
Class Name:	Journalism
Department Name:	English
Section Number:	1
Instructor:	Hernandon
Term:	2-94
Units:	2
Class ID:	5
Course Number:	105
Class Name:	Speech
Department Name:	Speech

E

Section Number:	1
Instructor:	Frank
Term:	2-94
Units:	2
Class ID:	6
Course Number:	202
Class Name:	Accounting
Department Name:	Business
Section Number:	1
Instructor:	Guffsaton
Term:	2-94
Units:	3
Class ID:	7
Course Number:	302
Class Name:	Physical Chemistry
Department Name:	Chemistry
Section Number:	1
Instructor:	Eiffler
Term:	2-94
Units:	3
Class ID:	8
Course Number:	150
Class Name:	Tennis
Department Name:	Physical Education
Section Number:	1
Instructor:	Lizzer
Term:	2-94
Units:	1
Class ID:	9
Course Number:	121
Class Name:	Basic Circuits
Department Name:	Engineering
Section Number:	2
Instructor:	Shockly
Term:	2-94
Units:	3
Class ID:	10
Course Number:	203

Class Name:	Composition
Department Name:	English
Section Number:	1
Instructor:	Mauffler
Term:	2-94
Units:	3
Class ID:	11
Course Number:	223
Class Name:	Political Talking
Department Name:	Speech
Section Number:	1
Instructor:	Reagan
Term:	2-94
Units:	3
Class ID:	12
Course Number:	330
Class Name:	Organic Chemistry
Department Name:	Chemistry
Section Number:	1
Instructor:	Curie
Term:	2-94
Units:	3
Class ID:	13
Course Number:	122
Class Name:	Resistor Theory
Department Name:	Engineering
Section Number:	1
Instructor:	Charged
Term:	2-94
Units:	3
Class ID:	14
Course Number:	130
Class Name:	Statistics
Department Name:	Mathematics
Section Number:	2
Instructor:	Counter
Term:	2-94
Units:	3

Books

Author:	Twain
Book:	Huckleberry Finn
Subject:	Travel
Author:	Cussler
Book:	Sahara
Subject:	Pollution
Author:	Brandon
Book:	Indians
Subject:	Am. History
Author:	McBain
Book:	Lightning
Subject:	Running
Author:	Woods
Book:	L.A. Times
Subject:	Movies
Author:	McCammon
Book:	They Thirst
Subject:	LA People
Author:	Bjorne
Book:	Internet Times
Subject:	Trivia

Completed Courses

Index Number:	10
StudentID:	888809292
Course Number:	4
Completed:	Yes
Grade:	a
Index Number:	11
StudentID:	999009800
Course Number:	4
Completed:	Yes
Grade:	b

Index Number:	13
StudentID:	999448887
Course Number:	1
Completed:	Yes
Grade:	c
Index Number:	14
StudentID:	999119800
Course Number:	1
Completed:	Yes
Grade:	a
Index Number:	15
StudentID:	999339837
Course Number:	1
Completed:	Yes
Grade:	b+
Index Number:	16
StudentID:	000348282
Course Number:	1
Completed:	Yes
Grade:	c+
Index Number:	17
StudentID:	777349993
Course Number:	2
Completed:	Yes
Grade:	f
Index Number:	18
StudentID:	777349993
Course Number:	6
Completed:	Yes
Grade:	a
Index Number:	19
StudentID:	777349993
Course Number:	7
Completed:	Yes
Grade:	c+
Index Number:	20
StudentID:	999-11-0000
Course Number:	2

E

Completed:	Yes
Grade:	d
Index Number:	21
StudentID:	999-11-0000
Course Number:	6
Completed:	Yes
Grade:	b
Index Number:	22
StudentID:	999-11-0000
Course Number:	5
Completed:	Yes
Grade:	c+
Index Number:	23
StudentID:	999-11-0000
Course Number:	1
Completed:	Yes
Grade:	a+
Index Number:	27
StudentID:	999-11-0000
Course Number:	3
Completed:	Yes
Grade:	b
Index Number:	28
StudentID:	000348282
Course Number:	2
Completed:	Yes
Grade:	a
Index Number:	29
StudentID:	000348282
Course Number:	3
Completed:	Yes
Grade:	b+
Index Number:	30
StudentID:	777349993
Course Number:	4
Completed:	Yes
Grade:	c+

Cross Tab Demo

Sale Number:	1
Salesman:	Smith
Category:	Canoes
Sale Value:	$30.00
Sale Number:	2
Salesman:	Jones
Category:	Yachts
Sale Value:	$30,000.00
Sale Number:	3
Salesman:	Doe
Category:	Canoes
Sale Value:	$500.00
Sale Number:	4
Salesman:	Smith
Category:	Canoes
Sale Value:	$100.00
Sale Number:	5
Salesman:	Doe
Category:	Boats
Sale Value:	$5,000.00
Sale Number:	6
Salesman:	Jones
Category:	Canoes
Sale Value:	$300.00
Sale Number:	7
Salesman:	Doe
Category:	Yachts
Sale Value:	$40,000.00
Sale Number:	8
Salesman:	Smith
Category:	Canoes
Sale Value:	$100.00
Sale Number:	9
Salesman:	Jones
Category:	Boats
Sale Value:	$5,000.00

E

Sale Number:	10
Salesman:	Doe
Category:	Boats
Sale Value:	$4,500.00

Sale Number:	11
Salesman:	Jones
Category:	Yachts
Sale Value:	$400.00

Sale Number:	12
Salesman:	Smith
Category:	Yachts
Sale Value:	$2,000.00

Sale Number:	13
Salesman:	Jones
Category:	Canoes
Sale Value:	$500.00

Sale Number:	14
Salesman:	Doe
Category:	Boats
Sale Value:	$325.00

Grade Values

Index:	1
Grade:	a+
Grade Value:	4.5

Index:	2
Grade:	a
Grade Value:	4

Index:	3
Grade:	b+
Grade Value:	4.5

Index:	4
Grade:	b
Grade Value:	3

Index:	5
Grade:	c+
Grade Value:	2.5

Index:	6
Grade:	c
Grade Value:	2
Index:	7
Grade:	d+
Grade Value:	1.5
Index:	8
Grade:	d
Grade Value:	1
Index:	9
Grade:	f
Grade Value:	0

Student Personal

Student ID:	999-11-0000
First Name:	Bill
Middle Name:	G.
Last Name:	Jones
Parents Names:	Joe and Mary
Address:	545 Oak Street
City:	Chicago
State:	IL
Postal Code:	39844
Phone Number:	(317) 555-9873
Major:	English
Email Name:	bjones@speedy.fictional.edu
Ethnicity:	Anglo
Note:	Hobbies include woodworking and skiing
Student ID:	999-00-9800
First Name:	Mary
Middle Name:	F.
Last Name:	Smith
Parents Names:	Marc and Shirley
Address:	6 Tempest Way
City:	Cairo

E

State:	IL
Postal Code:	35854
Phone Number:	(317) 555-9038
Major:	Mathematics
Email Name:	99955@compuserve.com
Ethnicity:	Indian
Note:	On full scholarship
Student ID:	999-11-9800
First Name:	Greg
Middle Name:	J.
Last Name:	Jefferson
Parents Names:	George and Martha
Address:	893 Main Street
City:	Daytona
State:	IL
Postal Code:	35888
Phone Number:	(317) 555-2983
Major:	Speech
Email Name:	gregj@speedy.fictional.edu
Ethnicity:	Black
Note:	Honor society candidate
Student ID:	888-80-9292
First Name:	Lizzie
Middle Name:	E.
Last Name:	Lytle
Parents Names:	Chet and Shirley
Address:	8220 Edward Street
City:	Raton
State:	NM
Postal Code:	87902
Phone Number:	(505) 555-9029
Major:	Pre-Med
Email Name:	N/A
Ethnicity:	Anglo
Note:	email to be assigned later
Student ID:	999-33-9837
First Name:	Jacob
Middle Name:	V.
Last Name:	Schwartz

Parents Names:	Moses and Jan
Address:	498 Tree Street
City:	Cairo
State:	IL
Postal Code:	35888
Phone Number:	(304) 555-9827
Major:	English
Email Name:	78282.2999@compuserv.com
Ethnicity:	Anglo
Note:	A fast swimmer
Student ID:	000-34-8282
First Name:	Tirilee
Middle Name:	Lynne
Last Name:	Lytle
Parents Names:	Chet and Shirley
Address:	490 Hermosa SE
City:	Albuquerque
State:	NM
Postal Code:	872222
Phone Number:	(505) 555-8837
Major:	Spanish
Email Name:	tlytle@hermes.fictional.edu
Ethnicity:	Anglo
Note:	
Student ID:	999-44-8887
First Name:	Jefferson
Middle Name:	B.
Last Name:	Donald
Parents Names:	Marian
Address:	9001 Avenue A
City:	Skokie
State:	IL
Postal Code:	34922
Phone Number:	(309) 555-9911
Major:	English
Email Name:	jeffd@hermes.fictional.edu
Ethnicity:	Black
Note:	Full academic scholarship

E

Student ID:	777-34-9993
First Name:	Anne
Middle Name:	P.
Last Name:	MacDonald
Parents Names:	Wilifred and Louise
Address:	7909 Pilgrim Ct.
City:	Cairo
State:	IL
Postal Code:	32998
Phone Number:	(309) 555-8899
Major:	Art
Email Name:	annie@speedy.fictional.edu
Ethnicity:	Anglo
Note:	Fast learner

Student's Current Courses

Index Number:	8
StudentID:	777349993
Course Number:	2
Completed:	No
Grade:	
Index Number:	9
StudentID:	777349993
Course Number:	6
Completed:	No
Grade:	
Index Number:	10
StudentID:	888809292
Course Number:	3
Completed:	No
Grade:	
Index Number:	11
StudentID:	999009800
Course Number:	4
Completed:	No
Grade:	

Index Number:	12
StudentID:	999448887
Course Number:	1
Completed:	No
Grade:	

Index Number:	14
StudentID:	999119800
Course Number:	1
Completed:	No
Grade:	

Index Number:	15
StudentID:	999339837
Course Number:	1
Completed:	No
Grade:	

Index Number:	16
StudentID:	000348282
Course Number:	1
Completed:	No
Grade:	

Index Number:	17
StudentID:	777349993
Course Number:	7
Completed:	No
Grade:	

StudentStatus Lookup

StudentStatus Number:	1
StudentStatus:	Full-Time

StudentStatus Number:	2
StudentStatus:	Part-Time

StudentStatus Number:	3
StudentStatus:	Visiting

E

Glossary

The following is a list of Access or database terms used in *Teach Yourself Access 2 in 14 Days*. For a complete Access glossary, search online help under the category "Glossary."

action query   A query that performs actions when run.

array   A finite set of variables sharing a common name and data type.

binding   Telling Access what table, query, or field a particular control, form, or report is linked to.

bound object   A control in a form or report that's linked to an underlying table or query.

check box   A control with two states: on (true) or off (false). Can be part of an Option group.

code   Usually source code. The English-like statements that you enter to write a computer program.

combo box   A control that combines both a list box and a text box.

concatenation   The chaining together of separate elements.

constant   A name assigned to a data storage location. Constants cannot change their value during code execution.

crosstab query   A query that performs a numerical process at its intersections. This query can also show summary information.

database   An orderly collection of data.

Database View   The view of your database through Access's database window.

Datasheet View   A window showing information in a grid.

declaration   A section of a module (Basic code) where, among other things, you declare the default data type for variables.

Design View   The mode in which an Access developer designs or changes the design of a table, form, report, or module.

function   A procedure that returns a value. Compare with Subs.

group   Records bunched according to a common criterion. Example: a report with records grouped according to the year in a selected date field.

information   Data collected into a database.

Label tool   A control for inserting unbound text into a form or report.

list box   A control giving you a list of choices.

module   Access Basic code containing one or more Subs and Procedures with one global declarations section.

normalize   To decompose data into logical groups.

null   An empty field or the end of the data set.

OLE (Object Linking and Embedding)   Using OLE with Windows, you can embed an object created in one application in another. An example of OLE is a voice annotation made with the Windows Sound System embedded in a Word for Windows document. The sound object appears in the Word document as a microphone icon. When you click the icon, the document calls the Windows Sound System to play the sound.

Option button   A button that can be on (true) or off (false).

Option group   A control with Check boxes, Radio buttons, or Toggle buttons. One control within an Option group must be selected. More than one control within the Option group cannot be selected.

QBE   Query by Example. A visual way to construct your queries using Access's query design grid. Using QBE, you drag the fields you want to query from a list box to the design grid and then optionally give Access an example of criteria to narrow the selection.

Radio button   A control with two toggled states: on (true) or off (false). Another name for an Option button.

referential integrity   The existence of a related value or attribute in a database depends upon another identical value or attribute.

relationship   An association between two data tables in a database.

row source   The source of an Access object's data.

sort   The order records appear in a database. For example, a table sorted in an ascending alphabetical sort would start with the As and move through the Zs.

SQL   Connectivity SQL, pronounced "sequel," stands for Structured Query Language. Certain relational database systems use this language to form their queries. Access can connect to many of these database systems. When you use Access to construct a query for an attached or connected SQL table, you can create the query using normal Access QBE methods, and Access translates your query to proper SQL syntax.

sub A procedure not returning a value. Compare with function.

text box A control that accepts text entry and editing.

toolbar A menu shortcut tool that appears directly under the menu bar. Although most people call this bar the Button bar, it's officially called the toolbar by Microsoft.

unbound object A control in a form or report that isn't linked to an underlying table or query.

variable A name assigned to a data storage location. Variables can change value during code execution.

Index

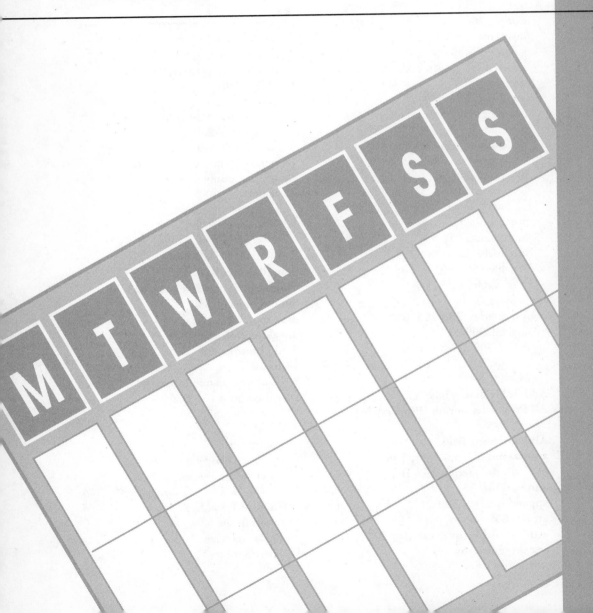

Symbols

forms

Sams
Learning
Center

SAMS
PUBLISHING

Property list box

Sams
Learning
Center

SAMS
PUBLISHING

Add to Your Sams Library Today with the Best Books for Programming, Operating Systems, and New Technologies

The easiest way to order is to pick up the phone and call

1-800-428-5331

between 9:00 a.m. and 5:00 p.m. EST.

For faster service please have your credit card available.

ISBN	Quantity	Description of Item	Unit Cost	Total Cost
0-672-30453-8		Access 2 Developer's Guide, 2nd Edition (Book/Disk)	$44.95	
0-672-30494-5		Access 2 Unleashed	$34.95	
0-672-30366-3		Absolute Beginner's Guide to Access	$16.95	
0-672-30378-7		Teach Yourself Visual Basic 3.0 in 21 Days	$29.95	
0-672-30447-3		Teach Yourself Visual Basic for Applications in 21 Days	$29.95	
0-672-30440-6		Database Developer's Guide with Visual Basic 3 (Book/Disk)	$44.95	
0-672-30345-0		Wasting Time with Windows (Book/Disk)	$19.95	
0-672-30385-X		Excel 5 Super Book (Book/Disk)	$39.95	
0-672-30384-1		Word for Windows 6 Super Book (Book/Disk)	$39.95	
0-672-30260-8		WordPerfect 6.0 Super Book (Book/Disk)	$34.95	
0-672-30383-3		WordPerfect 6 for Windows Super Book (Book/Disk)	$39.95	
0-672-30410-4		Paradox 4.5 for Windows Unleashed (Book/Disk)	$34.95	
		Shipping and Handling: See information below.		
		TOTAL		

❑ 3 ½" Disk

❑ 5 ¼" Disk

Shipping and Handling: $4.00 for the first book, and $1.75 for each additional book. Floppy disk: add $1.75 for shipping and handling. If you need to have it NOW, we can ship product to you in 24 hours for an additional charge of approximately $18.00, and you will receive your item overnight or in two days. Overseas shipping and handling adds $2.00 per book and $8.00 for up to three disks. Prices subject to change. Call for availability and pricing information on latest editions.

201 W. 103rd Street, Indianapolis, Indiana 46290

1-800-428-5331 — Orders   1-800-835-3202 — FAX   1-800-858-7674 — Customer Service

Book ISBN 0-672-30488-0